PACKERS
VS.
BEARS

PACKERS
VS.
BEARS

Glenn Swain

Charles Publishing
Los Angeles

PACKERS vs. BEARS
Library of Congress Catalog Number 96-86269
ISBN 0-912880-08-2

Cover Photo: Vernon Biever
Cover Design: Matt Hoerr, Conner Design Group
Consultant: Barbara Balch

October 1996
Manufactured in the United States of America

Contents

The 1970s

The 1980s

The 1990s

Acknowledgments

I would like to thank the following people who have all contributed greatly to this book. I am deeply appreciative. First of all, the players who were kind enough to submit to interviews:

The Bears

Sam Francis
Ray Nolting
Gene Schroeder
Joe Maniaci
Bill Geyer
Hugh Gallarneau
Clyde Bulldog Turner
Sid Luckman
George McAfee
Harry Clark
George Connor
Ed Sprinkle
Ken Kavanaugh
Al Campana
Harlon Hill
Doug Atkins
Bill Wade
Mike Pyle
Ted Karras
Gale Sayers
Gary Kosins
Bob Avellini
Todd Bell
Mike Hartenstine

The Packers

Tony Canadeo
Bob Adkins
Bobby Dillon
Deral Teteak
Gary Knafelc
Veryl Switzer
Jerry Kramer
Fuzzy Thurston
Jim Taylor
Paul Hornung
Jim Carter
Scott Hunter
Willie Wood
Bart Starr
Forrest Gregg
Gust Zarnas
Hal Van Every
Bob Long
Herm Schneidman
Harry Jacunski
Richard Wildung
Dick Deschaine
John Martinkovic
Ray Nitschke

The Bears

Russell Thompson
Waymond Bryant
Virgil Carter
Doug Buffone
Johnny Lujack
Lee Artoe
Mike Ditka

The Packers

Steve Luke
Ken Stills
Karl Swanke
Dave Robinson
Clayton Tonnemaker
David Whitehurst

Special thanks to Pro Football historian Joe Horrigan and the entire staff at the Pro Football Hall of Fame; Frank Woschitz, Executive Director of the NFL Players Association Retirees; and the voice of pro football, Ray Scott.

I would also like to thank all of those who were guilty of support, promotion, encouragement, love, and patience: Jim and Pat Swain (that boy of yours wrote a book!), Steve, Diane, and Andy; Ed, Emily, and Joanna Bazel; Mark, Carlena, and Erin Spencer; Phil and Amanda Swann; JoAnn Musolf (tickets ... we need two tickets!), Barbara Villaseñor for helping me give birth to this baby, Steve Bloch, Susan Hathaway, Mary Jane Herber and everyone at the Brown County Library in Green Bay, everyone at the Harold Washington Library in Chicago, Vernon Biever, Lee Lefebvre, John Biolo, Lee Remmel, and Annie.

Many resources were used in the writing of this book. I would like to thank David Neft, Richard Cohen, and Rick Korch, authors of *The Football Encyclopedia* (when checking statistics and the proper spelling of players' names, it was essential). Thanks to writer Richard Whittingham, whose book *The Chicago Bears, An Illustrated History*, was also essential. Thanks to Michael O'Brien, whose book *Vince* is one of the best researched books I've ever read. Special thanks go to author Larry Names, whose collection of books entitled *The History of The Green Bay Packers—The Lambeau Years Part One, Two, and Three*, were very helpful to my research. Thanks also to all the sports writers for the *Green Bay Press-Gazette* and the *Chicago Tribune* who, through the years, provided a detailed record of the Green Bay Packers and the Chicago Bears, and the players who made the rivalry the best in any sport.

Finally, this book is for everyone who loves the game of football and sees beauty in a graceful catch, a shattering hit, an open-field run, and a perfect spiral.

Glenn Swain

Preface

I think it was ex-New York Giants' star Frank Gifford who once said that pro football is like nuclear warfare: There are no winners, only survivors. For seven decades the Chicago Bears and the Green Bay Packers have waged a gridiron war of iron wills and bloodletting vengeance—and survived.

Both teams began playing when the National Football League was still the American Professional Football League. Much different than today's star-studded spectacle, the game back in the early 1920s was crude and primitive. Leather helmets (if any at all), cheaply crafted shoulder pads, heavy jerseys, and high-top shoes with rectangular cleats were the uniform of the day. Games were played on grassless, cinder-strewn fields that were often no more than pasture land. Fields, equipment, and uniforms may have improved since pro football's infancy, but the manner in which the Packers and the Bears play football has not.

We are all familiar with the old Postal Service adage, "Neither rain, sleet, hail, nor snow will deter the carrier from his appointed rounds." Well, the same could be said for these two storied franchises and their ball carriers. In a time of domed stadiums and artificial turf, the Packers and the Bears still play football in its most basic form: outside, on real grass, in rain, sleet, hail, or snow. It has been that way since their first meeting on November 27, 1921, at Cubs Park in Chicago, when the Bears were still the Chicago Staleys and the Green Bay Packers were in just their third year of operation.

It has always been big-city Chicago against small-town Green Bay. The cities' close proximity—a mere 207 miles' drive on I-94 and I-43—is alone enough tinder to spark a spirited rivalry. Being so close, you will find many Green Bay Packers' fans residing in and around Chicago, and just as many Chicago Bears' fans living in and around Green Bay. Adding to the heated war of words exchanged by the two teams' staunchly loyal followers is the fact that fans in both camps are among the most knowledgeable football aficionados anywhere.

Including the two regular season games of the 1995 season, Chicago leads the series overall with eighty-two wins, sixty-two losses, and six ties. In a water-cooler debate, Bear fans may use the leverage they have with their team holding the win-loss advantage, but most Bears' or Packers' fans could care less about the series' record. Fans are notorious for their "What-have-you-done-for-me-lately" attitude and bragging rights go to the side that won the last game.

A decade-by-decade analysis is interesting. Chicago gained its huge series' advantage during the 1940s and the 1950s. During the Forties, the Sid Luckman-led Chicago Bears dominated the Packers in sixteen of twenty-one contests The Fifties saw a less-talented Bears' team beating much poorer Green Bay teams fourteen out of nineteen times. The Bears have come out on top every decade but the 1960s when the powerful Vince Lombardi teams swamped George Halas' troops fifteen out of twenty games. Not surprisingly, by the mid-1990s, the teams are deadlocked 6-6 for the decade. After more than seventy years of football, the average score of a game between the Packers and the Bears is Bears, 17; Packers, 15. It's that close.

This book examines the rivalry in depth—from reviewing the games played to personal interviews with some of the legendary players of the game. These are the gridiron greats who strapped on those first helmets, went into battle, and made the Chicago-Green Bay rivalry what it is: the oldest and best in football.

We will look at the birth in the early 1920s of the battles between the Packers and the Bears and see how the Packers formed one of pro football's greatest teams by the end of the decade. We'll see both teams flourish in the Thirties, combining to win six of the ten NFL championships. The 1940s were the decade of the great Bears' teams that dominated the league. The Fifties will show both teams regrouping and rebuilding.

Vince Lombardi and the Packers ruled the Sixties, although the Bears won it all in 1963. While both teams were again unspectacular in the Seventies, the 1980s saw the Chicago Bears form one of the finest squads in the history of professional football. In the

Nineties, we find both teams starting the slow climb back to the top.

The interviews I conducted for the book were a real joy for me. I talked football for hours with some of the game's greatest players: Paul Hornung, Gale Sayers, Bart Starr, Bulldog Turner, Jerry Kramer, Sid Luckman, and many, many others. Truly a thrill.

The one constant I found throughout the interviews was the enormous respect each team's players had for the other's. Ex-Chicago Bears from the Forties spoke in reverent tones about Green Bay's great Don Hutson. Ex-Green Bay Packers spoke respectfully of Bears' linebacker Dick Butkus. Back and forth it went. Players on both sides admitted to me that, if their team was not in the championship run in a given year, they pulled for their arch-rival to win it all. I guess the players who fight you the longest and hardest are the ones who have the most respect for you.

For seventy-five years and in over 150 games, the Bears and the Packers have clashed on the football field and left a trail of broken bones, bloody noses, star players, and professional sports' oldest and most enduring rivalry.

The Green Bay Packers and the Chicago Bears ARE professional football!

The 1920s

Postgraduates, an Iceman, Jug, and the Hungry Five

The men who sat on the ground floor of the Odd Fellows Building in Canton, Ohio, on September 17, 1920, had no idea they were about to make history.

While many Canton residents spent that early fall Sunday enjoying a day of rest from their five and six day work schedules, the men, representing twelve football teams, had congregated in the automobile showroom of Ralph Hay to form a professional football league. In two short hours, they created the American Professional Football Association, which would change its name two years later to the National Football League. A. F. Ranney of the Akron Professional Football Team took the minutes at the meeting, and summed up the formation of the league in twenty-one words:

> "It was moved and seconded that a permanent organization be formed to be known as American Professional Football Association. Motion carried."

The infant league issued franchises for a fee of $100 each to an eclectic group of twelve teams named for towns, sponsors, animals, etc. The Canton Bulldogs, Racine Cardinals, Akron Pros, Cleveland Indians, Dayton Triangles, Hammond Pros, Massillon Tigers, Muncie Flyers, Rochester Jeffersons, Decatur Staleys, Chicago Cardinals, and the Rock Island Independents. In the end, however, two teams, Massillon and Muncie, never fielded a team.

The new league unanimously elected as its first president the greatest athlete of his time—Jim Thorpe. Using the legendary Thorpe's name gave the fledgling league some needed recognition and credibility. However, Thorpe held his office in name only; he was still playing for the Canton team.

1

Sitting on the running board of one of Hays' automobiles that Sunday was a 25-year-old skinny Bohemian who had briefly played pro baseball. He had grown up a huge Chicago Cubs fan, many times watching games through a knothole in the fence at Cubs Park. Although his dream of becoming a baseball star would never materialize, he was destined to be great. He would become the "Papa Bear" of Chicago.

George Stanley Halas became known as one the founding fathers of pro football. His impact on the game is immeasurable. From helping to keep the young league afloat, dividing the league into divisions, and devising critical rule changes through the years, George Halas has to be credited for the pro game we see today.

George Halas was born on February 2, 1895, in a Bohemian community about two miles southwest of downtown Chicago. A bean-pole as a youth, his speed made up for his lack of size on the athletic field and allowed him to compete with his more athletically talented brothers.

When he entered Crane Technical High School in 1909, Halas weighed only 110 pounds. He played tackle on the lightweight football team all four years, while also competing in track and indoor baseball. By the time he graduated, Halas was up to a whopping 120 pounds.

In the fall of 1914, Halas quit his job as attendance recorder at Western Electric in Cicero, Illinois. With three shirts, three pairs of socks, three sets of underwear in a suitcase and $30 to his name, he set out for Champaign and the University of Illinois to enroll in civil engineering. He immediately got a job waiting tables and joined Tau Kappa Epsilon fraternity. He was 140 pounds of taut muscle.

Halas' freshman coach was the smallish Ralph Jones who played him only as a relief back that first year. He was encouraged to put on more weight and acquire the brawn needed for playing the rough and tumble sport he so loved. During summer break he did just that, gaining twenty pounds and the attention of Illinois head coach Robert C. Zuppke.

His first scrimmage at trying out for Zuppke's starting halfback met with predicable results. The wiry Halas would crash into the line only to be flattened by the bigger, stronger linemen. Coach Zuppke, out of sheer pity, yelled for Halas to get out of there. Halas was quickly switched to offensive end. Later that year, while attempting a tackle, Halas broke his jaw when a runner's heel hit him flush on the chin. George Halas was yet to be the football star he wanted to be.

In 1918, with the United States embroiled in the war in Europe, George Halas felt a tug of patriotism and duty. Although his mother wanted him to get his diploma first, he enlisted in the Navy and went to Great Lakes Training Station where he was assigned to the sports program. It was 1918.

In that year, Halas helped Great Lakes to the Rose Bowl against Mare Island Marines. In the game, he returned an interception seventy-seven yards, scored a touchdown and, in his opinion, was cheated out of another TD. He was named the game's Most Valuable Player.

The following March Halas was discharged from the Navy. Soon after returning home, he told his mother he loved football, but would from then on devote his competitive self to another love, baseball.

Bob Connery, a scout for the New York Yankees, invited Halas to spring training in Florida for a tryout. Although he had good speed and a pretty good arm, Yankee Stadium would never become "the house that Halas built." Before being sent down to the Yankees' minor league squad in St. Paul, he played right field in eleven games and had a less than spectacular .091 batting average. With that, and a new man in right field named Babe Ruth, Halas' short pro baseball career was over.

He returned to Chicago and went to work for the Chicago, Burlington, and Quincy Railroad in the bridge design department. Halas remembered hearing of a doctor by the name of A. A. Young who operated a semi-pro football team across the border in Hammond, Indiana. Halas showed up and made the team. It was 1919.

That 1919 season with Hammond made the young Halas fall in love with football again. Halas knew there was no way he could stay with the railroad company until retirement. Enter A. E. Staley, who owned a corn products company and changed George Stanley Halas' life.

In March 1920, George Chamberlain, superintendent of the

A. E. Staley Company in Decatur, contacted Halas. Chamberlain told Halas that Mr. Staley wanted to form an employee football team to play other semi-pro and industrial teams. Staley needed someone who knew the game of football and who could build him a winning team around the better college players. Staley wanted Halas.

A. E. Staley had, during the 1919 Christmas holiday, contacted a University of Illinois running back by the name of Dutch Sternaman about helping to organize his football team. Sternaman was interested and, after graduating from Illinois, joined Halas in the search for players.

The following summer Halas and Sternaman agreed to be co-coaches and owners of the team and assembled a talented group of players to form the Decatur Staleys. Halas' friend from the Great Lakes team, Paddy Driscoll, joined up, as did Jimmy Conzelman, Pard Pierce, and Charlie Dressen. They also landed an All-American end from Nebraska University named Guy Chamberlin. The line consisted of Hugh Blacklock and Ralph Scott at tackles, Russ Smith and John "Tarzan" Taylor at guards, and George Halas at end.

The man they signed as center ended up playing an amazing thirteen years with Halas. In those early days, playing professional football was not a long-term occupation. The league was in confusion, as were the players who would often play for many different teams during a season. One exception to the rules of disorder and player migration was Chicago native George Trafton.

Trafton was a hard-hitting durable center who had been kicked off the Notre Dame squad by Coach Knute Rockne for playing semi-pro football. Known by an array of befitting nicknames, notably "Brute," "Beast," and "Cyclone," Trafton was a 6'2", 235-pound blood-spilling ruffian described by one teammate as one of the toughest, meanest, most ornery critters alive.

A sports writer once reported that Trafton was strongly disliked in every city of the league, except Green Bay and Rock Island. In those places "he was hated."

Case in point: In the Staleys' third game against the Rock Island Independents, Trafton got word that a player on the Rock Island team was going to try to remove him from the game by any means necessary. That idea didn't sit well with "Brute." In a span of twelve plays, four Rock Island players were taken out of the game, thanks to Trafton. Legend has it that one of the players taken from the field had the imprint of Trafton's cleats from his forehead to his chin.

Later in the game, with the Independents' fans already enraged at him, Trafton slammed into Rock Island back Fred Chicken, flinging him against a fence post and breaking his leg.

The fans came unglued. At the end of the game, they chased Trafton from the stadium throwing rocks, bottles, anything they could get their hands on. He escaped their wrath only by the grace of God and a passing motorist.

The two teams played another bloody game later in the year. When the game was over, Halas gave Trafton the Bears' share of the gate receipts, $7,000, for safe keeping. After seeing him run from that hostile crowd in the first game, Halas knew the money would be in safe hands.

Trafton was the first on offense to center the ball with one hand, and for good reason: he was missing the index finger on his left hand. He made All-NFL honors eight times in thirteen years, and defiantly wore Number 13 his entire career.

The Halas and Sternaman-led Decatur Staleys finished the year 10-1-2. The 1920 season had been a success but the joy would be short-lived. The economy took a sudden downturn and A. E. Staley faced tough times. He told Halas that the company could no longer afford to underwrite the team. Suggesting that Halas take the team to Chicago, Staley offered to put up $5,000 if the team would remain the "Staleys" for one more year.

Most of the team moved north with Halas and Sternaman to field the Chicago Staleys. Chicago Cubs owner William Veeck agreed to lease Cubs Park to the Staleys for fifteen percent of the gross gate receipts.

When the agreement with Staley expired in 1922, Halas and Sternaman renamed the team the Chicago Bears to forge a connection with baseball's Chicago Cubs. Halas and Sternaman no themselves in a big-time sports town with a new product to sell. They both knew the best sale's tool would be a winning team on the gridiron.

Folks immediately liked the guy with the infectious smile and mass of coal-black curly hair. His wide grin brimmed with wholesomeness, and honesty was written all over his handsome young face. He had a presence about him that immediately put people at ease. But beneath Earl L. "Curly" Lambeau's calm and tranquil exterior lay a fiery competitor and a heart burning with ambition.

Born in Green Bay on April 9, 1898, Lambeau was the child of Belgian parents who had settled there in the 1870s. The Green Bay, Wisconsin, of Curly's childhood was one of proper Victorian homes on tree-lined streets right alongside a bustling bar scene and red-light district. Green Bay was also fast becoming the largest cheese-packing community in the world.

Lambeau was a triple-threat back for Green Bay East High School where he lettered in football all four years. He also had his first coaching experience at East when he stepped in for the head coach who had gone off to find a book on football. During this time, Curly also briefly played for the South Side Skiddoos, a team of players from the immigrant families located on Green Bay's south side.

A freshman at Notre Dame in 1918, Lambeau played on the varsity team under the legendary Knute Rockne. As starting fullback, Lambeau was paired in the backfield with the immortal George Gipp. However, his time with the "Fighting Irish" was cut short when he came down with acute tonsillitis during his Christmas holiday in Green Bay.

Unable to return to school on time, Curly decided to skip the next semester and, in early 1919, took a job with the Indian Packing Company in Green Bay. Any thoughts he had of returning to school were quickly forgotten when he began making the incredible sum of $250 a month. Although he was making a lot of money at the packing plant, Curly still had a burning desire to play football. He realized the leaves would soon be turning from green to gold and the air would turn crisp; it would soon be fall. Curly could not imagine a fall without football. A chance meeting over a beer with a frustrated athlete-turned-writer would bring him back to his first love, football.

The frustrated athlete was George Whitney Calhoun, sports editor for the *Green Bay Press-Gazette*. The crude, grizzly, cigar-chomping, profanity-spewing Calhoun worked in an office that everyone called the "black hole." There Calhoun would bang out brash headlines on his E. C. Smith typewriter, chew John Ruskin cigars, and eat smelly Limburger cheese sandwiches, with his faithful Boston Terrier, Patsy Tootsie Tiger, by his side.

John B. Torinus, an aspiring journalist of the day, once said he learned the finer points of drinking beer from Calhoun. "He was the all-time champion," Torinus said. "He taught me early on how to drink a bottle of beer without swallowing. You merely tip your head back and open your throat and let the beer guzzle down."

Torinus, Calhoun, and any visitor to Green Bay during the live-it-to-the-hilt 1920s could easily find a hooch club in which to wet one's whistle. Clubs like the Rex, the National, the Office, and Jake Geurtz' freely poured drinks for one and all.

Calhoun thought being the paper's sports editor required him to get personally involved in the town's sporting teams. Cal (his preferred nickname) had been a good athlete at Buffalo (New York) University, but an attack of juvenile arthritis left him crippled in his hands, arms, and legs. John Torinus believes that Cal's gruff exterior may have been a mask to keep people from feeling sorry for him. Inside, he had a heart of gold.

Cal had known Curly Lambeau since the latter's playing days at East High School. Cal knew Curly missed football. They ran into each other one day at a local speakeasy over their beers.

"Why not get up a team in Green Bay?" Cal asked Curly between swigs of brew. He then added, "I'll help you put one together, and I'll give you all the publicity you need." How could Lambeau resist an offer to help organize a football team and have his own publicity director, to boot?

On August 11, 1919, in the news room of the *Press-Gazette,*
George Calhoun, Curly Lambeau, and some twenty-five players
gave birth to professional football in Green Bay. Lambeau was
elected captain and Calhoun agreed to be team manager.

Cal's column the next day noted, "Close to 25 pigskin chasers
attended the conference last evening and there was a great deal of
enthusiasm displayed among the candidates."

His column went on to pre-name the team the "Indians," noting, "Indications point to the 'Indians' having the greatest team in
the history of football in Green Bay and there is no doubt but that
gridiron fans will see a great exhibition of football chasing this fall."

In fact, Cal would call this new team by a number of different
names in its first few years. Most of the time he referred to them as
the "Big Bay Blues," because of the blue jerseys the team first wore.
However, the team's association with the Indian Packing Company
made it natural to call them the "Packers." (Soon thereafter, the
Indian Packing Company was renamed the Acme Packing
Company). Actually, Lambeau didn't like "Big Bay Blues" and even
tried to get rid of the "Packers" appellation, as well.

A football team needed uniforms, footballs, and a place to practice. Frank Peck, Curly's courteous and understanding boss at the
packing company, came to the rescue. Lambeau convinced Peck to
provide the team with jerseys and access to a field next door to the
company to use for practice.

The Packers played their home games at Hagemeister Park near
the Hagemeister Brewery. The park was little more than an open
field with a football gridiron marked on it. Because the park had no
bleachers, curious onlookers would congregate near a small fence to
watch, arriving on foot, by car, and even by horse and buggy. (In
1920, a small grandstand would be built to accommodate a couple
hundred people; Curly Lambeau's father helped build it.) George
Calhoun, with a little of his own unique verbal convincing,
retrieved money from the interested patrons by passing his hat
among them.

Following the plays up and down the field, the fans always had
seats on the 50-yard line! At half-time, both teams would retreat to
opposite end zones to rest and regroup. There they would be surrounded by fans who were not at all shy about sharing their opinion

or giving advice.

Today's fans would find American football as played in the early Twenties quite boring compared to the fast-paced and glittering spectacle we're used to now. In the old days, it was difficult telling one team from the other because uniforms were often similar. Jerseys were faded and numbers crudely sewn on. Some jerseys weren't numbered at all making it even tougher to distinguish one from another. Every player wore black high-top cleats and canvas pants hiked up high to protect the lower back. Headgear, which was optional, was made of cheap leather that offered little in the way of protection.

In the early days, brute strength counted for more than skill and ability. Most offense's used a single-wing or Notre Dame box formation. The idea was to run the ball into the line and place as many men as possible at the point of attack to improve the chances of gaining yardage. Having a hard head was a definite plus.

Receiving the ball directly from the center, an offensive player would plow head-first into the line in hopes of finding daylight. They rarely did. Most running plays ended up with twenty-two men in a huge pile-up with a squashed ball carrier somewhere underneath.

Punting was considered an offensive move. Pinning the opponent deep in his own territory with a punt and hoping he would make a mistake improved the odds of winning. Monstrous punts were normal, given the oblong ball of those days, and it was routine to punt on third down when no defensive player would be back to receive it.

There was passing but with only limited success because the football's egg-like shape made it difficult to throw. In those early days, if a team completed one or two passes in a game, it was cause for great celebration.

Curly Lambeau came to realize that the forward pass could surprise an unsuspecting defense and open up the game. In his first year in a contest against Upper Michigan's tough Stambaugh Miner's team, Lambeau watched as three players on three consecutive running plays ended up with fractures. Lambeau didn't call a running play for the rest of the game.

Lambeau quickly realized the full value of the forward pass and became the first pass-minded coach and player in pro football. During his many years associated with the Packers as a player and coach, Lambeau would tailor his offense around a passing combination matched with a competent running game.

Lambeau believed that using the forward pass defined the Packers and brought them instant notoriety. In his opinion, it is what would put the small-town Green Bay Packers on the map and keep them in the league, and he was right. (By 1935, the Depression was taking its toll and all of the small-town teams would be extinct—all, that is, except Green Bay's Packers. The team from the little Wisconsin town would stand alone.)

"I don't think we ever would have gotten into the National Football League without passing," Lambeau once said. "We took advantage of the defense, and it paid off. And, of course, it gave us a reputation."

Curly had heard of the September 1920 meeting of owners in Canton, Ohio, that had spawned the American Professional Football Association. He desperately wanted to be a part of the fledgling league.

Lambeau was not afraid of asking for what he wanted. Two years earlier he had persuaded Frank Peck to furnish jerseys and a practice field. Now all he had to do was to convince J. E. Clair, his boss at the Acme Packing Company, to apply for a league franchise. Curly's infectious smile and enthusiasm won over Clair, who applied for and was granted a franchise on August 27, 1921.

"Lambeau's Squad Only Pigskin Aggregation From Wisconsin in Famous Gridiron Organization," was the August 29, 1921, headline in the sports section of the *Green Bay Press-Gazette*. "Some of the biggest professional teams in the country will be seen in action here on the Hagemeister Park gridiron," George "Cal" Calhoun wrote. Adding that contracts for the games were in the mail and playing dates would soon be made public, Cal's column went on to warn that, "... any club guilty of tampering with college players will be expelled." In the very near future, the irony of that admonition would become clear.

Green Bay's first two seasons were very successful, although the opponents were almost always Wisconsin teams, and poor ones at that. In those first two seasons, the Packers finished with a combined record of 19-2-1, scoring 792 points and only allowing 36 against them! Seventeen games in that two-year stretch were shutouts. Teams like the Oshkosh Professionals and the oddly named Beloit Fairies were the equivalent of cannon fodder for Lambeau's young team.

Research reveals an odd discrepancy in the Packers' 1921 record. In his book *The Packer Legend*, John B. Torinus claims they finished the year at 7-2-2, while other sources list a 3-2-1 record. Apparently, Torinus included five independent games not recognized in official league records.

Howard "Cub" Buck was already a veteran of the game when Curly Lambeau coaxed him into playing tackle for the Packers in 1921. Cub began his football career in 1916 with Jim Thorpe's Canton Bulldogs, using "Moriarty" as his last name because his family didn't approve of football.

Cub was the first really big man in football, weighing in at a whopping 280 pounds. And he was strong—very strong. In true Paul Bunyan fashion, he once picked up two opposing players by the belts of their football pants (producing pro football's first, albeit unofficial, wedgie!)

A fierce competitor with a desire to win, Cub Buck was nonetheless a gentleman in every sense of the word. He never lost his temper and never uttered a cuss word in his life. He felt swearing indicated a lack of vocabulary.

Cub never engaged in an on-the-field fight. Years earlier, he'd been in a fight with another boy and beat the kid to the point onlookers thought he had killed him. That incident taught him to be careful with his superior weight and strength.

Cub Buck did, however, earn the first broken nose in the Bears-

Packers rivalry. A dubious honor, to be sure.

On November 27, 1921, 7,000 fans, including 300 cheering Packers' fans, took their seats in Cubs Park to witness the birth of professional football's oldest—and most famous—rivalry. While it was only the first meeting between the Chicago Staleys and the Green Bay Packers, events during that game would draw the first drops of bad blood between the two teams that continues to this very day.

It is only fitting that the first player to touch the ball and herald the start of the rivalry was George Halas. He took the opening kickoff back for twenty yards.

The Chicago Staleys totally dominated Lambeau's crew. Ohio State back Pete Stinchcomb scored the game's first touchdown on a beautiful 45-yard blast off tackle, shaking off six tacklers on the way. Halas himself would score the final touchdown, hauling in a pass from "Chic" Harley.

The Packers only chances to score came on two attempted field goals by Curly Lambeau. He missed one and the other was blocked.

The *Chicago Tribune*'s Monday sports page headline would spell it out in bold type: "Staleys Whale Green Bay Packers for 20 to O Victory."

"The Packers were beaten but not disgraced," Cal wrote in the *Green Bay Press-Gazette*. "Every man on the team played great football. The Packers met a better team."

Early in the game, small but feisty Chicago guard "Tarzan" Taylor sucker-punched Cub Buck and broke his nose. With most players, that would have started a donnybrook, but not with the disciplined and controlled Buck. He simply told Taylor, "You're supposed to be a college graduate and a gentleman, you know." Buck's restrained condemnation hurt Taylor more than a good punch could have. (Buck would, however, get his revenge in a 1925 game when one of the Bears tried to break Buck's nose, but Cub reached out, caught his opponent's arm, and snapped it like a twig.)

Coverage of the game in the *Chicago Tribune* and *Green Bay Press-Gazette* is interesting because of the differences in the articles' detail and length. The *Tribune* offered only a small two-column wrap up, including the starting lineups. Thanks to Cal, however, the *Press-Gazette* printed a thorough play-by-play commentary of the game in addition to the lineups.

In Chicago, the Staleys were not the only game in town. Besides competing for newspaper coverage against the more popular college football game, the Staleys also had to contend with baseball's well-established Cubs and White Sox teams. Chicago was a big sports town with lots to cover and the Staleys warranted little ink at the time.

It is no surprise that George Halas was the author of every article about the Staleys in the Chicago papers in 1921; none of the press corps' reporters attended Staley games.

Green Bay, on the other hand, had its Packers and little else. The Packers were the only game in the small town. Although college football and other amateur sports dominated the sports page, Cal kept the Packers alive and well almost by himself. His daily column provided just the kind of cheer leading the young Green Bay team needed.

Someone noticed three new faces on the Packers' sideline during that first Staleys' game that weren't listed in the lineup. Although two of them have long since been forgotten, the third would play a big part in the futures of the Chicago Bears and the Green Bay Packers. His name was Heartley W. "Hunk" Anderson and he was the starting guard on Knute Rockne's Notre Dame squad. And that was the problem.

Hunk, and the other two (anonymous) Packers had not yet graduated from college. The previous year, team owners had pledged not to play undergraduates in professional games, an agreement loosely obeyed at best. However, many college players had played for different pro teams under assumed names. Some would even go as far as to bandage their faces to hide their identities. Hunk and his two cohorts were certainly not the first collegiates to play pro football.

Someone squealed to the *Chicago Tribune* that Anderson and his two teammates had played for the Packers in the Staleys' game. Knute Rockne saw the *Trib*'s exposé and promptly banned the three players from college football.

George Halas wasted no time. At his behest, the league, now re-christened the National Football League, revoked the Green Bay franchise for playing undergraduates in the game against Chicago. Halas and every other manager had found—and used—loopholes in the agreement in order to use college players. Why was he being so self-righteous now?

Author Larry Names theorized in his book, *The Lambeau Years-Part One*, that Halas was upset that Curly Lambeau had managed to get Hunk Anderson first. Because Halas wanted Anderson on the Bears, he squealed to the league and got the Green Bay franchise revoked so he could then sign Anderson. After all, Anderson couldn't play for the Packers if the team didn't exist!

How surprised Halas must have been when, at the league's 1922 meetings in Canton, Curly and his friend Don Murphy showed up with an apology, a request to be accepted back into the league, and the required $250 franchise fee.

According to Names, the wily Halas then had the league hold up the Packers' franchise application until after Anderson's graduation and Halas had the opportunity to sign him to the Bears. Sure enough, the Packers' application was held up until the last week of June 1922.

In the meantime, the "stolen" Anderson graduated, signed with the Bears, and played six seasons on the line. Hunk Anderson went on to become one of football's greats innovators. He even coached the Bears in the mid-Forties while Halas served in the Navy during World War II.

There you have it. The greatest rivalry in football began because George Halas single-handedly engineered the revocation of the Green Bay Packers' franchise for the sole purpose of stealing Heartley W. "Hunk" Anderson away from Lambeau.

Ironically, three years later Halas would tamper with an undergraduate player. Although the result would be extremely beneficial for the league and the Bears, it still shows that Halas would do anything to gain an upper hand on an opponent.

The January 28, 1922, *Chicago Tribune* applauded itself for exposing the infraction. The sports page headline boasted, "FOOTBALL PROS SHOW GREEN BAY THE DOOR, TRIBUNE STORY CAUSE."

While the story included information on new rules adopted at the league meetings and that Halas had been granted a franchise for the newly christened Chicago Bears and would be operating out of Cubs Park, it concluded with, "The action of the American Professional Football Association was the direct result of an exposé by the *Tribune* of conditions prevailing on the Green Bay team."

Green Bay residents grumbled about Halas and the Packers' expulsion in whispers around town. A growing hostility and general feeling of loathing grew for Halas and his Chicago Bears.

Another event would soon add fuel to the fire and the *Green Bay Press-Gazette*'s George "Cal" Calhoun would find himself right in the middle of it all.

The 1921 Staleys were declared champions of the American Professional Football Association with their 10-1-1 record. The Staleys could only bask in the glory of winning the championship. It certainly didn't make them any money. The team had, in fact, lost money on the year.

At the recommendation of George Halas, both the Chicago Staleys and the league changed names in 1922. Wanting a connection with the baseball Cubs, his Wrigley Field counterparts, Halas renamed his football team the Chicago Bears. Also, his proposal to rename the American Professional Football Association to the National Football League was adopted.

The newly christened Chicago Bears beefed up their squad with some new faces. Dutch Sternaman cajoled his younger brother Joey into joining the Bears. "Little Joey," who played quarterback for eight years, also became one of the best drop-kickers in the league.

Another addition was tackle Ed Healey. Halas had played against him when Healey had starred with the Rock Island Independents. Healey was too big for Halas to control so he had resorted to holding him at the line, something Healey didn't care for. After that brutal game, Halas thought he would rather have Healey playing for him than against him.

In 1922, the Rock Island team owed the Bears $100, so Halas took Healey's contract in lieu of the money. Healey went on to make All-Pro five times and helped anchor the very tough Bears' line until his retirement at the end of the 1927 season.

Healey and the other newcomers, Laurie Walquist and Joe LeFleur, found playing with Chicago brought luxuries they had never known. Back then, most NFL locker rooms had but one shower for the entire team and players hung their clothes on a big nail in the wall. The Chicago Bears, however, had heat, showers, and even lockers in the locker room!

While the Bears sailed through most of their 1922 schedule beating up on opponents, the Packers had a much tougher time of it. Eventually, they limped through the season, finishing with a mediocre record of 4-3-3.

The second scheduled contest between the Bears and Packers had been set for Thanksgiving Day at Hagemeister Park. A huge turnout was expected. However, earlier in the season Halas had wired Lambeau demanding that Green Bay pay him $4,000 before he brought his Bears north to play in the November game. Although the two teams had already signed a contract to play, Halas now wanted an increased guarantee. Lambeau could do little about it. Halas reasoned that he could stay in Chicago, pack 10,000 fans into Cubs Park to watch them play their cross-town rivals, the Cardinals, make twice the money they would playing in Green Bay, and be home later that day for a turkey dinner and all the trimmings.

On Thanksgiving Day, the Packers' were forced to replace the Bears with the non-league Duluth Kellys. The game was a disaster. It began raining the night before the game and never stopped. Expecting attendance to be low, Curly and Cal discussed canceling the game. If they played the game, they would owe the Duluth team their guaranteed money. Yet, if no one showed up they wouldn't have the money to pay. Curly and Cal decided to call Andrew B. Turnbull, the *Press-Gazette*'s business manager, for advice. He advised them to play the game and work it all out later.

The game did go on as scheduled and less than 100 people showed up. Curiously, the Packers' press guide lists 2,000 fans in attendance. Only in Lambeau's dreams would 2,000 come out in a driving rain storm on Thanksgiving Day to watch a non-league team. The Packers won the meaningless game, 10-0.

The canceled Thanksgiving Day game was yet another incident that passionate Green Bay fans could blame on George Halas. Not only had Halas engineered the loss of Green Bay's football franchise and held up the application until he could sign away a Packers' player, now he had stabbed the Packers in the back by canceling a holiday game and forcing them to play a non-league team that cost them money! Cal couldn't put it in print, but he went around town calling Halas and his Bears all sorts of terrible names.

There was, however, a silver lining around those storm clouds that deluged Green Bay that Thanksgiving Day: Andrew B. Turnbull. Turnbull felt the only way to keep professional football in Green Bay was to put it on a firm financial base.

In the summer of 1923, Turnbull enlisted the aid of Lambeau, Leland H. Joannes, Dr. W. Weber Kelly, and Gerald F. Clifford to organize a corporation to provide financial support to the Packers. Sports writer Oliver E. Kuechle of the *Milwaukee Journal* dubbed the group of prominent and highly respected business men "The Hungry Five" because they all went begging for badly needed capital.

On August 18, 1923, the "Articles of Incorporation for the Green Bay Football Corporation" were filed with the State of Wisconsin. The document listed Andrew Turnbull as president, Joannes as secretary and treasurer, Kelly and George Delair as members of the executive committee, and George Calhoun as team secretary.

The Articles provided that stock would be sold for $5 a share and the purchaser had to buy at least six season tickets. The Green Bay Packers were then—and are still to this day—the only team publicly owned in the NFL. The stock certificates clearly stated that no dividend would ever be paid. The Green Bay Football Corporation's Articles declare that in the event of dissolution, the Corporation and all assets would go to the Sullivan-Wallen Post of the American Legion for the purpose of erecting a proper soldiers' memorial.

The only way Green Bay could lose its team would be through bankruptcy. No stockholder would ever vote to move the franchise and assets could not be sold without the approval of the stockholders.

The Green Bay Packers were here to stay.

1923-1924

As previously noted, a long career was a rarity during pro football's infancy. The aforementioned George Trafton had no peers, but the Packers' center for eleven years, Jug Earp, had an equally long career.

At a hefty 240 pounds, Jug was in charge of law and order on the Packers' line from 1922 until his retirement in 1932. Such responsibility came naturally. Jug was related to legendary lawman Wyatt Earp.

Jug began his professional career in 1921 with Ed Healey and the Rock Island Independents. After one season, however, Earp found himself in Wisconsin.

"I can't remember for the life of me the man who contacted me about coming to Green Bay," Earp once said. "Anyway, he talked to me in Rock Island and three weeks later Curly Lambeau wired me an offer. I was in Green Bay the next year."

Earp and Trafton would often butt heads during their unusually long careers. "We had some battles, old George and I," Earp recalled. "One thing they said about us was never true, though. They started a story that we used to spit in each other's eye with tobacco juice during a game. Some fan started that and I bet I've denied it fifty times and they still believe it. I don't think Trafton ever had a chew in his life and I know I never did."

Earp and the Packers played their home games in 1923 and '24 in Bellevue Park. Built primarily for baseball, Bellevue Park was a grossly inadequate football venue. The city and the team had to wait two more years for City Stadium to go up near the original site of Hagemeister Park. The Packers would call City Stadium home until 1957.

Due to Halas' cancellation of the Thanksgiving Day game, the Packers and the Bears never met during the 1922 season. 1923 began a run of sixty years in which the two teams played at least once each season. The streak ended with the strike-shortened season of 1982.

The two rivals buckled up their leather helmets for their second get-together on October 14, 1923, at Bellevue Park. Some 4,481 Green Bay fans paid to heckle the hated Bears, while another 200 fans nicknamed the "Knot Hole Gang" watched the game for free through the fence.

"Horseshoes aren't supposed to be part of gridiron equipment but the Bears sure had 'em in Sunday's fracas," the *Press-Gazette* reported.

A fumble in the second quarter gave Dutch Sternaman the opportunity to hit a three pointer that turned out to be the lone score in a 3-0 Bears' victory. Green Bay's two field goal attempts missed badly.

The *Press-Gazette* did provide a vivid account for its readers who were not at the game. "When the Bears pranced on the field, a chorus of 'Ohs' greeted them. Every man on the Bruin squad looked as big as a house and garbed in their orange sweaters, they sized up like giants. The Bears sure are 100 per cent in huskiness."

By the end of '23, the Bears weren't husky enough. Halas and Sternaman had put together a good squad but they finished second behind the Canton Bulldogs. The Bears' 9-2-1 record was good, but the Bulldogs' 11-0-1 record was better.

The Packers, in the meantime, finished a fine 7-2-1 season in third place right behind the Bears.

Hoping to make his Packers more competitive in 1924, Curly Lambeau recruited a lanky Nebraskan by the name of Verne Lewellen. Baseball's Pittsburgh Pirates had been ready to sign Lewellen until his pitching arm was injured in a train wreck.

When his spindle-like legs met the ball, Verne Lewellen could kick it over sixty yards. A number of his kicks sailed eighty yards in the air. Not only did he have distance, he was deadly accurate as well. It's unfortunate the league didn't keep records back then because Lewellen would certainly rank as one of the league's best punters.

Verne Lewellen was a versatile back who scored fifty touchdowns during his nine years with Green Bay. With 301 points, Lewellen ranked as the Packers' all-time scorer until 1942, ten years after he had retired.

In 1924, the Packers and the Bears joined sixteen other NFL teams vying for the chance to call themselves champions. The young league was experiencing growing pains, chaotic scheduling, low attendance, and transient players. At the July league meetings in Chicago, motions were considered to split the bulging league into an eastern and western division and to have the league, not the teams, schedule all games. (However, the division concept was not adopted until 1933, when the Depression thinned the league to ten teams.)

One motion that was adopted—and later to be regretted by its creator Dutch Sternaman—set the football season from September 24 through November 30. The championship would be determined by the games played between those dates.

On December 7, 1924, the Chicago Bears trounced the Cleveland Bulldogs, 23-0, in a game billed by many as a championship contest. After the game, four separate teams laid claim to the NFL title. League president Joe Carr settled the squabble by declaring Cleveland the champion. Carr had enacted Sternaman's season-setting motion so Chicago's win over Cleveland didn't matter. Cleveland, with the best percentage of the four protesting teams, was awarded the championship.

September 21, 1924, is a day that is forever etched into the memories of any die-hard Packers' fan. That was the day the Green Bay Packers defeated the Chicago Bears for the very first time. Even though it was just an exhibition game, it still meant a lot to Lambeau's squad to whip the big city upstarts from down south. The capacity crowd at Bellevue Park gleefully watched their beloved Packers blank the Bears, 5-0, in what the *Chicago Tribune* called a "bitterly contested game."

The rivals' third battle was played in Cubs Park just two weeks before the end of the '24 season. It was a carbon copy of the '23 game.

Dutch Sternaman won the 1923 game with a field goal, but Dutch's younger brother Joey won the '24 game with his toe. After the Packers' Warren Hendrian fumbled in the third quarter, the junior Sternaman stepped up to the Packers' 28-yard line and nailed the field goal. The Bears held on to win a second straight 3-0 victory.

"It was a fighting team all the way and the Green Bay fans in attendance were still mighty proud of their Packers," Cal wrote in the *Press-Gazette*. Calling the game "a grudge battle," Cal noted the Packers had died "with their boots on."

Lambeau's penchant for passing garnered applause from even the most ardent Bears' supporters. "Some Windy City scribes," Cal continued, "admitted that when it came to 'basketball football,' the Packers were in a class by themselves."

Pass-happy Curly Lambeau would become the first player to throw for over one thousand yards in one season. His record 1,094 yards in 1924 far outclassed anyone else in the league. As a team, the Packers would throw for 1,448 yards, more than doubling the output of the runner-up Milwaukee Badgers. Lambeau was passing from anywhere on the field and at anytime. To Curly, passing was the best and fastest way to get down the field.

Lambeau's lads finished the '24 campaign at 7-4, sixth place in the standings. After a slow start, the young Packers won six straight before splitting their final three games.

The 1924 edition of the *Green Bay Press-Gazette*'s annual All-NFL team, a poll taken by sports writers in NFL cities, placed one Packer and three Bears on the first team. Green Bay's end Tillie Voss was honored along with Bears' tackle Ed Healey, quarterback Joey Sternaman, and center George Trafton. Curly Lambeau only garnered second team honors.

1925

"Green Bay placed itself in bigger [company] than ever before on the National Football map Sunday afternoon at City Stadium when the fighting Packers scored a victory over the famous Chicago Bears by the score of 14-10, in a thrilling encounter which was witnessed by the largest crowd that ever attended an exhibition of pigskin chasing in Green Bay," wrote George Whitney Calhoun in the *Press-Gazette*. "It was probably the most sensational game ever played by the Packers."

The Bears received the opening kickoff and began a steady march downfield towards Green Bay's goal line. With the tip of the ball mere inches from the goal line, a touchdown seemed assured. However, Halas and the Bears didn't count on a stubborn Packers' defense that, as Cal put it, "... battled as they never battled before." Bears' ball carriers slammed into the line four times only to be rebuffed by the Packers' front wall. The goal line stand would be the deciding factors.

Green Bay's first score came on a blocked punt. Packers' right guard Moose Gardner slipped through and blocked the kick as four players dove for the ball. A Bear picked it up, fumbled it in the end zone, and Gardner jumped on the ball, as Cal put it, "like a hot potato."

After Chicago's Joey Sternaman drop-kicked a field goal, the Bears turned the tables and scored on their own blocked punt. Verne Lewellen's kick was blocked by George Trafton, and Bears' right tackle Richard Murray grabbed the ball and scampered in for the score. Bears 10, Packers 7.

The game-clincher came in the fourth quarter with the Packers' deep in the Chicago zone. Cub Buck asked for a towel from the sidelines to wipe off the ball. After a couple more stunts, he had the Bears' defense believing the Packers were going to try a field goal. Catching the Bears off guard, quarterback Charlie Matheys took the snap and lofted a rare pass in the direction of halfback Verne Lewellen who caught it in the end zone for a touchdown. Cub Buck booted the extra point, giving the Packers' their first-ever regular season win over the crew from Chicago.

While the invigorated Packers went on to win five of their next seven games, the Bears did even better. The Halas-led Bruins were 5-1-1 in their next seven games, giving up only sixteen points for the series.

Scheduled for mid-November, the next Packers-Bears encounter would reap more publicity than any professional football game in history, all because of a young man who used to haul ice blocks to make spending money.

In 1925, many viewed pro football as nothing more than a third rate, bargain-basement imitation when compared to the much more popular college game. It was quite common for 75,000 people to show up in Columbus, Ohio, for a Saturday afternoon college game, while a meager 4,000 would attend a pro game on Sunday. While the college patrons sat in huge bowl stadiums overlooking well-kept fields of green, the few hearty souls who turned up to watch the pro game did so in rundown ballparks with dirt and rock playing fields.

They sat in crude grandstands to enjoy an outcast game. Those early fans of pro football were mostly blue-collar working class folks who would scrape up $1.00 for a bleacher seat to see the likes of Jim Thorpe, George Trafton, and other pro ball players of the era.

For the most part, sports writers shunned the pro game. Why cover a low-class professional football game when they could write about a Gene Tunney knockout or the antics of the immortal Babe Ruth? Back then, pro football usually rated no more than a brief mention at the bottom of the sports page.

Many felt it was disgraceful to even play football on Sunday. Playing football on the Sabbath was bad enough but getting paid to do so was downright sacrilegious.

Some distinguished college coaches at the time spoke out openly and loudly about the evils of playing football after one's college career was over.

University of Michigan coach Fielding Yost publicly admitted to discouraging his athletes from pursuing a professional career as a player or coach. George Huff, Illinois' athletic director, denounced pro football, despite being an ex-professional baseball player him-

self. The controversy did not subside until the following year when
league Commissioner Joe Carr helped pushed through regulations
prohibiting any pro team to sign a collegiate player before his class
graduated.

Players were still paid meager salaries and conditions were mini-
mal at best. Players dressed for games anywhere they could. In
Pottsville, for example, the Packers would dress in the fire station
two blocks from the stadium. When they played the Staten Island
Stapletons, they would dress in their downtown New York motel
rooms, take a bus to the Staten Island Ferry, then take the ferry to
the island to play the game.

The year 1925 saw the introduction, at last, of a lined football
that held its shape. The heavy and fat earlier footballs were, basically, bladders covered in leather. To make matters worse, the early
ball had no lining, so the more the ball got kicked and bounced
around, the flatter it got. (George Halas once fielded a kickoff that,
by the time he got a hold of it, was nothing but a flat slab of leather.)

Yet, 1925 is remembered for more than the redesigned football.
It was also the year the pro game found its savior. He had been
lauded and glorified during his days at the University of Illinois
where he was All-Everything. (In 1991, *Sports Illustrated* put him on
its cover, calling him "an original superstar.")

In college he was known as "The Wheaton Iceman" because he
hauled huge blocks of ice during his summers in Wheaton, Illinois.
He was also called "The Galloping Ghost." This football Messiah
was Harold "Red" Grange.

Red Grange came to the pro game and immediately transformed
its image, putting pro football on the sports page above the fold.
Single-handedly, Grange legitimized the professional game when,
on November 21, 1925, after his last game for Ohio State, he
announced his intention to play professionally.

The idea for Red to go pro actually occurred a few months earlier. Red and a teammate went to see a movie at the Virginia Theater
in Champaign. An usher approached Grange in the theater and
handed him a one-year movie pass compliments of the owner,
Charlie Pyle. Red returned to the movie house a couple of days
later and happened to meet the nattily dressed Pyle in the lobby.
Inviting Grange to his office, Pyle stunned Red by asking him if he

would like to make a lot of money playing pro football. Red was, of course, intrigued, but Pyle swore him to secrecy. Pyle said he would be in touch.

The next day, Pyle went to Chicago where he met with Bears' co-owners Halas and Sternaman about signing Grange. It was agreed that Red would sign a pro contract directly after his last college game. He would then play in the season's remaining games. The Bears' squad would then tour from Florida to the West Coast playing a series of exhibition games. Pyle would book the tour himself. Most believed Red Grange would draw the same large crowds to the pro game as he had to his college games.

The day after the season closed between Illinois and Ohio State, Grange, Pyle, Halas, and Sternaman met at the Morrison Hotel in Chicago and agreed to the pact. Red was set to capitalize on his gridiron fame.

Later that same day, Red Grange, draped in a fur coat, sat on the sidelines and watched along with 6,398 freezing fans as his Chicago Bears thrashed the Green Bay Packers, 21-0, the Packers' worst defeat ever. *Green Bay Press-Gazette* writer George Calhoun opined that maybe Red Grange had jinxed the Packers; the peerless one had recently been getting more publicity than President Coolidge.

Cal wrote that Grange "made his bow to the shivering multitudes and got a hand that must have been heard in Green Bay." Cal added that the famous Red "looked every inch the college hero and whenever he moved there were a thousand hero worshippers pushing and shoving at his heels."

"I believe the public will be better satisfied with my honesty and good motives if I turn my efforts to that field in which I have been most useful in order to reap a reward which will keep the home fires burning," Grange told the crowd.

That night, the Champaign Rotary Club held their annual dinner for the University of Illinois football team and Grange and Coach Zuppke were there. Zuppke was not going to miss the chance to get in a few good barbs against his former superstar.

"I have nothing against professional football," Zuppke began. "The only thing I regret is that Red will no more graduate from Illinois than will the Kaiser return to power in Germany. From now on he will travel a different course than he was here. Grange is green, greener than when he first came to Illinois. He must watch out for persons who will try to make their own fortunes out of his tact and his talent. Grange will pass on. He will be forgotten."

Red Grange immediately got up and left.

Red's official debut came four days later on Thanksgiving Day against the Chicago Cardinals. Sports scribe Irving Vaughan wrote in the *Chicago Tribune* that "The whole town rose up on its hind legs and shouted we must have tickets!" When the tickets did go on sale, the crush for them became so great that mounted and foot patrol officers were called to restore a semblance of order. Meanwhile, those early birds who had already purchased tickets meandered through the crowd offering to sell their $1.75 seats for $5 apiece. Grange's overwhelming popularity drew 36,000 fans (at the time, the biggest crowd ever to attend a pro game) to his debut at Wrigley Field.

The allure of Red Grange can be compared to the box office lure of basketball's Michael Jordan. People simply wanted to see this bigger-than-life character in person. The spell Grange cast made them go out to the stadium in sub-freezing temperatures to watch him run between the chalk lines.

Like Jordan today, Grange was courted by many pitch men for product endorsements. 1925 saw an unusual assortment of products bearing Red's name: a candy bar, socks, a brand of cigarettes, a fountain pen, ginger ale, and even yeast-foam malted milk!

After the '25 season, Grange and the Bears set out on two brutal tours. They traveled more than 10,000 miles and played seventeen games, from the opener in St. Louis on December 2, 1925 to the finale in Seattle on January 31, 1926. Hordes of people came out to see the great Grange in Boston, Jacksonville, and New Orleans. Unbelievably, 75,000 people filled the Los Angeles Coliseum to watch Red play. Coral Gables, Florida, built a 25,000-seat stadium in only two days to showcase Grange. Ticket prices were as high as $18! The tours were very successful.

Although C. C. Pyle and Red Grange hit the mother lode in Grange's first year as a pro, they set their greedy sights on even more in 1926. Pyle suggested the only way Red Grange would wear a Bears' uniform in '26 would be for the Grange-C. C. Pyle Company to own one third of the team. Halas and Sternaman rejected that plan immediately.

Undaunted, Pyle created his own team around Grange, the New York Yankees. The team, however, was not allowed to play in the NFL. The persistent Pyle took it a step further: If his team couldn't play in the established league, he would just start his own.

The American Football League began with nine franchises. Pyle's new league was a major threat to the NFL in the beginning, but by year's end, only four teams remained active. The AFL survived just one season but, because of Grange's drawing power, the Yankees were invited to join the NFL.

Ironically, in a 1927 game against his former Chicago team, Red Grange suffered a knee injury on a pass play that sidelined him the entire 1928 season.

As Grange leaped for a pass he collided with Bears' center George Trafton. Grange's cleats caught in the turf as he fell. Trafton fell on top of him, badly twisting Red's knee.

Red Grange would never be the same.

1926-'28

In the *Chicago Tribune*'s "Speaking of Sports" column, dated September 27, 1926, writer Don Maxwell commented on the young pro game.

"Pro football is here to stay," he began. "It has something college football lacks and it lacks a lot that college football has. Pro football offers the public a chance to see gridiron stars, developed in the colleges east, west, north, and south. It offers one a chance to see team positions played by experts. It offers opportunity to thousands who are shut out from college bleachers.

"What pro football lacks is enthusiasm, and the power to make the fan feel that he is personally interested in a team's success," Maxwell added. "Promoters might develop enthusiasm if they provided bands at the games. And they might develop a personal interest in their team's success if they organized the fans."

Maxwell was correct. Pro football did provide a place for

"postgraduates" to continue to play and get paid to do so. The old days when a football player graduated and never again had the option to play football were over. Playing pro football gave them that opportunity.

Maxwell was also right about the pro game being bland and humdrum. Low scoring and scoreless ties were common. In the mid 1920s, the majority of games were shutouts or scoreless ties.

To say the offense was at a disadvantage is an understatement. Playing with what was essentially an oblonged basketball made passing difficult. Also, there were no hash marks on the field. If a player was tackled near the sidelines, the ball was spotted there. In order to move the ball toward the middle of the field, the next play was too often obvious. A passer could not throw inside the five yards of the scrimmage line and a team throwing an incomplete pass landing in the end zone lost possession of the ball.

A rule adopted in 1927 made scoring more difficult. The league moved the goal post from the goal line to the back line of the end zone. It did save players the occasional headache inflicted by a collision with the goal post but it didn't make scoring any easier.

It was not until 1933 that the league made passing legal from anywhere behind the line of scrimmage, marked the field ten yards from the sidelines, and planted the goal post back on the goal line.

In 1926 Green Bay and Chicago played three regular season games for the first time. The largest Wisconsin crowd to date—7,000 fans—filed into City Stadium on September 26 to watch the bitter rivals play to a hard-fought 6-6 tie.

"There was more honest-to-goodness football stuffed into those sixty minutes of gridiron skirmishing than has been seen here in many a year," George Calhoun extolled.

The game was typical 1920s pro football. It was a punting duel between Green Bay's Verne Lewellen and Chicago's Paddy Driscoll. The game also got riotous, as Green Bay rookie Carl Lidberg quickly learned.

"The opposing eleven's tackled in savage style," Cal wrote. "After 'Cully' Lidberg had been knocked 'cuckoo' and forced to leave the game, the Bays seemed to fall into a slump and it took a lot of driving by Capt. Lambeau to whip his club together again to stem the crashing Bear attack that seemed to get stronger as the fray progressed."

What wasn't so typical was that the game's only two scores came on passes. Both Curly Lambeau and the Bears' Laurie Walquist missed extra points, ending the game deadlocked.

An icy wind swirled around Cubs Park in November as the Bears' won the rematch, 19-13. Once again the game was exceptionally violent with, as the *Chicago Tribune* reported, "Each team determined to smash the other against the unyielding icy surface of the field." Trying to keep the game clean, officials ejected Packers' end Dick O'Donnell and Bears' end Frank Hanny for fighting in the fourth quarter.

Thanks to Curly Lambeau, the star of game three was the great Paddy Driscoll. With Green Bay leading 3-0 in the fourth quarter, Lambeau attempted a punt from his own 25-yard line. Lambeau fumbled, Chicago recovered, and Driscoll drop-kicked a field goal to tie the game.

The Bears had wooed Driscoll away from the cross-town Cardinals. Paddy set a NFL standard in 1926 by scoring eighty-six points, a season record that stood until broken by Green Bay's Don Hutson in 1941. Driscoll's twelve field goals that year set a record that stood until 1950.

Under George Halas, the 1926 Chicago Bears were a very strong squad but they would still finish second behind Guy Chamberlin's Frankford Yellow Jackets. The NFL championship was decided December 4 in Philadelphia when the Yellow Jackets edged the Bears, 7-6.

Lambeau's 1926 Packers finished with a respectable 7-3-3 record. Chicago, eclipsed by Frankford's 14-1-2 record, wound up 12-1-3, the only blemish being the one-point loss to the Yellow Jackets.

Bernard "Boob" Darling at center, Verne Lewellen at end, and Red Dunn and Charles Mathys at halfback joined Green Bay's first-year man Lavvie Dilwig for the 1927 campaign.

Dilwig was a straight arrow from Milwaukee's Marquette University. In 1926, his first year in the league, he played for the Milwaukee Badgers, an atrocious team whose only bright spot was Dilwig. His steady play earned him a good reputation around the league. When the Badgers folded after the '26 season, Dilweg signed with the Packers for what would be his greatest years.

Football researcher Bob Carroll once said Lavvie Dilweg was about as colorful as a hospital sheet. Not at all a flashy player, he would take the field, knock down any opponent he could, or block for a teammate. Lavvie would get up from a pile of players, walk back to his end position and await the next play. In a word, steady.

Dilweg received his law degree from Marquette in 1927, practicing football in the morning and law in the afternoon. "Most of the men in my day did nothing in the afternoons," he once recalled. "I was able to use law as a living, with football as a helper."

Dilweg eventually went into politics, once running against teammate Verne Lewellen for county attorney. Dilwig lost. In 1941, he was elected to the U.S. House of Representatives from Wisconsin. Years later he was appointed by President John F. Kennedy to the U.S. Foreign Claims Commission.

Lavvie Dilwig played the entire sixty minutes in just his third start for the Packers, a home game against the Bears. Chicago won, 7-6.

"It was a typical Bears-Packers game all the way," Cal wrote. "There was no love lost on either side and the players went after each other with hammer and tongs. When the fracas reached the sizzling point in the final stanza, several personal encounters enlivened the argument and the fans were yelling for blood."

George Whitney Calhoun may have been a crotchety, ill-humored, cigar-chomping geezer, but boy, could he turn a phrase!

On November 20, the Bears again defeated their northern rivals, 14-6, before the largest crowd of the season at Wrigley Field. Cal wrote that the game had thrill upon thrill and, "Even the final whistle found the thousands of fans pop-eyed with amazement."

The Packers just couldn't stop Chicago's hard-driving, elusive halfback Bill Senn. Green Bay's offense mainly consisted of Lewellen's kicking, who spent most of the day punting with his back to his own goal line.

The bright spot for Green Bay had to have been their marching band, the Lumberjacks. The *Press-Gazette* reported that the band marched around the field in their namesake outfits that included flaming red socks donated by Fred Burrall through the courtesy of the King Radio Company.

On Monday morning, October 22, 1928, Chicagoans thumbing through the *Chicago Tribune* saw a large display advertisement for the Oriental Theater at Randolph and State Streets boldly proclaiming, "He's Here TODAY!" The *Tribune* ad featured the likeness of the Galloping Ghost, Red Grange, and band leader Paul Ash with his Merry Mad Gang. "See Red and a big cast of entertainers in a rousing, rollicking revue packed with college spirit, syncopation, and fun!"

It was only one stop on the road of a vaudeville tour Red Grange had joined to try to put aside his troubling knee injury and the haunting fear that his football career was over. The 1928 season was the first fall since his childhood in Wheaton that he didn't don a football uniform. He felt like a duck out of water.

In the Vaudeville show, "C'mon, Red," Grange did a silly skit that got top billing and made him a nice chunk of change. Grange may not have been on the field dodging Green Bay tacklers or running for touchdowns, but his drawing power in Chicago was still strong.

While Red Grange the vaudevillian was packing theaters, Packers' and Bears' fans filled the stands for the three rival's games in 1928. Both teams finished just above mediocrity in the standings in the disappointing '28 campaign. Green Bay won the season's series by defeating the Bears twice; they tied once.

On September 30 at City Stadium, the two squads battled to a 12-12 tie. The Bears' jumped out to a 12-0 lead on a Joey Sternaman touchdown catch and a splendid 80-yard punt return by Dick Sturtridge. Unfortunately for Chicago, Sternaman missed both extra points.

The Packers' countered with two Verne Lewellen scores to tie the game but two missed extra points by the Packers' resulted in the deadlock. With just fifteen seconds left, Packers' kicker Harry O'Boyle attempted a game-winning field goal from the 30-yard strip. O'Boyle missed it to the left of the goal post by mere inches.

The air was spicy and cool and the sun was shiny and bright as the Bay's got the best of the Bruins, 16-6, at Wrigley Field just three weeks later. Of the 15,000 in attendance, the noisiest section came from where 2,500 Packer fans cheered their hometown heroes.

Green Bay Press-Gazette sports editor Arthur W. Bystrom had nothing but praise for the Bay's fans. He proudly wrote of the devoted Packers' fans who boarded the Chicago, Milwaukee, Pacific, and Northwestern railroads to travel to the game in Chicago, while as many as 900 Green Bay enthusiasts had driven to Wrigley Field.

The two rivals met again on the frozen turf of Wrigley Field December 9. A tough defensive battle, the game was scoreless with only two minutes left. The Packers' had the ball on their own 40-yard line when quarterback Red Dunn took the snap from center and drifted around end. It was a run fake. Dunn suddenly stopped, dropped back, and launched a bomb downfield for Dick O'Donnell. Surrounded by Bears, O'Donnell snagged the ball and raced to the goal line. The Packers' missed the extra point but it didn't matter. Green Bay won their season-ender, 6-0.

"The intense rivalry between the teams urged both in the vehemence of their defensive tactics," wrote *Chicago Tribune* scribe Wilfrid Smith. "Fleckenstein [Bill], Bears' center, ably filled the role of his predecessor, George Trafton, in fomenting miniature riots. He was argumentatively and physically opposed by Jones [Bruce] of the Packers and Dunn, whose control of his temper is notable for its absence."

Packers' fans wanting to cheer on their hometown boys now made it a habit to attend games in Chicago, traveling en masse to the Windy City. At the December 9 contest, an estimated 600 Green Bay fans came by train and car.

Those who stayed at home converged on the Columbus Club, a Green Bay haunt where players and fans often mixed. There, all eyes would be glued to the Playograph Board. The board was a large replica of a football gridiron with a life-sized football that moved up and down the field to visually represent the play-by-play account of the game. Game information would be sent by telegraph from Wrigley Field to Green Bay where an announcer would broadcast the action over a public address system, and the board operators would move the ball re-enacting the game. When the Packers won, an automatic electric phonograph serenaded the happy fans with a rousing version of "On Wisconsin."

1929

Before the 1929 season, Curly Lambeau realized he was a few bricks shy of the load needed to have a powerhouse football team in Green Bay. He found his "bricks" and quite possibly saved professional football in Green Bay.

Mike Michalske, Cal Hubbard, and Johnny "Blood" McNally completed the foundation on which Lambeau built his football powerhouse in the north.

"Iron" Mike Michalske, who had played for the New York Yankees, signed with the Packers after the Yankees folded. The 6'2", 210-pounder from Cleveland, Ohio, had wanted out of New York anyway because "... there were too many bright lights and I couldn't save any money."

Michalske was one of the NFL's first great pass rushers. He was a master at getting to an opponent's passer and knocking the hell out of him.

"We called it blitzing in those days, too," he once said. "Our target was the man with the ball, but especially the passer. It may not have been exactly ethical but it was legal, in those days, to rough the passer even after he got rid of the ball. We worked him over pretty good."

Iron Mike pioneered the idea of turning fast, explosive fullbacks into linemen. He had played at fullback himself but thought moving to the line to take full advantage of his cat-like speed would strengthen the Packers' offense. Lambeau was sold on the idea.

Cal Hubbard was another valuable acquisition for Lambeau. Nicknamed "The Enforcer," the 6'2" Hubbard was a rock-hard 270 pounds, and the biggest man playing pro football at the time. Russ Winnie, radio voice of the Packers, used to say Cal weighed between 265 and 280 pounds, depending upon what he ate for breakfast.

After one year with the Giants, he told the team, "Trade me to the Packers or I quit." Cal had decided he liked Green Bay after spending a week there the year before. "We played the Packers in Green Bay one Sunday and had to play the Bears in Chicago next, so we stayed in Green Bay that week to practice," he once commented. "I kind of liked Green Bay."

What he also liked was umpiring baseball, which he would do professionally from 1928 until 1951. Hubbard has the distinction of being enshrined in both the Pro Football Hall of Fame and the Baseball Hall of Fame.

In addition to his devastating power and strength, the mountainous Hubbard also had a sense of humor. Near the end of the 1936 championship game against the Boston Redskins, Cal stood and shouted across the line yelling that if anyone had a grievance they had a minute left to get even because he was retiring from the game.

John Victor McNally was the remaining player Lambeau needed to ensure a championship team. McNally played college football at St. John's University in Minnesota, but also played in semi-professional games there. In order to play semi-pro ball and still protect their collegiate eligibility, college players would disguise themselves and compete under an alias. One day while Johnny and a friend were walking to a semi-pro tryout, they passed a movie marquee advertising Rudolph Valentino's "Blood and Sand." McNally grabbed his friend's arm and said, "That's it, you be Sand and I'll be Blood." And Johnny Blood was born.

"In my negotiations with Curly Lambeau, I asked for $100 a game," McNally once recalled. "He came back with an offer of $110 a game, providing I would initial a clause in the contract forbidding any drinking after Tuesday of each week. I countered with an offer to take the $100 I had proposed and drink through Wednesday. Curly agreed."

Mike Michalske, Cal Hubbard, and Johnny Blood joined seasoned veterans to make the 1929 Green Bay Packers powerful, unconquerable, and one of the best football teams to ever walk onto a field. During a rugged thirteen game season, they held opponents to an astounding 22 points, recording an equally amazing seven shutouts. They were undefeated at 12-0-1: the only blemish in their record being a scoreless tie with the Frankford Yellow Jackets.

On Sunday, September 29, 1929, Boy Scouts, high school students, and policemen directed fans to their seats at City Stadium for the next installment of the Packers-Bears rivalry. It was no surprise that tickets were scalped as high as $10 for bleacher seats. This game not only featured the two league rivals but also showcased the return of Number 77, Red Grange.

Frank Zambreno, the man who had booked Grange's vaudeville tour, told Red he should try to play football again. Seeing that Red's true talent obviously lay in performing on a football field rather than on a vaudeville stage, Zambreno had talked to Halas and had found him to be positive about Grange returning to the Chicago Bears for the '29 season. Halas was enthusiastic about Grange returning to the Bears as a player and Red wanted back into football in the worst way.

Grange's serious knee injury had limited his cutting and darting ability, reducing him to a straight ahead, part-time runner. Obviously rusty after a year's layoff, Red played mostly on pass defense, where, at first, he missed many tackles.

Before the game, Grange took the field of Green Bay's City Stadium and addressed the crowd over the loud speaker. Grange announced that he was "... glad to have the opportunity to play in Green Bay and hoped that the best team would win." He got his wish.

"How the mighty have fallen," was the lead line of Arthur Bystrom's narrative of the game in the *Green Bay Press-Gazette*.

"The Chicago Bears, once powerful and ferocious rulers of the midwest professional football kingdom, have undergone an evolution and today are seeking shelter in the lowlands and the Green Bay Packers are perched upon the vacated throne," Bystrom proudly exalted. "They blocked like demons and charged like a hurricane, sweeping everything before it."

Early in the second period, the Packers' offense struck twice. After a fine exhibition of passing by quarterback Red Dunn, Hurdis McCrary plunged over for a score. On the next series, Dunn tossed a 15-yard pass to Tom Nash and the Packers led, 14-0.

Two mistakes by the Bears settled the game. The Packers blocked a Bears' punt for a safety. Later, the Bears had a pass intercepted deep in their own territory. From ten yards out, Packers' runner Bo Molenda slammed over the goal line for the score.

Thirteen thousand Packers' fans were thrilled to watch the hated Bears suffer their worst defeat ever, a 23-0 smearing. Packers ran through the Bears' line like it was tissue paper, while the defense never allowed the Bears' offense to even get close to scoring. It had been no contest.

Near the end of the game George "Brute" Trafton shouted to his teammates from the bench, "Get in there and get used to it, we've got two more games with them."

A drenching downpour greeted the two teams in Chicago on November 10. After only a few minutes of action, spectators could hardly distinguish the numbers on the player's mud-caked uniforms. In an effort to help the fans differentiate Packers from Bears, an announcer walked up and down the field identifying players for the crowd over the public address system.

In the 14-0 Packers' win, the majority of the damage done to the Bears came from the foot of Johnny Blood. In an amazing display of kicking, Blood booted the wet pigskin for an average of fifty yards, keeping the Bears pinned in their own territory. The Packers' only low point came late in the game when Red Dunn separated his shoulder and had to be escorted off the field.

Chicago writer Wilfrid Smith's account of a donnybrook late in the game between Cal Hubbard and Bears' lineman Bill Fleckenstein is sports writing at its best: "Fleckenstein of the Bears and Cal Hubbard, 250 pound man mountain at right tackle for Green Bay, played a game of fist-tag in the closing minutes to top off the performance. Fleckenstein, with enthusiasm and in quite legal fashion, smacked Hubbard above the eye. On the next play, Hubbard led with his right, which may be poor boxing, but it came close to being taps for Bill. Naturally, Hubbard left the game. It would have been more interesting to have drawn a circle and let the boys continue, since by this time the rainy dusk had shrouded the game from the spectators."

The season-ending game a month later was a carbon copy of the first game. Thanks again to marvelous punting (this time by Verne Lewellen), the Packers swept the Bears, 25-0. Lewellen averaged 60 yards a punt, booting 185 yards and another 75 yards.

Completely overpowered, the Bears' one and only first down in the entire game came on a shifty 18-yard scamper by Red Grange. On nearly every other running attempt Grange was stopped cold at the line.

"It wasn't that the Bears' didn't try," wrote *Chicago Tribune* sports scribe Wilfrid Smith. "They faced a team which had everything in a champion's repertoire."

In 1929, Green Bay dominated every minute of play in all three games and won all three games against Chicago.

The league championship had more or less been decided three weeks before when the Giants entertained the Packers at New York's Polo Grounds. The 9-0-0 Packers beat the 8-0-1 Giants, 20-6, with Lambeau playing his eleven starters the entire game. The star of the contest was Johnny Blood, who recovered a fumble setting up a touchdown and scored the game's final TD on a short run.

League standings at that time were simply one list of the team's records and their winning percentage. The team finishing on top was considered the champion. The first championship game as we know it today was not played until 1932.

Lambeau had his first championship! His shrewd acquisitions of Hubbard, McNally, and Michalske had produced the powerhouse squad of his dreams. The 1929 Green Bay Packers became the first undefeated champion in NFL history.

After their final game with Chicago, the Packers were welcomed home by a crowd of devoted fans holding kerosene torches and lining the train tracks for five miles from DePere to Green Bay. Greeting the train in freezing temperatures, 20,000 fans paraded the champs from the station to the Beaumont Hotel for a giant victory celebration.

There were no celebrations in Chicago that Sunday night.

During the year, Bears' owners George Halas and Dutch Sternaman had differed on how to run the team's offense. The end result was that Chicago went nowhere.

Entering the second game with the Packers, Chicago was 4-2-1. After their 14-0 shellacking by Green Bay, the Bears totally fell apart. In their final seven games, the Bears tied one and lost six.

Finishing ninth in the twelve team league, it was the first losing season for Halas and his Chicago Bears. There had to be massive changes made for the Bears to be competitive again. While Chicago had become an old and complacent team, Lambeau had injected new vitality into the Green Bay squad. Add to the mix the growing dispute between Halas and Sternaman, and you had all the ingredients for a lousy season.

Relief for the Bears came in 1930 with the additions of a muscled giant discovered working in a Minnesota farm field and a new coach who promised a championship within three years.

The 1930s

A Bronk, a Moose, an Antelope,
and a Frustrated Priest

The Chicago Bears had just finished their worst season ever and the two owner-coaches, George Halas and Dutch Sternaman, knew changes had to be made. By 1930, they didn't agree on much except that they needed just one coach and it couldn't be either one of them.

Enter the bald-headed Lilliputian, Ralph Jones. Jones had been an assistant to Bob Zuppke at the University of Illinois and had enjoyed recent success at Lake Forest Academy near Chicago. Jones was an innovator and possessed a great football mind. While most teams were running the single-wing, double-wing, and Notre Dame box offenses, Jones did an about-face and re-instituted the ancient T-formation. Jones' new version would dominate pro football for decades.

Jones fine-tuned the T-formation and made it a multi-faceted offense. It spread out the defense by sending men in motion, splitting the ends, and opened up the passing game. Also, the quarterback was now directly behind the center to receive the ball, as in today's game.

Some old faces were still around, eager to renew the Bears' pride. George Trafton, Link Lyman, Joey Sternaman, Laurie Walquist, Bill Fleckenstein, Bill Senn, and Red Grange all returned for the 1930 season.

The new offense called for new blood. Two recruits made the Chicago squad contenders once again.

The Bears acquired University of Florida halfback and potato farmer Carl Brumbaugh, who quarterbacked Chicago for eight seasons. They also obtained a mammoth running back from Minnesota who was, according to one Chicago sports writer, a one-man football team.

At 6' 2," and 230 pounds of pure muscle, Bronko Nagurski was a legend before he ever played a pro game. The story goes that when Minnesota University coach Clarence Spears was out scouting, he stopped to ask directions of a young man plowing a field by himself ... without a horse. The *farmer* was pushing the plow! The farmer was Nagurski. Rather than just pointing the way, Bronko lifted the entire plow and pointed it toward town. Spears had his directions and his new fullback.

Bronko had huge shoulders, a size nineteen collar, tree trunk legs, and a great desire to pound someone into the ground. If his team won the game in the process, all the better.

One NFL coach said tacklers to Nagurski were like flies on the flank of a horse: a nuisance, but not a very serious one.

Bronko was matched up with Red Grange in the Bears' backfield. Not only would the two team up to gain over half the Bears' rushing yardage and combine for ten touchdowns in 1930, they would equal the feat in '31.

The revitalized T-formation got off to a slow start in 1930: The Bears lost their first four games, scoring only twenty total points.

Chicago's second loss of the year was a 7-0 thumping by Green Bay. In his first game against the defending champs, Nagurski gained just 36 yards on ten carries. Packers' defenders Cal Hubbard, Whitey Woodin, and Mike Michalske had rudely welcomed the big rookie.

Veteran Grange fared no better. He gained a pitiful 12 yards on ten carries, and had to leave the game in the second period after a ground-shaking crash with Johnny Blood. Blood was attempting to catch a Verne Lewellen pass when he smashed into Grange, who was also going for the ball. Grange was knocked out cold and carried from the field. Blood, uninjured, trotted back to the huddle. Big Red would return late in the fourth quarter.

The 3,000 fans from Wisconsin who followed their undefeated Packers to Wrigley Field on November 9 witnessed one of the best games the rivals had ever played.

Packers' quarterback Red Dunn passed for two touchdowns and kicked a critical extra point, leading the Bays to a 13-12 win, their twentieth straight win over two years.

Nagurski showed his true potential by contributing 104 of the

196 yards gained by the Bears. Writer A. W. Bystrom of the *Press-Gazette* was especially impressed by Bronko. "The Big Nag, Bronko Nagurski, led the Bear attack and what a whale of a game he played," Bystrom wrote. "Smashing, driving, and ever fighting his way forward, the former (Minnesota) Gopher star loomed up like a man mountain in Green Bay's path to another pennant."

Cocky veteran Cal Hubbard decided to test rookie Nagurski during the contest. Cal had heard how tough Bronko was and figured rattling Nagurski's teeth would be a nice way to welcome the young lad to the NFL. Nagurski and Grange were positioned as blocking backs each time the Bears lined up to punt. Over and over, Hubbard tried to get a shot at Bronko but Grange always stepped in the way.

Secretly during the game Hubbard promised Grange he would not block the punt if Red would allow him to burst through and let him see for himself just how tough Nagurski was. With the punt snap, Grange stepped out of the way and Cal came charging through with Bronko as his target. Nagurski dug in his cleats, leaned forward, and walloped Hubbard back across the scrimmage line. Hubbard wanted no more of that.

The rivals' third meeting of the year finally brought a reversal of fortunes for the Bears. The 22,000 fans at Wrigley Field that day watched the Bears blank the Packers, 21-0.

Red Grange would show his defensive (and, perhaps, mind-reading) prowess by intercepting two of Verne Lewellen's passes, both leading to Brumbaugh touchdown throws to Luke Johnsos. On Johnsos' second score, he badly out-foxed Packers' defensive man Johnny Blood, caught the ball, and simply jogged into the end zone with Blood trailing far behind.

The game also featured a double knockout crash. In the second quarter, Green Bay's rookie halfback, Wuert Englemann, collided with defensive back Joe Lintzenich while the two were vying for a pass. Both were knocked unconscious and carried from the field, to be revived in the dressing room.

Chicago finished the season very strong, winning seven of their last eight games. Ralph Jones' T-formation had improved the Bears' record from 4-9-2 in 1929 to third place in 1930 with a 9-4-1 for the season. It was those first two close games with their rivals that cost the Bears the championship.

Even with the late season slump, the eight straight wins earlier in the year had clinched the title for the Packers. At 10-3-1, Green Bay won a second consecutive title over the Giants by the narrow margin of only four percentage points.

Verne Lewellen finished a close second in league scoring with fifty-four points, while quarterback Red Dunn won the league's kicking honors. Nagurski and Blood had each scored thirty points for the year, a statistic Blood greatly improved the following season, while Nagurski's numbers fell.

The Depression began taking its toll on the smaller franchises in the league. 1931 saw the demise of the Minneapolis Redjackets, the Newark Tornadoes, and the independent Ironton, Ohio, Tanks. By the end of 1931, the Frankford Yellow Jackets and the Providence Steam Rollers also crumbled under the pressure of an ailing economy.

But in Green Bay, Wisconsin, all was well. After two consecutive championships, the team was on solid footing and Green Bay's support and pride in the team had never been higher. Many were even predicting a third straight pennant for the Bays. If Lewellen, Molenda, and Dunn stayed healthy and Johnny Blood didn't end up killing himself, it just might happen.

Professional football has had its share of unique characters, those eccentric oddballs of legend. The history of pro football abounds with stories of free-spirits and curfew-breakers who walked on window ledges, ate glass, and perpetrated other mischief.

One of the league's first true nonconformists was Green Bay's Johnny "Blood" McNally. An extrovert all his life, Blood's earliest memory was of standing on the windowsill of his nursery, pulling up his nightie, and flashing a small audience across the street.

"Without knowing it, I may have pioneered a new art form," he once said.

Blood was a restive kid growing up in New Richmond, Wisconsin. "When I look back on it, I can see that some of my unorthodox behavior came out of my upbringing in Wisconsin and had nothing to do with the zodiac," he recalled. "I was a horrendous character."

A voracious student, he graduated high school at fourteen. He was too small to participate in athletics but he did like to climb. "I loved to climb trees, telephone poles, and the outsides of houses," he recalled. As a teen, he once scaled the outside of a hospital to the third floor and crawled through the window to cheer up a sick friend.

Johnny was seventeen when he entered St. John's College in Minnesota. It wasn't long before he traded his trademark brown suit, white shirt, brown tie, and white tennis shoes for football, baseball, track and basketball jerseys.

Johnny McNally went on to Notre Dame to finish his postgraduate work and to play football for the Fighting Irish. He ended up only playing one year. He walked away from Notre Dame in the spring of 1924, "absenting myself from the campus, along with some classmates," he once recalled. Johnny also had gotten into trouble around St. Patrick's Day by partying too much.

After his expulsion from one of the most prestigious universities in the nation, "I bought a motorcycle," he remembered. "I was just learning to drive it fairly well, when I happened to attend a party in South Bend. There was a girl there and we got to talking. I told her I had purchased a motorcycle and was planning a tour of the Eastern seaboard. She confided that she was married to a sailor who was due to sail from Norfolk, and she was anxious to wish him bon voyage. So we set out."

When McNally next played ball it was in the NFL. Johnny bounced around the league for a couple of years, spending time with the Milwaukee Badgers and the Pottsville Maroons. It was his alliance with Green Bay from 1929 to 1936 that brought him football stardom, and brought Curly Lambeau a few headaches.

Blood was quite possibly the very first player to be fined. During practice following a late night of drinking and nightclubbing, Blood attempted a punt, missed the ball completely, and landed hard on his ass. Lambeau sent him back to the hotel.

"Alcohol hangs on to me," he once told writer Myron Cope. "I don't sober up fast. It's a family characteristic. I have plenty of recuperative power, but alcohol doesn't fall out of me. It hangs on to me."

The Blood-Lambeau relationship is legendary in the NFL. In Los Angeles for a game, Johnny approached Lambeau in the hotel lobby for some extra spending money so he could do the town right. Lambeau refused and headed for the elevator to his eighth floor room, telling Blood that he wouldn't be answering the door. Johnny pondered the situation for a moment and then deduced that maybe old Curly didn't hear him right.

Deciding to plead his case again, Johnny made his way up to the eighth floor and out onto the fire escape. With his palms against the building, he slowly sidestepped his way along the ledge until he was six feet from Curly's half-opened window. As he prepared to leap to Curly's window ledge, he heard a teammate's voice ring out from a window two floors below.

"Is that you up there, Johnny Blood?" the teammate said.

"The same," answered Blood.

"Dear God in Heaven," screamed the teammate, "what are you going to do?"

"Coach wants to see me," Johnny answered. "Told me to drop in and talk over a matter of business."

He then jumped, landed cleanly on the window ledge, threw open the window, and announced himself. Wild-eyed, Lambeau clutched his heart.

"I thought perhaps I didn't make myself clear, Coach, about the advance I asked for," Johnny said. "Now the fact is ... "

"Take it, take it!" Lambeau cried as he fumbled for some money. "Go anywhere you want, Johnny."

"Thank you, Coach," Blood said politely. "I knew we could come to an understanding once we talked things over in a calm, reasonable way."

"Go, just go!" Curly cried.

"Have a good night's sleep, Coach," Johnny called as he walked out into the hallway and into the night.

On a different occasion the Packers were set to embark on an exhibition tour in Hawaii right after the 1932 season. The train to the West Coast would leave the Green Bay station promptly at 10:00 a.m. That morning, Blood found himself still in the company of a young woman he'd met the night before who "was a late-riser, putting great demands on chivalry."

"I got a late start for the depot and discovered the train had left without me," Blood recalled. "There was really no choice. Either I stopped the train, which was then just pulling out of the yard, or I got fined for missing the train."

Blood and his date jumped in his touring car, floored it for three blocks, and pulled across the tracks in front of the oncoming train.

"I couldn't imagine that the engineer was a callous man and would run the engine through the car," Blood recalled, "especially since the lady and I were still in it."

As the engineer was stopping the train, Johnny, as befit a man named for Valentino, kissed the woman good-bye, left her in the driver's seat, and valiantly boarded the train.

On the way home from Hawaii, Blood's teammates were stunned to find him swinging from the flagpole on the stern of the ship. It was the dead of night and the ship was pitching in the rough seas. It was quite apparent Blood had had a bit too much Okole Hao, a native Hawaiian drink.

Ex-Packer Herm Schneidman recounted another tale about Johnny Blood from around the time of the Hawaiian trip.

"Johnny had this idea to take two teams to England and play one half football and the other half rugby," Schneidman said. "He thought that anyone going to England had to be continental and everybody should wear a hat, and none of the boys he knew wore a hat. He went to a Stetson hat store and bought twenty-two hats and had them put in a big canvas bag. Now this was after the football season.

"They were ready to start practice the next year and they can't find Blood. They finally got a call from him. He was still in California and he was out of money. Lambeau sent him some money to get to Green Bay.

"When he gets there, all he has is this big bag with twenty-two hats. Well, Jug Earp was the center on the team at that time and he had the largest head on the team. The smallest hat in the bag was too large for Earp! And they never did get to England."

Stories about the infamous Johnny Blood go on and on. Once while staying in a motel room, he couldn't find ice with which to make a drink. He left the hotel and later returned carrying a huge block of ice on his shoulder through the lobby. When someone asked him what he was doing, he simply answered that he was going to make himself a drink.

Then there's the one where two girls asked him for an autograph. "I'll do better than that," he said. "I'll sign it in blood." And with that he cut his wrist with a knife and signed the game program in his own blood. The cut required four stitches.

In another such display, Johnny once cut himself, wrote on a sign, again in his own blood, "I am the great Johnny Blood," and paraded it down the aisle of the train he was aboard.

There was just something about Johnny Blood and trains. He once had a $10 pre-game bet with Bears' quarterback Carl Brumbaugh on which team would be victorious. The Packers won the game and Blood boarded the Bears' train to collect his winnings.

"All hell cut loose," McNally remembered. "I came on board to challenge the whole Bears' team, which wouldn't have been very bright considering the few escape routes open. I barely got out of there in one piece, and I didn't collect the money from Brumbaugh."

Milwaukee Journal sports editor Ollie Kucchle dubbed Blood the "Vagabond Back" after he hopped a train on his way to the Packers' training camp one year. Kucchle first wanted to call him the "Hobo Halfback" but Lambeau asked him to change it to avoid the suggestion that the Packers hired hobos.

An early 1930s Packers' game program listed Johnny Blood as the most colorful football player that ever flaunted the Packers' blue and gold. It added that he could be called on to play any backline position, "and on the defense when he tackles 'em they usually stay tackled."

Johnny Blood was just as exciting on the field as he was off. He was a sure-handed pass-catcher with a flair for the spectacular. He had complete confidence in himself which his teammates also felt whenever he played.

He was unusually adept at improvising on demand. As proof, Herm Schneidman tells of one play in which Blood took command.

"We were leading 7-0 with like a minute to go 'til the half," Herm recalled. "We were around midfield and Johnny Blood called a long pass to himself to the goal line. Everyone in the huddle said,

'Check, check, check!' He said, 'I'm the quarterback and I called it.' The captain said, 'Check it, Johnny, it isn't right.' He repeated, 'I'm the quarterback and we're going to play it.'

"Well, he ran down and caught the damn ball for a touchdown. He came back to the sideline and he said to all of us, 'You know, you have to give people their money's worth in this game.'"

Writer Gerald Holland once asked Blood to rate himself as a player. "Well, I always figured I was a pretty fair all-around back," he replied. "I could kick with almost anybody. I wasn't a real good thrower, but in my time I was as good a receiver as there was around.

"I was said to be an imaginative signal caller. I called signals for three championship teams. I scored thirteen touchdowns for the Packers in 1931, and that was a record for the time."

Blood was traded to Pittsburgh in 1937 and became a player-coach. In his first game, he ran 100 yards for a touchdown with the opening kickoff. When he retired in 1939, his thirty-seven career touchdowns and 224 points were league records.

Blood finally graduated from St. John's some twenty-six years after the rest of his class. He later taught economics and history at St. John's and wrote a book on Maithusian economics.

A true jack-of-all-trades, Johnny was, at one time or another, a seaman, a croupier in a gambling house, a feed salesman, a hotel desk clerk, a farmhand, a floor waxer, and a pick-and-shovel worker for the WPA.

In 1963, the same year he was chosen as a charter member of the Pro Football Hall of Fame, he was asked his occupation.

"Reading, studying, writing, and meditating," he replied. "Once meditation was an honorable occupation. Today, it would appear on a police blotter as a form of vagrancy, I suppose."

Blood also once ran for sheriff of St. Croix County, Wisconsin. His simple campaign platform promised honest wrestling. He lost.

"People have told me," Blood once stated, "that I'm really a frustrated priest."

A record crowd arrived at City Stadium on September 27, 1931, for the twentieth episode in the ongoing rivalry. After too long a wait to get into the park, twenty fed-up fans put their shoulders to the fence and crashed it.

"Like a mighty 'Big Bertha' pounding the enemy's line, the Green Bay Packers pummeled the Chicago Bears at the City Stadium Sunday until the foe weakened," Arthur Bystrom wrote of the game between the champs and the challengers.

"The Packers, monarchs of the midwest football world, won a smashing 7-0 victory before a record 13,500. It was their twentieth straight win on the home field. The lone touchdown was scored on a short Lewellen run, under an unmercifully hot sun. The temperature baked the combatants and the water bucket got a real work out, especially by Lavvie Dilweg and Mike Michalske, who played the entire sixty minutes of action."

The game's only score came after Bears' back Joe Lintzenich fumbled on his own 22-yard line. Just minutes into the second half, Verne Lewellen smashed into the defensive line going in from just beyond the goal line for the touchdown. Red Dunn added the extra point.

The rest of the game was power against power. If not for Lintzenich's fumble and Johnny Blood's superior punting, the game may very well have ended in a scoreless tie.

Game coverage in the *Green Bay Press-Gazette* noted the presence of five newspaper photographers who raced up and down the sidelines "... adding a cosmopolitan atmosphere to the field."

Veteran Packers' Mike Michalske and Red Dunn would become hero and goat in 1931's two remaining games with the Bears. In game two in Chicago, Cal Hubbard crashed into Bears' quarterback Carl Brumbaugh, forcing him to hurry his throw. Michalske intercepted the ball and raced 80 yards for what would be the only touchdown in a 6-2 Packers' victory.

Writer Bystrom described the game as "... tense, occasionally sensational, often thrilling and always dogged." He went on to add that tackling and blocking were vicious and hard. "Occasionally," he wrote, "it was rough beyond necessity, but the officials did nothing about it. All who played took punishment as they have seldom taken it in any game."

The accuracy of Bystrom's account of the game was proven

when Lavvie Dilweg entered the game for but a few minutes. Nagurski took the ball and was running around Dilweg's side. Lavvie splintered through the Bears' offensive line and pulverized the big Nag, knocking him out.

Chicago lost by not taking advantage of Green Bay's errors. The Bears would not make the same mistake again. With a frigid Lake Michigan wind at their backs, the Packers, behind 7-0 in the second quarter, recovered a Bears' fumble at the 15-yard line. On the next play, Johnny Blood ran into the end zone covered closely by Red Grange. Wrigley Field's surface, frozen and slippery, caused Grange to slip and fall on the seat of his pants. Now all by himself, Blood cradled an Arnie Herber-thrown pass and ran it in for a touchdown.

Red Dunn missed the point after attempt, hooking it past the upright by mere inches. It was a rare miss by Dunn, who finished 1931 second in league kicking. Explaining the miss, the *Press-Gazette* reported Dunn had entered the game "cold and stiff."

As a team, the 1931 Packers were far from being cold and stiff. Their only losses that year were to the Chicago Cardinals and their last game with the Bears. The eccentric Johnny Blood won the league scoring title with eighty-four points, leading the Packers to a 12-2 record and their third consecutive championship.

Shortly after the last Bears' game, the 11-3 Portsmouth Spartans tried to arrange a game with the Packers to challenge them for the title. Earlier in the year, the Packers had wanted to play the Spartans, who were keeping pace with them, but it could not be arranged. Now it was a different story. The Packers were not about to play the Spartans and risk tying for the championship. Green Bay had nothing to gain and everything to lose. They would have no part of it.

L. H. Joannes, President of the Green Bay Packers, put the whole issue to rest by noting Green Bay had never signed a contract to meet Portsmouth, and added that the team had played fourteen games and that was enough football. The game with the Bears would conclude the schedule.

The Green Bay Packers were champions once again, and that's all there was to it.

In 1932, the election of Franklin Delano Roosevelt and his promise of a "New Deal" brought Americans a ray of hope. They needed it. 1932 had been the worst year of the Depression. Bread lines lengthened, millions were unemployed, and hundreds of thousands were homeless. From the dust bowl of Oklahoma to the cardboard shacks of the inner cities, people felt helpless and hopeless.

Professional football suffered along with everything else in 1932. The league would have only eight teams that year: the Green Bay Packers, Chicago Bears, Chicago Cardinals, Portsmouth Spartans, Staten Island Stapletons, Boston Braves, New York Giants, and the Brooklyn Dodgers.

Green Bay was the team to beat, and their competition would come from the rival Bears and the vastly improved Spartans.

The Chicago Bears and the Green Bay Packers acquired new talent in 1932 that would immediately affect their futures. Joining the Bears was running back Johnny "Big Train" Sisk, quarterback Keith Molesworth sharing quarterback duties with Brumbaugh, and, for the first time, a new player would be under the ball at center. Charles "Ookie" Miller from Purdue was the first to do what many had tried before: beat George Trafton out of a job.

A future Hall of Famer also joined Chicago that year. He was known as the "Offside Kid" because some people thought he was perpetually offside on defense. He was that quick. On offense, he would become a great pass-catching end and a noted ball-slinger.

He was Bill Hewitt and he arrived from the University of Minnesota with average credentials, only to become an All-NFL end three of his five years with Chicago. Traded to Philadelphia in 1937, he went All-Pro and became the first player to win All-NFL honors with two different teams.

Writer C. C. Staph called Hewitt, "a lantern-jawed, 1930's Rambo." He's easy to pick out in old news reels or photos from that era. He's the one not wearing a helmet. He went eight years without a helmet until the league ordered him to put one on. Broken noses and lost teeth aside, he simply felt that a helmet handicapped his play.

Hewitt would also become known for thinking up gimmick

plays to fool the opposition. One was called the "Stinky Special," which would bury Green Bay in their opening game in 1933. But we'll get to the "Stinky" play later.

For Green Bay veterans Jug Earp and Verne Lewellen, 1932 would be their swan song. Second-year men Milt Gantenbein, Hank Bruder, and Wuert Engelmann would play every game and contribute to the Packers' drive for a fourth championship.

A bright-eyed rookie running back joined Curly's crew that fall and would become a Hall of Famer.

All-American running back Clarke Hinkle was a highly scouted prospect from Bucknell College who decided to join the Packers in an unusual way.

"One of the Mara's who owned the Giants invited me to stay over in New York after my last college game to see the Giants play the Packers," Hinkle recalled. "They [Green Bay] had a guy playing tackle named Cal Hubbard who stood 6-foot-5 and weighed about 265 pounds. As I watched the game, I thought to myself, by God, I believe I would rather be on his side than play against him.

"Curly came to my hotel room to talk to me about playing for the Packers. I didn't hesitate, and Lambeau offered me $120 a game. What he didn't know was that I wanted to play so badly that I would have signed for nothing!"

Coming from a small town in Ohio, Hinkle fit right into the village-type atmosphere of Green Bay. "I thought Green Bay would be like a college town with a lot of college spirit, and it was.

"They took their football seriously in Green Bay. If we won a game we were in all the bars that night and never bought our own drinks. We had a ball! Lambeau would say, 'The lid's off; just don't get thrown in jail.' But if we lost a ball game we never left the hotel. People were mad. If we had to leave the hotel we would go down the alleys," Hinkle remembered.

Hinkle played linebacker on defense where his encounters with Bronko Nagurski were nothing short of barbaric duels. He was also a reliable kicker, leading the league in field goals in 1940 and '41.

As a hard-charging running back, Hinkle had few peers in the 1930s. In his career, he rushed for 3,860 yards and scored forty-two touchdowns.

"My greatest thrill in pro football," Hinkle once said, "was every time I ran the ball."

In his rookie year of 1930 and his second year in '31, Green Bay hometown boy Arnie Herber played little, spending most of the season on the Packers' bench. A few of the veteran players, not ones to make a newcomer feel welcome, started calling him "dummy." After Lambeau threatened to fine $50 for the next offense, Herber's nickname became "Kid."

Growing up in Green Bay, Herber had sold Packer game programs so he could get into the games. He attended the University of Wisconsin as a freshman but then transferred to tiny Regis College in Denver.

He returned to Green Bay as an unheralded rookie, hanging out as a handyman around the Packers' clubhouse. Lambeau, thinking that a local boy like Herber might be a drawing card, gave the 6 foot, 200 pounder a chance at quarterback. Herber was ecstatic at the offer of a whopping $75 a game.

Herber, like Bill Hewitt, refrained from wearing head gear for his first eight years in the league because it was uncomfortable and he thought it slowed him down.

"Kid" Herber, cursed with very small hands and stubby fingers, possessed an arm more akin to a catapult than a human limb and could launch a football down the field with amazing accuracy. Despite his small hands, he became a great passer by placing his thumb, instead of his four fingers, over the laces of the ball.

"It was something I had been doing since my days in high school," he once recalled. "I felt I could get more on the ball by palming the laces." The result was a ball that spiraled without wobbling.

Arnie was a light-hearted and jovial guy who loved beer, pretzels, shooting pool, football, and the forward pass. He liked everybody and everybody liked him.

One of his admirers was Curly Lambeau, who put Herber in the backfield at the beginning of the 1932 season after the retirement of Red Dunn and the impending departure of Verne Lewellen. At the end of the 1932 season, "Kid" Herber would be ranked the league's best passer.

Arnie Herber and Clarke Hinkle were supposed to provide the Packers with a one-two punch on offense but, in their September 25th game against the Bears at City Stadium, defensive football reigned. 13,000 fans, including the recently retired Red Dunn, saw the two teams pound each other into a scoreless tie on a very windy Wisconsin day. The line of scrimmage trench-play was vicious and tough, as shown by a total by both teams of only thirteen first downs.

Arthur Bystrom noted the consistent but not dazzling play of the Packers' two new backfield mates.

"Clarke Hinkle," Bystrom wrote, "hit hard and often for short gains and did a Herculean job at backing up the line and Arnie Herber, at halfback, who did everything called upon him to do."

Since coming to training camp earlier that summer, Hinkle had heard the tales about the great Bronko Nagurski. He couldn't wait to go up against the Bronk to find out who would rule the roost. Their first encounter came on the opening kickoff.

Hinkle kicked off and Nagurski caught the ball on the five. The two bulls met head-on around the Bears' 30-yard line. For a few minutes, they both lay on the turf motionless. Suddenly, Hinkle got to his feet and found his way to the sideline. A couple of Nagurski's teammates carried him off the field.

In the rematch three weeks later, defense once again dominated. Packers' end Tom Nash, charging through unimpeded, blocked a Dick Nesbitt punt at the 20-yard line. Nash had the ball smack him with a dull thud full on the chest. The ball bounced beyond the end zone line for a two-point safety, the only score of the game.

The prettiest play in an otherwise non-offensive game belonged to Clarke Hinkle, who broke off a beautiful 37-yard romp in the third period. While being hauled down, however, one of the Bears' long, rectangular cleats caught Hinkle above his eye, causing a massive cut. Bloodied and bandaged, he would later return to the game.

Bronko Nagurski produced over half the Bears' total yardage on the day with 86 yards. The game marked the fourth consecutive week that the Bears had not scored a point. They fought to scoreless ties in their first three games and were now shut out 2-0 by the Packers.

Bears' coach Ralph Jones was not pleased. His stern post-game announcement was that, unless his team showed some scoring power, there would be changes made in the squad.

"Another great Green Bay team," was the comment of Joseph P. Carr, President of the NFL, who was in attendance. "It is remarkable how Curly Lambeau continues year in and year out to consistently produce a winner. Around the league, the other managers are rating him as a "gridiron magician."

Curly, nonetheless, needed some offensive hocus pocus in the December 11 season finale against the Bears. A dog team and some snow shovels may have helped also. Snow fell throughout the afternoon producing ankle-deep drifts and swirling winds, making field conditions atrocious.

Bears' kicker Tiny Engebretsen booted a 14-yard field goal in the fourth quarter for the first points of the game. Chicago writer Wilfrid Smith described the three-pointer as only he could:

"The kick might be called a miracle," he wrote in the *Chicago Tribune*. "Despite the snow and a wet, slippery shoe, Engebretsen lifted the soggy football in a perfect parabola well within the upright."

A perfect parabola? Only Winfrid Smith could turn a simple 14-yard field goal into a science lesson.

A few minutes after the "parabola" field goal, Nagurski nailed the door shut on one of his greatest runs as a pro. The Bronk rumbled down the field on a 54-yard run, outdistancing every Packer except one poor soul who tried to bring him down. Nagurski, on a dead run, simply gave the defender a nasty forearm, bounced him harmlessly out of the way, and coasted into the end zone.

Chicago's 9-0 win clinched a tie for the championship with the Portsmouth Spartans. Chicago had ended the '32 campaign with an odd 6-1-6 mark while the Spartans had notched a 6-1-4 record. Since ties did not count in the standings, they were deadlocked and would have a playoff for the championship.

Although having four more victories than either Chicago or Portsmouth, Green Bay could not be crowned league champion. The Packers finished a respectable 10-3-1, a .769 winning percentage. Chicago's .817 percentage ended Lambeau's chance for a fourth consecutive championship.

Chicago, winning the championship outright the next week by smashing the Spartans 9-0, made a prophet of Ralph Jones with his prediction of a championship within three years.

The championship game of 1932 became one of the most important games ever played because of the rule changes it would inspire. Played indoors at Chicago Stadium because of heavy snow in Chicago during the week, the playing surface was only 45 yards wide and 80 yards long. The field size necessitated special concessions.

Since the field was lined with a wooden fence only feet from the sideline, the ball was moved in ten yards following an out-of-bounds play. Then a play that ended 5 yards from the sideline was put into play at that spot. The ball's placement made for many plays being wasted by attempting to get the ball toward the middle.

A disputed pass play involving Bronko Nagurski in the fourth quarter fueled suggestions later that allowing passing from anywhere behind the line of scrimmage would be a rule improvement. At that time, a pass could only be thrown from five or more yards behind the scrimmage line. The rule was, at times, difficult to enforce.

Most of all, the game proved that the public supported a championship game to settle who was best. Gone were the days of a team winning championship by percentage points or simply staking claim to it. In 1933, at the suggestion of Washington Redskins' owner George Preston Marshall, the league was divided into two divisions, Eastern and Western, and plans were finalized for the two division winners to play a championship game. It would become the forerunner to today's mega-popular Super Bowl.

Some Packers' fans still believe Lambeau's 1932 Green Bay squad should have been awarded their fourth consecutive championship. Winning four games more than Halas' Bears and going 1-1-1 against them on the season is fodder enough for Packers' backers in any barroom debate.

"We really won four [championships] in a row," Cal Hubbard maintained, "but they didn't give it to us."

To this very day his opinion is shared by many.

Nineteen thirty-three was a year of many changes. After a low of only eight teams in the league in 1932, the NFL accepted three new franchises in '33 when Pittsburgh, Cincinnati, and Philadelphia joined. The league lost Staten Island, which folded after the 1932 season.

Another change was the ball itself. It was slimmed down to its present form, making it easier to pass (a fact not lost on Arnie Herber).

Even the look of the field changed. The goal post, which had been moved to the back line of the end zone in 1927, was now placed back on the goal line. Attempted field goals increased dramatically, which, in turn, helped rid the league of so many ties and low scoring games.

Truly, the NFL needed to liven up their game. Although the pro game had evolved into a better game during its first thirteen years, it was still not as popular as the college game. The ever-present spirit of a college contest was hard to find in a pro league game.

What was arguably the most vital decision the league made came at the suggestion of Washington Redskins' owner George Preston Marshall. After the successful Chicago-Portsmouth championship game in 1932, Marshall's idea of splitting the league into two divisions with a championship game to be played between the two division winners was adopted. It would end all debate about who had won the NFL championship, silencing those who, in the past, had simply laid claim to it.

The Depression blanketed the American landscape like a dark cloud and pro football suffered like everything else. Folks standing in soup lines and selling apples on a street corner thought little of spending their hard-earned money on a pro football game.

At the same time, the George Halas-Dutch Sternaman partnership was about to come to an agreeable end. They privately hammered out a deal for Halas to buy out Sternaman's share in the Bears for $38,000, but Halas had to borrow the entire amount from a bank and other investors. It was a very risky move on Halas' part but he wanted to own the Bears lock, stock, and barrel.

George Halas made another important decision in the summer of 1933. Telling reporters that it was "for one year only," Halas reinstated himself as head coach. Ralph Jones had resigned to return to Lake Forest College as athletic director.

For "one year only," except for a two year stint in the military, George Halas would be the Bears' had honcho from 1933 until 1968. Years later, Halas remarked, "It turned out to be an awfully long year."

At 6'2" and 270 pounds, George Musso was an imposing figure on the campus of Millikin University in Decatur, Illinois. Having starred in basketball, track, baseball, as well as football, one would think Musso would have been hotly pursued by NFL teams. But tiny Millikin University was not a hot bed of football so it never attracted a lot of attention from the pro teams.

George Halas had a sixth sense about football players. Many times he would choose a player on just a hunch. (A few years later, in the NFL's first draft of college players, Halas would choose a guard simply because he liked the guy's picture.)

Halas showed Red Grange a picture of a mustached Musso in his Millikin basketball uniform. "He'll never make it," Red quickly predicted. "He looks like a walrus!"

This was one time Halas went with his gut. He wooed Musso with an offer of $90 a game and $5 for the train fare from Decatur to Chicago.

"Chicago was $3 on the Wabash," Musso remembered. "This gave me $2 for incidentals."

Musso didn't immediately impress Halas. In training camp, Musso was fighting Minnesota University rookie Bob Wells for a place in the lineup. After getting wind that Halas was going to choose Wells, Musso asked Packers' coach Curly Lambeau to request his outright release.

"He told me I could play for him," Musso recalled.

The scuttlebutt that Wells was going to get the job was correct. Halas called Musso into his office to inform him of his decision. Musso recounted his conversation with Lambeau and asked Halas to release him so he could sign with the Packers.

Halas convinced Musso to stay with the team for a pre-season road game against New York. During the trip, Red Grange counseled the young Musso that he could make the club if he would just play up to his capability. Grange's pep talk was exactly what the young tackle needed to hear. Musso proceeded to have a great game against the Giants.

After the pre-season game in New York, George "Moose" Musso was a Chicago Bear, and would be for the next twelve years. In those twelve years Musso, at tackle and guard, would help the Bears win four championships, seven division titles, and compile a 104-25-6 record.

The 1933 Chicago Bears were the defending champs and league favorites to repeat as Halas brought together a team loaded with talent. Their '33 lineup is a *Who's Who* of the early NFL.

Chicago's gifted offense included helmetless Bill Hewitt and Luke Johnsos at end, Zuck Carlson and Joe Kopcha at tackle, Link Lyman and rookie Moose Musso at guard, and Ookie Miller at center.

The backfield was an opponent's nightmare. The running tandem of Grange and Nagurski would combine for 830 yards on the season. Carl Brumbaugh and Keith Molesworth handled the quarterbacking duties, with Molesworth being the team's designated passer. Then, thinking ahead, Halas added two other backfield hotshots who would both play out the decade with the Bears.

With the goal post back at the goal line, Halas knew a good kicker was a necessity. He signed "Automatic" Jack Manders from the University of Minnesota. A capable halfback, Manders was, first and foremost, a great kicker. From his first game against Green Bay in 1933 and continuing until 1937, "Automatic Jack" kicked seventy-two straight points after touchdown. He led the league in field goals in four of his first five seasons.

The acquisition of Marquette University's Gene Ronzani added a multi-faceted runner and passer to an already talent-ripe Bears' backfield. After his retirement in 1940, Ronzani became an assistant coach under Halas. Ten years later he would find himself coaching against Halas, when he became the head coach of the rival Green Bay Packers.

Green Bay entered 1933 with a solid core of veterans and up-and-comers, enough to make Lambeau optimistic they could oust the hated Bears from the top of the Western Division.

While veteran stalwarts like Verne Lewellen and Jug Earp had retired after the 1932 season, rookies Bobby Monnett and Charles "Buckets" Goldenberg took their rightful places in the backfield alongside regulars Johnny Blood, Clarke Hinkle, Arnie Herber, and Hank Bruder.

The Packers' line was bolstered by center Red Bultman, tackles Cal Hubbard and Claude Perry, guards Mike Michalske and Lon Evans.

On paper, Curly's 1933 gang should have challenged Halas' band of brigands for the Western Division championship. Talent-wise, the teams were fairly equal although the proficient Bears' backfield gave Chicago a slight advantage.

Three consecutive championships plus that disputed fourth one made Green Bay ripe for the picking. They would begin the 1933 season like they had ended the '32 campaign, in a dreary slump.

Following their season-opening tie with the Boston Redskins, Green Bay hosted Chicago at City Stadium. With five minutes to go in the fourth, the Packers led, 7-0, and looked like sure winners. Then they completely fell apart.

From the shadow of their own goal line, the Bears stormed the entire length of the field in just four plays. The blitzkrieg ended with a Bill Hewitt to Luke Johnsos TD pass. There wasn't a Packer defender within twenty yards of Johnsos as he caught the ball. Jumping from the bench, Coach Halas danced up and down the sidelines, accompanied by a chorus of boos by the Packers' faithful. "Automatic" Manders added the point after and tied the game.

In the following series, the Packers ran three plays, failing to gain a first down. Arnie Herber positioned himself to punt ... sort of. At the snap, Hewitt burst through from the left end and the ball smacked him squarely in the chest. Corralling the pigskin after a short scramble, Hewitt sprinted into the end zone for a Chicago 14-7 victory.

"Hewitt turned in a Frank Merriwell performance," wrote the *Chicago Tribune*'s Wilfrid Smith.

Packers' fans were stunned; never before had they witnessed such a heart-breaking loss. No one could understand how the same Packers' line that had played so well for fifty-five minutes of the game could fall apart so quickly. It was enough for a few pessimists to think the Packers had thrown the game.

The Packers' 6-3-2 defense held Bronko Nagurski in check all day, stuffing him at the line most of the time. There was more hard luck for the "Big Nag" on defense.

On a second period fake punt attempt, Clarke Hinkle ran the ball around end and spied Nagurski closing in. Just before he got to the sideline, Hinkle cut back and met the charging Nagurski head on and wide open. A sickening thud echoed through City Stadium.

The collision knocked Hinkle senseless and back ten yards. Dazed, Hinkle looked over at Nagurski stretched out on the ground. Bronko's nose was over on the side of his face, bleeding and broken in two places. Nagurski was out cold. A couple of his Bear teammates pulled him off the field.

After the game, Red Grange was involved in an on-the-field fracas with, of all people, the Packers' equipment boy! The Bears wanted the game ball as a victory souvenir but the lad refused to give it to them.

"We won the game, didn't we?" Grange queried. The Packers' representative clutched the ball to his chest and walked away.

History would eerily repeat itself one month later in Wrigley Field. With four minutes remaining, the Bears' Keith Molesworth first returned Hinkle's punt for 30 yards then caught a pass to the Packers' 22-yard line. On the next play, Grange took a pitch-out, faked a run and then threw a pass over the head of Johnny Blood and into the arms of Luke Johnsos in the end zone. "Automatic" Manders added the tying point.

After being stopped cold on three plays, Hinkle again got into punt formation. He got the kick away but not before it was partially blocked and downed on the Bears' 43-yard line.

The Bears' backfield did the rest, slashing through the Green Bay defense until they were resting on the Packers' 21-yard line. Manders was, once again, the hero, sailing the ball through the uprights for a field goal and the 10-7 win.

Chicago had taken complete advantage of Green Bay's mistakes once again. The Packers had the ball near the goal line three times but failed to score. An official signaled one of Hinkle's goal line lunges a touchdown but failed to see that he had fumbled before crossing the line. Another official called the fumble, giving the ball to the Bears on the turnover.

Hinkle lost another TD when he slipped on the wet field at the 11-yard line. Grange killed the Packers' third scoring attempt when he intercepted a third down pass inside the 10-yard line.

The *Tribune's* Wilfrid Smith again sang the praises of Bill Hewitt. "Bill Hewitt! There's a football player," Smith gushed. "Bill had gone to the bench just before the rally, almost unable to stand from exhaustion. But Hewitt must have inspired his team-mates. He was the greatest star in a galaxy of stars who played for both teams. From the first minute to the last, Hewitt performed faultlessly at left end.

"And when he left the gridiron," Smith added, "tears running down his face, in exasperation that his body no longer could pace his will, the throng accorded him a tumultuous round of applause."

The *Green Bay Press-Gazette* theorized "the Bears must have a carload of horseshoes in their last two games with the hometown Bays."

The Packers, their season now a total wash, limped through the remaining schedule and came back to Wrigley Field for the season's final game—and more bad fortune.

Hinkle took the opening kickoff on his own 4-yard line and dashed through Bear tacklers until he was pulled down by Bill Karr at the Chicago 4-yard line. However, four subsequent plunges into the line netted little yardage and was yet another lost opportunity for the Packers.

Karr literally saved the day by jumping on Hinkle's back around the 10- yard line and riding him like a rodeo bull, finally forcing him to the ground.

Chicago had a 7-0 lead going into the final quarter after Gene Ronzani's gallop into the end zone in the second quarter. Halas and company were confident that the defense, which had so far played splendidly, could hold on for the win.

In the fourth quarter, Molesworth punted and Packers' back Bobby Monnett gathered in the ball and took off from the 22-yard line. Dashing to one side of the field and then the other, Monnett zigzagged his way into the end zone. Officially an 88-yard TD, Monnett actually ran more like 130 yards.

Monnett held the ball for Roger Grove, whose extra point kick would tie the game. Grove made eight of the nine extra point attempts during the 1933 season. This was the one he missed.

Joe Zeller, the Bears' right end, slammed through the line and blocked Grove's attempt. The Bears hung on to win, 7-6, sweeping the series, 3-0.

Finishing at 5-7-1, it was Green Bay's first losing season in their fifteen year history, and it would be another fifteen years before it would happen again.

Halas and his Bears were on the verge of winning their second consecutive crown; only the New York Giants stood in their way. The game at Wrigley Field was one of the most famous football laterals in history.

With the Giants winning 21-16 late in the fourth quarter, Bill Hewitt took a Nagurski pass and started downfield. When he saw two New York defenders closing in, he lateraled the ball to Bill Karr who was running beside him. Karr raced untouched into the end zone and Chicago won, 23-21.

Compared to today's multi-million dollar game—where winning a Super Bowl is worth five figures to each of the victors—the money the Bears' received for the 1933 championship was a joke.

Each Bear collected less than $300.

In sports bars, on sports talk radio, and over office water coolers, the debate over who fielded the greatest pro football team ever has always been—and will always be—a lively one. Some think the Steelers' teams of the 1970s were best. Miami Dolphins' fans stand by with their undefeated 1972 team. How about Lombardi's Packers of the Sixties? Or those great early Fifties, Otto Graham-led Cleveland Browns? Folks in San Francisco can always cite the great Super Bowl teams led by quarterbacks Joe Montana and Steve

Young.

However, any serious such debate must include the 1934 Chicago Bears.

How good were they? In their first nine games, opponents never came within thirteen points of them. They amassed a total of 286 points in their season's thirteen games, granting only eighty-six measly points to opponents.

The 1934 Bears became the first NFL team to go through a regular season undefeated. They were that good!

Halas made an important acquisition in 1934: the fleet-of-foot University of Tennessee scat-back, Beattie Feathers. An elusive runner with power, he played in the backfield with the hard-blocking Nagurski. Chicago even brought back the single-wing formation to be used along side the T-formation. The combination of Bronko's blocking and the two offensive formations led to Beattie Feathers becoming the first runner in NFL history to gain a thousand yards in a season.

His season total of 1,004 yards is impressive enough, but his average yards-per-gain is mind-boggling. In 101 attempts, Feathers rushed for an astounding 9.94 yards per carry.

Add Feathers' 1,004 yards to Nagurski's 568 yards and Gene Ronzani's 485 yards rushing, and you have the Bears' merciless backfield.

Also adding to their opponent's woes was "Automatic" Jack Manders, the first kicker to make ten field goals in a season—a record that stood until Cleveland's Lou Groza made thirteen field goals in 1950.

For the first time since 1927, and for every season thereafter, the Packers and Bears would meet twice instead of three times during the regular season.

On Sunday, September 23, 1934, some 13,000 football fans braved a threatening Wisconsin sky to witness the twenty-ninth meeting between the rivals. Those in attendance saw yet another display of the fourth quarter jinx that had lately plagued the Packers in their games against the Bears. With the score tied, 10-10, Bronko Nagurski rumbled in for two fourth-quarter touchdowns, one on a short plunge and the other on a beautiful 34-yard run down the sideline to ice the game. He finished the day with ninety-three yards rushing.

Five weeks later the Packers again played the Bears tough but lost, this time, 27-14. The Bears' powerful offense ran up 420 yards. Beattie Feathers himself ran wild through the Packers' defense for 150 yards. Feathers' lone touchdown came on a 17-yard pass from Gene Ronzani late in the first period.

Describing the game, *Green Bay Press-Gazette* sports writer John M. Walter wrote that the Packers harassed the Bears throughout the game, "... until George Halas' cigar was chewed to a fragment and the timer's gun erased the wrinkles from the foreheads of the Bears' substitutes."

Walter's assessment of the game's rough play was downright bombastic, if not grandiose: "It was a dog-eat-dog affair, with bitterness rising from both sides and hatred spreading over the playing field like haze from Lake Michigan."

Chicago Tribune writer George Strickler took a simpler approach, stating the obvious that the Chicago Bears "possessed all-conquering power."

And all-conquering they were. Chicago destroyed their remaining six opponents for their first-ever undefeated season.

The Bears went into the championship rematch with the New York Giants at the Polo Grounds with two of their stars sitting it out. Guard Joe Kopcha and Beattie Feathers stayed in Chicago with injuries.

The game day weather was atrocious. A freezing rain turned the field into a sheet of ice overnight and footing was difficult. At halftime, with the Bears leading, 10-3, the Giants' equipment manager brought the team sneakers to wear. Coach Steve Owen had his Giants put them on to increase their traction. In what was later dubbed "the Sneaker Game," the New York Giants went on to trounce the heretofore undefeated Chicago Bears, 30-13.

Many have forgotten about the 1934 Bears and their accomplishments. This great Bears' team is generally overlooked in discussions of great football teams, and the loss against the Giants may be the reason.

On the year, Chicago led the league in touchdowns scored, total points, touchdown passes, rushing yardage, and field goals. They were talent-heavy, and, on paper, a better team compared to the 8-5

Giants.

Sadly, the harsh weather and sneakers proved to be the great equalizer for George Halas and his gridiron Bears.

1935

On September 22, 1935, some 13,000 spectators overtaxed City Stadium on a sunny day in Green Bay to witness the thirty-first meeting of the two rivals. It was the opening game of the year for the Bears, while a week earlier, the Packers had opened their season with a 7-6 loss to the Chicago Cardinals.

Green Bay was attempting to gain the old glory of the 1929, '30, and '31 championship teams. In the previous two seasons, the Packers had regressed somewhat, finishing third in the Western Division both years. 1934's 7-6 record had been an improvement on the previous year's 5-7-1 finish, but some were beginning to think the Packers were finished as leaders of the Western Division.

The mighty Bears had beaten the Packers six straight times coming into the game and looked to make it seven. The Packers, however, had a new weapon in hand and were ready to unleash it. Those lucky 13,000 fans at City Stadium were there for the birth of the first great passing combination in the NFL.

A skinny, long-armed kid from Alabama was nervously tucking his jersey into his game pants in the Green Bay locker room. He turned to the wily old veteran Cal Hubbard seated beside him and said, "I'm scared to death. I did all right in college, but these fellows are so much bigger and better. I'm not even sure I belong up here".

"Don't worry, kid," Cal bellowed. "You belong."

Did he ever!

Green Bay won the coin toss and returned the kickoff to its 17-yard line. Quarterback Arnie Herber called for Johnny Blood to line up in the wingback position on the right side and for the Alabama rookie to line up on the left. Herber got the direct pass from center and drifted back. Blood ran up the right side taking most of the Chicago defensive backs with him. The young rookie lazily shuffled down the left side, watching Blood's maneuvers all the while. Then Chicago defender Beattie Feathers made a big mistake by taking his eyes off the rookie for a split second.

Herber, taking his time, was hit twice before he fired the bullet-like pass to the left where the rookie was now streaking down the sideline. Never breaking stride, the Alabama newcomer caught the ball over his head at the Bears' 43-yard line and, in the most thrilling moment of his athletic career, raced into the end zone on a breathtaking 83-yard touchdown run.

"I didn't know he could run that fast and I didn't know Herber could throw it that far," the dejected Feathers admitted after the game. "I saw Herber throw this pass downfield, and I saw this lanky guy loping down toward me. All of a sudden, he turned on his speed and ran right by me."

Fittingly, it was the only score of the game. In that one striking and definitive moment, Green Bay had introduced the National Football League to Don Hutson. The record books would never be the same.

One Milwaukee sports writer dubbed Hutson the "Alabama Antelope." He was a scrawny six-footer who weighed around 175 pounds soaking wet. But he possessed, as *Chicago Tribune* writer George Strickler put it, "... tremendous speed, a pair of hands as big as umbrellas and arms that dangled almost to his knees."

Don grew up in Pine Bluff, Arkansas, a skinny, shy, and a real loner. As a kid his only burning passion was to raise rattlesnakes, which he did with his friend, Bob Seawell.

It was Seawell who talked Hutson into playing football in high school. While he was a good player, Hutson never became a high school star. Seawell, on the other hand, was courted by a number of Southern colleges to play football.

Bob finally agreed to attend Alabama on one condition: If they take him, they had to also take Hutson. Alabama decided to use a scholarship on Hutson; at least he could talk rattlesnakes with Seawell, the up-and-coming star. Hutson went on to become All-American at Alabama. Seawell dropped out of school after his junior year.

Packers' coach Curly Lambeau went to Alabama's practice field to scout a couple of linemen as the team prepared for their 1934

Rose Bowl appearance. Finding the gate locked, Lambeau climbed the fence and tore his new suit in the process. (Police then tried to eject Lambeau but a Notre Dame alumnus intervened and saved him.) Finally taking his seat, Lambeau saw Hutson running an end-around play.

"When I saw him cut, I reached for a contract," Lambeau recalled later. "I knew I had to have him. I hadn't seen anybody cut like that since [Red] Grange. I knew he was a complete football player. That's why I broke my neck to get him."

Hutson had several offers, including one from George Halas for $75 a game and another from the Brooklyn Dodgers football club. The Dodgers had promised to top any deal any other club proposed.

"I had offers from all the pro teams to come and try out," Hutson once told interviewer Myron Cope. "The strange thing is that until I started receiving letters from Curly Lambeau, I had given no thought at all to playing pro football. They didn't even have the results in the papers. It was a whole different country down there [Alabama]. For example, the first tavern I ever saw was when I got to Green Bay."

Curly sold Hutson on Green Bay when he told him his talents were tailor-made for the Packers' offense. Curly also reminded him that the Packers had the greatest passer in the world, Arnie Herber.

"Going to Green Bay was one of the smartest decisions I ever made," Hutson recalled. "If I had gone to Brooklyn I might never have played. I was very fortunate."

Over the years, many have thought that the 83-yard touchdown against the Bears was his first play in the pros. It wasn't. A week before, Hutson saw limited action against the Chicago Cardinals in the Packers' 1935 season opener. One incomplete pass was thrown at him and he attempted one run, fumbled, and recovered the ball for a twelve yard loss. Hardly a legendary debut.

Hutson certainly got Chicago's attention in his first game against the Bears. The mean and proud Bears were, however, amused by all the fuss over the lanky neophyte. They thought him an antelope and little else. "Wait 'til next time," a big Chicago tackle predicted after the game. Hutson just looked at him and smiled.

A month later, he would again frustrate the Bears and their

faithful followers at Wrigley Field with, as *Green Bay Press-Gazette* scribe John Walter put it, "... as thrilling a struggle as ever was waged on an American gridiron."

With three minutes remaining, Chicago was comfortably ahead, 14-3, and thousands were already heading for the exits, certain in the knowledge the Bears had this game won. Green Bay had the ball deep in its own territory when Arnie Herber huddled his weary troops for assault. Herber knew who his receiver had to be. He looked Hutson in the eye and said, "Let's shoot for the moon, Don." Hutson got loose, snared a Herber spiral, and left the Bears' defenders in the dust as he breezed across the goal line.

Johnny Blood stood on the sidelines praying, "Dear Lord, make them fumble."

Bears' quarterback Bernie Masterson obliged by coughing it up at the 13-yard line. Five plays later Herber found Hutson in the end zone for a touchdown and typewriters went into overdrive, clacking out the story of a legend in the making.

Broadcaster Russ Winnie of WTMJ Radio, Green Bay, got so excited by the game's turnaround that some newspapermen in a booth next to him feared he would have a stroke. An estimated 5,000 Packers' fans screamed themselves hoarse.

Hutson had four catches on the day for 103 yards, scoring two touchdowns in three minutes. Single-handedly, the "Alabama Antelope" had destroyed Chicago's season. But for Hutson, the Bears would have been undefeated after seven games and well on their way to another possible championship. Instead, they staggered through the remaining portion of the season, finishing 6-4-2. With Hutson in hand, however, the Packers went on to finish second in the Western Division with a 8-4 record.

Many forget that Don was a good defensive back and accurate kicker. He intercepted twenty-three passes over his final four seasons and kicked for almost 200 points, never missing an extra point. He was also the first to paint black shoe polish on his cheeks to cut the sun's glare. Although not the intention, it gave him a macabre appearance.

His defensive ability didn't go unnoticed, either. "If he never caught a pass for us he would have [still] been one of our most valuable men," Lambeau once said. "I have never seen him miss a tackle."

Lambeau wisely positioned his prize rookie on defense, putting Hutson at defensive back because he was less likely to be injured there. "They moved him from defensive end," Packers' tailback and defensive back Hal Van Every recalled.

"The poor guy was getting killed with these big guys coming around at him," Van Every added. "He only weighed about 170. They put him back at defensive halfback and that was sure a smart move because he could keep up with any end coming down the field. He was just as fast or faster as they were."

Hutson would go on to assault the record books. He caught 489 passes for over 8,000 yards; scored ninety-nine touchdowns; broke nineteen NFL records; was named All-Pro nine of his eleven seasons; led the league in receiving for eight seasons; and in 1963 became a charter member on Pro Football's Hall of Fame.

"The guy who really opened up offensive football was Don Hutson," Pro Football Hall of Fame historian Joe Horrigan contends. "Hutson is still the receiver all others are measured against. He was the first to require double and triple coverage. He caught seventeen touchdown passes in 1942, more than all but one team that year.

"Hutson was a receiver that no one could equal to that point," Horrigan adds. "He changed the face of the game. To that point, we're talking about the leading receiver in the league having seventeen receptions in a season. And suddenly Hutson is able to do that in a game. It was a tremendous turnaround. It was revolutionary."

After a loss to the Packers, many an opposing coach would find themselves explaining that although his team had fought a hard battle, there was "too much Hutson." Teams would literally concede two touchdowns to Hutson and hope they could score more.

Don Hutson revolutionized professional football. He dominated the NFL like no other player before or since. Sports writers and historians will always debate who was the greatest player to ever put on a uniform. Many believe it was the skinny, shy, rattlesnake-loving kid from Pine Bluff, Arkansas.

Don Hutson was the embodiment of athletic grace and beauty.

1936-'37

The NFL held its first draft of college players in 1936, and the team with the worst record chose first. Russ Letlow, a guard from the University of San Francisco, was the first of the Packers' nine draft picks. Letlow would see seven years of service on the Bays' line.

The Bears, however, would use the first draft to brilliant advantage. Halas choose Dan Fortmann from Colgate and Joe Stydahar from West Virginia University. Both would become Hall of Famers.

"Jumbo" Joe Stydahar, a raw-boned 250-pound tackle, was Halas' first round pick. Stydahar played nine seasons for the Bears, was All-NFL tackle from 1937 through '40, and was inducted into the Hall of Fame in 1967.

"That was the turning point of my life," Stydahar said of being drafted by Halas and the Bears. "Halas has been like a second father to me. I didn't know anything about football until I had a chance to play for him."

Jumbo Joe had an odd approach to tackling that would make only a dentist smile. "When you charge you gotta keep your head up," he once said. "You lose a lot of teeth that way but you also make a lot of tackles."

As head coach of the Los Angeles Rams in the early Fifties, Stydahar blasted his players after a huge loss by saying, "No wonder you guys got kicked around. Every guy on the team has still got all his teeth."

Halas made his final pick in '36 on a hunch. He chose guard Dan Fortmann because he liked his name. Fortmann joined the Bears as the youngest starter in the NFL and one of the smallest. At 6' 0" and 200 pounds, Fortmann was not expected to make the squad in a ball-rushing, trench-dominated game.

Fortmann on offense called the signals for the line; on defense he was a deadly tackler. He earned All-NFL honors six straight years and played beside Stydahar from 1936 to 1943. During that time, the Bears finished first in their division five times, second twice and third once.

"It helped me tremendously to play next to Joe for so many

years," Fortmann once said. "A true partnership built up. We got to know exactly what to expect from one another."

An experienced and promising Green Bay team entered the 1936 campaign with hardened veterans and optimistic rookies eager for the championship drive. The team's nucleus consisted of Herber and Hutson but many standouts remained from the championship years of 1929 through 1931.

Russ Lelow, Tiny Engebretsen, Ade Schwammel, and Buckets Goldenberg anchored a line that was one of the best in the league. The offensive backfield was deep in talent. Herber, Joe Laws, Bob Monnett, and Johnny Blood were top-flight pigskin carriers. Blood caused some concern when he held out until a contract was agreed upon. The season started without him.

One of the talented Packers' backs was a hard-hitting Iowa Hawkeye in his second year with the Bays. Herm Schneidman had been unsure about his future as his graduation approached. Former teammate Joe Laws advised him to tryout for Lambeau's squad. "He told me I should come [to Green Bay] because you could make the team," Herm said. "I had pretty good speed in those days, and I didn't know what I was going to do, so I gave it a shot."

Herm ended up playing blocking back on offense and right halfback on defense. He signed his first contract for $85 a week and received $10 a week in meal money. "Some of the guys would eat hot dogs and save the rest of the money," Schneidman recalled.

He quickly moved into the starting lineup after Hank Bruder was injured in the '35 season opener with Chicago.

"You know," Herm said, "I never made All-Pro but I can tell everyone I played with the best. I played against Bronko Nagurski, George Musso. I gave it my best and I'm pretty proud of that."

In those days it seemed every Packers-Bears game featured a donnybrook of some kind. Herm recalled one fight during his rookie year, 1935. Bears' back Beattie Feathers was in the middle of it.

"One of the Packers' tackles hit Beattie and Bronko came up and shoved the guy," Herm said. "I was in the middle of that. I can remember dropping on my hands and knees and crawling out between some legs, and standing on the outside watching them battle. I was too small to get into that."

Green Bay was then and still is a small town where everybody knows everybody else's business. In those days, Packers lived side-by-side with their fans. Their supporters praised them after a win or griped and gave unsolicited advice whenever they lost, especially if they lost to the Bears. There was one taxi driver in town, Moose Shibley, who used to haul the Packers around. Moose was a strong Packer Backer. "He'd take us in his cab," Herm recalled, "but if we'd just lost a ball game, he wouldn't talk to any of us."

Herm was the blocking back when his rookie cohort Don Hutson caught the winning 83-yard touchdown against the Bears in '35. "We worked on that (the play) for a couple of weeks," Herm said. "Herber would drop back, the line would hold tight, and I would hit the first man through.

"Hutson was great. He ran just as hard in practice as he did in a game. He could play with a bad ankle and still beat people."

Herm remembered vividly the second Bears' game that year when Hutson performed his heroics. "I remember that very well," he said. "Lambeau went up and down the bench saying, 'We're going to win this game.' Anyone who had a tough look in their eye he put in the game.

"After that first touchdown, Lambeau said he wanted the ball so get it back. Masterson fumbled and we scored another one and beat them."

Herm also had the privilege of playing with two of the all-time great backs, Clarke Hinkle and Arnie Herber. "Clarke was a superstitious fella," Herm recalled. "He'd get his ankles and wrists taped on the bus going to the game. In the dressing room he wouldn't want to speak to anyone. He was really keyed up. When that whistle blew he was ready.

"Arnie was just a happy-go-lucky guy. When he threw the ball he put his thumb on the laces of the ball instead of the four fingers like most throwers. He halfway palmed it.

"One year we were in California making a Pete Smith motion picture called Pigskin Champions, a short feature on the Packers that was a preview to the feature shows in picture houses across the nation. In one of the scenes they strapped a window on the outside of the goal post and they put three footballs on the 50-yard line and Herber was supposed to throw the ball through the glass. The first one he just missed by an inch. The second hit the wooden frame and broke the window. They put another one up and he threw one right through the middle of that damn thing. He'd been out the night before drinking beer and I don't think he could even see it."

In 1939, Schneidman pulled a muscle in his hip and went home. The Chicago Cardinals came calling in 1940 but he quit after he received a paltry $15 check for a very bloody game against the Redskins.

His football days weren't quite over, though. In 1942, he enlisted in the military and played on the Navy's Great Lakes championship team of '43.

"We just enjoyed playing back then," Herm said. "We played for the love of the game."

The Bears had assembled a formidable cast of players and were certainly in contention for the '36 championship. Bronko Nagurski starred in a backfield that included Beattie Feathers and John Sisk at halfback, Bernie Masterson at quarterback, and, in the twilight of his career at left end, Bill Hewitt.

Right tackle George Musso, center Charles "Ookie" Miller, and guard Ray Richards formed a tough, unforgiving line that was more than ready to put their cleats in the face of any Packer foolish enough to cross paths with them.

In 1936, the Bears' stunned the league with new pseudo-psychedelic uniforms. In one word, stripes! Three orange stripes were added to the helmet, two blue and one orange stripe on the shoulders, and two blue and one orange stripe around the sleeves. The pants were blue set off by really hideous blue and orange-stripped knee-socks. The Bears stood out, to say the least. That uniform didn't last long. The next year, most of the stripes were gone but the blue pants remained.

George Halas and his mighty Bears were lying low for their '36 season opener in Green Bay. They silently pulled into town, checked into the Northland Hotel, and waited. The 1935 season had been ruined by Hutson and the Packers and they had not forgotten about it. Chicago fans reminded them of it every day. They came ready to play.

The 14,312 fans who were there saw an ambush. Chicago controlled the first half and dominated the second, winning convincingly, 30-3. It was Green Bay's worst defeat at home in eleven seasons of pro football league play.

The Packers were completely flat. They missed blocks—or didn't block at all—and lacked any fire whatsoever. Their only score came on an Ade Schwammel 25-yard field goal but he also missed three others in the first half. It was a crushing defeat for Green Bay.

The one-sided loss did have at least one positive effect. After watching his team be so thoroughly humiliated, Johnny Blood signed a contract and returned.

In an amazing turnaround, Curly Lambeau directed his Packers to four straight wins and a rematch with the 6-0 Bears on November 1.

Intermittent showers couldn't dampen the spirits of the largest crowd to see a pro game in Chicago since Red Grange's debut in 1925. Green Bay spotted Chicago ten points on a Jack Manders field goal and Bill Hewitt's mud-splattering 53-yard touchdown gallop.

In the second quarter the Herber to Hutson combination finally lit up the scoreboard. It was Hutson's eleventh career touchdown.

Late in the game, Hinkle's personal duel with Nagurski would again prove painful to Bronko. Hinkle broke through a hole in the line but was met by Nagurski who threw his entire body at Hinkle, throwing him back across the line. Amazingly, Hinkle landed on his feet and ripped back through the same hole, stomping the prone body of Nagurski as he went. Hinkle burst by a diving George Musso and splashed down the sideline through the muck and mire of Wrigley Field for a 59-yard touchdown.

George Sauer added another score and the Packers had the revenge they wanted, besting the undefeated Bears, 21-10. Writer John Walter called the Packers, "One of the greatest teams that had ever stepped upon an American field." Chicago writer George Strickler called the Packers, "A greater football team than at any time since its three year championship reigns teams in 1929, 1930, and 1931."

Strickler was correct. Green Bay would win four straight, tie the Chicago Cardinals in the season's finale, and finish 10-1-1. The Bears would play out the rest of the season at 3-2, finishing 9-3.

Green Bay won its fourth championship on December 13, walloping the Boston Redskins, 21-6. The little Wisconsin town, known only for its football team and paper mills, could again claim they were football's best.

Incidentally, after the game, as the Packers filed out of their hotel to go home, they discovered Johnny Blood going around and around and around in the hotel's revolving door. Blood declared he wasn't going home, but teammates got him in a cab and to the train bound for Green Bay.

When Lambeau and his champion Packers arrived in Green Bay to a rousing welcome, Johnny was nowhere to be found. Blood had jumped off the train somewhere near Pittsburgh.

Pro football's draft system of 1937 was light years away from the sophisticated selection process of today. Much of the time, a professional head coach learned of a college player's abilities and skills from an alumnus or a friend of a friend who knew someone. Coaches had to rely on press clippings for information on potential prospects, and the result was that many players from less-publicized schools were overlooked.

One such player was Ray Nolting. Ray played halfback at the University of Cincinnati and was referred to George Halas by a man who would later become the sheriff of Hamilton County, Ohio. He had watched Nolting play at Cincinnati and suggested Halas take a look at him.

"I don't think George ever saw me play," Ray recounted. "He just took the guy's word for it. I came in as a tryout. Carl Brumbaugh, the Bears' quarterback, was the one who helped me make the squad."

Nolting was helped by one coach a player could really trust: "Red Grange was our backfield coach in '36," Ray recalled. "He coached for one year then went into doing radio. He helped me with my starts. I was one of the fastest starting backs in the league because I used to run a lot of quick openings from the T-formation.

"My first contract was for $100 a game," Ray admitted. "I got paid for a total of twenty-nine games that year, including exhibitions. I was rich. When I retired before the 1944 season, I was making $250 a game."

Nolting got his chance to start in the second Packers-Bears game of 1936. "Beattie Feathers got his ankle hurt so I had to go in the ball game," he said. "We ran an off-tackle play and Bronko Nagurski made about fifteen yards on it. I blocked and knocked down Clarke Hinkle because I was leading the play. Bronk came back to the huddle and said anyone who can knock that Hinkle on his ass can play on my first team. Halas used to listen to Bronko. Anything Bronko wanted, Bronko got. So from that time on I was a first string player."

When Ray was playing defensive back, he bore the burden of trying to cover Don Hutson. "I had him, that was my guy," Ray remembered. "I did pretty well against him. I don't think he scored any touchdowns on me. He had all the moves. Change of pace, slants, stop and go's, everything. He had three speeds. Fast, faster, and still faster."

In those days receivers were not coddled by the softer offensive rules of today. There was none of this 5-yard chuck zone and players can't be touched. Most receivers were harassed and mugged when running patterns, and being a star back didn't exclude them from it.

"Green Bay had a play from the single wing and they always shifted to the right," Nolting recollected.

"When Hutson would put his hand down, everybody went. That was their starting signal. One time Hutson put his hand down and he went out on this slant. I could have never caught him with my two hands. I knew I had to knock him some way so he didn't get the ball; so I made a fist and hit him right on the chin. His feet went up in the air, and he skidded along on his head for awhile. It was the only way I could bring him down. No penalty was called. I never got swung at so many times in my life. All the Packers were swinging at me. That's where I learned to duck."

Ray Nolting led the Bears in rushing in 1937, '38, and '40. He retired after an injury he suffered during the third exhibition game in 1944. He went on to coach at his alma mater until 1950, when newly named Packers' head coach Gene Ronzani asked him to be an assistant coach in Green Bay.

For the sixth straight year in Green Bay, Wisconsin, George Halas and his 1937 Bears began the season. After a quiet and score-less first half, the Bears' struck for two touchdowns in the span of seven plays. Bruising back Bronko Nagurski blocked into the Packers' line near the goal, allowing Ray Nolting to plow over for the first score of the game. Soon after, a 45-yard aerial from quar-terback Bernie Masterson to Jack Manders made the score 14-0. The Packers only score on the day was a safety in the third period. Don Hutson broke through on a Bears' punt, blocked Sam Francis' punt, and the ball bounced out of the end zone for two points. Bears 14, Packers 2.

When they met again November 7 at Wrigley Field, Chicago's defense had allowed only thirty-four points in their five wins and one tie. Green Bay was on its own five game winning streak. In those five games, the high scoring Packers, with the Herber to Hutson combination, had scored 139 points and only allowed forty-nine. A win would put the Packers right back in the divisional race with their dreaded rivals.

After a scoreless first period, Packers' defensive back Eddie Jankowski intercepted a Bears' pass and ran it in for a score. As Jankowski lumbered across for the TD, his momentum led him into the red brick wall in the southeast corner of Wrigley Field. "The collision," said *Press-Gazette* writer John Walter, "would have killed any man who wasn't raised on concrete hash."

Chicago spotted the Packers seventeen points before they scored on their own interception return for a touchdown. Jack Mander's 54-yard interception of Bob Monnett's pass made it 17-14 Green Bay. Then lightning struck again.

In the fourth period, Arnie Herber drifted back around his own 15-yard line, and let fly a pass that sailed fifty-five yards in the air. On the receiving end was the "Alabama Antelope," who blazed into the end zone for a 78-yard touchdown. When Don Hutson put the game out of reach, he put the Packers back in the divisional race.

Two hard-nosed rookies from the University of Nebraska watched on the sideline as Hutson performed his heroics. They were Sam Francis and Russell Thompson.

Francis was an All-American and a number one draft choice of the Philadelphia Eagles, a team he would never join. "Halas traded five players for me," Sam said. "I went to Chicago and Halas, me, the Big Ten commissioner, and Chicago Cardinals' owner Charles Bidwell met to discuss my signing. I went along with it and signed."

Sam backed up Bronko Nagurski. When Bronko, a notable professional wrestler, would be competing in the ring, Francis would fill in at fullback for Bronko.

Sam, like Bronko, was a multi-talented athlete. He was the runner-up for the 1937 Heisman Trophy and also made All-American in track. In the Berlin Olympic Games in 1936, Sam was the leading shot putter for the U.S.A. "I finished fourth there. I was nervous as hell and that was the first time I had been beaten," he admitted.

Halas traded Sam to Brooklyn in 1940. He played in the '41 championship game against the Giants, but soon found himself leading 850 troops through the Pacific in World War II. He spent a total of thirty years in the military.

Russell Thompson was a tackle on the Chicago Bears' squad that featured Sam Francis. Quarterback Bernie Masterson mentioned Thompson to Halas.

"Masterson came home after the [1936] season and Halas had him bring a set of contracts along for me to sign," Russell remembered. "It was for $90 a game. We thought that was good. We could make a thousand dollars in three months and the top guys in your class at school were working for a hundred dollars a month."

In his first training camp, Russell played behind tackle George Musso. But the Bears were a little short on guards, so Musso made the switch and Thompson filled his vacant tackle position.

"Playing on the line really wore you down," Russell said. "We played both ways [offense and defense] in those days. Today, the guys are always fresh. When they get tired they take them out. We didn't have the specialist like they do now."

Russell was traded to Philadelphia in 1940. "It was a depressing outfit," he said. "They had no game plans; not a damn thing. It was a bad situation. I would have liked to have stayed in Chicago. Green Bay tried to trade for me but Coach Bert Bell at Philadelphia wouldn't let me go."

In his own unique way, Russell summed up his playing days in the NFL. "It beat the hell out of sittin' out in the country and milking a cow."

1938-'39

1938 saw the Packers split the season's two games with their rivals. In the first meeting in Green Bay, played in a driving rainstorm, the score was tied 0-0 early in the fourth quarter. Green Bay's Arnie Herber positioned himself to punt from his own 15-yard line. Center Derrell Lester snapped the ball, sailing it over Herber's head. Running into the end zone, Herber tried to shovel the ball back onto the playing field but Chicago's Dick Plasman knocked the ball right back at him. Finally, Packers' guard Tom Jones fell on it in the end zone for a safety and the Bears led, 2-0. In the last minute of play, Clarke Hinkle attempted a desperation 37-yard field goal. Hinkle hit the ball well, but it fluttered to the right of the goal posts and the Packers lost.

Green Bay revenged the loss in November by scoring two touchdowns off Chicago fumbles in just eight plays at the start of the game and winning, 24-17. The 40,208 fans were also stunned by an incredible 80-yard punt by Arnie Herber late in the final period. The ball sailed over the end zone line and into the right field stands. Even the Bears' fans gave him a round of applause.

Chicago Tribune sports writer John Walter called it the season's "Game of Games," and the "roughest, toughest, most bitterly fought engagement in which the Packers have been involved this year. The contest which had loyal fans stammering and the heavily populated stands jittery as each attempt by the Bears to wrest the lead from the Packers was denied."

One player it was especially rough on was Bears' left end, Dick Plasman. He suffered a severe injury when he crashed into the south brick wall in Wrigley Field while chasing one of Bears' quarterback Ray Buivid's forward passes. Wrigley's infamous red brick barrier had claimed another victim.

On the Bears' sideline in the "Game of Games" was Ohio State rookie, Gust Zarnas. Gust would have a good rookie season substituting at guard on both offense and defense. It turned out that 1938 would be his one and only year with the Bears. Gust was one of the very few players to suit up for both Chicago and Green Bay in his career. "I had the opportunity to stay with Chicago," he said. "The money was better with Green Bay. I was fortunate to go to Green Bay because we won the World Championship in 1939."

Gust knows he was very lucky to have played for both George Halas and Curly Lambeau. "I admired both coaches," he said. "They were good people to work with. They were the pioneers of coaching in the pros. My memories of them are terrific."

Those early days of pro football were fierce and violent. Zarnas was there in the trenches and attests to how rough the line play really was in the late Thirties.

"It was pretty rough," he recalled. "We didn't wear these masks like they do today. Guys would do a side-body block and fling their legs in the air and catch you in the mouth with the heels of their cleats. This happened to a Chicago teammate, Russ Thompson. I was playing next to him during a Packers' game and saw this. His mouth was all bloody and four of his teeth came out but he stayed in the game.

"I went along with him to the dentist the next day. He got up in the chair and the dentist found there were nerves exposed. The dentist told him that he would have to extract some more teeth. The dentist asked Russ before he started if he wanted gas or Novocain and he bravely said he didn't want anything. Well, he started pulling his teeth and Thompson was just throwing his legs up and down in pain. He was in agony. I couldn't believe it. One of his teeth the dentist extracted was as big as a horse's tooth. I had to look the other way."

Zarnas went on to play for the Packers in 1939 and '40. "Then the war broke out and I enlisted in the Navy. I was there for four years. While in the service, I played on the championship Great Lakes team. We had a bunch of ex-pros and All-Americans. We had a great team.

"When I got out of the service, I got a few telegrams from Curly Lambeau wanting me to return as soon as I got my service release. But I just called it quits. I wrote Lambeau a nice letter of thanks."

When asked if he had any regrets about not continuing his football career, Zarnas replied, "I would have liked to have played more but I had responsibilities to my family. I could have played five or six years more I think."

Today, Gust Zarnas is a fan of both the Packers and the Bears. "When they play each other I stay neutral," he said. "I cheer for whoever has the ball."

Green Bay came within one game of becoming champions again in 1938. They won the Western Division, 9-3, and played the New York Giants in the championship game at the Polo Grounds. A record playoff crowd of 48,120 saw the Giants drive for the winning touchdown after being down, 17-16, and defeat the Packers, 23-17.

Green Bay's 1939 team has been called one of the best. Their backfield consisted of rookie Larry Craig, Arnie Herber, Clark Hinkle, Joe Laws and Cecil Isbell. Milt Gantenbein and Don Hutson were the ends and Russ Letlow and Buckets Goldenberg anchored the line at guard.

Halas leveled accusations of spying and cheating at Lambeau as the Bears practiced in Green Bay before the September 24 game at City Stadium.

Halas noticed the windows of nearby houses were full of binoculared onlookers as the team practiced. Halas actually went so far as to question some of the residents, all of whom claimed that they were "bird watchers."

Down 13-0 at half-time, the Packers capitalized on Chicago's mistakes and won, 21-16. George Strickler of the *Chicago Tribune* wrote, "It was a typical Packer-Bear struggle, with George Musso and Russ Letlow, rival guards, being ejected for fighting as early as the second period. The intense rivalry led to frequent altercations with officials and on nearly every play some gladiator arose limping, a victim of an especially hard tackle or block."

Chicago would get their revenge in the first week of November. Green Bay came into the game at 6-1, the only blemish being a three-point loss to the Cleveland Rams. The Bears had faltered somewhat and were 4-3, but their mid-season hobble was about to end.

As the Packers practiced at the University of Chicago's Stagg Field, Lambeau noticed white-coated men in the windows of an adjacent biology lab. Halas told him they were "biologists." Lambeau thought, "Biologists ... with binoculars?" Halas had his spies working again.

Actor John Barrymore and the 40,536 other fans at Wrigley Field saw a great offensive battle where the lead changed hands six different times. Green Bay's backs threw for 311 yards on only fifteen completions but lost a heartbreaker, 30-27.

"In the memory of the oldest observers, there is no equal for the sensational display of offensive football produced by this 40th meeting between these bitter rivals," the *Tribune's* George Strickler wrote.

Summing up the afternoon's drama was veteran Bear Dan Fortmann. After playing all but thirty seconds of the game, he said later, "It was one of those games where all you could do was go out there and pitch; the idea was to wind up with the most points."

Chicago featured a balanced attack of 183 yards on the ground and 132 via the air game. Filling in for injured back Joe Maniaci, was Bears' rookie fullback Bill Osmanski, who scored two touchdowns. Halfback Bobby Swisher added a touchdown and seventy-seven yards on the ground. Starting at quarterback and throwing the winning touchdown pass was a young kid from Columbia University, who would soon become a star of the Forties. His name was Sid Luckman.

The game also saw a makeup of sorts. George Musso and Russ Letlow met before the game and straightened out the disagreement they had in September when they had been ejected because of their "homicidal tendencies."

While the two rival teams came to blows on the field, loyal fans fought it out in the stands. One particular belligerent Bears' supporter made the mistake of picking a fight with none other than former Packers' end Lavvie Dilweg. By *Press-Gazette* writer Dick Flatley's account of the incident, Dilweg got the best of the grandstand fight. Flatley wrote that the Bears' fan realized picking the fight, "... was an error of ways, the lesson of which was learned painfully."

After the game, George Halas left no doubt where he thought the Packers' power was contained: Arnold Herber, Don Hutson, and Clarke Hinkle, the three "Hs."

In one of the best divisional races in years, both the Packers and the Bears went on to win their remaining four games. However, a Chicago three-point loss to the New York Giants in their sixth game cost the Bears a divisional tie with the Packers. Chicago finished the season at 8-3, while Green Bay won the division at 9-2.

On December 10, 1939, Green Bay and the New York Giants faced off for the championship at State Fair Park in Milwaukee. 32,000 fans sat in bitter cold and wind to witness the Packers make playoff history as they put the first shutout game in a NFL championship in the record books. Lambeau's lads routed the Giants, 27-0, for their fifth league championship.

The 1940s

A Bulldog, a Grey Ghost, Indian Jack, and a War

Bert Bell, the head coach of the hapless Philadelphia Eagles, glanced over the Chicago Bears' roster before the 1940 season and saw what he thought was the greatest team ever assembled.

Bell saw a lineup that clearly showed that the Western Division could not be dominated by any one other than Halas' Midway Monsters. The Bears had an exceptional rookie class. George McAfee, a halfback from Duke University, Ken Kavanaugh, an end from LSU, Lee Artoe, a tackle from the University of California, and Clyde "Bulldog" Turner, a center from Hardin-Simmons University, all joined a veteran Bears' squad already deep with talent.

Halas was a coach in high clover. He now had so much talent on his team he was able to field two teams a game. He broke his squad in half and the first team would play, for instance, the first and third quarters while the second team would play the second and fourth quarters. This gave the Bears the advantage of having fresh players in the game at all times. While the opposing players would be dead-tired from playing both offense and defense for most of the game, the Bears were full of piss and vinegar throughout.

"That's the way Halas functioned," running back Joe Maniaci recounted. "He had two teams operating and both of them were equal in power. For example, I would play the first and third periods and Bill Osmanski would play the second and fourth quarters. Even though the team that started would have their names in the paper as starting, it didn't mean much."

Along with the wonderful rookie class, the Bears fielded a veteran team that included six future Hall of Famers. The two-platooned Bears had a backfield full of talent: Sid Luckman at quarterback, and George McAfee, Bill Osmanski, Joe Maniaci, Ray Nolting, Harry Clark, Gary Famiglietti, and Ray "Scooter" McLean running the ball.

Blocking for them were Bulldog Turner at center, Ray Bray, George Musso, and Danny Fortmann at guard, Lee Artoe, Ed Kolman, and Joe Stydahar at tackle, and Dick Plasman, Ken Kavanaugh, and "Eggs" Manske at end.

Running back Joe Maniaci put it this way: "We had the smarter coach, the better system, and we had the personnel."

The offense would run what is the T-formation. Ralph Jones introduced the "T" in 1930 with the split ends and backs in motion. He also had the quarterback take the snap directly from the center. In 1940, Halas saw to it that the T-formation was perfected.

Credit goes to Stanford coach Clark Shaughnessy for helping to modernize the T-formation by introducing a signal calling system and the counter play. In 1935, Shaughnessy met Halas at a civic dinner where, after rearranging the place cards, they sat together discussing the formation in detail. Halas invited him to come up to the office to learn more about it.

Starting in 1935, Halas paid Shaughnessy $2,000 a year to assist with the implementation of the T-formation. Shaughnessy would later take the "T" to Stanford where he would transform a winless Cardinal team into the 1940 Rose Bowl champions.

After a stint as head coach at Notre Dame, Hunk Anderson came to the Bears as a line coach and defensive specialist. He became instrumental in designing new blocking assignments for the T-formation. He also invented the "blitz," or, as it was called then, "Red Dog." Red meant "be alert" and Dog meant "hound the quarterback."

Now, to run his new offensive scheme, Halas needed an intelligent, athletic quarterback to step in, learn a completely new system, and make it work. By happenstance, Halas had already found his quarterback at the 1937 Columbia-Syracuse game.

In New York for the Bears-Giants game, Halas attended the Columbia game at Baker Field and was impressed with Columbia's quarterback, Sid Luckman. Halas immediately saw the possibilities.

"I was a running back and I did the passing," Luckman recalled. "We did a tremendous amount of spinning to the halfback and the fullback in the single-wing formation. Some of the plays Columbia had designed, I would spin, hand off to the fullback, or fake to the fullback and give it to the running back. So, from what he [Halas] had observed that day, he felt that I could be the signal caller doing the spinning and part of the passing. He saw the possibility that I could fit into his system. It was very hard to come by a T-formation quarterback because the Bears were the only team using the T. Halas couldn't find quarterbacks. That's why he came down to see if I could do the job.

"I didn't think I was good enough to play; no way on God's earth could an Ivy League quarterback play in the NFL," Luckman continued. "Halas wrote me a letter and I wrote him back and told him I wasn't interested in playing. I was too small, and who had ever heard of Columbia University? An Ivy Leaguer in the NFL? They were few and far between."

In the December 1938 college draft, the Pittsburgh Steelers made Luckman their first choice. In a pre-arranged deal with Halas, Steelers' owner Art Rooney then traded Luckman to the Bears for another player.

"Halas came over to the house one night and we signed a contract for $5,000 at that time. My wife sort of enticed me into playing. That was really the turning point in me becoming a professional football player," Luckman continued. "I knew that I had her support and Halas' support, I figured I'd take a shot. When Halas left, he gave me the contract, put his arm around me, and said to Mrs. Luckman, 'I'm going to make sure that Sid Luckman becomes a T-formation quarterback and helps the Bears.' That stuck in my mind because he really did do everything he could to make the trade with Art Rooney.

"After signing the contract, Halas gave me some plays to look at. He and Clark Shaughnessy wrote me a long letter telling me what to look for and what to expect. During preparation for the College All-Star game, Halas came out to watch us practice one day and at that time he gave me the playbook and all the plays drawn up on cards so I could understand it."

After being a single-wing quarterback at Columbia, the complexities of the T-formation confused Luckman. At first he fumbled a lot and stumbled over his own feet when pivoting to hand-off the ball.

"In training camp, Carl Brumbaugh, who was a former T-formation quarterback for the Bears, and I would stay after practice for an hour just spinning, turning, twisting, and setting up the pass play," Luckman recalled. "I did that everyday for at least an hour if not more. That had a lot to do with my success."

Luckman got his first chance to be a T-formation quarterback in his rookie year of 1939 in a game against the New York Giants. Up until then, Luckman had been playing at left halfback. Down 16-0 to the Giants, Halas sent in the young Columbia star to lead the Bears. "It was a very stressful, emotional step for me," Luckman said. "I never realized that I was going in at a position I knew very little about."

Luckman rallied the Bears for thirteen points but Chicago lost, 16-13. His showing gave him confidence that he could run a T-formation offense.

Two weeks later, Sid worked his magic in a wild 30-27 win over the Packers. Luckman led the Bears down the field for a last minute drive that had won the game. From that point on, Luckman was the T-formation quarterback for the Bears. He spurred the squad to four straight wins to finish the 1939 season. Luckman, Halas, and the Bears entered the new decade with momentum.

Then, a new formation was often named for its originator: the Rockne Formation for Notre Dame's famed Knute Rockne; the Warner Double-Wing for coaching legend Pop Warner. Halas wanted no part of a "Halas Formation."

"I asked Halas one day," Luckman recalled, "why don't you call it the 'Halas Formation?' He said, 'No, no, it's the T-formation.' He was a very humble man. He certainly wasn't braggadocios about things like that."

While the Bears were forming a powerhouse club, things were pretty much status quo in Green Bay with the defending World Champs. The only real change involved Arnie Herber, who played a diminished role for the 1940 Packers.

Former Purdue offensive back Cecil Isbell, who had joined the Packers in 1938, was now seeing more playing time. Isbell threw for 1,037 yards and nine touchdowns in 1940. Herber was now about to abdicate his passing throne to Isbell.

The line was anchored by center George Svendsen. The tackles were Baby Ray and Bill Lee, Russ Letlow and Buckets Goldenberg were at guard, and Don Hutson, Moose Mulleneaux, Bob Adkins, and Ray Riddick played at end.

Along with Isbell and Herber, the backfield consisted of Clarke Hinkle, Andy Uram, Ed Jankowski, and the Packers first round draft choice from Minnesota, Hal Van Every.

As a left halfback, Van Every was a solid runner who also handled some of the punting duties.

"I was lucky to be the number one draft for Green Bay," Hal remembered. "And I got the great sum of $3,500."

Van Every turned out to be worth more than that to the Packers. In 1939, his senior year at Minnesota, he led the nation in pass interceptions with eight. "I never knew it until I picked up a book recently and found it listed in there," he said. "I thought, geez, isn't that nice to find out fifty years after you played that I did that."

Hal vividly recalled the hard-fought games with the rival Bears.

"Playing those Bears, it was like going to war three times a year," he said. "They had some terrific athletes. It was a dog fight out there. They weren't the cleanest club in the world. They knew every trick to get you to do things.

"Those Bears' teams of 1940 and '41, I still claim, are as good as a football team that has ever played the sport," Van Every admitted.

On September 15, 1940, the Green Bay Packers were hosting the Philadelphia Eagles at City Stadium. Out of the 11,600 people who came to see the Packers win, 27-20, were nineteen very inquisitive men sitting near the top of the stands. They observed, wrote on pads of paper, and spoke to each other in a whisper.

The nineteen observers were George Halas, his two coaches Luke Johnsos and Hunk Anderson, and sixteen of his Bears. The men were busy charting the plays Lambeau called so they could organize a defensive response. This was no ordinary scouting trip. Halas had a score to settle. He wanted to beat the Packers in their own back yard; he knew the road to the championship went through

Green Bay. The master charts the Bears made that day were going to be used against the Packers the next Sunday. During the week, Halas sent Lambeau a telegram asking Curly to take it easy on his poor Bears and not to run the score up. Lambeau jeered back, saying, "The Bears are coming up here to give us the going over of our lives, and if we let down for an instant, and believe any of this stuff, we'll take a bad beating."

The mind game—the game before the game—had begun.

The Packers led 3-0 in the first quarter on a Tiny Engebretsen field goal. Kicking off, Engebretsen put the ball into the hands of first year man George McAfee at the 7-yard line. McAfee, cutting across the field, straightened out along the sidelines, cut back into the middle of the field, and took it in for a 93-yard touchdown. The electrifying run left the Packers' partisans stunned.

Behind 14-3 at half-time, Lambeau tried to convince his troops they were still very much in the ball game, even though there was an air of suspicion the Bears had been overrated.

Engebretsen sailed the second half kickoff away from the speedy McAfee and into the waiting arms of Ray Nolting at the 3-yard line. Nolting swung across the field and streaked down the sidelines, bypassing Andy Uram in hot pursuit, for a 97-yard touchdown return. Everyone could hear the door slam shut for the Packers.

Writer George Strickler called Green Bay, "sluggish and at times stupid," after failing to connect on its celebrated passing game. Isbell and Herber each had three passes intercepted, while Hal Van Every had another picked off. Two of the steals lead to touchdowns for Chicago.

Looking at the game's statistics, one might think the Packers won. Green Bay garnered nineteen first downs to Chicago's five, and out-gained them in total yardage, 333 to 280. The difference was McAfee's and Nolting's dazzling kickoff returns.

Both teams came to rip up the sod of Wrigley Field in their rematch six weeks later, the 42nd meeting between the two teams. The 45,434 in attendance saw a great Bears' defense stymie the Packers' offense, stopping the Packers from scoring in the second half after Green Bay made a first down on the Bears' 21-, 23-, 12-, 32-, and 7-yard lines. In the second half, defensive back Bobby Swisher thrice tipped away possible Green Bay touchdown passes in an end zone of lengthening Indian summer shadows.

"For some reason, which rests only with the gridiron gods, none was fated to succeed," *Press-Gazette* writer John Walter said of the thwarted end zone passes. "The Packers lost, and to a great football team, one of the roughest, biggest and toughest which ever trod the American gridiron."

Chicago walked through the Western Division portal by slugging the Packers, 14-7. Short bone-crushing runs by Joe Maniaci and Gary Famiglietti were all the Bears needed to take a two-game cushion in the divisional race. Green Bay's only moment of brilliance came early in the second period when, as John Walter stated in the *Press-Gazette*, Arnie Herber "stuffed a touchdown pass down Don Hutson's ever-receptive throat."

After both teams played .500 football in their remaining four games of 1940, Lambeau's Packers found themselves where Halas' Bears had been one short year ago: in second place looking up. Both coaches knew finishing second in the Western Division meant that you went home with your tail between your legs while your arch-rival went to the championship game.

The Bears lost to the Washington Redskins, 7-3, on November 17. On the last play of the game and with the Bears on the Redskin 6-yard line, Luckman attempted a pass to Bill Osmanski in the end zone. Osmanski was in position to catch the ball for the win, but a Washington defender wrapped his arms around the Bears' running back, interfering with him. The foul was so obvious, the ball actually hit Osmanski in the chest. The referee didn't make the call, and the game was over.

Halas was livid. Rushing towards the referee, the Papa Bear let him have it in some choice Chicago street language, making up a few new cuss words in the process.

After the game, Redskins' owner George Preston Marshall called the Bears a bunch of crybabies and stupidly went on to call the Bears "quitters". He even had the audacity to send Halas a telegram saying he hoped to have the pleasure of beating Halas' ears off in the championship game and every year after that.

Big mistake. On Thursday before the championship game, T-formation genius Clark Shaughnessy joined Halas in Chicago to help him choose plays. Halas was confident the T-formation, with its man in motion, would destroy Washington. Marshall's "crybaby" remark gave Halas and his Bears a score to settle.

It became pro football's greatest trouncing. If ever a team played a perfect game, it was the Chicago Bears on that day. The 73-0 blowout sent Marshall back under a rock and George Halas and his beloved Midway Monsters to the top of the pro football mountain.

"Not since the British sacked this city more than 100 years ago", *Chicago Tribune* writer Winfrid Smith wrote, "has Washington seen such a rout."

The Chicago Bears of 1940 were the greatest team to rip up the turf at Wrigley Field.

There's a picture of Chicago Bears' center and linebacker Clyde "Bulldog" Turner that stands out from the rest. In it, Bulldog is poised over the ball ready to snap it. He looks like he's ready to explode off the line, his black high top cleats propelling him to bury a rival Packer. His head and chiseled chin are high, his stare deadly, his hair slightly wind-blown. His handsome physique is dressed in a tight-fitting white Bears' jersey with "66" on the chest. His stance and poise is reminiscent of the bulldog hood ornament seen on Mack trucks. That picture clearly shows the menace that was Bulldog Turner.

Bulldog retired at the end of the 1952 season as one of the greatest players in pro football history. He was a bulldozing hellion at the center position and a hard-nosed linebacker, making All-NFL six times, and leading the league in 1942 with eight interceptions. In 1947, he had an interception return of ninety-six yards. He was so versatile, he would even play running back in emergency situations. In a game that has seen its fair share of odd and entertaining nicknames, Clyde "Bulldog" Turner's did not come about quite as one might expect.

"When I was getting ready to go to Hardin-Simmons College, most everybody at that time was on a full scholarship," Bulldog remembered. "It was during the Depression, you know, and nobody had any money. So the only way we could go to college was on a scholarship. Me and a high school classmate of mine were invited down to try out for the Hardin-Simmons team. We trained a little bit that summer before going down there. While we were training, we devised this plan. If I wasn't looking too good, he'd holler, 'Come on, Bulldog, hit 'em like you did back home.' I was supposed to holler, 'Come on, Tiger, hit 'em like you did at home,' whenever I thought he wasn't doing his best. After we made the team, we told that story and they all got a big kick out of it. So, by golly, I got the name then and there. I even had classmates and first cousins who didn't know my real name. Everybody knew me as 'Bulldog.' It has just stayed with me all my life. Because of the nickname, after I went into business it got a little embarrassing, but it was too late. I couldn't shake the name.

"I was the number one draft choice of the Bears in 1940," Turner continued. "That year, George Halas had traded for someone else's first pick so he picked me and George McAfee in the first round. He chose George McAfee on the pick he traded for. I didn't know there was such a thing as pro football until I was a senior and saw a short subject on the Green Bay Packers at the movies. Even then I didn't understand what it was all about.

"That year I played in the *Chicago Tribune* All-Star Game. The College All-Star team played the pro champions of the year before. It was played at Soldier Field and there were always 100,000 people there. I was in training camp with the All-Stars and that night after the game I went with the Bears.

"I had talked to Halas over the phone before but had never met him. He flew me up to Chicago and that was just when commercial airlines were getting started. That was a big deal to be flown to Chicago to talk to someone about a contract. It was a big deal to me. Mr. Halas and his wife met me at the airport and I doubt he met many of his players like that. I also thought that was a big deal, the owner of the Bears meeting me like that.

"I was a two-way player. I started right out playing center and outside linebacker. I played two-way until my last year in 1952, when I only played offense. I really preferred to play defense. That was the only time you got any notoriety. In fact, I lead the league one year in pass interceptions and I'm the only linebacker to do that. I set a new league record at the time but it was broken the next year."

Bulldog had a good career against the Packers. Bears' running backs usually had a field day with the workhorse Turner leading the blocking up front. But, he admits, like most other defenders at the time the real thorn in his side was receiver Don Hutson.

"The guys I was blocking on offense didn't bother me," Bulldog said. "I could handle them. My headache was Don Hutson. I had to help cover him. It was my job to do that bump and run, try to slow him down, and cover him for a short distance. That guy was a mental monster. Even now I still worry about that guy. He was so good, you just couldn't cover him.

"His team designed some of the pass patterns they use today. Like that out pass where you catch it and step out of bounds? That was Hutson's play. There was no way you could stop him on that.

"I always seemed to have a pretty good day against the Packers. Green Bay had a guard playing in front of me by the name of Ed Neal. He weighed about three hundred pounds, and all muscle. He was big. I remember Neal broke my nose about every time we played. We didn't wear face masks in those days and as soon as I'd move the ball, Neal would ram me in the face. I got so I'd duck my head and he'd hit me on the helmet. It didn't take him long to crush that helmet. I'd take three helmets when we went to Green Bay because I knew he'd be cracking them up."

Bulldog decided to call it quits after the 1951 season but Halas asked him to come back as a player/coach in 1952. Just the day before the Bears broke camp in 1952, Halas traded off a player who had been playing at the tackle position. Halas put Bulldog in the last exhibition game and after that he played offensive tackle every play that year. After the season he retired and coached with the Bears for five years, in charge of the offensive line.

There is a story often told about Bulldog falling out of a three-story window. An awning broke his fall and he landed on the sidewalk. As he sat there dazed, a police officer ran up to him and asked him what was going on.

"I don't know. I just got here myself," Turner replied.

Clyde "Bulldog" Turner and his splendid career were rewarded in 1966 when he was inducted into the Pro Football Hall of Fame.

1941

And the rich got richer. George Halas had to look no further than his good friend at Stanford, Clark Shaughnessy, for a new tandem of fast runners for the 1941 season. Norm Standlee and Hugh Gallarneau were drafted by Halas because they were accustomed to the T-formation after playing for Shaughnessy. They knew the runner's duties in the T-formation better than anyone. Halas expected them to make an immediate impact in the lineup.

"That's why he drafted Standlee and myself," Gallarneau opined. "In the 1940 Rose Bowl game I was the high scorer and all the Bears were out and saw the game. Halas liked the fact that my first touchdown was a run and the second was on a long pass-reception."

Hugh Gallarneau had a banner year, finishing third in league scoring and amassing a productive 508 total yards in rushing and pass receiving.

Gallarneau's competition at right halfback was considered one of the most dangerous runners in the game, second-year man George "One Play" McAfee.

"He was a great football player," Gallarneau recalled. "He was the finest broken-field runner of all time. He was the original great scat-back. A lot of people don't realize that he was a great blocker."

The immortal Red Grange called McAfee "the most dangerous man with the football in the game."

Curly Lambeau paid him a great compliment by saying McAfee was "the most talented running back the Green Bay Packers had ever faced." Originally drafted by the Philadelphia Eagles, Halas traded for McAfee's draft rights. It was a great move for the young kid from Duke. He went from the doormat Eagles to the champion-caliber Bears.

Although Duke University didn't use a T-formation offense, its quick-hitting plays were tailor-made for the speedy McAfee and it was easy for him to learn. "I started off at right halfback," McAfee said, "It wasn't any problem. It was very easy to get onto."

McAfee was one of the fastest runners of his day. No one could catch him in the open field. He was a whirling, dancing runner who had a great hip shift that kept defenders grabbing air where he had been only a moment earlier.

"I always felt like I had good speed," the Corbin, Kentucky, native admitted. "I came from a family of twelve, so you had to have good speed to beat them to the table."

In 1941, McAfee would run through the league like it was the Thanksgiving Day dinner rush with his brothers and sisters. He led the Bears in rushing yardage with an impressive 7.3 yards per attempt, scored eleven touchdowns, and finished second in league scoring with seventy-two points behind Don Hutson's ninety-five. McAfee's stats are amazing when you realize he averaged only twenty-five minutes playing time per game in 1940 and '41. Hence, the label "One Play McAfee."

George McAfee also pioneered the use of low-cut shoes to increase his speed and make him ever more elusive. In practice, McAfee would wear the usual high-top football cleats. On game day, however, he would change to lightweight Oxford-type footwear.

Other than Ray Bray replacing guard George Musso, the 1941 Chicago Bears were essentially the same team that had destroyed the league the season before.

The Packers' 1941 seventh round draft choice didn't look like a pro football player, let alone a future Hall-of-Famer. He was from Gonzaga University in Spokane, Washington. At 5' 11", he was short by football standards and slightly overweight at 195 pounds. He wasn't fast nor did he possess the shifty, evasive moves of a George McAfee. Tony Canadeo was also prematurely grey, giving rise to his nickname, "The Grey Ghost."

However, the attributes Tony Canadeo did possess are evident in any great player. He had courage, tenacity, and an unrelenting desire to win. For eleven years Canadeo played a variety of positions. As an offensive halfback he ran and threw the ball, he was a receiver, he returned punts and kickoffs, punted, and intercepted passes. And he played defense. Although a highly respected player, Canadeo wouldn't get his just due as a great runner until 1949, when he became only the third back in NFL history to gain over a thousand yards in a season.

A Detroit University coach noticed Canadeo in a game against Gonzaga. He told Lambeau about the hard-rushing Canadeo and Curly liked what he heard.

"I was supposed to go to the Redskins," Canadeo remembers. "The Redskins trained out at Gonzaga and they were going to sneak me through the draft, but Lambeau grabbed me."

Like most other players of the era, Canadeo didn't become rich by turning pro. "I think I played for $175 a game," he recalled. "We played twelve league games and a playoff game against the Bears. I probably made $4,000 that year."

Canadeo shared halfback duties with Cecil Isbell in Green Bay's Notre Dame's box offense. "In those days there wasn't free substitution," Canadeo remarked. "You started and you played a quarter, then someone else came in. Isbell was primarily the number one passing halfback at that time, but I got in quite a bit though."

Even after more than fifty years, Canadeo vividly recalls those tough games against the Bears.

"We always hated them so much," he said with a laugh. "I was born and raised in Chicago so I used to hate the Packers when I was a high school kid. I was a Bears' fan because I was from Chicago."

That allegiance quickly changed when Canadeo faced the Bears for the 1941 season opener on September 29. Some 24,876 fans packed City Stadium for the 43rd Packers-Bears brouhaha. Early in the game, Canadeo got the ball and attempted a line plunge.

"The first time I carried the ball," the Grey Ghost ruefully recounted, "I went off-tackle and I came up spitting teeth. The first time I ever played against them!"

Canadeo had Danny Fortmann and Joe Stydahar to thank for the missing molars. The tough Bears' line decisively outplayed Green Bay's front wall most of the game. Putting great pressure on Canadeo and Hal Van Every, the Bears' line seemed to be in the Packers' backfield all day, and each meeting proved to be a punishing encounter.

"When the Bruins got mad," *Green Bay Press-Gazette* writer John Walter wrote, "when they elected to release all their pent up explosives, it was just a case of stand back or get hurt."

Chicago's execution of the "T" offense was deceptive and crisp. In the first quarter, Luckman lateraled to George McAfee, who stopped and threw a TD pass to Ken Kavanaugh waiting on the 7-yard line. The Chicago Tribune incorrectly credited the pass to Kavanaugh as thrown by "Bill McAfee."

With Chicago leading 15-0, Cecil Isbell mounted an aerial attack with eight straight passes. Catching three of the eight, Don Hutson snagged a 10-yard pass, broke free, and galloped the remaining thirty-five yards for the score. The multi-talented Hutson then added the extra point as well.

Although Green Bay stayed close, costly fumbles and Chicago's unequaled running game defeated the Packers that day. The Chicagoans recovered three of the six Packers' fumbles while their backs hammered the defenders' line for 258 yards and the 25-17 Chicago win.

"The Bears," wrote John Walter, "were extremely rough and great ball stealers. The Packers were charged with four fumbles, and better than half of them had the impetus of clawing tacklers in orange uniforms."

Back in room 707 of the Northland Hotel, a beaming George Halas held court with reporters during post game interviews. "It was finesse, nothing more, that beat the Packers today," he boasted. "Our power wasn't any better than the Packers' but we did come through when it counted. I'd like to have some of Curly's boys on my club. We could use them."

Leave it up to Papa Bear to humble you to death!

Halas picked up the phone and called his mother in St. Louis to tell her of the victory. Room 707 grew silent as mother and son gloried in the triumph.

In the Packers' locker room, the chorus of "Wait 'til Chicago" rang out. Lambeau knew his squad was on a par with Halas', and he vowed to prove it in the rematch.

Lambeau concocted a plan that let veteran guard Russ Letlow practice with the team during the week, then reconnoiter Chicago's games on Sunday in preparation for their next meeting. He would return on Monday to be debriefed by Lambeau. The early November rematch at Wrigley Field showed the Packers' strategy was the product of Letlow's spying excursions.

Lambeau implemented a seven-man line to counter the Bears' talented backfield. It worked. Stuffing eight Bears' backs for a total of eighty-three yards, the Packers held off a gallant Chicago comeback to win a 16-14 squeaker. Like the German army that was blitzkrieging over the Crimean peninsula, the Packers stormed the surprised Bruins to prove they, too, had what it takes.

It was a typical Bears-Packers game, with Chicago's Bulldog Turner, Bill Osmanski, and Bob Nowaskey, and Green Bay's Ed Jankowski all leaving the game with injuries.

Cecil Isbell had one of his best days ever as a pro, completing eleven of nineteen passes for 139 yards. Most importantly, he had the time to throw. The Packers' offensive line, notably guards Pete Tinsley and Buckets Goldenberg, held the brawling Bears at bay.

"Buckets romped over the field like an unshaven youngster," *Press-Gazette* scribe Ray Pagel proclaimed.

Clarke Hinkle, the "Bucknell Battering Ram," became the hometown hero after galloping for sixty-nine yards and kicking what would be the game-winning 44-yard field goal in the first quarter. During the game, Hinkle came to the sidelines with a deep gash in his leg. Lambeau was waiting for him.

"Hinkle, why are you coming out?" Lambeau asked.

"Coach, I'm hurt," Clarke shot back.

"No you're not," Lambeau countered.

"OK, I'm not," Hinkle said as he turned around and ran back into the game.

After the game, Coach Lambeau was so happy, he went around hugging his players. Many were at a loss for comment.

"Curly Lambeau," wrote the *Press-Gazette's* Ray Pagel, "was as happy as a schoolgirl bride. Curly took that over-rated T-formation and made Halas eat all the words that the Chicago sports writers had written in praise of his exploits."

It was a huge win for Green Bay. The Packers, now at 7-1, looked forward to sweeping their remaining four opponents and pushing into the championship game.

What Lambeau didn't count on was that the Bears, now at 5-1, would rip apart their last five foes. It was inevitable. The Packers and the Bears were on a collision course to again meet in the playoff game to decide the Western Division title.

On the morning of December 7, 1941, Comiskey Park was packed to its fullest for the season-ending inner-city rivalry between the Chicago Bears and the Chicago Cardinals. All eyes were on this league battle. It would decide whether the Packers, with a Bears' loss, would play the Giants in the championship game, or if with a Bears' win, they would be forced into a playoff with their arch rivals. Green Bay wasn't counting on any help from the pitiful Cardinals.

Curly Lambeau and his Packers were in the stands that day to see their futures decided by the inner-city foes. Would the following Sunday see them traveling back to Chicago for a playoff game or staying at home and hosting the New York Giants for the championship?

No one at the game was prepared for the entire world to change that day. The announcement came over the PA system at half-time.

"Ladies and gentlemen: The Japanese have bombed Pearl Harbor. The Japanese have bombed Pearl Harbor."

The crowd sat in stunned silence.

"Obviously, we were all shocked," Bears' back Hugh Gallarneau said. "We knew that a lot of guys would be leaving for the service and we knew a lot of them wouldn't come back."

Packer Tony Canadeo, like many others, didn't even know where Pearl Harbor was. "I thought 'Pearl Harbor...where in the hell is that?'" he recalled.

"After the game," George McAfee remembered, "we went over to a Cardinal player's apartment and listened to all the news on the radio."

"My wife was at the game," Bears' halfback Harry Clarke said. "She said people just sat there stunned, with no one talking. After that, we just sort of went through the paces."

After the announcement, the game's outcome seemed trivial. The Cardinals put up a good fight, but in the second half the Bears scored two touchdowns and won, 34-24, forcing a playoff with Green Bay. George McAfee scored two touchdowns, bringing his total to a league-leading eleven. Following close behind with ten TD's was rookie Hugh Gallarneau.

Only days before the game, the *Green Bay Press-Gazette* printed a headline that Lambeau was confident his Packers could beat the Bears like they had in November. It also reported the Bears were predicting they would win by forty points.

"The Packers tricked us once this season with their seven-man line, but they are not going to do it this time," a cocky Sid Luckman proclaimed.

It was a bitterly cold December 14 when the Packers and the Bears met in Wrigley Field to decide the Western championship.

The uncertainty of the newly declared war and what effect it might have on pro football was evident when *Chicago Tribune's* writer Edward Prell wrote, "It may have been the last time these two titans of the gridiron will meet for a long, long time. If so, the fans will have plenty to remember them by until this war runs its course."

Packers' runner Clarke Hinkle led off the scoring by plunging over from the 3-yard line. On their next possession, a Packers' punt landed in the hands of Hugh Gallarneau, who zig-zagged his way to an 80-yard punt return. A missed extra point kept the Packers in the lead, 7-6. Then it all fell apart.

Two touchdown runs by Norm Standlee, one by Bobby Swisher, and a field goal by Joe Stydahar amounted to a twenty-four point second quarter, making the remainder of the game anti-climactic. The Bears ran roughshod over the Packers, 33-14, sending them into the championship tilt against the Giants.

"The team wasn't fighting and they made a lot of mistakes," a dejected Curly Lambeau stated.

"I had a feeling we'd win this one," a confident Halas said afterward. "I figured it all along. We were better prepared, and the team was much more highly keyed than they were in November."

Another huge rushing game won it for Chicago. Bear backs had pounded the Packers' forward defensive wall for 267 yards. In November, the Bears had been held to eighty-three total yards rushing. This time, Halas and his T-formation had out-foxed Lambeau again.

To make Lambeau's nightmare complete, NFL Commissioner Elmer Layden fined Lambeau $100 for allowing two Packers to wear numbers that didn't correspond with the game program. Lambeau later got the fine returned after he pointed out the mix-up was the league's fault.

On December 21, 1941, in front of only 13,341 faithful at Wrigley Field, the Chicago Bears became back-to-back champions by routing the New York Giants, 37-9. The low attendance figure was not surprising. America's mind was on the war and the general consensus was that the championship had already been decided the week before in the playoff game with the Packers.

The war decimated the Chicago Bears, just as it had every other team in the league. Beginning in 1942, the wartime draft robbed most teams of their best and most talented players. For the next few years, teams would be stocked with draft-deferred men and over-the-hill players.

By 1943, Sid Luckman, Ray Nolting, and Bill Osmanski would be the few holdovers from the two-time champion Bears. By 1944, only Luckman remained.

Concern about the war led many to question whether the league should shut down until it was over. Some wondered how the league could go on while America was fighting a world war. Others rationalized that Americans on the home front needed some outlet from the dark news coming from Europe and the Pacific.

During the war years attendance fell off and interest in pro football waned, yet the league sputtered on somehow. Only ten teams took to the gridirons in 1942, followed by a league-low eight in 1943.

1942-'43

Places like Guadalcanal, Stalingrad, and Wake Island became household words in the fall of 1942 as newspapers and radio brought daily details and updates on the fighting in the Pacific and Europe. Americans began rationing gas, coffee, and, later on, leather shoes. Coastal "blackouts" became commonplace and everyone knew that the "Bataan Death March" wasn't a John Phillip Sousa anthem.

Like so many others after Pearl Harbor, George Halas felt the pull of patriotism and duty to his country. After his limited involvement in World War I, he had vowed that if ever again his country went to war he would make more of a military contribution.

Lieutenant Commander Halas was stationed at a large Naval base in Norman, Oklahoma, where he was third in command, but wanted more than anything to be in the Pacific fighting the Japanese. His wish was granted later that year.

Before leaving Chicago, Halas took care of team matters. He turned over the Bears' administrative duties to steel company president Ralph Brizzolara and his secretary Frances Osborne. He designated Luke Johnsos and Hunk Anderson as co-coaches, with Johnsos responsible for the defense and Anderson for the offense.

Chicago began the 1942 campaign with George McAfee, Norm Standlee, Joe Maniaci, and Bobby Swisher noticeably absent from the backfield. Ken Kavanaugh, Dick Plasman, and Young Bussey were off fighting the war.

Green Bay lost sixteen players to the war in 1942. Gone were stars Clarke Hinkle, Gus Zarnas, Hal Van Every, Moose Mulleneaux, Smiley Johnson, and George Svendsen.

"One of the reasons more of our players weren't drafted was that we were a bunch of broken-down stumblebums," Packers' guard Buckets Goldenberg once said. "A bunch of us tried to get in but were rejected. When we asked them how come we could play pro football and yet be rejected for the service, one doctor said, 'Well, if you're playing in a football game and your knee gives out, they can stop the game and take you out. In a war you can't call time-out during a battle.'"

The Packers got a break, for the time being, when Tony Canadeo was deferred. "I know I was deferred for a while because I was the sole support of my mother, wife, and child," Canadeo recalled.

Also deferred was running back Larry Craig, who was exempted because he was a farmer, an occupation considered vital to the war effort.

Pro teams traveling from city to city were also affected. "Travel was really different during the war," Canadeo noted. "Servicemen had priority on trains and in hotels, so a lot of times we would crowd up in day coaches rather than getting sleepers. Hotel reservations were hard to get but we just put a lot of people in a couple of rooms."

Green Bay residents browsing through the *Press-Gazette* on Monday, September 28, 1942, couldn't miss the huge H. C. Prange Co. ad saluting the "New men and popular veterans" of the '42 team and the sixteen Packers off fighting in the war:

"Old Mother Green Bay is mighty proud of her Packers, but this year when she expects to run up another National Championship Pennant ... she is already proud of this pennant ... the Packers' Service Flag. They're not in Packer uniforms this autumn because they're in other uniforms—Uncle Sam's Sailors, Soldiers, Marines, Coast Guard! Surely they belong in the annual community football tribute and we at Prange's salute the Packers."

Unfortunately, the *Press-Gazette* also had to print the story of an opening day loss to the Bears, who, in winning, posted the highest point total ever in the forty-seven meetings between the rivals.

The game started off on a negative note for Chicago. On the first series of downs, running back Bill Osmanski was nearing the sidelines when he saw the trainers' kit in his path. As he sought to avoid it, he was hit hard by two Packers, injuring his left knee. Done for the day, he spent the night in Green Bay's St. Vincent Hospital. Also hurting was Sid Luckman, who hadn't practiced all week because of a sore shoulder.

Lambeau's legion held steady with Halas' hooligans for three quarters, leading Chicago, 28-27, into the fourth. Then all hell and high water broke loose. After the smoke cleared, the scoreboard read Bears 44, Packers 28.

It was a bittersweet day for the pigskin-tossing Isbell. This was the twelfth straight league game in which he completed one or more touchdown passes. On the bitter side, four of Isbell's lobs were picked off, two by Bulldog Turner on consecutive sets of downs. All four takeaways led to Bruin touchdowns.

Bears' fullback Gary Famiglietti was the hero, scoring three touchdowns in a game marred by fights and ninety-one yards in Bear penalties. "The crowd thought Lee Artoe was a bad boy," wrote Edward Prell of the *Chicago Tribune*, "especially when referee Ronald Gibbs warned him to cut down on this enthusiasm." Packers' center Charley Brock found his own way to warn Artoe— he took a couple of swings at him.

A 38-7 Bears' triumph seven weeks later saw no improvement in Artoe and his mates. The Bears were penalized four times for unnecessary roughness. One foul was attributed to Artoe. "Lee Artoe, the Bears' big bad man, hit Lou Brock so hard in the stomach that the Packers' fullback was out for three minutes," wrote the *Green Bay Press-Gazette's* Art Daley. "What's worse, Brock was hit after the play was stopped."

When the Bears weren't taking cheap shots, they were having fun with the punchless Packers. With the game safely in hand, Chicago added a ludicrous in-your-face touchdown on a razzle-dazzle play. Center Bulldog Turner hiked the ball on an angle to back Harry Clark, who then lateraled to Luckman, who then passed to halfback Scooter McLean for a 15-yard score. The odd play was in the Bears' playbook, but was to be used only as comic relief. With twenty-one straight wins, Chicago was laughing its way to another championship.

During the game, the crowd cooperated by returning footballs kicked into the stands to the officials. It had been announced that all such footballs would be sent to various military service posts. One of the footballs used in the game was auctioned off to purchase war bonds. An unnamed business firm bid $20,000 for the ball.

Green Bay had come into the game all nicked and banged up. Don Hutson was among the running wounded. The "Alabama Antelope" had sprained his ankle the preceding week against Cleveland but had kept it a secret. He scored the only points the Packers put on the board with a 6-yard pass catch from an also ailing Cecil Isbell.

One veteran scribe in the press box declared, "I never saw a Green Bay team play that badly."

Fellow writer Ray Pagel summed it up best by saying, "A summary of [Packer] mental lapses and poor tactics would be boring."

Fact is, Green Bay wasn't a bad team. They finished second in the Western Division in 1942 at 8-2-1. The truth was that Chicago had a great squad. Once again, the Bears proved they had the better players and coaches than any other team in the league.

George Halas, still stationed in Oklahoma, heard the details of his Bears' smashing victory. Interim Bears' general manager Ralph Brizzolara arranged for a telephone line from Norman, Oklahoma, as soon as the game was over. When Brizzolara revealed the score, Halas hollered, "However it was done, it was done right!"

The entire 1942 season had been "done right" in Chicago. They breezed through their eleven game schedule, amassing 376 offensive points and giving up only eighty-four. In 1942, the Bears beat their opponents by an average score of 34-7! They punted only thirty-four times all season. They obliterated all opponents.

One team they hadn't faced in the regular season was the Eastern Division champ Washington Redskins. The 10-1 'Skins had a great team, featuring quarterback Sammy Baugh and fullback Andy Farkas.

The two divisional winners met in Washington on December 13 to settle the score as 36,008 looked on. Bears' co-coach Luke Johnsos kept thinking of their undefeated 1934 team. Johnsos was the only member of the undefeated 1942 team to play on the squad that lost the championship game to the sneaker-adorned New York Giants in 1932. Johnsos didn't want to be a part of another Bears' team that would have its undefeated season ruined by losing the title game.

Coach Johnsos' Bears would be thwarted again. With George Halas on leave and in attendance, an inspired Redskins' defense stuffed the Bears' running game, silenced the T-formation, and won the championship, 14-6. Chicago's only points came on a 52-yard fumble recovery by the genial and sweet-tempered Lee Artoe.

Not having Halas' every day pushing and prodding had affected the team. The co-coaching of Johnsos and Anderson had appeared, on the surface, to be successful, yet Sid Luckman saw the loss of Halas had hurt the Bears in the long run. He recalled that the Bears had begun to think of themselves as unbeatable. Adding that Halas would have never allowed that, Luckman said the team didn't work as before and the inevitable occurred. The Bears were no longer champions.

In the fall of 1942, the *San Francisco Chronicle* ran a picture of Packers' pass catching wizard Don Hutson snaring a pass thrown by Cecil Isbell. What caught everyone's attention was that the picture was purposely printed upside-down. *Chronicle* sports editor Bill Leiser was the guilty party. When a rival paper scoffed that Hutson was good, but not that good, Leiser replied, "The fellow who has caught passes enough to lead the professional leagues in scoring year after year, Don Hutson, DOES catch 'em that way, upside down."

The dashing Hutson had just finished his greatest season ever. In 1942, Hutson led the league in (1) Most passes caught in a season: 74; (2) Most touchdown passes in one season: 17; (3) Most net-yards receiving: 1,211; (4) Most yards in one game: 209; (5) Shortest touchdown pass: 4 inches; (6) Most points: 138; (7) Most points after touchdowns: 33; and (8) Most points after touchdowns in one game: 6. At the time, he also held league records in passes caught, most yards gained on passes, and most career touchdown passes. He was the greatest scoring machine the league had ever seen.

What's forgotten is that Hutson was also a great kicker, although it was only a sidelight to his pass-catching. He didn't kick an extra point until 1938 when he hit three. He added only two in 1939, fifteen in 1940, and twenty in 1941. He made two field goals in his career, and it's no surprise that they both were game winners.

Catching the football was Hutson's specialty, and no one knew that better than the Chicago Bears. Hutson had scored at least one touchdown in each of his eight years against the Packers' most hated rivals.

Hutson's league record of 138 points was not broken until 1960 when another Packers' Golden Boy bettered it by thirty-eight points.

The war continued to take its toll on both teams in 1943. A total of thirty-one Bears' suited up in military uniforms instead of the team's orange and blue. At the same time, twenty-five Packers were also playing for Uncle Sam. Chicago's backfield, already hit hard by the absence of George McAfee, Joe Maniaci and Bobby

Swisher, also lost Hugh Gallarneau, Ken Kavanaugh and Lee Artoe in 1943. Green Bay suffered less than Chicago, losing notable linemen Russ Letlow and Bill Lee.

Trying to find good players was becoming a real challenge. "We held tryouts at Cubs Park and signed up anybody who could run around the field twice," co-coach Luke Johnsos recalled. "We had players forty and fifty years old."

The draft-depleted Bears, so in need of players, even coaxed old Packers' nemesis Bronko Nagurski out of retirement to play at tackle. They found the old "Nag" working on his farm in International Falls, Minnesota. Bronko considered himself a little old to be running around the gridiron again but decided to attend the Bears' training camp in Delafield, Wisconsin. Later in the season he even played some at his old fullback position.

Lambeau picked up two impact players in the college draft in 1943. Beefing up the line after the loss of Letlow and Lee, Curly drafted tackle Richard Wildung from the University of Minnesota and added Irv Comp from St. Benedict College to the backfield.

The league fielded eight teams in 1943, down two from the previous season. The Cleveland Rams suspended play in 1943, while the Steelers and the Eagles merged to become the Steagles.

In dire need of intensive care, the league was still breathing, albeit barely.

Some 23,675 fans crammed into City Stadium on September 27, 1943, to watch the war-weakened rivals play to a 21-21 "kiss your sister" tie. It was the first time they had played to a tie since 1928.

Tony Canadeo, the Gonzaga Grey Ghost, had a huge day, rushing for ninety-nine yards on thirteen attempts and tossing a 26-yard TD pass to Hutson, who snagged the pass with two Bears' defenders right on top of him. Also singled out for their outstanding play were old veterans George Musso, in his eleventh season, and the dusted-off retiree, Nagurski.

Don Hutson made a great sacrifice to be in Green Bay that day and played under a heavy burden. Don left for Arkansas immediately after the game to attend his father's funeral while, at the same time, dealing with the tragic news that his brother had been killed in action in the South Pacific.

The hard-driving Bears went on to reel off five consecutive wins before their rematch with the Packers on November 8 in Chicago. The second largest crowd in the history of the rivalry saw the Bears gun down the Packers, 21-7, in, as the *Chicago Tribune's* Edward Prell described, "a rain playing a soft and steady accompaniment."

Through the muck and mire of Wrigley's muddy field, Tony Canadeo splashed his way to a 20-yard touchdown run to open the scoring. Shortly after, Bears' halfback Ray "Scooter" McLean dashed off for a 60-yard touchdown to even it up. Eventually, the Bears' line-driving rushing attack wore down the Wisconsin defenders, gaining a total of 213 yards.

As usual, the Midway Monsters' defense stuffed the Packers when they had to. Sid Luckman's defensive play was exceptional. Two times during the game, Luckman slammed into Hutson simultaneously with the pass reception. As the great Hutson struggled to his feet he recognized Luckman. "When did you start tackling people?" Hutson asked him.

"They [the Bears] came off Wrigley Field's mud-churned field, smiles breaking the caking on their faces after a bitter battle," wrote Ed Prell. "At the finish of battle, the only color showing on the twenty-two mud-splattered warriors was the bobbing light yellow of Green Bay helmets. The big numbers on the jerseys were completely obliterated."

The Chicagoans kept their winning streak at Wrigley Field intact. Chicago had not lost at home since the 16-14 defeat by the Packers in 1941.

Bears' quarterback Sid Luckman's had his greatest season in 1943. He threw for twenty-eight touchdowns and 2,194 yards, averaging almost twenty yards per completion. In New York for a game against the Giants, Luckman threw six touchdown passes and tallied 433 yards passing. He couldn't have picked a better time to do it: New York had officially been declared "Sid Luckman Day."

Sid finished off his masterful season by leading his Bears to a 41-21 victory over the Washington Redskins in the championship game at Wrigley Field. Luckman attempted thirty passes and completed twenty-three for 508 yards and five touchdowns. He also ran for another sixty yards.

His incredible year earned Sid Luckman the league's Most Valuable Player award in 1943. Every day in Chicago was now "Sid Luckman Day."

1944-'45

By 1944, another three Packers, including offensive back Andy Uram, had replaced their Packer uniforms with military ones. The three new inductees brought the number of Packers serving overseas to twenty-seven.

The Bears were still the hardest hit of the two teams. Stars Harry Clark, Danny Fortmann, Bill Geyer, and Bill Osmanski all left for the war, leaving co-coaches Hunk Anderson and Luke Johnsos with a roster of veterans, rookies, and old-timers all scrambled together. Even Sid Luckman was not spared. As a Merchant Marine, Sid was usually away during the week, but he generally got to play on Sundays. His backup was the thirty-five-year old Gene Ronzani who had retired in 1938. In 1944, a total of forty-three Chicago Bears were away at war.

A chance meeting in a Chicago restaurant brought Packers' coach Curly Lambeau and ex-Bear George "Brute" Trafton together to discuss their favorite subject, football.

"What's wrong with that club of yours?" Trafton inquired. "They don't scrap back like that old Green Bay crowd. Why, right now, in this dinner jacket, I could chase those mugs out of the park."

Coach Lambeau was both amused and impressed. "You've got a job," Lambeau declared. "Show up in Green Bay August 20th."

Trafton, who had once been the most hated player in Green Bay, did just that and became the Packers' new line coach. Author Larry Names, in his book *The Lambeau Years-Part Two*, claims Trafton held a grudge against Halas, Hunk Anderson, and his former team for denying him the head coaching job in 1932 after Ralph Jones quit. Trafton had very much wanted to be head coach of the Bears, the team he had helped build into a champion. How better than to get his revenge by coaching against Halas and his old team.

Don Hutson was also a Green Bay assistant coach in 1944. Hutson had wanted to retire for a couple of years but Lambeau and the fans would heap on just enough guilt to make him stay in uniform another year.

"It's hard to retire in Green Bay," he once said. "Everybody is crazy about football up there and playing the way I had, it was hard to quit. Finally, I told Lambeau after my eighth year that I'd sign another contract with the Packers if he would agree that he wouldn't ask me to play after the contract terminated."

Hutson was concerned he would become a "football jerk," a tarnished player who would continue to play after his skills had diminished. He was also leery of injury. "I had played eleven years on offense and defense, sixty minutes every week, and I hadn't been hurt," he said. "The odds were against my going on and not getting hurt."

Also buckling under the coaxing and cajoling of Lambeau was Charles "Buckets" Goldenberg. Like Hutson, Buckets had also retired but both men now decided to return to the gridiron for one last hurrah.

The 1944 Packers were a mediocre squad of retirees, veterans, and draft-deferred players. At center was Charlie Brock, Pete Tinsley was at guard, Baby Ray at tackle, and Don Hutson and Harry Jacunski were the ends.

The backfield consisted of Larry Craig, Joe Laws, and Lou Brock. Also returning were Ted Fritsch and Irv Comp. It was a competitive team in 1944, but not in the same class as some of its predecessors.

The 1944 Chicago Bears began to practice at a new facility. The campus of St. Joseph's College in Rensselaer, Indiana, became the Bears' training camp for the next thirty-one years. Surrounded by cornfields, grasshoppers and little else, Halas thought Rensselaer would be far enough away from the lights of big city Chicago to keep a player's mind on football. Over the next three decades, Halas found many a curfew breaker to test his theory—and his patience.

The Bears' coaching staff grew by one, with the addition of the ageless Paddy Driscoll. He joined Anderson and Johnsos, who were once again directing the Bears' attack with Halas now in the Pacific.

Chicago's line was a hodgepodge of new and old. Bulldog Turner was a veteran fixture at center, along with George Musso at tackle in his final year. The newly acquired Ed Sprinkle, from Hardin-Simmons University, joined the remaining lineup of unknowns.

The backfield returnees were Sid Luckman and Gene Ronzani at quarterback, Scooter McLean and Jim Fordham at halfback, and Gary Famiglietti at fullback.

On September 24, 1944, a capacity crowd of 25,000 packed City Stadium to boo the cursed Bears in the 49th contest between the rivals. The fans got their money's worth.

The Bears came out flat and fell behind early. Irv Comp broke free from some hard-charging Bruins and lobbed a perfect pass to Lou Brock who, throwing tacklers aside, dashed down the sidelines for a 30-yard touchdown. After Chicago lost the ball on downs, Green Bay quickly capitalized as Comp darted his way into the end zone from nine yards out.

On the next series, Luckman tried to lateral the ball to Henry Margarita but he fumbled it away to Green Bay lineman Charlie Brock. Fullback Ted Fritsch rammed his way over to score from the 1-yard line. Later in the first half, Comp lofted a spiral to Don Hutson who cradled it into the end zone for the score.

Behind, 28-7, at half-time, Halas was a raving lunatic in the locker room. Blasting his players, Halas minced no words about his team's horrible performance. Halas must have been convincing.

"Like the slow onrush of a volcano," Ed Prell wrote, "the Bears inexorably fought their way back into the battle."

After a march of eighty-seven yards, Bears' end George Wilson leaped to catch a Luckman pass for a TD, drawing Chicago closer, 28-14. The Bears then recovered a Green Bay fumble and George Wilson dove over for a score. In the fourth quarter, Margarita slid through a line of Packers' defenders from five yards out to tie the game, 28-28.

But the Bears' valiant comeback try would be for naught. With the score knotted, Luckman intercepted an Irv Comp pass returning it to the Packers' thirty-two, setting up the Bears to win the game. However, a holding penalty nullified the play and gave the Packers the break they needed. On the next play, Lou Brock broke wide to his left behind terrific blocking and raced for a touchdown.

Luckman's attempted assault to again tie the game in the closing minutes was thwarted when he was intercepted by Ted Fritsch. Fritsch corralled the ball at the 45-yard line and ran down the sidelines pushing Luckman and other Bears out of the way for the unnecessary touchdown. Green Bay 42, Chicago 28.

Curly Lambeau was overjoyed with their first victory at home over the Bears since 1939. "The second half," he added, "proved again that you can't let down against a club like the Bears. We relaxed with a twenty-one point lead and they tied it up on us."

On a cold and blustery November 5 in Chicago, it would be a different story. The Packers were as cold as the north wind and were shutout, 21-0. Green Bay never made a serious scoring threat the entire game. It was the Packers' first shutout since 1938 when the Bears goose-egged them, 2-0, in a downpour at City Stadium. Also ending was Don Hutson's scoring record of forty-one consecutive games. He had scored one or more points in each game since midway in the 1940 season.

In a game fraught with penalties, the oddest moment came in the fourth quarter when Bears' running back Gary Famiglietti and Packer Tony Canadeo squared off near the sidelines.

"It was late in the battle," wrote Ed Prell, "and during a mix-up on a Bear blast into the line, Famiglietti and Canadeo, two lads of Italian extraction, had a verbal tete-`a-tete. All of a sudden they were making wild swing[s] at each other. In explanation, Gary said, 'No one can call me a dumb dago; least of all a guy named Canadeo, and that's what I told him.'

"To avoid further rancor, the Bears immediately removed Gary but only after he had invited Tony, an army sergeant on furlough, to step out of bounds.

"'Get out here, they can't fine us,' said Gary in explaining his challenge."

That was about all the fight Chicago had. Finishing at 6-3-1 for the season, the champion Bears were to be dethroned.

Green Bay didn't set the league on fire in its last four games, either. They sputtered towards the end. Their only saving grace was their hot start to begin the season.

At 8-2, Curly Lambeau's troops won the Western Division and a right to meet the New York Giants in a rematch of the 1939 championship game. Quarterbacking the Giants was a pudgy pigskin tosser by the name of Arnie Herber. The ex-Packer had joined the Giants earlier that season and had led New York to a 24-0 regular season win over his old team three weeks earlier.

Lambeau had a plan to use Hutson as a decoy. Don the Decoy would draw most of the attention from the Giant defense, while the Packers' backs would slam into a weakened New York line. Ted Fritsch, Irv Comp, and Joe Laws pounded into the Giants' line for 173 yards. Fritsch scored on a short plunge and a 28-yard pass, leading the Green Bay Packers to a 14-7 win over New York and their sixth NFL title.

A huge crowd was waiting for the champion Packers as the train carrying their heroes pulled into the depot on Washington Street in Green Bay. A celebration began that went long into the night. No one had any idea that Green Bay's faithful would not celebrate another championship for eighteen long years.

A dapper Lambeau was very full of himself after winning the 1944 championship. He could be seen strutting around town like a returning king while the Packers were mere subjects.

"By 1945, Curly Lambeau had built a fantasy world around himself where he saw himself as God's gift to professional football," author Larry Names wrote in his book *The Lambeau Years-Part Two*. "He seemed to forget that Green Bay had a pro football team before he joined it in 1919 and that had he gone back to Notre Dame that fall, Green Bay would most likely have had a pro football team anyway."

To many of the down-home residents of tiny Green Bay, the swank and ritzy Lambeau had "gone Hollywood." Pushing fifty, he had started spending more time in California, where he had courted and married an attractive young blonde.

The decisions he began to make would cause him to lose dear friends, money, the town's support, and, eventually, the backing of the team's executive committee. Lambeau was beginning a downward spiral that would send him crashing to the ground.

In late February 1945, Lambeau suddenly announced the release of George Trafton as line coach. Lambeau said that Trafton had been told of the release in January, before he had hired Walt Kiesling to take his place. "I think a great deal of his ability and I'm sorry that circumstances are such that he is leaving us," Lambeau stated.

Lambeau's sincerity was questionable. Lambeau may have thought Trafton was getting too much press coverage. Also, Trafton began to give Curly advice and he didn't like it. Trafton had to go.

Lambeau got rid of Trafton in a very underhanded way. He waited until Trafton signed a year's lease on an apartment in Green Bay; it was too late in his wife's pregnancy for them to move. Then he fired him.

Lambeau welcomed thirty-five players to training camp in '45, hopeful that some of the forty-four Packers still serving in the military would be discharged in time to see some action on the playing field.

The first football and military veteran to return was end Carl Mulleneaux, who would tally thirteen TD receptions for the Packers during the 1945 season. The talented Irv Comp, Ted Fritsch, Joe Laws, and Larry Craig returned to the backfield. The line was anchored by vets Charley Brock, Baby Ray, Tiny Croft, and Pete Tinsley.

Number two draft pick Clyde Goodnight, an end from the University of Tulsa, would become a solid end for the Packers through the remainder of the decade.

Before the usual season opener at City Stadium, the Packers' Lumberjack Band, led by William Burke, played the Packers' fight song as the pennant for Green Bay's sixth NFL championship was raised. That pennant would join the others from 1929, '30, '31, '36, and '39.

The champion Packers began 1945 where they left off the previous season, with a 31-21 victory over the Bears. Jumping out to a 28-0 lead, the Packers saw their lead shrink throughout the game. In the end, they recovered like a boxer about down for the count and held on for the win.

The game saw the return of Hugh Gallarneau and Lee Artoe, home on furlough from their service duty. Things quickly got back to normal for the rabble-rousing Artoe. On the Packers' opening drive, Navy Lieutenant Artoe lost his temper when Green Bay's Larry Craig fell on him. The street-fighting Artoe cut loose with a flurry of punches, all of which the referee saw. The ref then proceeded to toss Artoe out of the game before the defensive giant had even broken a sweat.

A month later, the 4-1 Packers prepared to meet the wounded and winless 0-5 Bears at Wrigley. The 45,527 there watched as the officials lost control of the game. The game turned into a slug-fest.

"It is doubtful," *Press-Gazette* staff writer Dave Yuenger reported, whether there has been a more bitterly contested game in the series between these two elevens. The rough and ready Bears, keyed to a mayhem pitch through reports of dissension on the team and five straight losses, threw the rule book out the window."

Once again, Lee Artoe would be the pied piper in the free-for-all rumble. Joined by linemen Al Barbartsky and George Zorich, they punched, kicked, and elbowed their way through, what Yuenger called, "unorthodox football." They smashed halfback Roy McKay's nose and loosened some of his teeth with two well-aimed punches and an elbow. In the third quarter, they injured halfback Irv Comp's leg and he had to leave the contest. Artoe wouldn't get away unscathed. A number of revengeful Packers ganged up on him. The battered Artoe was sent to the hospital for X-rays to determine if his jaw had been broken.

Near the end, Packers' end Clyde Goodnight and lineman Pete Tinsley were sent to the sidelines for fighting. Even there it wasn't safe. Soon thereafter, Bears' center John Schiechl was running down the sideline when Tinsley suddenly stood up and whacked him with his helmet. Fighting aside, Chicago chalked up its first victory of the season, 28-24. The win did little to jump start the Bears for their next two games, however; both were losses.

Then came light at the end of the tunnel. As the Bears practiced Thanksgiving morning, George Halas walked onto the field in his Navy uniform and again took command of his beloved Bears. Then at 1-7, they won their remaining two games, finishing with their worst record ever at 3-7. It was their first losing season in fifteen years.

Green Bay, finishing the season at 6-4, relinquished their Western Division title to the Bob Waterfield-led Cleveland Rams, who narrowly defeated the Redskins for the 1945 championship.

The Packers were about to go through some major changes. Don Hutson was going to be true to his word and retire from playing to coach. The greatest pass catcher the league had ever seen made his plans but then decided just days before the opener against the Bears that he couldn't retire. The man who a year earlier had said he'd jump off the Empire State Building before playing again, had one of his finest seasons in 1945. Hutson snagged forty-seven balls for 834 yards, for an 18-yard average. Hitting thirty-one of thirty-five extra points and two field goals, the great Hutson went out on a high note, finishing second behind Philadelphia's Steve Van Buren's ninety-seven points.

1946-'49

The postwar boom brought new life and fans back to the NFL that had been lost during the conflict. With the return of the better players from military service, a higher caliber, more competitive game sent attendance figures soaring. This breath of fresh air, however, did not translate into a cash windfall for the owners. The league suddenly found itself embroiled in another war—this one with the newly formed All-American Football Conference, the AAFC.

Organized by *Chicago Tribune* sports editor Arch Ward, the AAFC began play in 1946 with eight teams: the New York Yankees, the Brooklyn Dodgers, the Buffalo Bisons, the Miami Seahawks, the Cleveland Browns, the Los Angeles Dons, the San Francisco 49ers, and the Chicago Rockets.

Chicago was a curious choice for an AAFC franchise. Although the Rockets drew some 51,962 fans to Soldier Field for a September clash with the Browns, the team still had a real uphill battle to establish itself. Not only were they in competition with the long-standing northside Bears and the southside Cardinals of the NFL, they would also be the worst team in the league, winning only eleven games in four years. Even changing their names to the Hornets in 1949 didn't help.

The Paul Brown-led Cleveland Browns were the new league's classiest act. They had captivated the city after the Rams had left Cleveland for the palm trees and sunny weather of Los Angeles. Quarterbacked by Otto Graham and behind the kicking of Lou "The Toe" Groza, the disciplined Browns would win four consecutive championships in the AAFC.

The Green Bay Packers Corporation began to find it increasingly harder to field a competitive team. Due to the new AAFC league, players' salaries were starting to increase, posing a real problem for the non-profit Packers. The formation of the AAFC began a bidding war between the two leagues that diminished any profits the NFL was now seeing with its higher gate receipts.

Curly Lambeau lost only one player to the new league, guard Bob Frankowski. Others flirted with the idea of leaving, but didn't. Fullback Ted Fritsch came the closest to deserting. He actually signed a contract with the Cleveland Browns but they let him out of it after he had a change of heart. Irv Comp was offered a couple of contracts by AAFC teams but he turned them down to return to Green Bay.

Noticeably absent in the group of fifty-seven hopefuls who showed up on the first day of the 1946 training camp were any African-American players. The league had unofficially banned them; no black player had suited up in the NFL since 1933. Beginning with Rams' owner Chili Walsh, however, the league slowly began to recruit black players in 1946. Lambeau was one of the last owners to sign a black player to his team.

With a housing shortage in the Green Bay area, Lambeau started to worry his players wouldn't have a place to stay. Still in control of all Packers' operations, Lambeau went over the edge when he somehow sold the Executive Committee on the idea of buying the large, Tudor-style Rockwood Lodge on some acreage fifteen miles north of Green Bay. It had been built by the Catholic Diocese as a recreation center but it had not been a success. Appreciating its cachet, the Packers bought the property for $32,000 plus another $8,000 for some pre-fabricated houses. It was Curly's idea to have the married players who couldn't find housing live there with their families. He also planned to house the team during training camp. One big happy family.

Trouble began when the Packers' Executive Committee found out that the practice field had a thin layer of topsoil over hard ground and rock. Suddenly, players began started suffering shin splints, sore feet, and other leg injuries. Eventually, the whole team would have to be bussed back into town to practice.

"It was a hard field," Packers' great Tony Canadeo confessed. "It was built on the rock ledges along the bay. We used to call it the 'shin splint special.'"

The hard field notwithstanding, Canadeo defends Lambeau's decision to buy the lodge. "Curly was before his time," Tony says. "Hell, they all have training camps now. I think he did the right thing. Housing was hard to get. Us town kids were able to live at home and just commute to practice. But if you came from out of town, you had a hell of a time trying to find a place to live. He got housing for a lot of married guys who didn't have it."

The basic idea was for the players to live together in a tightly knit group that would produce a team spirit reminiscent of college. It didn't work. The players lived, played, and slept football. It was overkill.

Divorced and remarried by this time, Lambeau gave his new wife carte blanche to decorate their cottage at the Lodge. Marshall-Fields in Chicago provided the elaborate furnishings at a pricey sum. It was then that the Executive Committee began to be suspicious of Lambeau. He was now under the watchful eyes of the higher-ups.

Wearing a big grin and a brown suit, George Halas walked across the bright green field of Green Bay's City Stadium fresh from trouncing the Packers, 30-7. It was Chicago's first victory there since 1942.

The opening kickoff was the only time the Packers were close. It was all down hill from there. The Bears held the ball for nearly nine minutes on the opening drive, resulting in a Frank Maznicki 27-yard field goal. The rout was on.

The Osmanski brothers, Bill and Joe, took turns battering the Packers' defensive line into submission. It was a blood and guts, meat-grinding Bears' offense that quickly wore down the weary Packers.

Whenever Sid Luckman drifted back to pass, he usually made the completion. He tossed a 15-yard TD pass to Ray McLean and later tossed a touchdown pass to Ken Kavanaugh, who caught the ball on the tips of his fingers in the end zone.

"It's always glad to get this Green Bay game out of the way," Halas said as he walked with his victorious troops. "We had a definite edge today," he added. That was an understatement.

Green Bay's once feared passing game was now gone, much of it standing on the sidelines. Don Hutson's absences were quite noticeable to everyone when the Packers failed to even complete a pass until the fourth quarter. Ahead 24-0, the Bears were barely awake by then.

After the game, the three Packers' coaches, Lambeau, Hutson, and Walt Kiesling, acted like the three monkeys who see no evil, hear no evil, and speak no evil.

"I have nothing to say," read the austere post-game statement from Lambeau. Curly, inaugurating his twenty-eighth season at the helm of the Packers, was disgusted with his team's inability to execute the fundamentals of football—blocking and tackling. The locker room aura was proof enough. *Press-Gazette* scribe Lee Remmel reported that "you could hear a pin drop" in the Packers' locker room and that the players talked "in hushed tones that would have done credit to a morgue."

The only real time the Green Bay crowd cheered loudly was during the half-time entertainment. A fine exhibition by four-time state champion baton-twirler Rosemary Schwebs, a sixteen-year-old from Menasha, Wisconsin, brought the crowd to its feet. Joining Schwebs was eight-year-old twirler Carol Jean Collard.

The Bears' sideline did provide the game's lighter moments. As the game began, an "unauthorized and unsober" fan found himself sitting on the Bears' bench beside Sid Luckman and Ed Sprinkle. Ushers and the police failed to notice the hooch hound sitting there in street clothes. He probably could have watched the whole game if he hadn't pulled out a game program and pencil and started asking for autographs. When discovered, he was ushered out.

Later, with his Bears leading, 17-0, in the second half, a relaxed Halas was standing on the sideline when a vociferous Packers' fan directed an off-color tirade at no one in particular. All of a sudden, self-righteous Halas retorted, "Here we don't use that kind of language in Chicago." Quite a stretch for Halas, former Navy man, tough Chicago northsider, and fluent speaker of foul language.

Although the Packers stumbled the next week against the Rams, they brought a three-game win streak into Chicago to face the 3-1-1 Midway Monsters on November 3.

Before the opening kickoff, the 46,321 in attendance paid tribute to the memory of Bears' quarterback Young Bussey, who had been killed at Lingayen Gulf in the Philippines in March 1945. Two buglers played Taps in the simple ceremony.

"The Bears were lucky to win," said Assistant Coach Luke Johnsos after Chicago squeaked by Green Bay, 10-7, on the muddy field at Wrigley. Two defensive linemen, Mike Jarmoluk and Ed Sprinkle, were the heroes that day. In the second half, Jarmoluk slammed Packers' fullback Ted Fritsch with a shoulder-high tackle. The ball popped loose, Ed Sprinkle scooped it up and ran thirty yards for the touchdown.

The game's only real casualty was Bears' center Bulldog Turner. Turner ran full-tilt into a Packers' helmet and broke his nose. Blood gushing from his face onto his jersey, Bulldog made his way to the sidelines to sit out the rest of the game.

Chicago was now firmly in control of the Western Division and for the remainder of the season, that's where they stayed. Winning four of their final five games, the Bears found themselves in the championship game facing the Giants in New York.

With the game tied 14-14 early in the fourth quarter, Sid Luckman shocked the Giants. All season the Bears had practiced a play called "Bingo Keep It" in which Luckman would fake a hand-off to McAfee, pivot to the right with the ball under his arm, and run himself. It worked perfectly. Luckman ran nineteen yards for the go-ahead touchdown.

Maznicki added a late field goal and the Chicago Bears, at 24-14, won the 1946 championship, the seventh in their storied history.

It would be seventeen long years before they would do it again.

With many of the superior football players fighting in Europe and the South Pacific, the war years provided the perfect opportunity for players who may not otherwise have gotten a chance to play pro ball to showcase their talents and win a spot on a team's roster. Many became Hall of Famers and All-Pros.

In the 1944 season one of these players was Ed Sprinkle. Simply put, Ed Sprinkle played football with an intense, two-fisted, ferocious spirit. He came to the attention of the Chicago Bears by way of a referral. Eventually, he starred at the defensive and offensive end positions until his retirement in 1956.

Sprinkle got an initial first taste of line play when he went in at guard his first time out. Not a real big guy at only 6' 1" and around 205 pounds, the end of the war and his physique would prove to be his undoing on the interior line. The story goes that George Halas took one look at Ed and said, "The big boys are coming back. We'd better move this kid out to end before he gets killed." Halas saw the potential in his aggressive guard and years later proclaimed him tougher than the Bears' legendary Dick Butkus.

Sprinkle was labeled a dirty player early on. Talk to some of his Bears' teammates and they say he didn't play dirty. Talk to some of the Green Bay players he lined up against and they'll tell you he was a cheap-shot artist. Teammate George Connor confirms that Sprinkle's reputation as a dirty player has kept him out of the Hall of

Fame. "He should be in the Hall of Fame," Connor declared. "Ed Sprinkle went 110% every play. I pushed for him when I was on the [Hall of Fame] committee years ago and their answer was that he was a dirty player. He never hit anyone from behind. It's unfair. He's a real gentleman and a quiet guy. He just got labeled that way. I think it made him a little more money with the pros but it's keeping him out of the Hall of Fame."

Ex-Packer and four time All-Pro defensive back Bobby Dillon says he's not surprised Sprinkle has not been honored in Canton.

"He was not liked at all when he was playing," Dillon admitted. "From an opponent's point of view he was not considered to be a very good player. He was considered to be a very dirty player. I'm sure he has a different view point. I saw him do some things that if they caught you doing that today, you would be out of the game. Things just uncalled for. He got away with it. Sprinkle would clothesline backs, hit late, and hardly ever got caught. His reputation was bad before I played at Green Bay. I can see why the Bears would defend him. I'm sure they liked what he was doing. It created a lot of havoc on the opposing team. Guys were scared wondering where Sprinkle was going to be."

Whichever side you choose to believe, one thing is certain: Any player who went up against Ed Sprinkle agrees that he possessed an unkind temperament and was one of the most physical players ever to step onto a football field.

Sprinkle himself was quick to dispel the unflattering tag.

"I was aggressive," he said defiantly. "I loved the contact and I went out there to do the best job I could do. I loved playing and hitting guys. I played rough but I didn't play dirty. Clean hits.

"There was an article in *Colliers' Magazine* that some guy wrote that picked up on it. Most of the guys I played with or against respected my ability as a football player and my guts and determination and not playing dirty. There were a few guys who said I was dirty but I never deliberately tried to hurt anybody. I would hit them as hard as I could hit them. They were out there and it's a contact sport. If I had an opportunity to belt somebody, I'd do it. It's not a game for sissies, you know.

"I was from Hardin-Simmons University in Abilene, Texas, and I played one year at the Naval Academy. I joined the Naval Air

Corps and I wasn't quite old enough to go when the war broke out so I joined the reserves.

"Teammate Clyde 'Bulldog' Turner graduated from Hardin-Simmons and he was playing with the Bears. He's the one who brought me up with the Bears. The Bears brought back [Bronko] Nagurski and he had been out of football for six years, I think. There were a lot of guys who would have never made the teams in the regular season if the war wasn't on. If I had come up during peace time, I probably would not have made the squad. It was fortunate for me because I wasn't a real big guy and I came up as a tackle and I was only 210 pounds.

"Bulldog was instrumental in keeping me with the Bears. They were going to send me home even in the war years. They were going to cut me and Bulldog said, 'You cut him and you cut me, too.'"

Ed Sprinkle played in an era of iron men. It was a rough, rowdy, and wide open game. It was commonplace for players to get their nose broken or their teeth knocked out. Face masks were new-fangled devices just starting to be used in the league.

"They never had face guards until I left the Bears," Ed recalls. "A few guys had them but they weren't mandatory. They first started out with one bar across. I had [my] nose and jaw broken in 1944 or '45 when we played the Rams. I caught an elbow and broke my jaw. They had to wire my teeth together. A lot of guys, while tackling someone, would swing their foot around and catch a guy in the mouth and knock [his] teeth out. I was lucky. I never lost any teeth."

With the start of training camp in 1946, Ed Sprinkle got his first look at Halas. "At that time, Halas was the top coach," Ed remembers. "As he went along in his later years though, I think he overstayed his time. He was a great guy but not a great innovator in his later years. One of the things Halas had was respect. All the players hated him but yet they loved him. When Halas walked on the field, he demanded respect. You listened to him. Later on, after I was gone, he stayed on as other teams came up with different ideas and innovations and maybe the Bears under Halas didn't adjust to them."

Ed spent twelve seasons being aggressive and administering

"clean hits" to the arch rival Packers of the north, and he compiled an impressive 19-6-1 mark against them over his career.

On Monday morning of Bears-Packers week, Halas and his coaching staff would start gearing up for the battle to come that following Sunday. "They [the coaches] would really concentrate on winning the game," Ed says. "They'd put in special plays and defenses. We put in some long practices for Green Bay."

Every game was a battle, but it seemed the Green Bay game was the roughest and it didn't take Ed long to realize the intensity of the rivalry. During his second game against the Bays, he was taken to a Chicago hospital with a suspected fracture in the vicinity of his left elbow.

"I played against a lot of their great players," Sprinkle recalled with pride. "Tony Canadeo, the Grey Ghost of Gonzaga. We had some great games. Don Hutson was still playing. They had a blocking back by the name of Larry Craig. I played defensive end so Larry Craig was the guy I would be meeting up with when I was rushing the passer.

"I played offensive end. I wasn't noted as a great pass receiver but I could block. I caught a few passes. I caught the first touchdown pass Bobby Layne ever threw in the NFL, and it was against Green Bay. I think that was in either '47 or '48.

"We played at old County Stadium when we went to Green Bay. We'd stay in the Northland Hotel, dress there, go play, then catch a train home. The Packers' fans would raise cane trying to keep you up at night. Blow horns, tooting, and all of that. It was quite an experience. Fans would be right behind you when you were on the bench. They'd be cussing you out and throw a bottle at you once in a while. I never took my helmet off when I was up there. You'd walk down the street and kids would spit at you. It was pretty well ingrained in Green Bay to hate the Bears.

"They used to have a rule that a running back could get back up and run. Green Bay had a running back from Texas Tech by the name of Walt Schlinkman. I tackled him and he was kicking trying to get up and we got to fighting and they threw us out of the game. We were fined $50 for it."

Sprinkle's small size and a change in defensive philosophy combined to spell an end to his career. He knew, like many other athletes, when it was time to give it up.

"I was ready to retire," he admitted. "I'd had twelve years and it had taken its toll. Then the Bears lost a guy and Halas was asked to bring me back and he said no. One of the reasons was that they went to a four-man line. So that eliminated a guy my size from the outside. The four-man line would mean me lining heads up on a big tackle. They went with the 4-3 and I was out."

It's been forty years since Ed Sprinkle retired and the NFL's inner circle debate about him continues. If the "dirty player" brand is deserved, then Ed's paying for it now. But if his reputation as a "cheap-shot artist" tag is unfounded, the blackballing of Ed Sprinkle should stop and he should be busted bronze in the Pro Football Hall of Fame in Canton, Ohio.

Along with Sprinkle, Halas had a solid cast of players return in 1947 to defend the championship. Bulldog Turner and Ray Bray were the pillars of the line. In their last year as players were backs Bill Osmanski, Hugh Gallarneau, and Scooter McLean. Second-year men Fred Davis at tackle and Jim Keane at offensive end proved to be needed acquisitions for the Bears.

All signs pointed to another solid season for the Northsiders.

Then came the College All-Star game at Soldier Field. Halas and his squad were completely embarrassed by the collegians, 16-0. Notre Dame coach Frank Leahy directed the All-Stars to the upset in front of an amazed 105,840 fans. It was the end of an era and change was in the wind.

A flamboyant Curly Lambeau continued to bask in his own self-made glory. Some folks around Green Bay were starting to tire of Lambeau's egotism. Talk at the corner store was that he had gone Hollywood. It would get worse. He was about to make another perfidious decision.

In early 1947, Curly hired George Strickler, a sports writer for the *Chicago Tribune*, to be publicity director for the Packers. In a prepared statement, Lambeau said Strickler would replace George Whitney Calhoun, who had retired.

Lambeau was lying. Actually, he was firing Calhoun, his old friend and drinking buddy, but Lambeau didn't want to tell him to his face. Calhoun learned the news while tending to the Associated Press teletype machine at the *Press-Gazette* one morning. Curly Lambeau had made a bitter enemy of a once-trusted friend.

Many in town took Calhoun's side. Despite his gruff demeanor, George Calhoun was well liked in town. Just one more example of Lambeau distancing himself from the fans who had supported him. He was on a roll.

Worried about Lambeau and expenditures, the Executive Committee decided in June of 1947 to start meeting every Monday to get a report from vice-president and general manager Lambeau. They also decided to split up into five groups to supervise the finances and other business matters.

"Tomahawked!" was the headline beside Art Daley's column in the *Press-Gazette* on September 29, 1947, describing the Packers' 29-20 massacre of the Bears at City Stadium. It was Curly Lambeau's first game directing a T-formation offense, the Packers being one of the last teams to make the change from the old single-wing and Notre Dame box formations.

Leading the way for the newly T'ed Packers was University of Oklahoma quarterback "Indian" Jack Jacobs, who threw for two TD's and ran for another.

"'Indian' Jack Jacobs," Daley wrote, "whose ancestors taught him the rudiments of skinning bears and lifting attached toupees, presided at the killing before 25,461 partisan fans."

In addition, Jacobs intercepted two Sid Luckman passes while defensive teammates Herman Rohrig, Irv Comp, and Bob Forte nabbed one each. Jacobs also punted five of six punts and averaged forty-nine yards.

Along with the damage Jacobs did to the Bears, running back Ted Fritsch slammed the line for good yardage. "Ted Fritsch, football's bull of the woods, rams for eighty-eight yards and twice carries two Bears on his back in wild plunges," the *Chicago Tribune's* Ed Prell wrote.

A devious air hung over Wrigley Field for the November rematch. Lambeau and his aides were fuming. Their radios with the press booth were dead. Phones had been installed but they didn't work. Lambeau figured Halas was up to his furtive ways. Curly blamed two failed Packers' drives on the non-working phones

Among the 46,111 in the stands that day sat the immortal Jim Thorpe, the NFL's first commissioner and Canton Bulldogs' great. He and the other football fans witnessed one of the hardest hitting games in recent memory. Vicious hitting and tackling were responsible for ten fumbles. In the second quarter, Packers' back Roy "Tex" McKay smashed into Hugh Gallarneau after the Bear tried to catch a Luckman pass. Gallarneau went down hard. Still groggy, he was helped to the sideline where he stayed until the third quarter.

With the Bears leading, 20-17, Packers' kicker Ward Cuff attempted to tie the game with a field goal from twenty-nine yards out and twelve seconds remaining. It never came close.

Chicago's Noah Mullins burst through the Packers' front wall and blocked the kick. Mullins saved the victory, the Bears' fifth win in a row.

It was a season of missed opportunities for both Green Bay and Chicago. Two losses to the cross-town Cardinals forced the Bears into a second place finish while the good but unspectacular 6-5-1 third place Packers' lost all five games by four or fewer points.

The war with the rival AAFC was going strong in 1947 with no relief in sight. While a good number of NFL players were jumping to the new league, George Halas had done a good job keeping his players happy in Chicago. Stars Sid Luckman, George McAfee, and Bulldog Turner were all courted by teams in the AAFC but the Papa Bear came up with the money to keep them in the Windy City. Also, as close as those Forties Bears' teams were, it would have been treasonous to walk out on Halas.

Only one major Chicago Bear decided to jump ship. Packers' nemesis Lee Artoe went west to play for the Los Angeles Dons in

1946, then moved on to the Baltimore Colts in 1948, his last season as a player. Artoe tried to convince some other Bears, like Hugh Gallarneau, to join him, but none would.

Even football in Green Bay came under attack after the 1947 season. In cities like New York, Chicago, and Los Angeles, NFL teams were competing with AAFC teams for fans. Of all the franchises that owners in both leagues worried about, the one in tiny Green Bay, Wisconsin, caused the most concern. Why?

"Simply because every single professional team owner outside Wisconsin believed that Green Bay could not survive the war between the leagues," theorized Larry Names in his book *The Lambeau Years-Part Three*. "To the thinking of the owners, the Packers were the pivotal pawn in the conflict."

According to Names, the NFL bosses were unanimous in their desire to move the team to the West Coast, probably San Francisco.

The move never materialized. The AAFC folded after the 1949 season and all talk of moving one of the oldest and most successful franchises in football quickly ceased.

George Halas' gift for choosing great talent would once again benefit him and Chicago in 1948. In the draft, Halas chose two quarterbacks to groom as successors to Sid Luckman. He had to dig deep in his wallet for the opportunity to keep Notre Dame's Johnny Lujack and Texan Bobby Layne from signing with the AAFC. He reportedly signed the free-spirited Layne for $22,500 a year for three years plus a $10,000 signing bonus to keep him from going to the Baltimore Colts. Halas came up with $18,000 a year for Lujack. In comparison, Luckman had signed a contract for $6,250 in 1939. During 1948, Halas continued to start Luckman at quarterback, while putting Lujack at defensive back and keeping Layne in reserve. Lujack would garner eight interceptions for the 1948 Bears.

Also joining the Bears at 6' 3" and 240 pounds was George Connor. The future Hall of Famer had more on his mind in 1946 than playing in the AAFC.

"I was a number one draft choice of the New York Giants in

1946 but I elected to go back to school," Connor said. "I told them I didn't want to play in New York, so they traded me to the Boston Yanks. When I got out of Notre Dame, I signed with the Bears because the Yanks had traded my rights to them."

Connor became the first, and remains the only player, to make All-Pro on both offensive and defensive squads.

So the three Ls—Luckman, Lujack, and Layne—led a powerful group of Bears into the 1948 season hoping to dethrone the cross-town Cardinals in the Western Division.

Their old rivals from Green Bay were also ready to dethrone the Cardinals. On the Friday before the game at City Stadium, Lambeau was concerned about his team's disposition. "We'll be shellacked unless we snap out of it and get fired up," he warned. He went on to compare the 1948 Bears to the great '41 team.

George Connor, playing in his first pro game, quickly found the amenities and surroundings of pro ball quite different than what he had experienced at Notre Dame.

"When we got to Green Bay, two thousand people would be there to greet us. The night before the game Halas told us to take our equipment bag to our room and we'd get dressed there for the game. I looked at Johnny Lujack, my teammate from Notre Dame, and asked, 'This is the big leagues?' Halas would say put your uniform on except your helmet and shoes, take the elevator down, put on your shoes outside on the curb, get in the bus and go to the stadium. When I first started playing against the Packers in 1948 they played their home games at City Stadium, a high school field. There was no dressing room for the visiting team. We would have our pre-game pep talk in the boiler room of a grade school near there. We'd go back there at half-time, also.

"Towards the end of the first half, Luckman threw a screen pass to J. R. Boone and I was out front blocking, without a face mask. I went to block Jack Jacobs who was a great defensive back for the Packers. He kicked me in the chin and opened a deep gash.

"At half-time, we retired to the boiler room. I don't think Halas carried a doctor with him. I think it was a veterinarian. He sewed me up with twenty-two stitches and I went back out to the field to play. I got out there but the gate was locked. Of course there were a bunch of Packers' fans there and I finally yelled up to the top row and got the attention of some Bears' fans up there. They came down and got in a fight, but they got the gate open. I ran out to the little fence surrounding the field and the Bears' bench was on the other side of the field. During a time out, I ran across the field and Halas yelled, 'Where the hell have you been, rookie? That'll cost you fifty dollars because you're late for the second half.'"

Halas had no reason to be angry with Connor or his team because they were in the process of walloping the rival Packers. As Connor strode onto the field, the scoreboard read Packers 0, Visitors 31. It was the worst defeat in Packers' history. Chicago eventually won, 45-7. Packers' players were shocked when they began hearing catcalls and boos from the hometown crowd as the score mounted.

Green Bay entered the game a three-point favorite because of an undefeated pre-season. Things quickly went to hell in a handbasket. On the second play of the game, Packers' back Bruce Smith fumbled and the Bears recovered on the 28-yard line. The Bears showed they meant business when Smith had to be helped from the field and was not able to return to the game.

Johnny Lujack made his NFL debut in grandiose style, intercepting three Jack Jacob passes all in the first half. All led to touchdowns.

"What happened today has nothing to do with the real ability of the Green Bay team, I want that to go on record," Halas said repeatedly. "Those first two touchdowns were lucky breaks."

A chain-smoking group of Packers' coaches sat silently for five minutes until Lambeau found courage to speak.

"We all played a very poor ball game," he mumbled, "but we're a lot better than we showed today."

The fact is Green Bay was not a good team. They lacked a skilled Sid Luckman-like quarterback. Jack Jacobs was good, but he wasn't Cecil Isbell. Clyde Goodnight was a steady player, but he was no Don Hutson. Mostly, they lacked the leadership of a good head coach. Things wouldn't get any better.

Two weeks later, after a 17-7 loss to the Chicago Cardinals, Lambeau fined the entire team half of one week's salary for "indifferent play." After blanking the Rams the next week, 16-0, the players thought they'd get their money back. Lambeau wasn't about to return it, and a near mutiny occurred. The players were understandably furious.

From that point on, team morale was lower than the muddy bottom of the Fox River that ran through town. Sitting on a 3-2 record, the Packers fell as far as a team could fall, losing their final seven games in a row.

The only game they kept close was the mid-December clash with Chicago, a game the Bears won, 7-6. The Packers held the Bears scoreless until the third quarter when quarterback Bobby Layne threw his first NFL touchdown pass, a 34-yarder to end Ed Sprinkle.

With five minutes remaining, Jack Jacobs connected with Nolan Luhn for a touchdown but, incredibly, kicker Ed Cody missed the extra point. After the game, veterans Tony Canadeo and Bob Forte cried as they plodded off the field. The rest of the team, heads bowed, headed for the locker room.

Lambeau's squad found some comfort when they returned home. Some 3,000 Packers' fans turned up at the railroad station to welcome their boys in yellow. At that point, they had lost four straight but to Packers' fans they were still heroes.

Green Bay's 3-9 record in 1948 was the team's worst season ever and Lambeau had to accept much of the blame for it. His irrational decision to fine the whole team five games into the season and then not return their money had been a dagger through the team's heart.

Many also blamed the Packers' dismal performance on the team being removed from the townspeople. In a speech the week before the Bears' game, businessman Jerry Atkinson of Prange's Department Store noted, "Many of us in Green Bay have somehow dropped our close affection for the team." Atkinson blamed the disillusionment on the Packers' living and practicing out of town at Rockwood Lodge.

The Green Bay Packers' losing ways were beginning to show in the team's profit and loss statement. The Executive Committee met in December 1948 to review the financial situation. At the same meeting, George Strickler was stripped of his title as assistant general manager.

It was becoming apparent that the Committee was flexing its muscles against Lambeau. The result would set the Packers' coach and the governing committee on a collision course, culminating in a fiery end to the decade.

George Halas had a hard decision to make in the summer of 1949. He knew the playing days of future Hall of Famer Sid Luckman were numbered. He had primed and tutored Johnny Lujack and Bobby Layne to fill Luckman's shoes.

After great deliberation, Halas decided to sell the colorful Layne to the New York Bulldogs, a move that would return to haunt him. Halas would later confess that it was one of his biggest blunders.

Halas still had a formidable squad to field in 1949. With Bulldog, Connor, Fred Davis and Ray Bray on the line, and Luckman, Lujack, McAfee, George Gulyanics and Don Kindt in the backfield, and Jim Keane, Ken Kavanaugh and Ed Sprinkle at offensive end, the Northsiders would certainly contend for the Western Division crown. Another welcomed addition was a rookie quarterback and place kicker from the University of Kentucky named George Blanda.

The Packers were another story. Things were at rock bottom in Green Bay as the Executive Committee and Lambeau fought a tug-of-war over control of the team. The surrounding controversy hurt the team's morale as they readied themselves for the upcoming campaign.

The quarterback duties would be shared by three players in 1949: Jack Jacobs, sophomore Jug Girard, and number one draft pick from Nevada-Reno, Stan Heath.

It was not, however, an All-Star Packers' line. Consisting of mostly unknowns, it was questionable they would be able to play against some of the other lines they would face in the coming season. They would prove many a critic wrong when they began to open holes for running back Tony Canadeo. Scissoring his way through an undistinguished line, the "Gonzaga Grey Ghost" rushed for 1,052 yards and into the record books as one of the only three men in NFL history to gain over a thousand yards in a single season. He finished second in rushing in 1949 to Philadelphia's Steve Van Buren who galloped for 1,146 yards.

The five officials working the September 25 Packers-Bears season opener had their hands full ... full of yellow flags. Nearly 130 yards in penalties were assessed to both teams in a contest *Green Bay Press-Gazette* writer Art Daley described as a "combination of boxing and football." It was back to simple roughneck football for these two.

After a scoreless first half that saw Bears' QB Johnny Lujack's clock cleaned by the Packers' defense, Lujack reentered the game in the third quarter and rallied the Bears to a 17-0 victory. The Packers' defense had played with a spirit many hadn't seen at City Stadium in a while, holding the Bears in check for most of the game.

"For 53 minutes the grid rivals battled back and forth in a bruising display of rock-'em-sock-'em football," wrote Art Daley. "Then, when it appeared that the Packers might overcome a 3-0 deficit, the Bears exploded two quick touchdown bombs within two minutes midway in the fourth quarter, for the final version."

The once-feared Packers' passing game was now a distant memory. Between Jacobs, Girard, and Heath, not one pass had been completed in thirteen attempts. There was one pass the Packers completed but it didn't count. In the second quarter, Jug Girard lofted a pass in the general direction of end Clyde Goodnight. Grossly overthrown, the ball sailed into the crowd and was caught by an unidentified fan who promptly took off running with it, never to return.

The worst assault may not have happened on the field but on the west end of the field just before the second half. For fourteen years, Frank Dain, the Bears' mascot, had the relatively safe job of dressing in life-like bear paraphernalia and waddling up and down the sidelines cheering on Chicago's eleven. On this day he almost became a casualty. While strutting around during half-time, he was tackled by a group of young hooligans who pummeled the "grizzly" for no other reason than to attempt to disrobe him. Dain fought off the smooth-cheeked ruffians, living to wear the "bearable" costume yet another day!

"This is only one game," Lambeau said to his team afterwards. "Only one game, and there are eleven more to go."

What Lambeau didn't count on was his Packers going 2-9 in those eleven games, their only wins coming on a two-point win over

Detroit and a shutout over the hapless New York Bulldogs, who were in their first—and last—year of operations.

The Bears' game on November 6 became an early epilogue to the season. Green Bay arrived at Wrigley Field still in the race with a 2-4 record. They left there a frustrated and heartbroken team.

The Packers found themselves inside the Bears' 20-yard line four times, only to come up with three points in a discouraging 24-3 loss. Although Tony Canadeo and the Packers would out rush the Bears by twenty-eight yards, the blown opportunities were too much to overcome.

As previously noted, the Packers' poor performance over the last couple of years had caused financial concerns for the Executive Committee even before the season began. In 1949, the money situation became critical.

Shortly after the Bears' game, the committee ordered Lambeau to shorten the roster and renegotiate the contracts of the remaining players. Other maneuvers in the committee's power play were to fire George Strickler as publicity director and to close the albatross Rockwood Lodge and put it up for sale.

In a move to increase revenues, a special exhibition game was scheduled for Thanksgiving Day where some of the old Packer greats would put on a show. Don Hutson, Jug Earp, Arnie Herber, and Verne Lewellen were a few of the veterans who donned the Packers' uniform one more time.

A heavy snowfall kept some away but there was enough paid attendance to raise $50,000 to pay off some pressing debts. Another stock sale was commenced to rescue the team from further financial trouble.

Now Lambeau was ready for his own power play attempt. At a meeting with the Committee, he told them he knew of four investors who would put up $50,000 for stock if the Committee would convert to a profit corporation from a non-profit one. Sticking to their guns, the Committee refused, maintaining the community non-profit corporation.

It was later learned that Lambeau had wanted the conversion to a profit-making Packers' corporation so he and a few old cronies could own the franchise. The four investors he mentioned were friends of his. It was a failed attempt to undermine and buyout the corporation.

At the same meeting, Lambeau was reluctantly given a two-year contract extension. Three of the original members of the "Hungry Five" voted not to keep him. Although officially head coach and general manager for another two years, Lambeau's days were numbered and he knew it.

On a bitterly cold day January 25, 1950, fire companies from all around the Green Bay area were called to the north of town to answer a four-alarm fire raging by the icy waters of the bay. When they arrived they found Rockwood Lodge completely engulfed in flames and not worth attempting to save. Faulty wiring in the attic was blamed, according to the caretaker Melvin Flagstead, but it was joked about in town about which Committee member had actually lit the match that made ashes out of the place.

By this time nobody cared. The property that had no takers on the open market, would, in its smoking embers, profit the team. The Packers collected insurance money of $75,000.

It had been an unstable, erratic, and frustrating half-decade for Curly Lambeau, the Packers, and their faithful. They had entered the 1950's on shaky ground, but there was still one last earthquake to come.

The 1950s

Tuffy, Saint Vincent, One-Eye Dillon,
and the Claw

Joking at the January 1950 NFL league meetings that the Packers would play two games with the Chicago Bears as long as he had two legs and a big mouth, Lambeau was one of the thirteen club representatives voting to continue the two-game Packers-Bears series. The league meeting was being dominated by proposals of new scheduling, and for good reason.

After the 1949 season, the NFL and the rival AAFC merged into one league, with the NFL dictating the terms. Three teams from the AAFC were accepted into the NFL: the Cleveland Browns, the San Francisco 49ers, and the Baltimore Colts. The remaining teams in the AAFC would be dissolved.

The new thirteen-team league would consist of two conferences: the American and the National Conference. Joining the Packers and the Bears in the National Conference were the Los Angeles Rams, the New York Yanks, the Detroit Lions, the 49ers, and the Colts. The American Conference included the Chicago Cardinals, the Pittsburgh Steelers, the Washington Redskins, the Cleveland Browns, the New York Giants, and, rounding out the league, the two-year champion Philadelphia Eagles.

It's hard to speculate what Curly Lambeau was thinking in that January of 1950. The man who had been in charge for almost thirty years was now on the hot seat. With the Packers' steady fall from the league's elite, poor draft choices, and the Rockwood Lodge incident, the once untouchable Curly Lambeau was now being questioned and second guessed. It must have been tearing him apart.

He loved the Packers, the town's people, and Green Bay. It was also his hometown.

The very idea of Lambeau coaching anywhere else seemed unthinkable. His name was synonymous with the Green Bay Packers. He had stalked the sidelines in 344 league games, winning 217, for a winning percentage of .686, and had won six world championships. And besides, where else would he go?

It was in this air of speculation that the shock came. On February 1, 1950, Art Daley reported in the *Green Bay Press-Gazette* that Curly Lambeau had sent a letter of resignation to Packers' President Emil R. Fischer. In it, Lambeau said that the "growing reluctance to alter policies" was not something to which he could subscribe. He spoke of the "disunity of purpose within the corporation" and called it divided. With his resignation, Lambeau hoped it would "restore the harmony necessary if the Packers are to keep their place in major league football," and that his decision was in the Packers' and the fans of Wisconsin's best interest.

Daley reported that Lambeau and his wife had rather mysteriously disappeared on the afternoon of January 31, and by the next morning were in Chicago. It wasn't a coincidence.

A week before, Lambeau had visited the suburban home of Ray Bennigsen, President of the Chicago Cardinals. There, it's believed, he had been offered and accepted the job as the Cardinals' next head coach.

Lambeau spent three forgetful years as coach of the Cardinals and two with the Washington Redskins in 1953 and '54. Curly won his 271st pro game as a coach with a 10-0 win over Philadelphia in the eleventh game of the 1954 season. It would be his last.

The job to resurrect the once-proud Green Bay Packers fell upon a man who for more than sixteen years had done his best to beat them. In February, Gene Ronzani was named the new head coach of the Packers. The former Chicago Bear had played halfback and T-quarterback for George Halas, coached two Bears' farm clubs in Newark and Akron, and had been an assistant coach with the Bears.

Ronzani made some heads turn in Green Bay when he announced his new staff of assistants were Ray Nolting, Ray "Scooter" McLean, John "Tarzan" Taylor, and Chuck Drulis. All, like Ronzani, were ex-Chicago Bears. The new staff was not welcomed by some of the players.

"Gene was a former Bears' player which probably was one strike against him," veteran Tony Canadeo said. "People (Packer fans) hated the Bears. Being from the Bears, it was easy to fight against him."

Clayton Tonnemaker, the Packers' number one draft pick in 1950, had his own theory about how Ronzani was hired.

"The Committee went to George Halas for a recommendation of who the coach should be," Tonnemaker recalled. "My guess is that he tried to unload a guy (Ronzani) that he didn't want anymore, and it was a win/win for him. He probably put an incompetent coach in charge of a rival for a few years. I always thought it was one of the dumbest management moves [by Green Bay] I've ever seen."

Lee Joannes, one the original "Hungry Five" and long time Executive Committee member, spoke to Ronzani about succeeding Lambeau. When several Committee members questioned Joannes on any other coaching prospects, Joannes said, "We're not taking a chance on Ronzani, he's taking a chance on us. Hell, he doesn't even know if he is going to get paid."

Getting paid was a concern to Ronzani. Before the 1950 season, the Green Bay Packer Corporation had nearly $75,000 in debts. The Committee, at the same meeting that they announced their new coach, authorized the sale of additional Packers stock at $25 per share, with a 200 share limit intended to prevent one person from taking control. The action raised $150,000, successfully rescuing the Packers from financial disaster once again.

In many ways Gene Ronzani is a forgotten figure in the history of the Packers. He was really in a no-win situation. Not only had he inherited a team that had been stripped of most of its talent, he was trying to fill the shoes of an arrogant but still successful and respected Curly Lambeau. To many, and to himself, Curly Lambeau was a legend. He had nursed the team along in pro football's infancy days, won six championships, and had forever made his stamp on the game. That alone was a tall order for the new incoming coach to fill.

"Gene knew his football," Canadeo recounted, "but getting it across was tough. I'd say that was the biggest thing."

Even though history shows that Ronzani was not a successful pro coach, he in many ways turned out to be the best man for the job at the time. For one, he was a nice guy. Most everyone liked the meaty-faced Iron Mountain, Michigan native when they first met him. He was jovial, kind, and a fine gentleman.

Secondly, he was to be a transitional coach. The Packers were in a deep hole when Ronzani took the job as coach. Attendance and that old Packers' spirit was sinking to new lows. The four-year Ronzani regime was the band-aid to stop the bleeding. The wounds were still there, but it was going to take time to heal. The Ronzani years were a healing bridge from the old to what would be the very prosperous future to come.

After his reign as the Packers' coach ended after the 1953 season, he continued to be an active Packers' supporter. He would often be seen at Green Bay's home games.

If Gene Ronzani could be remembered for one thing and nothing else, it would be for his hiring in 1950 of full-time talent scout and old friend Jack Vainisi.

Jack Vainisi, the son of a Chicago northside grocer, grew up in the shadows of Wrigley Field. Vainisi, a huge Bears' fan, had the opportunity to meet and befriend many of his idols when they came in and shopped at his father's store. George Musso himself gifted the young Vainisi a complete Bears' uniform. One of the more frequent visitors was Gene Ronzani. They struck up a friendship that would pay great dividends for the Packers later on.

Vainisi went on to play freshman football at Notre Dame, where his coach was none other than Gene Ronzani. Gene was impressed by the young Italian, whom he had befriended on the Bears' bench at Wrigley Field and at his father's store. Vainisi's playing days ended, however, after he was called into the Army and was stricken with rheumatic fever that enlarged his heart.

When Ronzani was contemplating who should be an assistant to head up the Packers' talent scouting program, he immediately thought of Vainisi. Desperately wanting to still be a part of the game, Vainisi quickly accepted the job offer and became the first talent scout in the club's history.

Jack Vainisi's diligent research, recommendations, and draft choices would not pay much of a dividend for Gene Ronzani, but it would become the foundation for one of the greatest teams in pro football history.

A thankful George Halas didn't have the off-the-field distractions that his rivals to the north were having, but he did have reasons to be concerned about his own team's on-the-field developments.

Halas saw three of his superstars make 1950 their swan song. Quarterback Sid Luckman, hurting all season from injuries, passed the team leader torch to Johnny Lujack, who garnered over 2,100 total yards in rushing, passing and kickoff returns. In the early season, Lujack also hurt his shoulder, but with Luckman out he continued to play, damaging his shoulder and throwing arm for good. After 1950, he would never be the same.

Running back George McAfee and end Ken Kavanaugh had a mediocre final season. "One Play" McAfee's role diminished drastically, being mostly delegated to returning punts. Kavanaugh managed to snag seventeen receptions and a couple of touchdowns.

"I just ran out of gas," an honest Kavanaugh admitted. "When defenders start catching you, it's time to get away. You could feel yourself slowing down."

Shortly after returning from military service, McAfee hurt his leg and he was never the same. "I banged up my knee and I think I lost a lot of agility and speed," McAfee confessed. "I ended up playing safety on the defense."

By no means was this a case of Halas being left high and dry. His 1950 Bears' squad was still full of talent. Bulldog Turner started the decade at center as he had in 1940, Ed "The Claw" Sprinkle dominated and terrified opponents, George Connor, Ray Bray, Gene Schroeder, and Fred Davis filled out an outstanding defense, while halfbacks George Gulyanics and Julie Rykovich handled the running chores on offense.

The Green Bay Packers' 1950 press guide noted that Gene Ronzani was starting again to "build Packer football fortunes with a whole galaxy of new stars." Pumping even more hot air into the proceedings, it went on to say, "Every time the team steps out on the field this fall, there will be thousands in the stands rooting for the 'Little City That Leads 'Em.'"

Typically, press guides accentuated the positive and ignored the negative. The 1950 Packers were thin in talent and bench strength. Their only returning stars included back Tony Canadeo, lineman Dick Wildung, and quarterback Paul Christman.

The only real excitement was in the new talent the Packers had picked up. For the first time in years, the draft yielded some real play makers. Chosen in the first round was 6'2", 240-pound Minnesota center Clayton Tonnemaker. Picked second was Tobin Rote, a rugged quarterback from Rice University. Rote accounted for more than half the snaps in 1950, throwing for 1,231 yards and seven touchdowns. Coming over from the AAFC's Los Angeles Dons was Billy Grimes, who gained some 2,400 all-purpose yards that first season.

The Green Bay Packers set sail on a new course in a 1950 season that promised to be a rough and potentially disappointing one. Before the beginning of training camp, Ronzani announced, "We'll need at least nine league games and maybe more to get our machine to working."

"I'm no miracle man," Ronzani kept telling the Packers' faithful, "but I do promise to put a team on the field with the old Packer spirit."

"The return of the Green Bay Packers from the football dead was completed today in the most dramatic setting possible," reported writer Edward Prell in the *Chicago Tribune* on October 2, 1950. "The Packers, guided by thousands of sideline gestures from their new coach, Gene "Tuffy" Ronzani, took the Chicago Bears apart with neatness and dispatch, 31-21."

"They deserved to win," a somber George Halas told the waiting press. "You can't take it away from them."

Press-Gazette scribe Art Daley got caught up in the hoopla by saying the Packers were, "... positively savage in their every move. This one tugged at your heart," Daley added. "It made you want to cry as the huge throng, wild with unbelievable joy and anticipation for sixty minutes, sat stunned, choked up, for a brief moment at the final gun, unable to grasp the real meaning of what had happened. Today, the Packers had to be pegged as a championship contender."

The early October crowd assembled at City Stadium saw one of best wide open Packers-Bears matchups in the sixty-one meetings between the grid giants. Packers' kicker Ted Fritsch led off the scoring with a 20-yard field goal. Just before the half, Bears' rusher Julie Rykovich slammed over for a touchdown and put the Bears ahead.

The second half was full of fireworks. Early in the third, former Bear Wally Dreyer intercepted a Johnny Lujack pass on the Bears' 28-yard line, and whizzed his way downfield for a score and a Packer lead, 10-7. Three minutes later, Lujack was hijacked again, this time by Rebel Steiner. Steiner stepped in front of a pass intended for Ken Kavanaugh at the Packers' 6-yard line and followed great blocking down the sideline for an electrifying touchdown.

The enraged Bears fought back with a 72-yard drive, capped off with Lujack atoning with a 1-yard quarterback sneak for a score: Packers 17, Bears 14.

On the last play of the third quarter the Bears punted to Packers' back Billy Grimes. Grimes cleanly fielded the ball on his 32-yard line, veered to his right, and raced up the field for a back-breaking Packers' touchdown.

On the Packers' next series, running back Larry Coutre broke through the right side of the Bears' defensive wall and ran like the wind until being hauled down by Harper Davis at the Chicago 14-yard line. Moments later, Breezy Reid caught a Paul Christman lob for another score. Chicago's Rykovich added a final touchdown, but it was not enough. Gene Ronzani and his Packers had won a big one.

The optimism would, unfortunately for the Packers, be short-lived. Only two weeks after their exciting win over the Bears, they met again in Chicago for the rematch. Some 4,000 Packers' fans were in Chicago to see their team battle the Bears to a 7-7 half-time score, but slowly lose steam and go down in defeat, 28-14.

The top thrill for the Northmen was a dazzling 73-yard scamper by Wheelin' Willie Grimes. Grimes took the hand-off from Rote, dashed through the Bears' line for ten yards, then fumbled. Fielding the ball on the second bounce, he scooped it up and headed for the end zone.

But Grimes and the rest of the Packers could not contain Bears' quarterback Johnny Lujack. The former Notre Dame star ran for three touchdowns and kicked four extra points to lead the Bears to victory before a record crowd at Wrigley Field.

The *Green Bay Press-Gazette* reported that the Bears had lost a total of twenty-six footballs—$576 worth—to "handy" fans in the end zones and along the sidelines. Unlike nowadays, where netting is hoisted behind the goal posts to keep the ball from going into the crowd, in those days nothing kept the ball from being kicked or thrown into the seats. Twenty-six fans went home with a pigskin souvenir.

After the win over the Bears in the third week of the season, the Packers came down to earth and began to crumble. Living up to what many had predicted, the Packers proceeded to lose eight of their last nine games to finish 3-9 in Ronzani's first year. The sputtering offense was bad enough, but the defense was horrendous, having allowed forty or more points in five different games. They couldn't stop anyone.

The Bears meanwhile went on to win seven of their last nine games, finishing 9-3, and tying the Los Angeles Rams for the National Conference crown. The playoff game would pit the teacher against the pupil. The Rams' head coach was none other than Joe Stydahar, Chicago's former standout lineman.

This time, the student would out-smart the teacher. Behind the generalship of quarterbacks Norm Van Brocklin and Bob Waterfield and the pass catching of Tom Fears, the Rams beat the Bears, 24-14, for the chance to play the Cleveland Browns in the championship game.

Both the Bears and the Packers were about to enter a deep

recession. The Packers, lacking any real talent, had fulfilled dismal expectations and obviously had some serious rebuilding to do. The Bears and their fans were having a tough time accepting their gradual fall from grace. It was time for George Halas and his Bears to pay the piper for the trading of Texan quarterback Bobby Layne.

While watching a football game today, one may see a certain offensive alignment that's called the "Shotgun Formation." It's where the quarterback stands seven to ten yards behind the center and receives the ball directly. Usually he's the only back in the backfield, although occasionally a fullback will stay behind to provide blocking.

The intention is to place the quarterback where he would end up anyway on a seven step drop-back position to pass the ball. It allows the quarterback to immediately see a defensive formation and decide what play would work best against it. Usually, there are at least four or five players going out on different routes to receive the pass.

The Green Bay Packers unveiled this new offensive formation on opening day against the Bears on September 30, 1951. It was a tactic used to mask the talent they were lacking. The Packers had a poor running attack in 1951, finishing dead last in the league in team rushing totals. Third round draft choice Fred Cone from Clemson was a good acquisition for the Packers at fullback, but would only rush for 190 yards for the season. An aging Tony Canadeo did what he could, but wasn't much help either. The offensive line tried valiantly to block and open holes for the Packers' backs, but it rarely happened.

On the Tuesday before the Bears' game, Ronzani installed the then-unnamed "Shotgun Formation" to try to generate some offense and to save quarterback Tobin Rote's neck. Most of the time Rote was running for his life. Rote did garner 523 yards rushing for the season, but he took an incredible beating for it. Tobin Rote and second string quarterback Bobby Thomason threw the ball well, combining for 2,846 yards on 231 total completions. Unfortunately, too many completions went to opposing defenders as interceptions.

Clearly, the Packers had not had enough time to work out the kinks of the new offense. They fell behind early, 17-0, but mounted a comeback with Rote and Thomason filling the air with passes. By game's end, the two quarterbacks had thrown thirty-eight times, completing twenty-two, enough passes to win most games, but not this one.

Two interceptions by rookie defensive back Gene Schroeder silenced two Green Bay scoring opportunities. The Bears won, 31-20, crowning their thirty-eighth victory, against twenty-three defeats and five ties in the sixty-third game of the series.

Physically, this contest was just as rough as the sixty-two games that had come before. The Bears were hit with 114 yards in total penalties while the Packers drew 109 yards in penalties. Two different dirty incidents by Chicago drew calls of revenge from the Packers' camp. Ed Sprinkle jumped feet-first on a Packers' blocker, and guard Paul Stenn was caught kneeing Thomason, with both cheap-shot episodes seen by all in the open field.

"Keep your daubers up," Ronzani encouraged after the game, his voice echoing in the funeral quiet of the Packers' locker room. "Boys, the season is long. We play them (the Bears) in November."

In the November 18 game, Tobin Rote again was like a man running from a burning building. He gained 150 yards rushing from the new offensive setup, but it still wasn't enough, as the Bears swept the series with a 24-13 hard-fought win. Wrigley Field had become a hex joint for the Packers. They hadn't won there in ten years.

The Packers, leading 13-10, had the Bears on the ropes early in the third quarter when Rote swept around the end for a 32-yard jaunt to the Chicago fifteen. The husky quarterback from Rice quickly learned why Chicago's George Connor was an All-Pro linebacker. Connor slammed into Rote with a vicious hit, jarring the ball loose, which allowed guard Frank Dempsey to recover it. That was the game's turning point, as the Lujack-led Bears marched eighty-nine yards for the go-ahead score.

It wasn't only Rote who was stopped cold on the day. Packers' rookie back Dom Moselle became yet another victim of the Wrigley Field's south end brick wall. Wildly chasing after a Tobin Rote pass in the fourth quarter, Moselle slammed into the bricks full speed.

After a couple of minutes with his nose firmly planted into the pasturage of the end zone, he left the field under his own power.

As well as some of the players being stopped cold, the Packers' Lumberjack Band, which was performing for its thirtieth straight year at Wrigley Field, was literally silenced by the below freezing weather. The frozen bass players complained to the *Press-Gazette* that they "couldn't get a sound out of our horns."

In 1951, Chicago Bears' rookie end Gene Schroeder made quite a splash in the NFL when he led the Bears in interceptions and receiving yards for the year. The speedy, talented Virginian would average eighteen yards per catch while playing for Chicago from 1951 to '57.

"Coming out of college I was a world class sprinter," Gene said. "I was at 21.2 seconds in the 220 yard dash. The Olympic committee came to me wanting me to go to the Olympics, but I decided to play football instead."

Like most players at the time, Gene played both offense and defense in college. In the pros, early on, an injury restricted him to playing offensive end.

"I only played both ways in 1951," Schroeder recalled. "I had a bad shoulder coming out of college and I kept dislocating it and they decided I couldn't tackle anymore. After 1951, I only played wide receiver."

Gene remembers the Packers-Bears rivalry too well.

"Coming out of college you think the toughest thing you've ever seen is a NFL exhibition game until you get into the season," Gene said. "The very first game I ever played was in Green Bay. I was on defense and I was standing around. A guy by the name of Dick Wildung just took off and clobbered me. He must have knocked me five yards. It was way after the whistle. Afterwards, I was standing next to George Connor and he said, 'Rookie, you have to keep your eyes open around here, even after the whistle in Green Bay games.' I was a rookie and I wasn't used to that.

"In my rookie season we were getting ready to go up there and Halas tells us that in Green Bay you keep your helmet on while on the bench. We played at old Green Bay East High School and the Bears' bench was very close to the stands. Halas said keep your hats on up there because people will throw beer cans at you. The field was so close to the stands that if you got knocked out of bounds you'd end up on the cinder track.

"Also in my rookie year we played in Wrigley Field. I was playing defense and I intercepted a pass. As I came up with the ball I fell to the ground and someone just raked me with two knees and an elbow to the head. It just absolutely ripped me. I turned around to find it was a college teammate of mine from Virginia! And we were good friends. I said, 'Stretch, why did you do that for?' He said, 'Well, you might have gotten up and run.' In those days, even with contact, you could get up and run. You sort of had to be pinned down. That's what kind of rivalry it was.

"Again in my rookie season, I was safety on the kickoff team. In those days we only had thirty-three people on a team. We had to do a lot of things. Anyway, Tony Canadeo catches a kickoff and brings it straight up the middle. He's coming right at me. I'm just playing on my toes waiting for Tony to fake me one way and go the other. He runs right over me and puts me on my back. Fortunately, I grabbed a leg and brought him down. He was a hard-nosed player. What a competitor. I knew Tony for many years afterwards. He was one of those guys who would bleed Green and Gold."

Injuries shortened Schroeder's career after a very promising first few years in the league. "I hurt my knee real bad while in the service," he said. "I had two great years my first two years in the league. I made All-Rookie team my first year, leading the Bears in interceptions and yards receiving. My second year I led the Bears in receiving and I made the Pro Bowl. Then I hurt my knee real bad at Great Lakes. I came back and played but I wasn't what I was before. The pain became so bad that I couldn't stand it. I'd play a game on Sunday and I'd have to go to the hospital on Monday and get fluid taken from my knee. I'd practice for a few days and then have to go back Saturday to have fluid taken out again.

"When I was fifty years old, I had to have my knee completely reconstructed. I was crippled at age fifty. Dr. Fox, the Bears' doctor, completely built my knee. Now it's fine. I'm walking today because of Dr. Fox. I saw him a couple of years ago and he asked me how the knee was doing. I said great. Then he said, 'You know, the warranty has run out on that.'"

In his rookie season, Gene found out just how tough and agile old man Halas was, shortly after the opening day game in Green Bay.

"In those years we beat them most every time. It was such a rivalry, and people hated the Bears so much in Green Bay that after the game we were at the train station waiting to go back to Chicago. Some Packers' fan walked up to Halas and punched him. I don't how old Halas was at that time but he started chasing him. The old man wanted to fight him!"

Jack Vainisi's expertise at choosing talented draft picks began to show in 1952 with a talented rookie crop that finally brought some relief for Ronzani's talent-poor team. Chosen number one was Kentucky quarterback Babe Parelli. Parelli shared quarterback duties with Tobin Rote in 1952, leading the team in passing with over 1,400 yards and thirteen touchdowns. Drafted second was Rice University receiver Billy Howton, who became the Packers' leading pass catcher with fifty-three grabs for 1,231 yards. Chosen third was Bobby Dillon, a defensive back from Texas, who shored up a very porous defense. Dave "Hawg" Hanner, a bald-headed, rough-neck defensive tackle from Arkansas would pillar the line for the next twelve years.

One area that Ronzani knew the Packers had to address was a tendency for the Packers to go on long losing streaks. In his first two seasons, he had seen the Packers go on six- and seven-game losing slides after early on posting respectable records. It seemed that midway through the season, the team would tire and fall apart.

Ronzani was also facing an intrusive problem, and this one was not on the field. The Packers' Executive Committee held a meeting every Tuesday morning with Ronzani at the downtown YMCA to discuss, play by play, the previous Sunday's game. It wasn't a coffee and donuts get together, either. It was a perfect setting for a Tuesday morning quarterback to second guess a Sunday afternoon decision. To make matters worse, the meddling Committee members even talked to individual players to assess the team's progress. It was a destructive wrestle for control, a case of too many cooks in the kitchen and too many hands in the pot.

"It was not a social event," Clayton Tonnemaker said of those Tuesday morning meetings. "It was, 'How come you're not playing the first draft choice more?' or 'How come you threw a down and out on third down instead of a fly pattern?' People had been watching football up there for years. This was the big thing in their lives, and they had been allowed to second guess coaches forever."

Ronzani quickly learned to brief the Committee on the team's effort and play calling, then to keep his mouth shut.

In 1948 the Chicago Bears had been rich in quarterbacks with the three Ls: Sid Luckman, and rookies Johnny Lujack and Bobby Layne. Halas knew in 1948 that the superstar Luckman would be retiring soon, and saw Lujack and Layne as qualified heirs to Sid's throne.

After Layne was traded in 1949 and Luckman retired after the 1950 season, Lujack had to shoulder the responsibility of the Bears' offense, preparing to carry it through the decade. His statistics were impressive in 1950, throwing for 1,731 yards, four touchdowns, and adding 397 rushing yards.

In 1951, Lujack was plagued with a hurt shoulder but continued to play with the injury. He admits that he should have had an operation to correct the injury instead of playing on. It very well may have cost him a Hall of Fame career. With his bad shoulder, his rifle arm turned into a riddled arm, turning his projectile throws into floating ducks.

"I had a partial separation on my right shoulder but a full separation on the left," Lujack recalled. "The one that was partial was the throwing arm and, of course, that interfered an awful lot with throwing.

"I was supposed to be out like five to six weeks, but in ten days with Novocain shots, I'm practicing with my arm in a sling. I'm under center with my arm in a sling and handing the ball off with one hand.

"Four days later, I took Novocain shots prior to the Green Bay game (the opening day game in 1949). I threw two touchdown passes, kicked both extra points and a field goal and we beat them, 17-0."

Lujack has mixed emotions now about playing with the injury and about George Halas' insistence on him playing. "He was a great pioneer of the sport, no doubt about it," said Lujack. "But you know, I can't admire anybody that says get a Novocain shot. Today you can't get away with things like that, but he (Halas) was able to. I don't think that he had the person's well being at heart. I think it was a sport, he was paying you, and he wanted you to play hurt or well, it didn't make a difference to him."

Halas and the Bears suffered in 1952 without a quality, proven quarterback. George Blanda, Steve Romanik, and Bob Williams shared the quarterbacking duties while Curley Morrison and Kayo Dottley handled the rushing chores.

The Bears still had a formidable line that featured the ageless Bulldog Turner, Dick Berwegan, George Connor, and the aggressive Ed Sprinkle. It was Sprinkle who became the catalyst in the Bears' opening day win in Green Bay.

Leading 10-7 in the fourth quarter, Sprinkle and the Bears had their backs against the wall with the Packers threatening on their 20-yard line. On third down, Tobin Rote went back to pass and was planted in the ground by the hard-charging Sprinkle. Ronzani decided to go for the game-tying three points and sent in kicker Bill Reichardt. As Reichardt's foot met the ball, the towering Sprinkle burst through and blocked it. The pigskin bounced back to the 40-yard line where the Bears recovered it.

Chicago marched downfield, closing the drive with a Bob Williams' touchdown pass to Gene Schroeder, who had eluded Packer defensive back Bobby Dillon. Another Green Bay fumble on their ensuing drive allowed the Bears an extra touchdown and the win, 24-14.

With the Packers ten-point underdogs, the two clubs met again in the second week of November at Wrigley Field, where eleven years of Green Bay frustration came to a spectacular end. Green Bay's stingy defense and a wide open offense stunned the Chicagoans, 41-28, with the Packers gaining almost 400 yards in total offense.

"Never in their glory days were the Green Bay Packers more devastating than yesterday in Wrigley Field," wrote Chicago writer Edward Prell. "Seldom in their thirty-odd years in the same arena were the Chicago Bears so inadequate."

The 66th game of the rivalry was highlighted by two kickoff returns, both by Chicago. Leon Campbell galloped eighty-six yards to tie the game at 7-7 in the first quarter, and rookie Eddie Macon raced eighty-four yards after the Packers were safely ahead, 24-7.

Offensive end Bill Howton, whom Prell called the Packers' "new Hutson," caught six balls for eighty-four yards and a touchdown, while the Packers change of pace offense—Tobin Rote's running threat and Babe Parilli's accurate long passes—kept Ed Sprinkle and the Bears' defense off-balance the entire afternoon.

The 2,000 Packer fans at Wrigley Field let out a collective war whoop as their heroes exited the field to the locker rooms beneath the stadium. Overjoyed that the Packers had ended the Wrigley curse, some 300 fans stayed behind to form a long conga line and snake-danced the entire length of the field.

In the locker room, Tony Canadeo, blood streaming from cuts under his right eye and forehead, was presented the game ball. It was his final Bears' game. Holding the ball aloft, with tears in his eyes, he said, "Well, I said we were going to beat 'em today—my first year and my last year."

It was an emotional victory for the entire team and town of Green Bay. In twenty-three degree temperatures, a crowd of 6,000 fans jammed the North Western Train Station platform, spilling into Dousman Street and lining the tracks on the west side to Arndt Street, to greet their heroes. After an eighty minute delay, sirens blared and fireworks flared as the train pulled to a stop. As Ronzani and the team exited, the crowd strained forward congratulating them with cheers and back slaps. It was the perfect salve to soothe any aching muscle.

Green Bay had improved on the 3-9 squads of Ronzani's first two seasons. Unfortunately, another losing streak would cost them dearly. In the thick of the National Conference race at 6-3, they lost to the Bobby Layne-led Detroit Lions and then headed to the West Coast to play the Rams and the 49ers.

Beginning in 1950 and continuing to the end of the 1959 season, the Packers played their two season-ending games in Los Angeles and San Francisco. For the Packers, it was the road trip from hell. In that span, Green Bay amassed a 3-17 record on the coast, with two of those wins coming in 1959. Trips to the coast were a season killer for them, and 1952 would be no different.

They lost to the Rams, 45-27, then ended the year with a 24-14 drubbing by the 49ers. At 6-6, they finished fourth in the National Conference, behind Detroit, Los Angeles, and San Francisco, the same three teams that beat them in succession.

Meanwhile, in Chicago it was soul searching time. Behind two untested quarterbacks, the Bears had sputtered the entire year, highlighted by an unforgivable loss to the hapless Dallas Texans. A season-ending win over the cross-town rival Cardinals did little to ease the mind of George Halas. Finishing at 5-7, the Bears dropped below the .500 mark for the first time since 1945, and only the second time since 1929.

George Halas fought the notion that maybe the game was passing him by.

In 1952, Deral Teteak was a rookie linebacker and guard for the Packers. He was recruited by Vainisi, who didn't have to drive a long distance to see his ninth round draft choice. Teteak had been a standout at Wisconsin University.

"Jack Vainisi, the Packers' talent scout, came down and watched me," recalled Teteak. "He's really the one who drafted me. I played at linebacker, though they also in those days called it a guard position. I started the first season and played until 1956.

"Our first year was pretty good. In fact, we went out to the coast for two games and if we'd won those we'd have been in the playoffs. We were 6-4 when we went out there and we lost both games and finished 6-6. We could have won our division.

"Ronzani was a different kind of coach," Teteak observed. "I remember in my first year we were playing the Bears and Ronzani didn't do much coaching. He was looking around to see if there was anyone from the Bears' system watching what we were doing. He was plugging up holes in fences and looking up in the air for planes. He was very afraid of George Halas and his spies."

One of Deral's many rookie memories include a first encounter with the time-hardened Bulldog Turner.

"I was the middle linebacker and he was the guy who was blocking me all the time," Teteak said. "It was his last year and I was a pretty young guy. He was one of the best blockers I played against. I recall on one screen pass he pulled out and I went to hit him. He turned on me and I just hit him in the back. The official was right there and he knew it. We intercepted the pass but I got a 15-yard penalty. He laughed about it. He knew what he did.

"Dave "Hawg" Hanner, he chewed tobacco and he'd come out and play over the guard and a couple of times the Bears would come up over the ball and Hanner would spit a wad of juice all over the ball. Bulldog Turner would come up and put his hands on the ball and find tobacco juice!"

Teteak recalled the games he played against the Bears in Chicago.

"I remember the white field lines at Wrigley Field. They were not white chalk. The lines were sand. White sand. By the time you got into the game you didn't know where the sideline was. I couldn't believe it.

"Another thing about playing in Chicago is that the fans better have had earplugs because of that George Halas. He was the most intimidating guy to the officials that I've ever been around. He would call those officials every name in the book. Very salty. I couldn't believe some of the things he'd call those officials. They would never throw a flag at him. I knew Don Kindt who played for the Bears and he was a Wisconsin man, too. He said he didn't end that with the officials. He went right to the players with the same kind of language. They were a wild bunch."

Teteak played in an era when players had to put up with hits by the likes of Bulldog Turner and Ed Sprinkle, and endure the scurrilous language of Halas, all for very little money.

"There was no money," Teteak simply said. "You played for fun. My first year contract was for $5,000 and I made the Pro Bowl. I wanted a thousand dollar raise and I had to hold out. They made me sign two contracts, one for $6,000 and then $6,500. In my last year in 1956 I made $8,500."

There were some lighter moments, though.

"I remember we had a guy on our team named Chubby Grigg who we got from the Cleveland Browns. A big guy about three hundred and something pounds. He played offensive tackle. We were playing the Bears in 1952 and we were leading at half-time. His locker was next to mine. Well, he had his head stuck in his locker. I thought what the heck is going on here. I mean, we were winning the game at half-time. You don't have to feel bad. I tapped him on the shoulder and said, 'Chubby, are you all right?' He said, 'Keep your mouth shut.' I looked in there and he was eating hot dogs! He had the ball guy go out and get him a half dozen hot dogs to eat at half-time."

Chubby Grigg, incidentally, goes down as being one of the lost Packers. The official Green Bay media guide doesn't include the hot-dog eating Grigg on their all-time roster, a list of Packers who have been active for at least one league game.

Ray Stanley, a Packers' fan from Milwaukee, was sitting in section J at City Stadium on October 4, 1953 ready to watch his beloved Packers play the hated Bears in the two team's 67th meeting together. Stanley had traveled with twenty-four other Packers' fans from Milwaukee to see the game, but during the first quarter he found himself sitting alone. He grew so concerned about his missing companions that he had Jim Cofeen announce over the P. A. system, "Ray is in section J. He's not lost—you are!"

The same could be said for the Packers, who were about to embark on a truly lost season.

It was not the typical Bears-Packers matchup. Both teams were inept and played sloppy football. The officials were kept busy throwing fifteen penalty flags, evidence of two poorly disciplined teams. A combined six interceptions and five fumbles made the 17-13 Chicago victory a comedy of errors.

"The case of the People vs. Gene Ronzani was argued out on the sun bathed gridiron of little City Stadium here today by an embattled aggregation of Green Bay Packers who fought the

Chicago Bears to the final minutes," wrote George Strickler in the *Chicago Tribune*.

The Packers had a bad case of "Last-Halfitis." This was the sixth consecutive game in which Green Bay's offense had not scored in the second half. Leading 13-10 late in the fourth, the Bears began moving downfield behind the play calling of George Blanda. Near the goal line, Blanda drifted back and threw a pass to end Jim Dooley. Dooley, who had dropped several balls earlier, jumped in between two Packer defenders and came down with the ball.

A last ditch effort by the Northmen would suddenly come to an end. After Tobin Rote had led his troops deep into Bears' territory, an errant throw was intercepted by John Hoffman icing the game for Chicago.

Ronzani was on the coaching hot seat. The Packers had the three-game skid at the end of 1952, followed by losses in their final four pre-season games in 1953, and then were blanked by Cleveland, 27-0, in the 1953 season opener. The team was in a terrible tail-spin ready to crash. People were now calling for Ronzani's head. Everyone was guessing when the Committee's hammer was going to fall.

Before the Packers-Bears Wrigley Field rematch, word leaked out that Halas had offered $50 to any of his Bears who could knock the mustache off of Packer receiver Bob Mann. Mann, who was Green Bay's first black player, made it through the game, but he took many vicious hits.

The first six minutes of the first quarter were thrilling for the Packers. The lightening-quick Dillon ran an interception back forty-nine yards for a touchdown and, soon after, Cone rumbled forty-one yards for a touchdown making it 14-0. The Packers' good fortunes started to turn, however, when Cone missed two field goal attempts from thirty-one and thirty-four yards out.

With two minutes remaining in the hard fought game and the score Bears 21, Packers 14, Green Bay end Billy Howton faked out Bears' defender S. J. Whitman on the 15-yard line and caught a Babe Parilli pass for a 23-yard touchdown, ending the game with a 21-21 tie. Packers' kicker Fred Cone's field goal attempt from the 45-yard line missed, assuring the tie.

The tie did little to soothe the impatient, football-loving com-

munity of Green Bay. In their next three games, the Packers lost to
Detroit twice and to San Francisco. Soon after the 34-15 loss to the
Lions on November 26, the hammer finally came down on Gene
Ronzani. The Executive Committee decided to fire him before the
final two-game road trip to the West Coast. Assistant Coaches
Hugh Devore and Ray "Scooter" McLean were named co-coaches
for the final two games.

"Everybody thought he was going to be fired before the
Thanksgiving Day game in Detroit," center Clayton Tonnemaker
recalled. "Ronzani paid his own way on the team train and took the
trip with us to the West Coast. He sat up in the press box during
the games. That was really bizarre."

Co-coaches may have been fairly successful for Chicago in the
mid-Forties, but the short coaching stint of McLean and Devore
would not prove to be successful for Green Bay. The team traveled,
along with Ronzani, to San Francisco and were blasted, 48-14, by
the 49ers. Heading south to Los Angeles, the Packers were again
toppled, 33-17. At 2-9-1, it was the worst Packers team other than
the horrendous 2-10 squad of 1949.

"I always felt badly about Ronzani's unsuccessful career with the
Packers," John B. Torinus said in his book *The Packer Legend*. "He
was a fine gentleman and continued to be one of the Packers' great
supporters in the years after he had given up coaching. He coached
the team at a very inopportune point in Packer history when they
were short of both players and money."

Center Clayton Tonnemaker, the Packers' number one draft in
1950, recalled a couple of his more hurtful Bear memories.

"The only time in my life I got knocked out was against the
Bears in 1950," Tonnemaker remembered. "We played two weeks
apart and the game in Green Bay they had worked me over pretty
good. I tried to defend myself but in the process I got thrown out of
the game.

"We go down to Chicago and Chuck Drulis, who was a guard
with the Bears, had gotten cut (thrown off the team). Ronzani
picked him up, I'm sure, to get all the information on the Bears

because we were going to play them in two weeks. It was the only year Durlis played for us and he became a coach after that.

"On the train down there he told me that I should be careful, because they were gonna get me. So, I had my head bent over snapping on a punt and Fred Davis, the Bears' defensive lineman, was lined up to my left. As I snapped, he threw the neatest right cross to my jaw and it knocked me out. He got thrown out of the game, and I was out for about a minute and a half. I saw on film afterwards that when the referee threw Davis out, he went over to the sideline and Halas was shaking his hand and congratulating him. I learned later that Halas paid his (league) fine. In those days it was $50, and that was a lot of money.

"The only thing that bothered me about the Bears was Halas. Every time you played at Wrigley Field, Halas would intimidate the officials and you never got a break down there."

Downsizing was the key word with the Green Bay Packers' Executive Committee in 1954. The directors appointed Jerry Atkinson, general manager of Prange's Department Store, to recommend changes in management structure and to hire a business manager.

Atkinson suggested reducing the Committee's size from thirteen to seven persons, and he hired former Packers' great Verne Lewellen, a lawyer who had served as District Attorney for Brown County, as business manager.

Lewellen's first job was to seek out a new coach. Hugh Devore was being pegged for the job but he turned the offer down. Lewellen finally chose Lisle Blackbourn, a head coach from Marquette University.

Blackbourn certainly had the football credentials. After being a successful high school coach, in 1948 he took over as backfield coach at Wisconsin. In 1950, he was named head coach at Marquette University, leading the Hilltoppers out of mediocrity to national prominence.

The Green Bay Packers' press guide painted a rosy picture of things to come with Blackbourn in control.

"The wedding of Blackbourn and the Packers should provide numerous offspring in the form of National Football League victories," the guide proclaimed.

"I thought Lisle was going to be a good coach," Clayton Tonnemaker recalled. "He was a very decent human being and I thought he was a leader. But the system of the huge board of directors and the micro-managing of the board finally got to him. My friends that played with him in 1954 said he was a totally different person in his last year of coaching (1957) than he was his first year. That was unfortunate."

All told, Blackbourn's leadership suffered from the same problems that Ronzani had faced. Although the Committee had been chopped in half, its hold on the team hadn't lessened any. With thirteen members or seven members, they still wanted to put in their two cents' worth.

Both Green Bay and Chicago, in an effort to dig themselves out of the doldrums, began to stock pile solid draft picks. After a 3-8-1 season in 1953, Halas and the Bears began to rebuild at the quarterback position, an area that needed dire attention. Ed Brown, from San Francisco University, and Georgia quarterback Zeke Bratkowski, were chosen to beef up the position.

The Bears also acquired linemen Stan Jones from Maryland, All-American defensive end Ed Meadows from Duke, and Larry Strickland from North Texas State.

One of their best finds was wide receiver Harlon Hill, from a little school in northern Alabama. Halas' old friend Clark Shaughnessy was the one who convinced Halas to take a chance on Hill.

"I went to Florence St. Teachers College, now known as the University of North Alabama," Hill recollected. "I guess Halas found me by accident down there. They have the Blue/Gray game in Montgomery every year. Coach Clark Shaughnessy, one of the Bear assistant coaches, was there scouting and spotted one of my opponent's coaches. They got to talking and he told him the best receiver in the area of the South wasn't playing. Shaughnessy asked why and he said he was from a college up in northern Alabama. He took him for his word and Coach Halas called the coach at Florence St. and asked for some film. Undoubtedly he liked what he saw on the film and I was drafted in the last round. Back then they had fifteen rounds. It was sheer luck. I started the first pre-season game and stayed there throughout the whole year.

"We were in the pro offense then and we had two receivers but we didn't throw like they do today. The defenses then were not as complicated and there was more man coverage. I was usually double covered. Back then, we had one old single bar on the helmets and they could hit you anyway they wanted until the ball was in the air. They'd tackle or block you while you were chugging down the field. It was pretty tough-going for receivers back then.

"Ed Brown was quarterback most of my career. We started off with George Blanda and then he got hurt. So it was Brown and Zeke Bratkowski, Brown more than Bratkowski. Ed Brown had a great arm. He could throw the long ball with great accuracy."

Harlon recalled his days playing against the Packers and old one-eyed Dillon!

"One of the best defenders I played against was Green Bay's Bobby Dillon. He had one eye! I could never figure out which one was he was blind in. I never had any, what you would call, great games against the Packers because of him. He was an excellent pass defense man. He was one of the best the Packers ever had.

"One year we were playing in Green Bay and it was third down and about four yards to go. We called a hitch pattern; I was supposed to go out five yards and make sure I got a first down. I went about three yards, caught the ball, and failed to make the crucial first down. We needed to keep the ball because we were behind. Coach Halas chewed me something awful.

"Right before the half one year up there, defensive coach Johnsos put me in at deep safety. The Packers had a great receiver by the name of Bill Howton. Johnsos told me not to let Howton get behind me. Well, he came down the field and cut all the way across to the corner. I just kept going back to the middle. He caught a touchdown pass right before the half. Johnsos just chewed me out. I reminded him that he had told me not to let him get behind me and to stay in the middle of the field. He said, 'You were supposed to go with him if he came to you and stay with him.' I'd never played any defense. I remember those two mess-ups.

"I really wasn't a two-way player. I had practiced some prevent defense. That Green Bay game was the first time I'd ever gone into a game. But I did practice a little bit at the free deep safety position.

"The Packers' games were probably more physical than most other games because they were such a rival. You read the papers all week long and the coaches are all talking about this player and that player, and it gets intense. Both teams then would leave everything out on the field."

Did Halas coach any differently during the week before the Packer game?

"It seemed like he always had security people around the stadium, but I think he would double up on security and be looking around the stands thinking some Green Bay people were spying on us. He seemed to be more uptight and suspicious. He was also a little tougher and more intense."

Jack Vainisi continued his, what time soon proved to be, mastery of the NFL draft for the Packers. In 1953 he chose halfback Al Carmichael from USC in the first round. Three years later Carmichael recorded one of the longest kickoff returns in NFL history, and it came at the expense of the Bears. Vainisi had also picked up a huge defensive tackle from SMU, Bill Forester, and a hard-nosed center from Syracuse named Jim Ringo.

The 1954 draft yielded some promising prospects also. Veryl Switzer, a speedy halfback from Kansas State, was chosen in the first round. Also picked to light up the offense was a free-wheeling offensive end from Tulane University, Max McGee.

After a 2-4 pre-season, Blackbourn and his troops opened the season with a loss to Pittsburgh, then took on the Bears in Green Bay. Halas and his men, arriving by train on Saturday, should have brought an ark. They stepped off the train just in time for a rare autumnal monsoon that brought 3 1/2 inches of rain to the area.

Packers' fans literally had to wade their way through the flooded streets of town to get to the stadium on Sunday. The slickered crowd watched in disappointment as the Bears recorded a 10-3 win, their forty-first victory in the rivalry.

What's surprising is that both offensives were not hampered by the elements and the ankle-deep mud at City Stadium. Green Bay tallied almost 300 yards in total offense while Chicago garnered 230 yards. But, as usual, games played in adverse conditions are decided by turnovers and mistakes. Chicago's Paul Lipscomb, a 250-pound tackle and once a Packer in the late Forties, recovered a Green Bay fumble on the Packers' 9-yard line to set up a George Blanda-to-Billy Stone touchdown.

Rote had a good day passing, completing twelve passes for 192 yards. One of his incompletions actually brought a cheer from the crowd and embarrassment to a Milwaukee pressman. A bullet pass from Rote in the second half sailed over the head of a Packers' receiver and knocked the hat off Milwaukee photographer Neils Lauritzen. The stunned and abashed shutter bug retrieved his now muddy fedora and placed it back on his head.

The mud-caked Packers entered the locker room tired, bruised, and battered. Stout-hearted Tobin Rote had a particularly tough afternoon after he had been pressured and knocked down by the physical Bears' line. While throwing a pass in the fourth quarter, Rote twisted his ankle with his foot planted firmly in the ground. He made it to his hands and knees and was helped off the field.

An elated George Halas was happy with the win, but was extremely peeved at the field conditions on which the game was played.

"The Packers are in the big leagues," Halas said, pulling no punches. "They have been for a long time. I think it's disgraceful they didn't have a tarpaulin to cover the field.

"We pay $90,000 to $100,000 rent a year at Wrigley Field; they pay nothing," he continued. "Yet, we have a tarpaulin, they don't. If they'd expend $7,000 for a tarp, it would help conditions terrifically. The competing teams and the fans are entitled to a game played under the best possible conditions."

It was a dry track in November for the Wrigley game that saw the Packers fall behind, 14-0, early on, then score two touchdowns in three minutes and nineteen seconds to tie it.

Rote hit rookie Max McGee for a 4-yard TD pass to make it 14-

7. With five minutes left in the half, Bears' punter Zeke Bratkowski punted the ball to the Packer 7-yard line where rookie Veryl Switzer was waiting. Switzer scooped up the ball running left, faked a hand-off to Al Carmichael, then tore up the Packers' sideline, his cleats kicking dirt in the face of the pursuing Bears. Switzer never stopped until he reached the end zone for the Packers' longest punt return in their history. The record stood until 1974, when the Chicago Bears were the victims once again.

Tobin Rote once again proved to be the fearless leader, playing most of the game with a broken nose.

"Somebody hit me a glancing blow just as I put my head down," Rote said, "and I don't have any idea who it was." Once again he was helped off the field, but he soon returned to lead the Packers, albeit with a patch over his nose and the front of his uniform blood-splattered.

In 1954, under Blackbourn's rule, the Packers improved with a 4-8 record. Once again, like his predecessor Gene Ronzani, Blackbourn suffered through a season-ending losing stretch, losing four out of their last five.

The Chicago Bears, meanwhile, were showing great improvement. People began thinking of Halas' men as Midway Monsters again after posting an 8-4 record. The complete opposite of the Packers, Chicago won six of its last seven games, finishing second behind the Bobby Layne-led Detroit Lions.

Even with the second place finish, Halas had a reason to smile. His 1954 team had been led by rookies, promising a bright future for the Papa Bear. Zeke Bratkowski, sharing quarterbacking duties with George Blanda, threw for 1,087 yards and eight touchdowns, and punted for an average of forty-one yards per boot.

Receiver Harlon Hill, many calling him the next Hutson, scored twelve touchdowns on forty-five catches and 1,124 yards. Leading the Bears' rushers was Indiana rookie Chick Jagade, who ran for 498 yards and a couple of scores.

During Halas' reign with the Bears, dating back to the Staleys in Decatur, and through Red Grange and the great teams of the

Thirties and the Forties, the Midway Monsters had won seven NFL championships and eight division titles. This was more than any other team. His Bears had won the most games, scored the most points, and made the most touchdowns.

When Halas was fifty-five years old he thought of retiring, but he changed his mind. Now in 1955 he had turned sixty. So it came as really no surprise that before the '55 season Halas announced this would be his final year on the sidelines. He would retire and settle into a position in the front office.

He informed his coaching staff and told them to prepare for one last season with him at the helm. He wanted to go out with an NFL championship in the worst way, and the team's acquisitions promised that the Bears would be a competitive club.

In a trade, the Cleveland Browns released the mountainous Doug Atkins, a 6'8", 255-pounder from Tennessee. The eccentric Atkins starred on the defensive line for the Bears until 1966. Floridian running back Rick Casares was chosen in the draft along with Bobby Watkins from Ohio State and linebacker Joe Fortunato from Mississippi State.

The two rookie running backs played a major role in the Bears' reversal of fortunes in 1955. Casares and Watkins would combine for 1,225 yards on the ground and would gain the Bears some much needed backfield respect.

That respect would have to come in time, however. The Bears began the season with three straight losses and in the second week met the Packers in Green Bay.

"It appears that little old Green Bay has itself a hard-fighting, highly-spirited, smartly-coached, up-and-coming Packer football team," Art Daley announced in his Monday morning *Press-Gazette* column after the Northmen had dismantled Halas and the Bears, 24-3. It was the first time the Packers had held the Bears without a touchdown since 1938, when Chicago had won on a 2-point safety. It was the widest Packers' victory margin on their rivals since the Pack had won 25-0 way back in 1929. The 24,662 in attendance couldn't have been more happy for their team and Coach Blackbourn.

With pinpoint passes to Billy Howton and second-year man Gary Knafelc, Tobin Rote had one of his best games as a pro. Along with the running of back Howie Ferguson, the Packers' offense amassed 411 yards total, tearing through the Bears' defense like it was tissue paper.

"I had some damned good blocking," Ferguson declared. "No kidding."

The Packers' defense had stuffed the Bears, intercepting four passes and never allowing more than two first downs in a single series.

"We played a bad game today," Halas said afterwards. "I have no excuses."

Ironically, it was Blackbourn and his Packers who were searching for excuses a month later when the Midway Monsters leveled them, 52-31, matching the highest total ever scored against Green Bay. It wasn't as close as the score indicates. Entering the fourth quarter, Chicago was coasting with a 45-3 lead.

The star of the day was linebacker George Connor. Twice on kickoffs, Connor shook the girders of Wrigley Field by pounding the Packers' return men with vicious, sledge hammer hits causing two fumbles, both resulting in touchdowns for the Bears.

"Offensively, it was our best game," Halas remarked afterwards, and for good reason. Chicago's backfield, namely Bobby Watkins, Rick Casares, Chick Jagade, and Ron Drzewiecki combined for a shattering 399 yards on the ground against a dismal Packers' defense.

"They've just got too much line for us," a disappointed Coach Blackbourn said after the game. "Their offensive line outplayed our defensive line at every stage of the ball game."

Chicago Tribune writer David Condon wrote amusingly of what was possibly the best run attempt of the game—by Bears' coach George Halas after the game!

"Near 4:00 p.m. yesterday," Condon wrote, "George Halas attempted to rush the approximate fifty yards from his team's lockers to a room where many were awaiting his analysis of the 52-31 triumph over Green Bay.

"Halas had to grind out yardage in bursts. He broke loose for seventeen yards before running into a wave of autograph seekers. A plunge through center netted Halas three additional yards, with more autograph seekers stopping forward progress.

"George advanced seven yards on a quick-opener, cut wide to the left for another seven yards, and may have gone all the way had not two newspapermen forced him toward a steel pillar, out of bounds.

"Two thrusts netted Halas six yards, he spun clear until two Wisconsin newsmen got him a yard short of the goal. Seconds later, he advanced the final yard into the clubroom door.

"After all, when a Bear sighted a goal yesterday, he reached it."

Unfortunately, Halas' goal of a championship in his last season as head coach suffered a crippling blow three weeks later on the south side of Chicago. At 3-5-1, the underdog Chicago Cardinals seemed no match for the 6-3 Bears, riding a six-game winning streak. Once again, the unpredictable Chicago weather became an equalizing factor. A snowstorm before game time turned into a brutal blizzard, helping the Cardinals to shock the disbelieving Bears, 53-14.

The Chicago Bears ended the season 8-4, a frustrating half game behind the Los Angeles Rams at 8-3-1. The Bears had defeated the Rams decisively during the regular season, 24-3. Coupled with the Cardinals shellacking of the Bears and the Rams' tie against Baltimore, Los Angeles went on to play in, and eventually lose, the championship game against Cleveland.

George Halas and his Chicago Bears watched the game on TV like everyone else.

On any given fall Sunday in the NFL over the years there has been many shattering hits, with some being caught on film and others only in the memories of the players, coaches, and fans who were there in the stadium that day. The sound of a great hit is memorable. The untempered crash of helmets and bodies unmistakable. You don't have to see a great hit. You can hear it.

For everyone in Wrigley Field on November 6, 1955, the memory of one such hit is still vivid.

"It was the hardest hit I've ever seen," said ex-Packer Gary Knafelc. "The crowd was just dead silent. It was unbelievable."

Then-Chicago wide receiver Gene Schroeder said, "I'm a football addict and I've watched a lot of football. That was the hardest tackle I've ever seen."

Fellow Bear Harlon Hill added, "It almost killed the running back. That's just an example of how hard the hitting was with the Bears and the Packers."

Jack Brickhouse, WGN radio announcer, claimed the hit could be heard all over Wrigley Field.

The deliverer of this pulverizing crash was Chicago Bears' linebacker George Connor. The recipient was a fleet-footed running back from the plains of Kansas. His name was Veryl Switzer.

Switzer was very physical for his size. He grew up on a farm where he worked in the fields loading hay, and broke horses and wrestled steers. He also lifted cement on construction sites.

He was drafted in the first round by Green Bay via the New York Giants in 1954. The Giants owed the Packers a first round draft choice, so Green Bay had New York draft him for that pick.

He preferred Green Bay over New York because of the density of population. Green Bay was more open and he was a farm boy and was a little nervous about the prospect of going to the Big Apple.

In his rookie year he led the league in punt returns, ranked high in kickoff returns, and played offense and defense from time to time. He was a dependable utility player.

George Connor was a number one draft choice of the New York Giants in 1946 but he elected to go back to school. He told the Giants he didn't want to play in New York so they traded him to the Boston Yanks. When he got out of Notre Dame in 1948, he signed with the Bears because the Yanks had traded his rights to Chicago.

Connor started playing tackle on offense and defense. In 1949, Bears' line coach Hunk Anderson placed him at linebacker to specifically stop the World Champion Philadelphia Eagles and their great runner Steve Van Buren. Although the Eagles would go on to win another title, Connor inherited the linebacker position.

He made All-Pro on offense and defense for five years, winning honors at linebacker, tackle, and guard. He's the only player in the league to make All-Pro on both sides of the ball. In these days of player specialization, it's certain the achievement will never be matched again.

Both men possess an amazing memory of this one play, a play that happened over forty years ago.

The ferocious hit was caused by a blocking mix-up on the Packers who were receiving the ball. It was George Connor's job to run down on the kickoff and bust up the wedge. The wedge is a group of four or five receiving team players who stick closely together and form a blocking wedge for the runner. Sometimes wedge blocking can cause a hole for a kick returner to slide through and gain big yardage. They routinely assemble around their own 20-yard line when the back is receiving the ball.

Veryl seemed willing, almost eager, to discuss the play. It seems as if he has worn the memory of the hit to this day like a badge of honor.

"In my opinion, George Connor made All-Pro that year for this one fluke tackle," Veryl said.

"I got the ball on the 5- or 10-yard line and the contact took place on the twenty-five. I was running full speed behind the wedge because I thought we were breaking it when I saw them speed up. They sped up to get out of the way. I don't know what they were thinking. Why didn't anyone take on Connor? I just think they wanted to get out of his way! Anyway, I raised up to really put on the burners and by that time here came this big, black blur right in front of me. I couldn't even avoid him. It was George Connor's job to come down and break up the wedge. He threw his body into the wedge. Well, the wedge sidetracked him. He threw his body right into me. He hit me about shoulder high, in the chest and straight on. I was able to twist my upper extremities just slightly to where he kind of glanced off but he still hit me pretty center. I went up into the air, my helmet went off my head with the strap still intact, and I didn't know what had happened. He came in with his head down and running low. He didn't even know what he had hit. In fact he said, 'What happened, where's the ball?' He didn't know he'd knocked me down and the ball with it. It was a lucky hit but he basically destroyed me on that play."

"I loved to run down on kickoffs and punts," George Connor recalled. "I suspected that 1955 was going to be my last year since I was having trouble with my legs and I had a knee operation the year before. That day I wanted to do something outstanding since my brother Jack and my mom and dad were there.

"We were kicking off from the south to the north. I always changed position in line when I was going down because opponents would watch game films for the guy who came down the hardest they would key on. I came running down on the right side and ran into the wedge. All of a sudden the wedge opened up and I was running right at Al Carmichael, who was the other back with Veryl Switzer. Well, Al disappeared—I guess those USC guys didn't want to get in the way—and I never saw Veryl. I hit him going full speed with my shoulder. He was out before he hit the ground. He fumbled and Bill George recovered and ran the ball in for a touchdown. I kept running through the end zone because I didn't want anyone to know my shoulder hurt. I ran up the sideline and Halas said, 'Nice tackle, kid.'"

Many in the hushed Wrigley Field crowd thought Veryl Switzer might have been dead. Finally, he came around and began to roll on the ground. As he walked off the field, even the partisan Bears' fans applauded.

"About five minutes later I heard applause," Connor said. "Veryl had gotten up and walked off the field under his own power. I thought, I guess it's about time to retire because I'm losing my stuff."

Amazingly, Veryl would only miss five minutes of the game before returning. He found himself once again setting up to receive a kickoff.

"Our players called a return up the middle again," Veryl said. "No, we're going right or left I told them. We're not going up the center again! So, the play went left. Al Carmichael took the next kick. I went to block and looked for Connor. I threw my body into him and he caught me in mid-air. He said, 'What do you think you're doing, you big ass.' That was kind of how we looked at each other. I was looking for him to let him know I wasn't fearful of that play.

"It didn't keep me from playing though," Switzer continued. "I went ahead and played the rest of that game on kickoff and punt returns. I did start to stiffen up towards the end of the game, though. The next day I could hardly walk. At our next practice, Coach Blackbourn wasn't happy with the wedge play. He chastised the guys. Blackbourn didn't play me real hard for a game or two after that game. But for six weeks after every time I got bumped in the chest I'd spit up blood. My sternum had been torn lose."

After the 1955 season, Veryl went into the Air Force and played football. When he got out of the service, and during the off-season, he had knee surgery. Unfortunately, his knee didn't rehabilitate very well. When he got back to training camp in Green Bay, he twisted the same knee. He laid up a couple of weeks but it hurt his chances of making the team again.

"They played me in a exhibition game against the Redskins for one quarter," Veryl stated. "I thought I made the team in that quarter. Scooter McLean (then Packers' coach) would practice me on offense and play me on defense in a game. So I could sense something was happening. In that game I made seven tackles and knocked down two balls in one quarter. On Monday I was called into the office and I was cut [from the team]."

Packer talent scout Jack Vainisi got Veryl lined up with the Calgary team in the Canadian Football League. He played there for one year and then was traded to Montreal where he played fullback.

Veryl Switzer's football career was nearing its end, though. In the third game of the season, he pinched a nerve in his neck and was temporarily paralyzed. "It was scary," Veryl confessed. "After that, every time I'd hit someone on defense I'd go paralyzed. So I decided that was enough for me."

Nineteen fifty-five would also be George Connor's last year in the NFL. "After the '55 season," George said, "I went to see Halas. He said, 'George, you're our captain and we're counting on you next year.' But I had this business friend of mine who asked me why I was going back and if I was going to be any better. Plus, I was having leg problems. I decided that if I wasn't the best player out there I didn't want to play. I stayed on a few years as a part-time coach. The toughest thing a pro athlete has to figure out is the time to get out. You want to leave at the top of your game."

After his short stint in coaching, in 1958 he teamed with announcer Ray Scott on CBS to broadcast Packers' games. He even had to travel to Green Bay the summer before to assure the Packers that he wasn't going to spy for the Bears!

A year later he joined the Bears as a broadcaster and worked with old veteran Red Grange. Connor did the color commentary and Grange did the play-by-play for CBS.

In the culmination of a great career, George Connor was inducted into both the College and Pro Football Halls of Fame. "Up until Packer running back Paul Hornung went into the Hall of Fame, I was the only Notre Dame player in both of them," Connor said. "I think now there's only four of us Notre Dame players in both Halls of Fame. It's a great feeling."

George Connor's final words put the entire collision episode into a simple summation: "I never saw him and he never saw me. In that way it was a fluke. It was just two people at the wrong place at the wrong time."

1956-1958

Before the 1956 season, Packers' scout Jack Vainisi performed another bit of draft magic. In what would be considered one of his best recruiting years, Vainisi, along with head coach Lisle Blackbourn, chose SMU tackle Forrest Gregg and Indiana tackle Bob Skoronski to strengthen-up the offensive line.

"I signed Gregg out at the All-Star camp and he only weighed 218 pounds at the time," Blackbourn remembered. "I was afraid we'd gotten one who was too small, but he came into camp that year weighing 230."

When it was Green Bay's turn to choose in the seventeenth round, they selected a little known, unheralded quarterback and punter from Alabama. He had led the NCAA in punting in his senior year but many clubs were leery of drafting him because of a back problem.

"We drafted [him] as a punter," Blackbourn recalled. "We had him punting in training camp, but he was having twinges in his back and the doctor suggested he cut out the kicking. I felt he was going to be a good quarterback, though, when I heard his voice that first day. He's got a great voice."

The owner of that great voice was a man named Brian Bartlett

Starr.

Once again, the Notre Dame connection would prove very beneficial to the Green Bay Packers. Johnny Dee, the basketball coach
of Alabama in the mid-Fifties and a Notre Dame grad, took a shine
to the young quarterback and thought Bart's talent was being wasted. During Alabama's dismal 1955 football season, Dee wondered
why football coach J. B. Whitworth didn't put Starr in more games.

Dee sat down and wrote a letter to his old Notre Dame friend
Jack Vainisi. In it Dee tried to convince Vainisi that Starr was a
good prospect and would make a good quarterback, adding that
Starr was a good passer and kicker.

At the time many ball players considered Green Bay the
"Siberia" of all football. The team and the weather were terrible.
Many players didn't even know where Green Bay, Wisconsin was.
The few who did know where Green Bay was didn't want to go play
there. Plus, it was Small Town USA. Outside of football, there was
nothing to do there. It was Squaresville.

For Bart Starr, it was perfect.

In February of 1956, Halas named his old friend Paddy Driscoll
to become the third head coach of the Chicago Bears. It was the
same Paddy Driscoll that had starred with the Bears as a running
back and drop kicker from 1926 to '29 and had been on the Bears'
coaching staff since 1941. The rest of the coaching staff was a close-
knit family consisting of Clark Shaughnessy, technical advisor; Luke
Johnsos, Phil Handler and George Connor, assistants; Sid Luckman,
quarterback coach; Chick Jagade, fullback coach; and Bulldog
Turner, coach of centers.

This experienced and talented cast of coaches would lead the
Chicago Bears back to the top of the Western Conference, and
make many compare them with the great Bears' teams of the early
Forties.

Runner Rick Casares came into his own in 1956, rushing for a
league-leading 1,126 yards and twelve TDs. The multi-talented Ed
Brown took most of the snaps at quarterback along with handling
the punting duties. Catching Brown's pin-point throws was Harlon

Hill, who snagged eleven TD passes.

Oddly, the Bears began the season with a unpardonable loss to the Colts and then prepared to meet the Packers in Green Bay on October 7th.

Press-Gazette writer Art Daley theorized that the game, "... must have been a pistol to watch on television, [because] it was tremendous enough in the flesh."

After Chicago opened the scoring with a 9-yard pass from Ed Brown to Rick Casares, George Blanda kicked off to Green Bay halfback Al Carmichael. The ball sailed over the goal line where Carmichael caught it six yards deep in the end zone. Figuring he would simply down the ball, the Bears' kickoff team let up. Some even began a slow trot to the sideline.

Carmichael daringly took off, zoomed out to the ten, cut toward the south sideline, picked up a great block by Forrest Gregg around the twenty, and streaked down the sideline for a shocking 106-yard kickoff return. To this day, it remains a Green Bay team record.

Slowly, the superior Bears' squad began dominating the Packers, scoring twenty-seven points the first five times they had the ball. Ed Brown and Rick Casares had one of their best days as pros, leading Chicago over Green Bay, 37-21.

A contented George Halas confided after the game that he "... had more butterflies in my stomach sitting in the press box than I ever did as a coach. I could work it off on the sidelines," he added. "Seriously, though, I don't miss it."

The 74th renewal of the rivalry was a wide open affair pitting the 2-4 Packers against the 5-1 and streaking Bears before 49,172 sun-bathed fans at Wrigley Field. In what writer George Strickler called a "carnival of spectacular passes and sensational runs," Chicago scored three of its five touchdowns on passes of more than fifty yards, while the Packers scored two TDs on long aerials.

When Tobin Rote completed his first pass midway through the second period for Green Bay's initial first down, the Packers were already behind, 21-0.

The Bears' defensive line, Doug Atkins, Fred Williams, Bill Bishop, and Ed Meadows, along with linebackers Bill George and Joe Fortunato, harassed and chased Rote all day long, pressuring him into three interceptions. Rookie quarterback Bart Starr came in, completed five of nine passes, and had two others picked off.

One of Rote's two touchdown passes on the day landed in the hands of end Gary Knafelc, who caught the ball in the corner of the end zone and crashed into the brick wall near the right field line, badly shaking himself.

"I can remember hitting the wall at Wrigley Field," Knafelc recalled. "Tobin Rote was our quarterback and he threw a ball to me very deep in the end zone. I was running full speed and I dove to catch the ball. I was conscious about keeping my feet in bounds. I continued on and hit the wall. The wall is only about two feet from the end zone. I stopped very abruptly. That was in my second year so I think I was wearing a single bar on my helmet. It knocked me out for just a moment. The wall I hit is by the first base dugout used by the Cubs. I hit the brick wall and just missed the dugout. If I'd been a foot to the left, I would have gone into the dugout and really got messed up."

The 38-14 win was Chicago's sixth straight victory placing them in a tie for first place in the Western Conference with the Detroit Lions. The deciding game for the conference championship came in mid-December when the Lions came calling on Wrigley Field.

With four Detroit policemen guarding their bench, the Lions walked into a Bear trap. In a game marred by fights and a near riot that involved hundreds of fans, the Bears earned the right to play the New York Giants in the championship game by knocking Lions' quarterback Bobby Layne out of the game and thrashing Detroit, 38-21.

The Chicago Bears would become a "sneaker" victim. Twenty-two years before, the 1934 Bears' squad played the Giants in the championship game after posting a perfect regular season. At half-time the Giants changed to sneakers for better traction on the icy field and upset the Bears. On this day the Giants, who obviously remembered the 1934 championship game, wore sneakers to start the game while the Bears wore cleats. After falling behind, the Bears changed to sneakers in the second half but it was too late. The Giants embarrassed the Bears, 47-7, and won the championship.

Although they had been thumped in the championship game, the Bears' season had been a great success. Running back Rick

Casares had a league-topping year, Harlon Hill had a league best yards-per-catch average, and quarterback Ed Brown led the league in passing. The Bears, as a team, led the league in four categories, including most points scored.

The Packers, on the other hand, finished 4-8, and were second to last in rushing. Their passing game, behind Tobin Rote and the lesser-used Bart Starr, was second in the league in total yards. The Packers ranked first in passes attempted, only because of the team's inept running game.

In his book *The Packer Legend*, former Executive Committee member John B. Torinus noted that Lisle Blackbourn suffered the same problems that Ronzani had inherited from Lambeau, mainly a lack of overall talent. He was only half right. The Executive Committee members were back to their old nosy, meddling ways. A few members began calling for Blackbourn's head, blaming the coach for the team's poor record and his decision to sparingly play the Packers' number one draft choice, halfback Jack Losch. One committee member was angry because Blackbourn had traded defensive end John Martinkovic.

It's normal for any losing team to have player dissension and finger-pointing. Tobin Rote showed his petulance after Blackbourn called him inconsistent and blamed him for the team's dismal season. Blackbourn handled the situation by simply trading Rote to Detroit.

When Bears' receiver Harlon Hill played against the Packers, he usually lined up across from a soft-spoken Texan defensive back named Bobby Dillon, whom the Packers drafted in the third round of the 1952 college draft. Bobby Dillon possessed great speed, Texas toughness, and a keen eye for the ball. And when I say "a keen eye," I mean one eye. Bobby Dillon played pro football with only eye. A series of childhood accidents culminated in his left eye being removed the summer Bobby turned ten years old. His parents wouldn't let him play football until he was fifteen years old.

Many have inquired about Dillon's challenge of trying to defend against the pass with the use of only one eye.

"People always commented on that," he said, "but I don't have anything else to compare it with. I can't remember having two eyes. I know from my left side I had to be extra cautious and had to turn my head a lot more and you had to be more active. And depth perception, people always commented on how could I catch a ball? I don't know how I did it but it wasn't hard."

Shortly before the 1952 College All-Star game, Dillon was standing in line for the physical when he was suddenly grabbed by the arm by the Illinois State Boxing Examiner, there to make sure every player could safely participate in the game.

"Son, you can't play in this game. You just have one eye!"

"Well, I know that," Bobby answered.

"I'm the Illinois State Boxing Examiner and I can't allow you to play football."

"I've gone through college," Bobby said.

"I don't care," the examiner said. "You can't play."

"Well, this gives me three or four extra weeks to work out with Green Bay," Bobby said.

"You're gonna play pro ball?" the examiner asked in disbelief.

"Yea," Bobby said.

"Get back in the line!" the examiner said.

Dillon played for four Green Bay coaches: Gene Ronzani, Lisle Blackbourn, "Scooter" McLean, and Vince Lombardi. Not one of them ever questioned the Texan's ability to play with his handicap.

"The coaches never expressed anything," Dillon remembered. "In fact, they had me playing on the wrong side. I played right safety where the middle of the field was on my blind side. Looking back, I probably should have been playing the left side. Then the sideline would have been on my blind side. I played left corner and right corner and I really couldn't tell any difference. The only thing was that it was more difficult catching the ball over my left shoulder."

During his career, Bobby usually had the difficult task of covering Bears' receiver Harlon Hill. Hill admits he never had a good game against Green Bay, and Bobby Dillon was probably the reason why. Dillon, in turn, had an enormous amount of respect for Hill's abilities.

"Harlon was a heck of an end," Bobby said. "I had some good

days against Harlon, especially in Green Bay. It seems like he couldn't do much in Green Bay but he did better when we played in Chicago. He was taller than me   and I'm sure he was faster than I was. Hill's cuts and moves weren't as sharp as someone like [Baltimore receiver] Raymond Berry, but he had speed, great hands, long strides, and he was difficult to gauge. He was hard to guard."

Bobby had a ritual before every Bears game of moseying over and talking to Hill during the pre-game warm-ups.

"We knew Halas didn't like his guys visiting with opposing players prior to the game," Bobby recalled. "Knowing that, I would make it a point to go over to talk to Harlon before the game. I remember Harlon saying, 'Bobby, get away from me, Halas will kill me if he sees me talking to you.' I'd do it just to harass him.

"Harlon and I never talked to each other during a game. Occasionally, I'd say nice move or nice catch. One time we were playing in Chicago and he got five yards behind me on a play and they threw the pass. It was going to be a sure touchdown. Now this was when the goal posts were still on the goal line. Well, the ball hits the cross-bar of the goal post. Harlon yelled, 'Goddamn!' I said, 'Harlon, I had you all the way!'"

Dillon was taunted by ex-Bears' quarterback and wild man Bobby Layne. When Layne was with the Bears, he would approach Bobby before a game, point his finger, and say, 'Alright you one-eyed son-of-a-bitch, I'll get you today.' Layne, and the rest of the league's quarterbacks, didn't "get" Bobby often.

Bobby Dillon's stats are impressive. He holds the record for most interceptions a game, four; he intercepted nine balls in three, twelve game seasons; he was named All-Pro four straight years; and he ended his career after the 1959 season with fifty-two interceptions. Dillon's interception totals are better than Hall of Fame Packers' Willie Wood and Herb Adderley.

On Monday, October 30, 1956, a young man with golden hair and an All-American physique sat down at a desk on the Notre Dame campus, pulled out two pieces of "University of Notre Dame" stationery, and wrote a reply letter to Green Bay Packers' head coach Lisle Blackbourn. It read:

> Dear Mr. Blackbourn,
>
> In answer to your letter of last week—I would be glad to answer your questions. First of all, I am very interested in playing pro ball, upon graduating from Notre Dame. If drafted by the Green Bay Packers, and arrangements made, I would be glad to play for Green Bay. I'm sure you know Mr. Tucker and since he has been a very close friend to me, he is going to handle my contract.
>
> You also inquired about my draft status. I dropped out of the Air Force ROTC, and I have yet to be reclassified. For all I know a mix-up may have occurred and the draft board may believe I am still in ROTC.
>
> Thank you again for the nice things you have said to me. I appreciate the fact that I have been placed in the top of your preferred list.
>
>   Sincerely,
>   Paul Hornung.

Blackbourn had written the Notre Dame quarterback and Heisman Trophy winner asking if he would be interested in playing pro football for Green Bay. Even in the mid-Fifties it wasn't certain a college player would move on to play in the pros. Salaries were still on the low side, although it wouldn't be long until they would skyrocket.

The scouting report on Hornung was impressive. Scout Julius Tucker called Hornung "one hell of a boy" and a "great natural athlete." Although Tucker noticed he needed to work on his passing, he went to praisingly write that Paul "Vernon" Hornung had "wonderful poise," was a "real good runner," and added that he could "withstand punishment."

Another important piece of information for Blackbourn was Tucker's underlined assurance that Hornung would not play football in Canada, thus eliminating any possibility of a bidding war for the talented star.

Julius Tucker also noticed what he believed was a weakness in

Hornung, important enough he thought to mention at the bottom of the scouting report.

In an obvious non-football observation, he noted and underlined that one of Hornung's weaknesses was that "He likes girls!"

In the 1957 draft, Green Bay had a first round pick and a bonus pick. Blackbourn and Vainisi's first round choice was offensive end Ron Kramer from Michigan. They made Paul Hornung their bonus pick. Ironically, it would be the subject of Paul Hornung that would be the undoing of Lisle Blackbourn in Green Bay.

The Packers weren't the only club stocking up for the future. The Chicago Bears obtained a speedy halfback from Florida A&M. Willie "the Wisp" Galimore became one of the game's newest breakaway runners. Evidence that the pro draft and recruiting process in 1957 was unsophisticated and often relied on word-of-mouth gossip is clear in the case of Galimore. Bears' assistant coach Phil Handler heard about Willie by, of all people, a jockey at Hialeah Racetrack in Miami. Who said a horse jockey couldn't be a good judge of football talent?

Since 1925, the Green Bay Packers had played their home games at City Stadium adjacent to East High School. Then, seating capacity was around 6,000, it was increased to 15,000 by 1934, and 25,000 later on.

After years of use the stadium had gone from a league favorite field to one with the worst conditions. Foremost was the lack of any toilet facilities for women who attended games. Sales of beverages to women at games were rare, indeed. Even the toilet facilities for men were inadequate. At half-time, men regularly relieved themselves under the stands, leading the women not to have roving eyes between halves. Also, there were no real locker rooms in the stadium. Both the Packers and the visiting team dressed inside locker rooms in East High School.

The underpinnings of the all-wooden stadium were also suspect. Built on the banks of the East River, the ground was poor footing for any structure. Inspections proved that a major replacement of the wooden fixtures was necessary. Simply, City Stadium was an accident waiting to happen.

Push began for the construction of a new football-only stadium. The *Green Bay Press-Gazette* organized a public voting effort for the citizenry to vote yes or no for a new stadium. The weekend before the vote, a pep rally was held at the Columbus Club where the Packers' old foe made an appearance in favor of a new Green Bay stadium: George Halas. The Papa Bear bluntly stated the only way Green Bay could continue to compete in the NFL was to build a new facility. The vote carried by a 2-1 margin and the first cement was poured in February 1956 at a sight in the southwestern part of town.

The dedication of the new City Stadium on the weekend of September 29, 1957 was a proud moment for the town and the whole state. It was a weekend of parades and pageantry with famous dignitaries converging on tiny Green Bay, led by Vice President Richard Nixon, Wisconsin Governor Vernon Thomson, Green Bay Mayor Otto Rachals, and Miss America Marilyn VanDerBur. Also, *Gunsmoke*'s James Arness rode in the parade and reenacted scenes from the popular western TV show. The fun didn't stop there, however. Featured in the weekend festivities were Leo Lefebvre's clown act, Diane Desohaney's acrobatic act, and the singing group Spud City Four. All of this, of course, being supported by city businesses like Posey's Hi-way Furniture and Izzy's Ambulance Service.

The inaugural game for the new stadium was the season opener against the Bears, in a game that could have been scripted by a Hollywood writer. After a long Bears' drive netted a touchdown on an Ed Brown keeper, a 38-yard pass to Billy Howton from the newly re-acquired Babe Parilli tied the game, 7-7. With 8:21 left in the game and the Bears ahead, 17-14, Parilli tossed a 6-yard pass to receiver Gary Knafelc for what was the winning touchdown and a 21-17 Packers' upset victory to the delight of the partisan 32,125 Packers' fans.

Vice President Nixon spoke to the crowd at half-time, praising the city of Green Bay for building the stadium without looking for financial help from the government. Nixon said helping dedicate the stadium was among the more pleasant duties he had experienced and called Green Bay "the best known little city in the United States today." The icing on the cake was a visit from Nixon to both locker rooms after the game.

With the new stadium, beautiful weather, visiting dignitaries, and the huge win, the *Press-Gazette* boastfully stated that, "Green Bay has produced a lot of spectaculars in its long history, but never anything like this. Anybody who wasn't satisfied is the kind of fellow who would growl about not getting eggs in his beer."

Sadly for the Packers, the egg would be on their face for the remainder of the season. Winning only one of their next five games, the Packers prepared to meet the equally punchless 2-4 Bears in Chicago, where Blackbourn's crew had won only six games in twenty-two years.

Poor penalty calls from the officials aided Chicago in a 21-14 win. With the game tied, 14-14, and facing a third down and twenty-two, Bart Starr threw a pass that was caught by receiver Joe Johnson, bobbled, then hauled into the end zone for an apparent touchdown. But an official wrongly ruled the pass incomplete and the Bears held on for the victory.

Another incident brought the wrath of Lisle Blackbourn down on the officials. In the third quarter, Chicago defensive end Doug Atkins took his fist and punched offensive guard Jim Salsbury in full view of an official. Not only was Atkins not ejected from the game, a penalty wasn't even called.

It would be that kind of season for the Packers. Inconsistency, bad calls, blowouts, and a lack of team unity dropped the Packers into last place in the National Conference at 3-9.

Towards the end of the season a heated exchange between Blackbourn and the Executive Committee signaled a parting of the ways. Blackbourn was called to the carpet by the Committee about not playing Paul Hornung enough. One committee member felt they were owed an explanation on why the high-priced Hornung was sitting the bench. Blackbourn basically told them it was none of their business.

Plainly seeing that his contract would not be renewed, Blackbourn decided to return to Marquette to coach football. He even asked Bart Starr to follow him to Marquette to be an assistant coach. Blackbourn approached Starr, bluntly predicted his future, and tried to sell him on the idea of coaching.

"I don't think you'll ever make more than backup quarterback,"

Blackbourn told Starr. "I think you could be a great help teaching. You're a natural. How about coming with me to Marquette University as an assistant coach?"

Although Starr declined the offer and was determined to make it as a pro quarterback, his exchange with Blackbourn certainly didn't produce a rise in his confidence level.

In 1954, the Packers acquired pass catcher Gary Knafelc from the Chicago Cardinals for virtually nothing. This was clearly a case where an injury helped bring the talented receiver from Colorado University to the tiny hamlet of Green Bay, where he became a starter until 1962.

"I was drafted out of Colorado by the Chicago Cardinals in the second round in 1954," Gary remarked. "I joined the Packers in the same year. I started the first three ball games for the Cardinals. Then I got a badly pulled hamstring injury. It wouldn't heal because they kept playing me. I just couldn't get well. I was let go by the Cardinals and I was picked up by the Packers. The Packers let me rest for almost four weeks and didn't play me much that first year, but they kept me."

Playing against the hated Bears produced some of Knafelc's most painful memories.

"Joe Fortunato was the linebacker outside and Bill George was the middle linebacker and I had to block them a lot," Knafelc said. "They were the ones I played against mostly. All the Bears were rough. Bill George especially. Then, of course, Doug Atkins. I remember one play when he came to hit me and actually picked me up and threw me. I came down on a crack-down block and he hated for someone to clip him or hold him. All I could do was to hold him because I wasn't big enough to block him. I'd clip him or hold him whenever I could. He didn't take kindly to that at all. He was a tough guy.

"My first game I went up against Ed Sprinkle. He was still playing my rookie year. He was very aggressive. He'd really let you have it on every opportunity.

"At flanker, I came down against Don Kindt mostly. When I

played against Don as a rookie, he gave me a 'welcome to the NFL' deal. They always baptized a rookie. I ran an 18-yard turn-in route, caught the ball, and Don was coming up hard on my outside. He was about six foot, 225 pounds and could run the hundred in about 9.1 seconds. I made a fake to the inside and he went to the outside and missed me. So about four plays later I caught the ball on a 12-yard turn-in pattern and I made the same move. He just came right down the field and didn't try to tackle me at all. He hit me in the head with his elbow and just flattened me. In fact, my head hit the ground before my cleats got out. I was sitting on my fanny with my hands over my mouth because I was bleeding. I thought I'd lost all my teeth. He just walked by and looked at me and said, 'Welcome to the NFL' and kept walking. I just shook my head and from then on I called him Mr. Kindt."

Gary was one of the many players in that era who was just thankful for the chance to play pro ball.

"I enjoyed every bit of it," he said. "I couldn't believe I was getting paid to play. I even loved practice. I just loved to get out there to run and play. I would have played for nothing. There are some players these days who play for the love of it, but not many.

"We made more money playing basketball in the off-season than we did playing football, when we were winning that is. That's why many of the Packers in my era stayed around town because we had to make a living and have another job in the off season. It was cheaper to live in Green Bay and you could get a job in the off season and take advantage of your name. That's why we were so nice to everybody. We were hoping they were going to buy something from you later on."

Gary had no problem recalling the City Stadium dedication game. That's the day the Vice President of the United States waved hello to him while he was standing in the shower buck naked!

"The dedication day for new City Stadium in 1957 was against the Bears," he said, choking back a laugh. "The Vice President was there and all. Babe Parilli was playing quarterback at that time. I caught a touchdown in the last minute of the ballgame and we beat the Bears. Anyway, Al Carmichael was playing for us. Al was one of these guys who always could do better or knew something better. I knew Miss America who was from Colorado. So I was telling everyone that I knew her and all this stuff. Well, Al said he knew Richard Nixon. I said, 'Come on, Al, what the hell is going on?' He kept saying, 'Dick and I are real good buddies.'

"After the game, Al and I are in the shower and we hear a commotion. The Vice President was coming into the locker room. So I'm thinking since I caught the winning touchdown that he naturally wants to meet me. We saw this head come around the corner and Nixon made that smile and that wave like he always did. I waved back at him and he yelled out, 'Hey, Al, how ya doing?' Al *did* know him! Nixon did say hello to me but not the way I thought he was going to. I said, 'Al, I'll be goddamn.' "

George Halas was sitting in the Wrigley Field press box during the finishing moments of the Bears' final 1957 season game with Detroit watching his beloved team lose their seventh game of the year. He writhed at the depths to which his Bears had fallen. Only a year ago they had competed for the championship, now they were about to finish in fourth place.

Halas was tired of spending his days behind a desk, pushing paper, and manning the phones in the press box during games. Even though the distance between the press box and the playing field was not far, to Halas it might as well have been the distance of the Lake Michigan shoreline.

Halas promoted Coach Paddy Driscoll to a vice-president position in the front office and took back the head coaching job. Papa Bear Halas would once again be ruling the sidelines, giving officials and his opponents hell. He also hired two new assistant coaches, Chuck Mather and an end coach from the Los Angeles Rams, George Allen.

With a defense led by linebackers Bill George and Joe Fortunato, and linemen Doug Atkins, Bill Bishop, and Fred Williams, Halas had the nucleus of a good team expected to compete.

Two important offensive acquisitions were running back and receiver Johnny Morris from the University of California, and offensive guard Abe Gibron. Morris would wear a Bears' uniform for the next ten years. Gibron, acquired through a trade with the Philadelphia Eagles, would play two more years, become an assistant coach, and later the Bears' head coach.

Before resigning the head coaching job, Lisle Blackbourn and Jack Vainisi got together for the 1958 draft of college players, a draft that would be most fertile for Green Bay. Blackbourn and Vainisi agreed they needed to make toughness a top priority in the '58 draft.

"I never got a chance to use those kids," Blackbourn said once. "But I can remember going over our situation that year with Vainisi. We talked about how this club we had—that 1957 club—had run-down quite a bit. It got so they weren't tough enough. Whatever our choices were to be that year, it was going to be somebody mean and tough."

Four of the Packers first seven picks were fullback Jim Taylor from LSU, linebacker Dan Currie from Michigan State, fullback Ray Nitschke from the University of Illinois, and guard and kicker Jerry Kramer from the University of Idaho.

Taylor was a bone-smashing runner known to run over defenders rather than around them. He made people pay for tackling him. In scouting reports, Taylor was described as "tough as hell but lazy in his blocking." Currie would be a defensive standout until 1964. Nitschke would be switched from a fullback to a bruising and deathly feared linebacker, and became one of the game's greatest at his position.

In a scouting report in 1957, Kramer was said to have "good speed and mobility." He was also called "a good looking kid who does not choke." The rap against him was, a scout wrote, dropping his head on pass blocks and his smallish size. "He should go in the service and come back for signing," the scout noted. Finally, the scout rated Kramer about where he thought the Packers should draft him. "If you consider field goals, PAT's, and kickoffs, draft 5-10," meaning that they should draft him between the fifth and tenth rounds. "If not," the scout wrote, "15-25 because you will have to wait some on size." Jerry Kramer was drafted in the fourth round and was a stalwart on the offensive line until 1968 with his near perfect play, and became a reliable kicker. He would single-handedly win the 1962 championship game with his kicking. He also made what became one of the most famous blocks in NFL history in the 1967 championship game.

It was a stunning array of talent for a new coach to control. That job of new Packers' head coach went to Blackbourn's assistant coach Ray "Scooter" McLean. McLean had played running back for the Bears in the Forties and had been named an assistant coach by Gene Ronzani in 1951. The Executive Committee's decision was a popular one with Packers' fans the players, the latter being the reason McLean wouldn't be around for long. A confident McLean boasted that his Packers were shooting for a good season and were going to be in the fight for the championship.

To look at the Green Bay Packers' squad on paper in 1958, it was easy for any Packers' fan to be excited about the upcoming season. This team would be the nucleus of one of the greatest teams in pro football history. On offense was quarterback Bart Starr, Paul Hornung and Jim Taylor at running backs, and receivers Max McGee, Gary Knafelc, and Billy Howton. The line was solid with center Jim Ringo, Jerry Kramer and Hank Bullough at guard, Forrest Gregg and Norm Masters at tackle.

The defensive line had veteran Dave Hawg Hanner, with Ray Nitschke, Dan Currie and Bill Forester at linebacker, and Bobby Dillon, Hank Grimminger, and Jesse Whittenton at defensive back. Missing from the squad were end Ron Kramer and offensive tackle Bob Skronski, on military leave.

So how in the world did this talent-laden team become the worst team in Green Bay Packer history? Simple. Head Coach Scooter McLean had no control over the team. He allowed players to set training rules and abide by them by the honor system; and wanting to be one of the boys, he often played poker with players the night before a game. His disciplinary problems centered around a few certain but important players. Many portray handsome "Golden Boy" Paul Hornung as a mischievous pied-piper leading other players out to break curfew for a wild night on the town. Granted, Hornung always had an audience. Hornung could visit the North Pole and a party would break out. But Max McGee, Jerry Kramer, Dan Currie, and others were ready and willing participants.

McLean tried to take control by fining five of the players during training camp. He wanted to keep discipline matters private from the press. Some members of the Executive Committee disagreed with him, arguing that making the news public just might act as a deterrent for other players. McLean got his way, but his role as an authoritarian and taskmaster was a joke. His disciplinary problems steadily worsened as the season began.

McLean debuted as head coach against the Bears on September 28 at new City Stadium in front of 32,150. Fumbles and Willie "the Wisp" Galimore were the Packers undoing, leading to a, 34-20. Chicago victory. The fleet-footed Galimore scored on rushes of one and eight yards, a 79-yard pass, and added 130 yards in total offense. Leading, 21-13, at half-time, Galimore and the Bears totally dominated the second half.

"We'll come around," a positive McLean said after the game. "We played probably the greatest team in this league today—we'll come around."

The Packers didn't "come around" as McLean predicted. After a tie and a three-point win over Philadelphia, the 1-4-1 Packers traveled to Chicago to play the 4-2 Bears on a sunny but cold day at Wrigley Field. This was an important game not so much for in the standings, since the Packers were out of the race anyway, but just for the mind-set of the team. The Packers came into the Chicago game after being totally decimated by the Baltimore Colts a week before, 56-0. The shattering loss and the team's discipline problems threatened to unravel the whole season. A win against their rivals would loosen the pressure on McLean a bit.

Green Bay fought bravely and found themselves behind only 7-3 at half-time. The hometown Bears, hearing the jeers and boo's from the partisan 48,424 in attendance, came out in the second half, dominated the Packers, and won, 24-10. Two mistakes by Bart Starr, a fumble in the end zone and an interception return, and a fine rushing performance by Bears' veteran runner Rick Casares, led to the crushing defeat. Green Bay's only scores came on a 45-yard field goal by Paul Hornung and a Jim Taylor plunge for a touchdown.

McLean barred the press from the Packers' locker room after the game, but he did tell them that, "If they give that kind of effort from here on in, they'll start hitting. If they keep going all out, we'll be all right."

It's safe to say that Scooter McLean was not one of the more superlative fact divulging and communicative orators.

He was also not a very good head coach. The Packers, now totally coming apart, hit rock bottom when they lost the remainder of their games; one to the Lions, and two apiece to Los Angeles and San Francisco. At each game's final gun, the Packers were never even close.

The 1-10-1 record posted by the 1958 Green Bay Packers is the worst in franchise history. The only season of futility that comes close to it was the Lambeau-led squad of 1949 that went 2-10.

It had been a disastrous season. The team was in total disarray, going nowhere, and the promising talent the Packers had was going to waste. Something had to be done. It was plain to see that the Executive Committee had a difficult decision to make on whether to keep McLean on board or to look somewhere else for a coach.

McLean made the decision for them. Soon after the season ended, McLean resigned the head coaching job and was hired by the Detroit Lions as an assistant coach. He's remembered in Green Bay as being a real gentleman and good guy, but his downfall was his inability to control the players on the team. This was a team of cliques, poor attitudes, and the aforementioned curfew problems. They all contributed to the dismal performance of the Green Bay Packers of 1958.

To say that Chicago Bears' defensive end Doug Atkins was one of the game's most colorful characters is a gross understatement. Humorously odd stories have always surrounded and followed Atkins. At any NFL reunion get-together you can bet on a Doug Atkins' story being told. His country bumpkin-like delivery was strangely calming, particularly because the mountainous Atkins was a man among men on the field, ferociously dominating line play in every game he played.

"Playing opposite Doug Atkins," Detroit offensive tackle John Gonzaga once said, "is like having your pants taken down in front of 60,000 people."

Doug began his career in Cleveland under the tutelage of the masterful Paul Brown. Weeb Ewbank, Brown's assistant, traveled to Knoxville to sign the Humbolt, Tennessee All-American. "He was probably the most magnificent physical specimen I'd ever seen," Weeb once recalled. The story goes that Atkins took Ewbank out to a bar to get him drunk so he could sign a contract for his price. Atkins' plan backfired when Ewbank turned the tables. It wasn't long before Atkins was the one who was under the table full to the back teeth!

"Hell, the true story is that I signed for $6,800, eight beers, and two hamburgers," Atkins remembered.

Doug played in Cleveland in 1953 and '54, then was traded to the Bears in 1955. It had always been rumored that he didn't fit in at Cleveland under the strict disciplinarian Paul Brown

"I don't know how all these stories start," Doug said honestly. "If you're outspoken and say what you think, you've got a lot of problems in this world. I never gave Paul Brown any problems at all. He never talked to me about misbehaving. I wasn't fined, I wasn't called in. I never got caught out after curfew. I don't know what they're talking about. It's all bullshit. You hear all these things—they have me riding tractors in camp when I've never driven one. It's bullshit."

There had been another rumor about Doug shooting apart a rookie's radio in New Orleans in the late Sixties when he playing for the Saints.

"That's another lie," Atkins said. "It was in San Diego by the ocean. I carried a little gun with me all the time. One night the rookies were raising a little racket and I hollered at them. I was on the second floor and they were on the third. I got the old gun out, took the screen off and shot up the side of the screen. It sounded like a cannon going off. It did quiet down. I don't know how all of these things get started but I did fire two or three shots up towards the window."

What about the story that he used to shoot at pigeons at Wrigley Field during practice?

"I did not carry a gun into Wrigley Field. Nobody goes to practice with a gun in Wrigley Field. It's all bullshit."

Atkins was one of the Bears' players who often tangled with George Halas, but both men had great respect for each other. Atkins mixes praise with criticism when the subject of Halas comes up.

"I got along with Halas," Doug stated. "Coach Halas was a pioneer of the game but football had begun to pass him by when I got there. We had a few disagreements and he was hard to deal with but I got along with him. He was a likable man. He was lots of fun to talk to. I didn't have really any problems with Halas."

Contract discussions with Papa Bear were notoriously heated.

"Halas just didn't want to pay you anything," Atkins maintained. "I had to fight for five hundred dollars. Five hundred raise was big back then. He was a real businessman. He made Scrooge look like the Good Fairy."

Atkins claimed that Halas hired sleuth hounds to trail players and even coaches around, having the amateur gumshoes report back on any curfew breakers or players breaking rules. Characteristically, it was Doug Atkins' scheme that got one of Halas' "H Men" drunk to have him confess the identify of his employer.

"Halas had the Burns Detective Agency follow us around after practice to see where we would go and write reports on us," Atkins recalled. "Where you were, how many beers you had, and what you did. One time I got fined a half a game's salary for drinking beer.

"One night at a local watering hole a detective who worked for Burns came over nosing around. I got him three-fourth's drunk and he tells me what's going on. Then Halas would tell us a true Chicago Bears' fan turned you in. It wasn't a fan. It was a guy who worked with the Burns Detective Agency."

Some of Doug Atkins' best games came against the Packers. He recalled traveling to the games in Green Bay, Halas' paranoia, and iced-down beer.

"I remember we took the train up there and all the Bears' fans took the same train. On the way back, the fans' car had beer iced down. We weren't supposed to go to their car but we'd sneak over there and sometimes it took us a while to get back. We always enjoyed the trip back from those games.

"When we went to Green Bay, the wind was always a little different in that new stadium. Halas always had a weather man up there with a balloon in the end zone checking the wind. Before the game, Halas would tell us which way the wind was blowing. He did this just for the Green Bay game."

It was Doug Atkins' job to shut down the famed Packer Sweep. It was a play that Vince Lombardi designed to get his running backs to the outside and into the open field. Both offensive guards would pull in the direction of the play, blocking for the back. Opponents knew it was coming, but rarely did they stop it.

"If you have the right defense you could stop it," Doug said. "The Packers charted our plays and we charted theirs. We tried to anticipate what they were going to do. If Green Bay called an audible on you, and you had a defense where you're expecting something else, there was no way to stop them. When they came back to the weak side, Paul Hornung would be leading the play. If I had inside responsibility, all Hornung had to do was to make contact and by the time I got rid of him and started outside, the runner would be gone. I'd have to stay inside and take a hit from him. We'd stop them one time, two times, then they'd catch us in a rinky-dink defense and they'd pop it."

Doug finally had his fill of Chicago and Halas, and in 1967 he got his wish to be traded to the expansion New Orleans Saints.

Even though Doug Atkins and George Halas had what could be described as a love/hate relationship during the twelve years Atkins played in Chicago, in summing up Doug spoke sentimentally about his old coach.

"He was very charitable," Atkins said. "He gave a lot of money away. A lot of players needed help at times and he helped them. He was quite a character. I think if I had ever had to have had some money, he would have helped.

"You have to understand that he started the league," Doug added. "He had to sell all the tickets. He went in on a shoestring and that was just the time he was raised up in. He was conservative because of the way he started out. But he had to be. It was hard to understand that when you were playing there, but after reading a book or two, you saw how he had to work and you understood better."

One year during training camp Halas fined Atkins $100 a day for holding out for more money. When Doug finally returned nine days later, the fines had accumulated to $900. Atkins had the money taken out of his salary at the end of the season.

"Years later, I think it was the Bears' 1978 reunion, Halas comes up to me and says, 'How ya doing?' I said. 'I'm doing fine, but I'd feel better if you gave me that $900 you fined me a long time ago.' He said, 'Kid, I might just do that.' Sure enough, it wasn't a week later that I got a check. Halas gave it back to me."

1959

The Executive Committee of the Green Bay Packers had to once again find a new head coach to lead the Packers back to a respectable level. They had tried two insiders, assistant coaches Ronzani and McLean, and a successful college coach, Lisle Blackbourn. Now the Committee thought it best to try for a pro head coach or an assistant coach outside of the organization. They also wanted to hire a general manager to conduct the team's affairs. One man who threw his name in the hat to be general manager was none other than Curly Lambeau, who had returned to Green Bay in 1959 after living in California.

When any coaching job becomes vacant, rumor and speculation run rampant. Many names were being batted around including Blanton Collier, head coach of Kentucky, former Cleveland Browns' quarterback Otto Graham, and Forrest Evashevski, head coach of Iowa.

"We were lobbying for Curly Lambeau to come back," guard Jerry Kramer recalled. "We knew Scooter was gone the last couple of games. We were in Los Angeles and four or five of us had dinner with Curly: Hornung, McGee, Taylor, Ron Kramer. We talked about him coming back. We were all kind of excited about his record and his history. Then they named an assistant coach from the New York Giants that no one had ever heard of and we wondered how the hell they could do that."

Once again, Jack Vainisi was at the heart of a decision that would drastically change football fortunes in Green Bay. He suggested the name of New York Giants' offensive coach Vince Lombardi to be the next head coach. Packer President Dominic Olejniczak phoned Giants' owner Wellington Mara asking permission to talk to Lombardi. Mara suggested he talk to their defensive coach Tom Landry instead, but Olejniczak insisted on Lombardi.

The Executive Committee heard rave reviews from respected coaches and friends about Lombardi. Reluctantly, even George Halas gave Lombardi a glowing review and recommendation

Lombardi flew to Green Bay in late January and was interviewed for the job in Prange's Department Store. Two days later the announcement was made. Vince Lombardi was the head coach and general manager of the Green Bay Packers.

The first question out of everyone's mouth was, "Who the hell is Vince Lombardi?"

Vincent Thomas Lombardi was born on June 11, 1913 in Brooklyn, New York, where he spent most of his childhood with skinned-up knees and elbows playing sandlot football. He played offensive and defensive guard at St. Francis High School and entered Fordham University where he became one of the famous Seven Blocks of Granite.

Graduating in 1937 with a B.S. degree, Lombardi got his first head coaching job at St. Cecilia High School, where he stayed from 1939 to '47. He, like most everyone else at the time, adopted the T-formation offense after seeing the great success that George Halas had had with it in Chicago.

From 1947 to '48 Lombardi returned to Fordham to coach the freshmen recruits. In 1949 he moved on to become an assistant coach at West Point under Army's legendary coach Earl "Red" Blaik. Lombardi won Blaik over the first time the two met.

In 1954, Wellington Mara, a top executive with the New York Giants, called to ask Blaik's permission to talk to Vince about becoming an assistant coach there. Lombardi didn't like the idea of leaving his mentor coach at West Point but it was an offer he couldn't refuse. Vince coached the New York Giants' offense from 1954 to '58.

On February 2, Vince and his wife Marie were met at Green

Bay's Austin Straubel Field by a flock of media and onlookers as they arrived to be officially introduced to the Board of Directors. Lombardi addressed a luncheon at the Northland Hotel and let the Board of Directors know immediately where he and they stood. He told the gathering that he was in complete command and that he expected full cooperation from them, adding that they would have his.

He went on to say that the board had only two decisions to make. They had already made one in hiring him as head coach. The only other decision they had would be to fire him. He was simple and to the point. He wasn't going to be second guessed at the Board's weekly meeting like Ronzani, Blackbourn, and McLean had been. There would be no more Monday morning quarterbacking by anyone except him and his assistant coaches.

He was the boss!

Lombardi had his work cut out for him and he knew it. His first order of business was to eliminate any player who had a bad or defeatist attitude. He knew it was essential to have players who believed in his system and who would fight together side-by-side as a close-knit group and family. He needed them to make the sacrifice.

In April, Lombardi traded receiver Billy Howton to Cleveland for defensive tackle Henry Jordan, defensive end Bill Quinlan, and offensive back Lew Carpenter. It was an enormous trade for Green Bay. All three players were valuable participants in the Packers' rise back to the top, and it was Henry Jordan's stellar career with the Packers that eventually earned him that honor. Howton languished in Cleveland for one year then moved on to the Dallas Cowboys where his playing career silently ended.

Before training camp, Lombardi spoke to his new team about what he expected of them. He reminded them of the many ways they could be shipped out of town and how he was going to find players who would sacrifice to win. He assured them that he would find the players.

One of Lombardi's first priorities was to decide what to do with Paul Hornung. He was a great talent going to waste. Under Blackbourn's direction, Hornung had played halfback, fullback, and quarterback for the Packers. Lombardi simply told Hornung that he was going to be a halfback because of his ability to run, pass, and catch. Hornung's ability to run, pass, and catch reminded Lombardi of Frank Gifford, the versatile New York Giants' running back whom Lombardi had molded into a superstar. He also told Hornung that he had heard of his reputation of being a night owl womanizer but told him that he thought much of it was fictional and that he trusted him.

Vince Lombardi began weeding out the workers from the loafers the very first day of training camp. The players had never been through any training camp so vigorous and tough. They ran laps upon laps, endless wind sprints, and they suffered the fate of an exercise from hell called a grass drill. A player ran in place, lifting his knees as high as he could for maybe thirty seconds. When Lombardi yelled, "Down!" the players threw themselves on to the ground, landing on their face and stomach. When Lombardi yelled, "Up!" they quickly got to their feet and began running in place as before. While many teams had a grass drill to get players in shape, they would only do maybe eight or ten at a practice. If Vince was in a ill mood, it was common for him to make his team do sixty. It was pure torture. Players became exhausted, one was sent to the hospital for sunstroke, and all of them lost weight by the tons.

Jerry Kramer remembered his first encounter with Lombardi and that hellish first training camp.

"I went into training camp a few days early and Joe Francis, a quarterback from Oregon State, and I thought we'd play some golf and piddle around a few days before camp. We showed up without a hotel or anything. We were standing in the Packers' offices talking to Jack Vainisi, the general manager at the time. We told Jack we needed a room and he said camp didn't open for a few days and we'd have to get a hotel. We were bitching about having to pay for a hotel and trying to talk him into getting us a room.

"Well, Coach Lombardi walked by. 'What's the problem?' he asked. Vainisi explained we needed a place to stay because we're a couple of days early. He barely got the words out of his mouth and

Lombardi said, 'Find them a place to stay,' and went on. He didn't stop to say hello or introduce himself. It wasn't much of an impression.

"Francis and I got our golf clubs and were heading out to golf when Lombardi met us on the steps and asked where we were going. When I told him we were going to play golf, he said, 'Like hell you are! You're in the dormitory so you make all meetings, all practices, all curfews, all meals just like everyone else. Now, come to practice!' We thought, 'Who in the hell is this guy?'

"There must be a theory of military tactics in history about uniting a group of people against the leader by putting them through pure hell, because he put us through pure hell and made just about everybody there dislike him. But we were united together with one another in our resentment of him. From the very first day you could see his no-nonsense, business-like attitude of 'let's get to work and get after it.'"

Lombardi and his Packers "got after it" in the pre-season, winning four of their six games, quickly establishing a winning attitude. Still, heading into the season, the trouble spot on the team was Lombardi's choice of a quarterback. Lamar McHan, Bart Starr, and Joe Francis were all fighting for the starting position, with no one of the three standing out from the other. Starr was the real mystery. Many thought, like his former coach Lisle Blackbourn, he would never make it in the NFL. He was shy, he was withdrawn, he didn't say much. His physical skills seemed too limited and critics questioned his toughness to be a big league quarterback. As Starr admitted later, his real problem was a lack of confidence. He had shown signs of good play in his first two years but nothing spectacular. He was a player who needed a caring coach who would take him under his wing and give him the confidence he desperately needed.

In the last pre-season game, the bigger and tougher Lamar McHan performed better than Starr and Francis, and got the starting nod when the Packers opened the 1959 season against Halas and the Bears.

Lombardi gave a rousing pep talk before the game. It was amazing some players didn't injure themselves attempting to get out the door so fast.

The Packers could have made it a rout early on. Instead, they narrowly missed three touchdowns by mere inches. With an on-again off-again rain falling in the first quarter, Hornung barely over-threw a pass to Lew Carpenter in the clear; Gary Knafelc suffered the same fate after he got behind Bear defender J. C. Caroline; and lanky rookie Boyd Dowler dropped a certain TD pass on the Bears' 15-yard line.

The Packers' offense was sloppy, having a slew of dropped pass-es, fumbles, and penalties that killed drives. Along with those bad breaks, Hornung darkened the day by missing three field goals from thirteen, nineteen, and twenty-six yards out.

While the Packers' offense struggled, the defense held the Bears at bay, eventually beating them. Green Bay defenders completely snuffed out Chicago's running game, allowing Casares and Galimore only fifty-seven total yards rushing.

With the score 6-0 Chicago in the fourth quarter, Bears' rookie halfback Ritchie Petitbon fumbled a Max McGee punt on his 26-yard line and Jim Ringo recovered for the Packers. Moments later, Bart Starr called 28-Weak, a play that resulted in Jimmy Taylor rumbling over Bears' linemen Doug Atkins and Earl Leggett scor-ing the only touchdown of the game, and a 7-6 Packers' lead. With forty-seven seconds left in the game, Ed Brown was tackled in the end zone for a safety by Packer veteran Dave "Hawg" Hanner. Like a script out of Hollywood, Lombardi and his Packers beat the rival Bears, 9-6.

The stunning upset made all of Packerland delirious. City Stadium looked like the end of a military graduation ceremony as hats, cushions, and game programs few into the air as the Packers' faithful let loose with joyous abandon. Lombardi was so excited that he planted a big kiss on the mouth of Max McGee. In a great show of emotion, a group of Packer players swept Lombardi off his feet and carried him off the water-sogged turf on their shoulders.

After his impromptu ride Lombardi relaxed after the game, say-ing, "It's just like I told you when I first came here. You have to have a defense to win in this game. Our defense did a tremendous job.

"We played a very emotional game," he added. "We have a ten-dency to get too emotional. That's all right defensively but it's no good offensively."

A saddened George Halas congratulated the Packers and their new coach after the game. "You have to hand it to Vince Lombardi, he did a splendid job," Halas said. "The Packers have made a great transition under him and are going to be a powerful factor in the Western Division race."

Amazingly, the Packers went on to win their next two games and were 3-0, which put them in first place, but not for long. A disheartening three-game losing streak brought Lombardi's Packers down to earth and on to the turf of Wrigley field on November 7 for the rematch.

The mistake-prone Packers gave the Bears two touchdowns on fumbles, as Hornung had what would be his worst day as a pro, rushing the ball four times for a minus three yards and three fumbles. To finish off a "game of threes," Starr led the Packers inside the Bears' 5-yard line three times but failed to score a touchdown. Green Bay's passing offense was pathetic, with Starr and McHan combining for only 72 yards in the air.

The Bears' overpowered the Packers, 28-17, in the 80th meeting between the two teams. Offsetting their weak season opener, the Bears' running game returned with a total of 172 yards.

With twenty-seven seconds left, Lombardi paced the sidelines muttering to anyone who cared to listen that, "The best team didn't win today, I'll tell you." After the game he boldly stated, "We should have won the ball game, in fact, we should have had at least thirty-five points."

Halas disagreed, saying, "The Packers were just as good today as they were in that opening 9-6 victory at Green Bay in September, only we were better than we were in Green Bay." He also went on to graciously call the Packers "a tough bunch of *hombres*."

1959 was a pivotal year for Green Bay. The Packers finally found their offense in their remaining five games, winning four of them, while running up consistent scores of 24, 21, 24, 38, and 36 points. They finished a respectable 7-5 on the year, their best since 1944, winning top honors for Lombardi as NFL's Coach of the Year.

The 1960s

Guardian Angels, the Wisp, a Golden Boy, and a Kansas Comet

Every man who reported to the Green Bay Packers' training camp in mid-July 1960, came better prepared than they had the year before. No Packer needed to have a fortune teller to predict what it be like at Vince Lombardi's Training Camp From Hell, Part Two.

The difference in this training camp from the previous one was the attitude of the entire squad. Behind the incessant driving of Lombardi, the defeatist and loser mentality had vanished with the success of the '59 squad. Lombardi was the most intense person anyone of them had ever come into close contact with. He had the personality and conviction that made his team believe in him, follow his direction, and completely sacrifice themselves heart and soul to a common goal. To achieve this, Vince simply worked their asses off. No team had ever worked so hard—and no team would have the success they were about to have.

The quarterback question was finally answered during the pre-season when Lombardi ended the flip-flop of the team's signal caller by telling Bart Starr that he was his quarterback and there would be no more waffling on the matter. For a player who severely lacked confidence, "You are going to be my quarterback" were the seven greatest words Starr had ever heard. He could now comfortably settle into the job with the assurance that he wouldn't have his pride hurt by being pulled from the game.

A little known fact is that after the 1960 season, Lombardi would try to trade Bart Starr away. Vince had contacted the Dallas Cowboys and offered any two Packers—Starr, Jim Taylor, whomever—for quarterback Don Meredith. The Cowboys refused. It can be only speculated how differently the fortunes of the Green Bay Packers and Vince Lombardi would have turned out had the trade been consummated.

The Packers' breezed through the pre-season winning all six games. Although it was the team's tenth straight victory, Lombardi knew it didn't mean anything. He was about to be proven correct.

The 32,150 fans who packed City Stadium to see the season curtain-raiser with the Bears witnessed the first loss by the Packers on home turf since November 1958. It would be a frustrating game for the Pack, who had the upper hand on the Midway Monsters most of the day but couldn't put them away. They scored three separate touchdowns, only to have them all nullified by penalties.

Bruiser back Jim Taylor rumbled over from the 1-yard line to give the Packers a 7-0 lead at half-time. Backfield cohort Paul Hornung added a 2-yard run in the third period, and the game seemed well in hand until the fourth quarter when the Packers suddenly became generous. Bears' back Willie Galimore scampered eighteen yards for a touchdown, edging Chicago closer, 14-7.

On the next series, Jim Taylor fumbled and the Bears' swarming defense recovered the ball. Three plays later Rick Casares galloped twenty-six yards for the tying touchdown, the Bears' second touchdown in less than two minutes.

With three minutes left in the game a Bart Starr pass was batted up in the air by Bears' defensive tackle Earl Leggett, intercepted, and downed on the Packers' 32-yard line. With thirty-five seconds left, kicker John Aveni booted a 16-yard field goal and the Bears had the win, 17-14.

Lombardi offered no alibis, simply saying, "We made too many mistakes, that's it in a nutshell."

George Halas had less praise for his team and more condemnation for the field conditions, which he saw as deplorable. A high school game had been played the previous Friday night at Lambeau Field in a pouring rain, turning the field into slop. "It is a beautiful stadium and, therefore, it's a pity to let such a thing happen," Halas said after the game. "It would be just like building a beautiful home and putting sawdust on the floors for carpeting. Allowing the high schools to play in the stadium over the weekend was the first serious mistake the city had made in years."

Life Magazine photographer George Silk, seeking to capture a panoramic view of the game, was permitted to position a camera on the 40-yard line just to the left of the ball before the second half kickoff. Set at a 180-degree angle, the camera was operated from the sideline. It vividly captured Paul Hornung's kickoff, the advance of players, the vicious collisions, and the bulging stands. As soon as Chicago's Johnny Morris was tackled on the 29-yard line, a Packers' property man sprinted out to retrieve the camera.

In the return match, the Packers brought a 5-4 record to Chicago while the Bears bested that with a 5-3-1 mark. This game would show the rise of Lombardi's Packers and the beginning of the end for Halas' 1960 squad.

Paul Hornung would become a record breaker on this day. The "Blonde Bullet" scored twenty-three points to bring his season total to 152, erasing Don Hutson's eighteen-year-old record of 138 points. The 41-13 victory was the worst beating the Packers had ever given their rivals and elevated them into a three-way tie with Baltimore and San Francisco for the Western Division lead. The win was the first for the Packers in Chicago since 1952 and only the second win there since 1941.

It was also an emotional victory. Jack Vainisi, an architect of Lombardi's budding championship squad, had begun having chest pains more frequently. "I think they probably came from the stress and strain of the job," his brother once said. "He was working until 11:00 or 12 o'clock every night preparing for the draft at the time. All those hours caught up with him."

The week before the second Packers-Bears game, Vainisi succumbed to a heart spasm, unjustly ending his life at thirty-three years old. His death was widely felt by the Packer players because Vainisi had been instrumental in drafting many of them to Green Bay. He had scouted them, drafted them, and went out of his way to treat each player well on a personal level. He was a hands-on guy and he would be sorely missed.

Before the Bears' game, Lombardi addressed his squad. "You have three good reasons for winning today," he said. "For Jack, for the tradition of this great game, and for the title. Now let's go and get it!"

"Did that set everyone off!" Bart Starr remembered. "I've never seen anything like it."

An inspired Paul Hornung played for Jack Vainisi that day in Wrigley Field. It was unfortunate, Hornung and the others thought, that Jack would never get to see the results of his hard work. For on this day, the Packers played errorless football, clearly showing the Bears and the entire league what they could do as a unit.

On the first play of the game, Jim Taylor ran the ball out of bounds on the Bears' sideline and ferociously hit a Bear simply standing there. A fist-slinging donnybrook ensued that took officials awhile to break up. Taylor didn't stop hitting anyone in a dark blue uniform the whole day. He pounded out 140 yards, one touchdown on the ground, and personally injured three Bears' defensive backs.

But it was the brilliant Paul Hornung who stole the show. Hornung caught a 17-yard TD pass from Starr, ran ten yards for a score, kicked two field goals of twenty-one and forty-one yards, and booted five extra points. He tallied 68 rushing yards and caught three passes for 32 yards. It was a stunning performance.

"He won it for us," Hornung said of the late Vainisi. "His death was weighing heavily on us all week. He wanted this game more than anything, and we knew it."

After the devastating loss to Green Bay, the Bears traveled to Cleveland, got swamped, 42-0, and then got shellacked by Detroit, 36-0, in the final game of the season. It was a terrible way to end what had started out to be a good year. At 5-6-1, the Bears weren't going anywhere.

Green Bay, on the other hand, was going somewhere. After the Bears' game, the Packers made their usual West Coast swing, beating the 49ers and the Rams, and headed for Franklin Field in Philadelphia for the 1960 Championship Game with the Norm Van Brocklin-led Eagles.

The bitterly fought game ended with linebacker Chuck Bednarik tackling Jim Taylor at the 9-yard line on the last play of the game. "This game's over!" he bellowed as he stood over the prone Taylor. Philadelphia had won, 17-13.

Addressing his players in the locker room afterwards, Lombardi quietly told them that they could have won the game and a loss like this would not happen again.

And it never would.

George Halas knew he had to rebuild his team. It gnawed at him to have the rival Packers to the north grabbing all the glory. He wanted it back.

The Bears' defense, that had been second best in 1959 but had allowed 299 points in 1960, was still considered a solid group. Dave Whitsell, Rosey Taylor, Richie Petitbon and J. C. Caroline were outstanding defensive backs. The linebacking corps was one of the best in football. Bill George, Joe Fortunato and Larry Morris made many a blocker and ball carrier pay for coming into their area. Doug Atkins and Fred Williams anchored the line.

It was the offense that had suddenly become inept. To beef up his scoring machine, Halas acquired Los Angeles Rams' quarterback Bill Wade. It would be a profitable trade for both Halas and Wade.

"I wanted to be traded from the Rams because of the circumstances out there," Wade recollected. "Bob Waterfield was the coach of the Rams. I could never get any satisfaction. In 1960, when I would make a mistake, he would pull me out of the game. So, my ultimatum was either let me play every play I was physically able to play, or trade me.

"I had a very close friend, Hall Bartlett, who produced and directed seventeen major movies. Hall had asked me to be a godparent to his oldest daughter. The NFL rules stated that I could not make a trade for myself, therefore, I asked Hall to intervene for me and we narrowed the choice to two teams: the Chicago Bears and the Cleveland Browns. Those were the two clubs that Hall contacted to see if they were interested in me. George Halas and the Chicago Bears allowed the quarterback to call most of their own plays, consequently, Hall and I decided that Chicago would be the best place for me. A trade was arranged with the Bears.

"I never asked Coach Halas for one penny in the seven years I was with the Bears. I always let him tell me what he wanted to pay me. I had no agent. I'd say: 'That's fine, Coach, I'm here to play football.'

"I admired Coach Halas. He was an extremely hard-working man who had to run an organization as well as coach. Vince Lombardi just had to coach. There's quite a difference. Halas had

George Stanley Halas

Earl "Curly" Lambeau

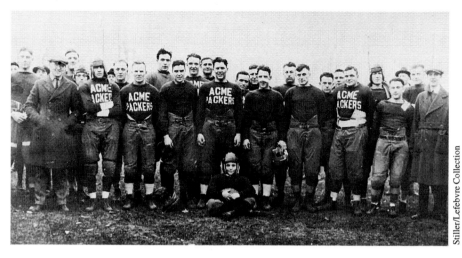

1921 Green Bay Packers (Lambeau center front row)

1924 Chicago Bears pose in Cubs Park
From left: George Trafton (3rd), George Halas (12th), Hunk Anderson (13th),
Dutch Sternaman (15th), Joey Sternaman (16th)

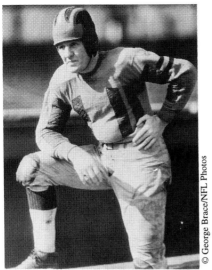

Harold "Red" Grange

Bronko Nagurski

Don Hutson

Johnny "Blood" McNally

Packers-Bears action at Green Bay, October 14, 1923

Bears vs. Packers at Wrigley Field, 1939 — Clarke Hinkle (30) ready to tackle Frank Bausch (54)

Packers' Cecil Isbell is pursued by a host of Bears

Bears' Bill Osmanski eludes Packers' Ed Neal (58) and Don Wells (43); Sid Luckman (42) in background

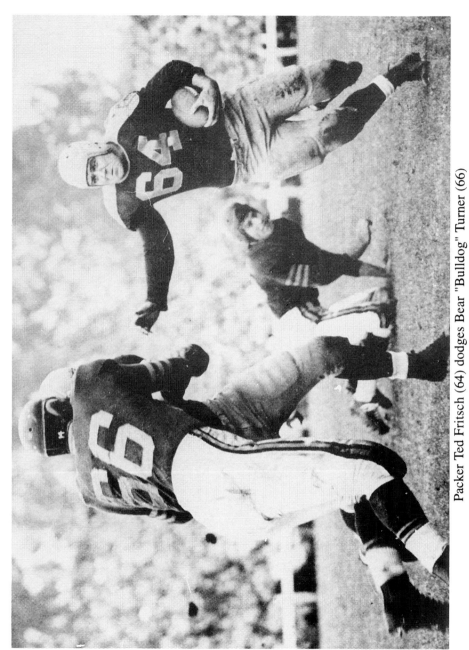

Packer Ted Fritsch (64) dodges Bear "Bulldog" Turner (66)

Stiller/Lefebvre Collection

Bear George Connor (81) running for yardage, Packers Carl Schuette and Steve Pritko (23)

Packers' Tony Canadeo stiff-arms a Bear defender

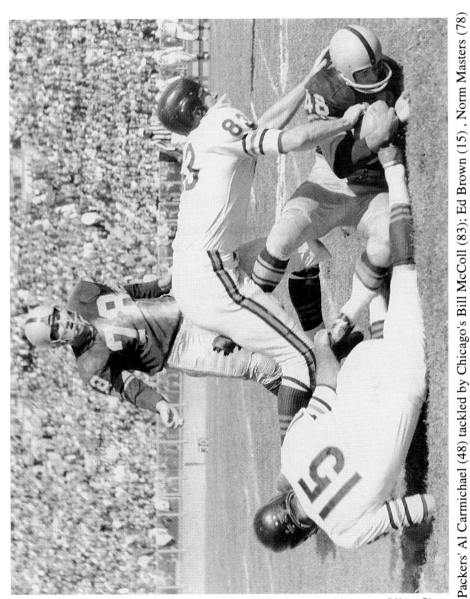

© Vernon Biever

Packers' Al Carmichael (48) tackled by Chicago's Bill McColl (83); Ed Brown (15) , Norm Masters (78)

Billy Howton (86) picks up yardage against the Bears.
Packers' Babe Parelli (10), Max McGee (85), Gary Knafelc (84);
Bears' Doug Atkins (81), Bill George (61), Joe Fortunato (31)

Vince Lombardi (L) enjoys a pre-game moment with "Papa Bear" Halas

Green Bay's Bart Starr

Mike Ditka cradles a pass

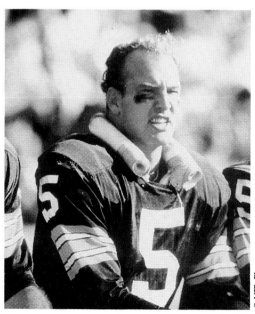

"Golden Boy" Paul Hornung

Burly Bear Dick Butkus (51) hammers Packer quarterback Don Horn (13)

Ray Nitschke (66) towers over Bears' quarterback Rudy Bukich (10)

© Vernon Biever

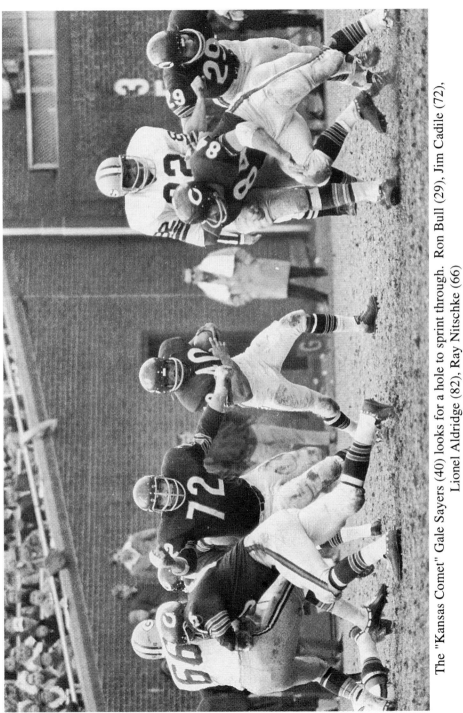

The "Kansas Comet" Gale Sayers (40) looks for a hole to sprint through. Ron Bull (29), Jim Cadile (72), Lionel Aldridge (82), Ray Nitschke (66)

Chicago linebacker Doug Buffone (55) bear hugs Green Bay's
John Brockington (42)

Walter Payton (34) breaks free from the grasp of a Packer defender

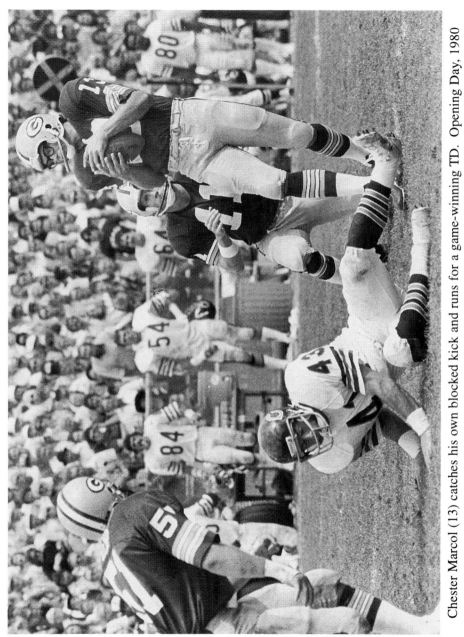

Chester Marcol (13) catches his own blocked kick and runs for a game-winning TD. Opening Day, 1980

William "The Refrigerator" Perry (72) is ready to pounce on a Packers' ball carrier

Chicago quarterback Jim Harbaugh (4) hands off to Neal Anderson (35)

Brett Farve (4) sets his Packers. The tough Bears' defense readies for battle.

"Minister of Defense" Reggie White (92) helps corral a Bears' ball carrrier.
George Koonce (53) assists.

responsibilities that Lombardi didn't have to worry about. Coach Halas would leave a lot of the coaching to the assistants but he kept up with all the things that were going on. Halas was an amazing human being. He loved the Bears; he was "Papa Bear," and it was an honor to work for him and with him."

Also added to the offense was a hard-nosed tight end from the University of Pittsburgh who loved walloping any opponent and enjoyed being hit himself. His name was Mike Ditka. *New York Post* writer Milton Ross once called Ditka a cross between a rhino and a battering ram. Writer Roy McHugh labeled him pro football's Ty Cobb.

Ditka was drafted by the Houston Oilers of the rival AFL but opted to play for Chicago for less money because he wanted to play in the NFL. He considered the league to be far superior to the upstart AFL.

Ditka went on to win Rookie of the Year honors after catching fifty-six passes for over a thousand yards and twelve touchdowns. He was also a crushing blocker, punishing defenders with a murderous drive and power, he became the pro game's first great tight end. Until then, an end's role was mainly blocking. He virtually made the tight end position what we know it to be today.

"Generous to a fault and confused in the clutch, the Chicago Bears squandered two excellent scoring opportunities, set up three touchdowns for the Green Bay Packers, and retreated from City Stadium roundly trounced, 24-0," *Chicago Tribune* writer George Strickler reported the day after the Packers had shut out the Bears for the first time since 1935.

A most prophetic moment had come in the pre-game warm-ups. As Halas and the Bears entered the stadium, the Packer Lumberjack Band began playing the song "It's the Wrong Time and the Wrong Place." It certainly would be.

Touchdown passes to lanky receiver Boyd Dowler and tight end Ron Kramer, and two scoring runs by Taylor and Hornung, gave the Northmen a convincing win. The Packers intercepted four Bear passes, stopped Chicago twice on fourth down plays deep in

Packers' territory, and returned a punt for a touchdown.

Chicago, bolstered with four consecutive wins, hosted the 6-2 Packers on November 12 at Wrigley Field. Before the game, Lombardi got peeved at the Lumberjack Band who had set up shop on the right side of the Packers' bench. For some reason, he wanted them to play on the left side. In a perfect example of Lombardi ruling the roost, he immediately "suggested" that the band move to the left. They did in a chorus of, "Yes, Sir, Mr. Lombardi, right away Mr. Lombardi."

In the first quarter, Mike Ditka caught a 15-yard touchdown pass from Bill Wade to open the scoring. From there, Bart Starr took command, throwing three touchdown passes, two to Ron Kramer and one to Hornung.

With the score, 28-7, peerless Paul lined up to attempt a field goal at mid-field. With Starr holding, Hornung's golden toe smacked the ball, making it tumble seemingly in slow motion, end-over-end across the bar for a 51-yard field goal. It would be the game's deciding points.

The Bears mounted a furious comeback to turn a sure rout into a spectacular contest. Quarterback Bill Wade suddenly went on a rampage, connecting with Ditka on two TD passes from fifteen and twenty-nine yards out. With three minutes left in the game, running back Rick Casares blasted his way nine yards for a score bringing the Bears within three, 31-28. The Bears got the ball back with one minute left but the Packers' defense rose to the occasion and snuffed the Bears' last drive.

Lombardi and his Packers rolled on to win the Western Division with a 11-3 record, winning it by three games over the Detroit Lions. The Bears finished in third place with a respectable 8-6 record. Adequate, but outclassed again by their rivals to the north.

On New Year's Eve, 39,029 heavily bundled football fans shivered in sub-freezing weather to watch the Packers play the New York Giants in the first pro football championship game played in Green Bay, Wisconsin. Although the Packers had won five Western titles before 1961, Green Bay had never hosted a title game.

After a scoreless first quarter, the Packers exploded in the second, scoring twenty-four points with two Bart Starr touchdown passes sandwiched in between a TD run and a 17-yard field goal by

Hornung.

With the Giants' running game now gone, Y. A. Tittle and Charlie Conerly began throwing the ball. Packers' defenders merely sat back and awaited the passes, intercepting four on the day.

Another scoring pass to Ron Kramer and a game-icing 19-yard field goal by Hornung settled the matter, 37-0. The Green Bay Packers were pro football champions once again! It had been eighteen years and fourteen days since Curly Lambeau had led his Packers to their last championship with the 14-7 victory over the Giants in 1944.

Green Bay celebrated its most memorable New Year's Eve as Packers' fans danced in the street holding banners that read "Titletown USA," causing massive traffic jams throughout town. It was a tremendous release of emotion.

The Green Bay Packers had become the greatest team in the history of the National Football League.

It is eye-opening to read through old newspaper articles and game recounts of just how valuable Paul Hornung was to Vince Lombardi and the Green Bay Packers. It's common to read in the game summaries where Paul had rushed for two touchdowns, gained seventy yards rushing, kicked four extra points, added a field goal, and booted three kickoffs over and through the end zone. He was a one man offensive machine. Add to that the fact that he was the inspirational leader of the team, and you can see why Paul Hornung was one of the most loved, respected, and honored football players to snap on a helmet.

The Green Bay Packers and the Chicago Cardinals flipped a coin to determine which would choose first in the 1957 college draft. There was little doubt that Paul "The Golden Boy" Hornung from prestigious Notre Dame would be the first choice.

"With Notre Dame located where it is, and with Chicago such a big Notre Dame town, I knew I was going to be the pick of either one of them," Hornung said. "I was sort of hoping the Cardinals would win the flip so I could be in Chicago. The way it worked out was probably best for me."

Growing up around Louisville and playing college ball near Chicago, did he ever yearn to play for Halas and the Bears? "That would have been great," he confessed. "I loved the Bears and Chicago. Chicago has been kind of like my second home. If I would pick anywhere to live outside of Louisville it would be Chicago.

"I loved Halas. Halas is the greatest name in the history of the game. Lombardi really admired him. He (Lombardi) knew that Halas had started the league and if it wasn't for him there would not have been pro football. I loved to beat him. To look over there on the sidelines and see the Papa Bear; that was a great thrill."

Hornung had no trouble coming with the one Bear who was the toughest he had ever faced.

"Doug Atkins was probably the best defensive end that's ever played," Paul said. "Doug was the toughest guy to block as far as I was concerned. I was a pretty good blocker. I always kidded Doug that in nine years I probably blocked him four times, and that was four more times than anyone else. He was almost impossible to block. He was six foot nine and could high jump six foot nine. If you blocked him low he would jump over you and if you tried to block him high he'd take you and throw you over. He's a hell of a man."

The infamous Packer Sweep play was usually run to Atkins' opposite side. "Thank God we ran the power sweep away from Doug most of the time," Paul said. "When you have a guy like that, you have to take advantage of him. You've got to find out if there is any weakness at all. But he had none."

Hornung believes the Bears, instead of playing a basic defense, would continually out think themselves. "We felt the Bears probably had the best individual talent of any of the defense's in the league but they played such screwy defenses. We always felt that gave us an edge since they weren't that well organized defensively. Lombardi used to always say that if they would put the Bears' defense in a 4-3 (four linemen and three linebacker set) and defied you to beat them man to man, nobody would beat them."

Hornung's career would be shortened in an encounter with Chicago Bears' linebacker Doug Buffone in a game on October 17, 1966. Hornung was handed the ball near the goal line and was following Jim Taylor into the line. "I was diving over to score a touch-down in Wrigley Field and Buffone came from the weak side of the defense and clothes-lined me, knocking my head back," Paul recalled. "That was it. That was really the hit that caused me to retire. I played a couple more games and I really should not have. I had a slight pinched nerve before that; but that hit did the whole deal. Doug and I are great friends. I've always kidded him about it."

Hornung summed up the Packers-Bears rivalry. "They wanted to beat us a little bit more than we did them. When you're playing your rival and a team in your division that you have to beat, that makes it a little extra special. We used to play them three times a year. Our players were very familiar with their players. Rick Casares and I were great friends. We hung around together and had a few drinks after the game. I had a lot of friends on the Bears. If we hadn't won it (the championship), we always hoped the Bears would win it."

The 1962 Green Bay Packers became one of the greatest teams ever assembled. Lombardi, now referred to as Saint Vincent, had taken a rag-tag bunch of under-achievers in 1959 and transformed them into a team for the ages. A look at the All-Pro team that year shows it overloaded with Packers. On offense Jim Taylor, end Ron Kramer, and linemen Jerry Kramer, Fuzzy Thurston, Jim Ringo, and Forrest Gregg were all named to the All-Pro team. On defense, linebackers Dan Currie and Bill Forester, linemen Willie Davis and Henry Jordan, and cornerback Herb Adderley won top honors.

Lombardi acquired Willie Davis from the Cleveland Browns in 1960. A Grambling grad, Davis was a high-powered, forceful defensive end at 6'3", 245 pounds. His teammates started calling him "Dr. Feelgood" because he was always happy and cheerful. Growing up in Texarkana, Arkansas, he had to hide his football playing from his worrisome mother. "My mother was afraid I would get hurt so I played my first two high school games without her knowing I was on the varsity," he recalled once. "The only reason she found out was that our third game was on the road and there was no way I could stay out that late without her knowing what was going on."

Willie was chosen in the seventeenth round by the Browns who proceeded to shift him from position to position on both offense and defense. In mid-spring of 1960, Lombardi traded offensive end A. D. Williams to Cleveland for Davis. Davis actually thought about quitting football. He didn't want to go to frozen Green Bay. Until Lombardi, no player wanted to be traded there.

"Willie, we have seen some films of you where your reactions are just incredible," Lombardi told Davis upon his arrival in Green Bay. "We feel with your quickness you can be a great pass rusher."

Davis made All-NFL honors five times from 1962 to 1967, was a Pro Bowl choice five years in a row, and had never missed a game at the time of his retirement in 1969. In 1981, Willie Davis was inducted into the Pro Football Hall of Fame.

What happened to A. D. Williams? Williams caught one pass for the Browns and finished his short career the following year in Minnesota.

Another great find for the Packers was Michigan State running back Herb Adderley, drafted in the first round in 1961. Hit with injuries in his rookie year, Adderley saw most of his action on special teams. As the season went on, it was obvious that he wasn't going to steal a running back job from Paul Hornung or Jim Taylor.

In the Thanksgiving Day game with Detroit in '61, starting cornerback Hank Gremminger became injured. Lombardi sent in Adderley to replace Gremminger since Adderley had played safety on defense at Michigan State. Adderley picked off a pass and the Packers had found a position for the exiled running back. "Defense is in my blood now," he said at the time, "and nothing could make me even want to think about going back to play on offense." Adderley became a fixture in the Packers' defensive unit from that point until 1970, when a personal dispute with Coach Phil Bengtson forced a trade to the Dallas Cowboys. Along the way, Adderley stole forty-eight interceptions; he was inducted into pro football's Hall of Fame in 1980.

George Halas' squad came into the season with some new blood on offense and defense. The Bears acquired defensive end Ed O'Bradovich from Illinois to booster an already talent-heavy defending team. On offense Halas added two talented runners in rookie Ron Bull from Baylor University and ex-Ram Joe Marconi.

Their acquisitions proved vital to the Bears' football fortunes in 1962 because of injuries to the starters. Another important addition was Bobby Joe Green, who would handle the punting duties in Chicago for the next twelve years.

The Bears opened the season on the West Coast where they defeated the Rams and the 49ers. After a 181-yard rushing performance against the 49ers, Willie Galimore was injured in the Rams' game. That caused him to be sidelined most of the season and finish the year with only 233 rushing yards. Rick Casares also spent most of the year injured and ailing. Marconi and Bull were left to shoulder the load in the backfield.

The Packers began the season with a 34-7 thrashing of the Vikings and a 17-0 shutout of the Cardinals. Both rivals brought 2-0 records to a sun-drenched City Stadium for the showdown on the final day of September.

After the Rams' game, George Halas was uncharacteristically cocky when asked to compare his memorable 1940-'41 teams to the present day Packers. "I never compare teams," he humbly said, but added that, "the Packers do not yet walk upon the water."

Maybe not, but the Bears themselves were about to land in the deep end.

After a scoreless first quarter, the explosion began. Green Bay's Jimmy Taylor plunged for a 1-yard touchdown and Starr hit tight end Ron Kramer for a 54-yard touchdown near the end of the half for a 14-0 lead.

In the third period Elijah Pitts, filling in for Hornung who had pulled a thigh muscle in the first quarter, rammed through the line behind a great block by guard Fuzzy Thurston, and sprinted twenty-six yards for a touchdown.

On the Packers' next two possessions, Taylor would score from the 11- and 1-yard lines. He would finish the day with 126 yards on seventeen carries, scoring three times.

After Starr added a rare run for a TD, the Bears' inserted second-string quarterback Rudy Bukich to finish up this debacle and take some game snaps. With a 1:40 left in the game, he threw a pass downfield that was picked off by Herb Adderley. The speedy defensive back burst up-field zigzagging his way fifty yards for the exclamation point touchdown.

As the gun sounded, the scoreboard at City Stadium glowed "Packers 49, Visitors 0." It was the worst beating Green Bay had ever given the rival Bears, and happened to be the worst defeat in the team's history. It was the Packers' fourth straight win over the Bears, a feat not seen since Lambeau's champion Bay's had done it in 1929, '30, and '31.

Lombardi was quick to down play the embarrassing total of points and his domination over Halas' hurting troops, and rightly so. The Bears' had been stripped of talent due to injuries. Along with Casares and Galimore, linebacker Bill George had stayed behind in Chicago with a back injury. Lineman Fred Williams and tight end Mike Ditka played but were also hurting. The Bears had marched into Green Bay like a bandaged and limping drum and fife corp. "You can't take people like George and Galimore out of there and not have it make a difference," Lombardi stated after the game. "How did we know they were really in such bad shape? All we knew was what we read in the papers."

"They were just too good for us today," a shocked Halas said softly in the locker room. "That's about all you can say... the Packers were really a great team out there today."

The headline in the *Green Bay Press-Gazette* above the box score of the game said it all: "Pall-Bearers."

The game was a most humbling experience but Halas wasn't about to let it ruin the season. They were still very much in the race and looked forward to the rematch five weeks later in Chicago. Some 48,753 fans packed a rain-swept and chilly Wrigley Field to watch their 4-3 Bears take on the perfect 7-0 Packers.

Jim Taylor opened the scoring on a 2-yard run, but in the second period the Bears' John Adams caught a pass from Bill Wade off his shoe tops and scored a 4-yard touchdown tying the game, 7-7. Before the half, Jerry Kramer, filling in for the injured Paul Hornung as place kicker, toed a 17-yard field goal to give the Northmen the lead at half-time.

After a long offensive march in the third period, Taylor rumbled over a driving Packers' front five from 1-yard out, for his second score. He added two more short touchdown runs to finish the day with four rushing TDs. Rookie Earl Gros added an insurance touchdown run in the last minute of play to cap a 38-7 "Taylorizing" of the Midway Monsters.

Tribune writer George Strickler wrote that the Bears helped the champion Packers by their own "giveaway program." The slippery-handed and mistake-prone Bears were cursed with nine fumbles and three interceptions by Herb Adderley, Willie Wood, and linebacker Ray Nitschke. It got so bad that it bordered on being comical. One of the fumbles happened during a Bears' punt. Bobby Joe Green kicked the ball and the Packer receiver was just going to let the ball drop to the ground. Instead, the ball hit Chicago's Roosevelt Taylor in the back and Packer Jim Ringo recovered the fumble. It would lead to a Kramer field goal.

After the game Lombardi was asked if his team, now 8-0, could go undefeated the entire year. "It's highly improbable we can go undefeated," he said. "Each opponent seems to be aroused against us and makes the maximum effort."

In the Bears' locker room, accolades abounded. "They're the greatest, absolutely the greatest," Mike Ditka praised. "In their own minds they can't be beaten. We played the best team I've ever seen, the only team in the league better than the Bears."

Papa Bear Halas was conciliatory in defeat, telling the writers that the avalanche of mistakes, added with the Packers' great play, had been too much for them. He ended the proceedings with one last comment to the sports scribes surrounding him under the stands of Wrigley Field. "Gentlemen," Halas said, "it will require the combined literary excellence of all of you to make our effort today appear even slightly adequate."

Halas' Bears would be more than adequate for the remainder of the season, going 5-1 in their games after the Packer loss. It had actually been a good season for the Bears, who would finish third in the Western Conference with a 9-5 mark.

Highlights of the season were the excellent play of Ron Bull and Bill Wade. Ronny Bull's 363 yards on the ground and 331 yards catching passes earned him Rookie of the Year honors. The outstanding showing of the "Baylor Bull" and Joe Marconi, who added 950 all-purpose yards on rushes, catching passes, and punt and kick-off returns, saved the Bears. Quarterback Bill Wade had his greatest season as a pro, passing for 3,172 yards, scoring eighteen touchdowns and completing fifty-five percent of his passes. They were certainly a team that would be formidable in the '63 campaign.

Lombardi's Packers continued on a roll until their Thanksgiving Day meeting with Detroit, where a swarming Lions' defense ransacked Bart Starr and the offense for a 26-14 upset, proving to the football world that the Packers were, indeed, mortal.

Green Bay handily disposed of its final three opponents to finish with a brilliant 13-1 record and traveled to New York's Yankee Stadium on December 30th to defend their championship, again opposing the Giants. At game time the temperature was twenty degrees but it dropped steadily throughout the day. The bone-chilling 35 mph wind squall that blew through the entire game brought the wind-chill factor down to 41 below, making the playing conditions almost unbearable. Even Green Bay, Wisconsin sounded warmer compared to this!

The game was an exercise of attrition. Since conditions made passing the ball very difficult, the ground game took center stage and this was where Lombardi's superior offensive line and runners dominated the game. Simple, old fashioned blocking and tackling techniques instilled in the Packers by their fiery coach won the game.

Jerry Kramer booted a 26-yard field goal in the first period and added a 29- and 30-yarder in the third and fourth quarters. In the second period, Taylor ran 7 yards for touchdown. The Giants only score came in the third quarter when they recovered a blocked punt in the end zone. Final: Packers 16, Giants 7!

It had been an incredibly bruising game for all participants but more so for Jim Taylor. In a collision with Sam Huff early in the contest, Taylor bit his tongue and spit blood the entire game. Towards the end of the game, Taylor noticed that most of the skin on his arms, elbows and knees had been scraped raw from hitting the frozen turf so often.

Lombardi knew it was entirely possible his Packers could win a third-straight championship with this team he had assembled. They were one of the best teams that had ever stepped on a gridiron. He knew it, and deep down he believed they could do it again.

In Green Bay, Lombardi's legend had grown to a scale of that of Curly Lambeau's. Lombardi was, in an unspoken way, in competition with the Lambeau legend. He once begrudgingly agreed to be photographed shaking hands with Lambeau for the cover of Packers yearbook.

Vince Lombardi wanted to make it three championships in a row in the modern era, but storm clouds were on the horizon.

Green Bay's Jimmy Taylor was one of the toughest fullbacks the game has ever seen. Taylor came rumbling out of the bayous of Louisiana and onto the gridirons of the NFL to punish tacklers and defenders. Often, he would taunt tacklers by saying, "Is that the hardest you can hit me?" From his rookie year in Green Bay in 1958 to his return home to play one year with the expansion New Orleans Saints in 1967, Jim Taylor trounced and leveled defenders.

Jack Vainisi and Lisle Blackbourn, in their attempt to make the 1958 Packers' team tougher, drafted Taylor out of LSU in the second round. In his rookie season Taylor substituted for veteran ball carriers Howie Ferguson and Don McIlhenny and played on the punt and kickoff return teams. In the final two West Coast games of the year, he started in the backfield and would be there through the 1966 season.

Taylor quickly found a vast difference between college ball and pro ball. Jim had played fullback at LSU, where he usually lined up behind the quarterback. When he became a pro, he really became more of halfback instead of a fullback.

"At LSU, you mainly ran the ball tackle-to-tackle and very little toss plays," Taylor explained. "You hardly ever had to catch a pass. As you move on into the pros, it was a transition to come out of a stance, run right or left, verses going straight ahead. I became more of a running back [at Green Bay] because I moved over to the halfback position where you have splitbacks in the backfield. That was a big transition for a runner, which of my ability, I'd probably say I had average ability. I had good balance and quickness to the line. I had good second effort and could read holes."

Taylor's clashes with defenders are still remembered by those who tried to stop him. Instead of trying to fake some would-be tackler to get downfield, Taylor would turn into a battering ram and bowl right over them.

"He'd kick you, gouge you, spit at you, whatever it took," said Hall of Fame linebacker Sam Huff. "He ran hard and he loved to kick you in the head with those knees." Huff, when he was playing with the Giants, even claims that Taylor dented his helmet when he tackled him in the 1962 championship game.

"Each individual runner has his own personality and maybe I developed a straight ahead style in college," Taylor explained. "I certainly didn't try to intentionally run over each defender. You pick up more yardage by not taking on a defender. There were stories in print about how I just wanted to sting players and this and that. That was never my intent, but I was a very aggressive runner."

The arrival of Lombardi signaled a drastic change in the football fortunes of Taylor and the other Packers.

"He was a very firm and strong disciplinarian and you believed in him," Taylor said. "He put it together and made you believe in yourself and built your self-esteem. He let you have your own identity. Hornung had his identity, Starr had his, I had mine. I was one he could really motivate. He knew how to intimidate, threat, and cuss, and that would get you moving to a higher level."

While at Green Bay, Taylor won All-NFL honors in 1961 and 1962, and made the Pro Bowl five straight years from 1960 to '64. In his pro career, Jimmy gained 8,597 yards rushing and tallied ninety-one touchdowns. Cleveland Browns' Hall of Fame runner Jim Brown won the rushing title every year he played, every year that is except in 1962, when Taylor surpassed him with 1,474 yards. Taylor also set a record for touchdowns that year with nineteen to his credit. Taylor eventually become the first Packers' player from the Lombardi teams to be inducted into the Pro Football Hall of Fame.

Taylor ran behind a great offensive line that lead him to a five yards per carry career average. Tough nut center Jim Ringo was sandwiched by two of the best guards in the game, Fuzzy Thurston and Jerry Kramer. Tackles Forrest Gregg and Bob Skronski, and tight end Ron Kramer filled out an offensive line that was clearly the class of the league.

"They had wonderful blocking skills," Taylor said. "They had great technique. Running at people was our strong point. We just defied them to stop us. We liked to run right into people and they knew we were coming. We used this technique earlier in our careers, like in 1961 and '62."

Taylor had some of his best games against Chicago. He recalled his encounters with the Midway Monsters.

"Linebacker Bill George was an outstanding player," he said. "Then you had Earl Leggett, Doug Atkins, Joe Fortunato, Larry Morris, they were all aggressive. They had a particular defense called the "George Defense" where Bill George would jump down and get on either side of [center] Jim Ringo and try to blitz and upset our plays. If the guards had any kind of split, he could get through there and get an arm on Bart. I had to pick him up on a blitz so Bart could get the ball away."

It's well documented that there was animosity between Taylor and Lombardi towards the end of the 1966 season. Taylor essentially became a free agent and went to Lombardi to discuss a new contract. When they couldn't come to an agreement, Taylor was sent packing to New Orleans. Vince saw Taylor as having no loyalty towards him or the Packers.

"He turned around and did the same thing, too, with the Packers by going to coach the Redskins," Taylor said with a bit of acrimony in his voice. "But we became closer after he became [the Packers'] general manager. If I had to do it over again, I would have done it the same way."

1963

On August 25, 1962, NFL Commissioner Pete Rozelle visited the Green Bay Packers' in a Milwaukee hotel before their exhibition game with Chicago. Rozelle was visiting every NFL training camp to warn players that severe penalties awaited those who might be gambling on games. As Paul Hornung listened to Rozelle, he silently told himself he had placed his last bet.

In the past, Hornung had bet on Packers' games. From 1957 to 1962, he had, on occasion, discussed NFL games with a West Coast gambler, through whom he began placing bets around 1959. "My bets averaged about $100, during some periods, $200," he once said. "Whenever I thought the point spread was right, I bet on Packers' games, but always on the Packers to win, never against them. How honest that seemed at the time."

Hornung came clean and told his story to Rozelle. "Well, Paul," Rozelle said, "I've got a very important decision to make. I want to check everything out. You'll either get a reprimand, a fine, or a suspension. I'll get in touch with you."

On April 17, 1963, Rozelle announced that Green Bay's Paul Hornung and Detroit Lions' defensive tackle Alex Karras were being indefinitely suspended for betting on games and associating with undesirables. After a four-month investigation that included lie-detector tests and interviews, a number of unidentified players in the league were fined for placing small bets. Hornung and Karras were the only ones suspended.

Rozelle had made it clear that no player, not even the league's leading scorer in Hornung or a defensive star like Karras, could escape harsh penalties for gambling. The message was loud and clear.

The 68-year-old Papa Bear looked expectantly at the upcoming '63 campaign, confident that his Bears could compete with the Green Bay Packers. Also, his squad had won five of their last six games in 1962, only losing to the Giants.

Chicago had a formidable team ready to do battle. The offense would be lead by quarterback Bill Wade. Wade would general the Bears through most of the season, calling most of the offensive plays himself. Receiving passes from Wade were tight end Mike Ditka and receivers Johnny Morris and Bo Farrington. Running behind the talented line of Mike Pyle, Bob Wetoska, Herm Lee, Ted Karras and Jim Cadile, were Willie Galimore, Rick Casares, Joe Marconi, and Ronny Bull.

The defense would be by far the most stubborn in the league, allowing only 144 points the entire season. Earl Leggett, Stan Jones, Ed O'Bradovich, and Doug Atkins formed the front defensive wall. Larry Morris, Bill George and Joe Fortunato stood their ground at linebackers. Defending the pass were defensive backs Dave Whitsell, Richie Petitbon, J. C. Caroline, and Rosey Taylor. The 1963 Chicago Bears were loaded and ready to fire.

Shortly before the season started, Halas told his team: "If we're going to win this thing, we're going to have to beat Green Bay twice." Halas was re-enforcing what the entire team already knew.

"I'm sure the rest of the team felt that way," quarterback Bill Wade concurred. "And, it ended up that way. If we hadn't have beaten Green Bay twice, they would have won the championship in our division. It ended up very close."

It would be very close, indeed.

On September 15, some 42,327 fans, the largest crowd to witness a game in Green Bay, settled into City Stadium for the season opener with the Bears. In the first quarter of battle Jim Taylor fumbled on his own 33-yard line. Six plays later Chicago kicker Bob Jencks booted a 32-yard field goal for an early 3-0 Bears' lead. Just before the half Jerry Kramer's 41-yard kick deadlocked the game.

In the third period, with the Packers driving, Bart Starr's pass to Boyd Dowler deflected off the receiver's hands and into the waiting arms of Roosevelt Taylor. The Bears proceeded to drive sixty-eight yards, culminating in Joe Marconi's 2-yard dive into the end zone, giving the Bears a 10-3 lead.

Packers' fans were now getting impatient. The game was being dictated by Halas and his Bears. Their two-time champions had met a team who was soundly beating them. Green Bay was being out-played and out-hustled.

The major damage was being done by quarterback Bill Wade's dump-off passes to his backs who were circling out of the backfield. Halas had noticed in game films that Green Bay's linebackers had a tendency to drop back on defense. Helping even more was the crushing blocks of Ditka and end Bo Farrington. In the process, Marconi and Casares caught four passes, Ron Bull six, while Ditka and Farrington had one each. It wasn't flashy football by any means but it allowed Chicago to control the ball and eventually to win the game.

"If you want to go back and see how we beat the Packers, we did so by little short passes because the Packers would drop off," Bill Wade revealed of the Bears' strategy. "It was discovered by [offen-

sive coach] Jim Dooley that ninety-four percent of the time, the
Packers did not red dog (blitz their linebackers). Ninety-four percent of the time they only rushed two men. Their key rusher was
Willie Davis. The interior rusher was Henry Jordan. Jim Dooley
was the one who discovered all of this, which means you're throwing
against nine people at a time. So, where were those nine people?
You've got to figure out where you can throw a pass you can complete. We were able to move the ball consistently with the short
passes. The Packers had a way of taking away all of your downfield
passes with nine men. So, that's why they were able to destroy us
the other games we had been playing them."

As Lombardi paced the sidelines and chained-smoked cigarettes,
Starr began moving the Packers down the field late in the fourth
quarter. The Packers' faithful held their breath for a miracle. They
began breathing again when a Bart Starr pass floated into the hands
of Dave Whitsell for an interception, ending the game.

The Bears had done it! Every Midway Monster that walked out
of City Stadium that day was a foot taller. The Bears' locker room
was a riotous place as players celebrated and hugged each other.

"We did it!" screamed Earl Leggett. "I didn't think we could
but we did!"

"I knew damned well we'd do it!" yelled linebacker Bill George.
"We wanted this game and had to have it."

Over a rousing team chant of, "We want beer, we want beer!"
Halas, game ball in hand, quieted his warriors and apologized for
the absence of the spirits they desired. Then Halas drew quiet, and
in a hoarse voice said, "Gentlemen, this was the greatest team effort
in the history of the Chicago Bears."

Later he told reporters circled around him that, "This effort
today culminates months of planning. The coaches have worked
hundreds of hours toward this one game. We knew they would drop
their linebackers back twelve to fifteen yards deep. So we figured to
try some swings. They didn't adjust their defense, so we kept doing
it."

"We didn't change the defense because they were only gaining
two and three yards at a time," Lombardi explained to another collection of sports scribes. "We put it up on the blackboard at half-
time but we didn't change the defense. They weren't really hurting

us."

"What told us we had a championship team was when we beat the Packers, 10-3, in the first game of the season," Bears' center Mike Pyle said. "That was probably the most sure game I can ever remember playing. It was the best preparation of any game and all of us felt the same way."

"When we won that opener," Bill George once said, "all the old-timers, Doug Atkins, Larry Morris, Fred Williams, and myself, knew we had a shot at the title. Yet, we always had a strange feeling after every game that year, a feeling that the bubble had to bust sooner or later. It never did."

Chicago Tribune writer George Strickler put it best in his opening paragraph the day after the huge win. "Venerable George Halas' Chicago Bears went swinging through Titletown USA today. The place will never be the same."

The big Bears' machine marched on, winning their next five games, before losing in San Francisco, 20-14. Three more wins against Philadelphia, Baltimore, and Los Angeles brought the Bears back home to Wrigley Field for their monumental rematch with their rivals from the north.

The Packers, in the meantime, hadn't rolled over and died. They were still the defending champs and showed it by winning their next eight games leading up to the trip to the Windy City. Once again they were completely destroying the rest of league, winning the eight games by scoring an average of thirty-one points a game.

As the players arrived at Wrigley about 10:15 a.m., they pushed their way through a small crowd on their way to the locker room under the stands. A couple of kids, obviously Bear fans, yelled out, "Wow, are you in for it today. We'll break both your legs!"

The 88th meeting between the two rivals on this gray November day was viewed by many as a battle just below Pearl Harbor in stature. Green Bay had to win the game so the Bears wouldn't sweep the two-game series. Chicago, being one game out of first place, had to win to prove they weren't laying down and conceding the championship to a team many thought walked on water.

The Packers were concerned about their quarterback situation. Earlier in the season Bart Starr had broken his hand. Finding it hard to grip the ball and to prevent the risk of more injury, Starr was to stay on the sidelines this day. In his place was backup John Roach, who would later be relieved in the third quarter by former-Bear now-Packer quarterback Zeke Bratkowski.

The Bears capitalized early in the first quarter, scoring thirteen points the first three times they had the ball. Two Roger Leclerc field goals quickly made the score 6-0. On the ensuing kickoff, the Packers' Herb Adderley caught the ball in the end zone and came tearing up the field holding the ball, in the elegant words of writer Red Smith, "in his right fist like a half-eaten sandwich." Adderley fumbled and Leclerc recovered. Two plays later, Willie Galimore ripped off a 27-yard touchdown run and the Bears led, 13-0, at half-time.

After Roach's departure in the third quarter, Bratkowski came in and completed three of eleven passes. Unfortunately for Green Bay, three others were completed to Bears' defensive backs for interceptions.

Once again Chicago's ball control offense stymied the Packers. The Bear's ground game shredded Green Bay's defense for 248 yards on the day. Leclerc added two more field goals while Bill Wade ran for a 5-yard touchdown, giving the Bears a commanding, 26-0, lead. The Bay's only score on the day was an 11-yard run by Hornung's replacement back, Tom Moore.

As the final gun sounded sealing the Bears' victory, the electrified 49,166 fans rose in a thunderous roar. Incredibly, the Bears had done it again. They had taken the ball right to the defending champs, rammed it down their throats, and were staking their claim as the imperious group of the Western Division.

"Our week of preparation before the second game in Chicago was one of those buildups where the entire city was a part of it," Mike Pyle recalled. "By the time we hit that game, nothing in the world was going to stop us. On the opening kickoff, we kicked to the Packers and Herb Adderley returned it. J. C. Caroline knifed in behind the wedge and just decked him. We knew from that time on there wasn't any question who was going to win the football game."

After the game, a beaming George Halas stated that, "This is our greatest victory since we beat the Giants for the world championship in 1946. The offense had a game plan and the defense had a game plan and I gave them the war plan," he grinned.

Lombardi, ever conciliatory, praised the Bears' effort and their coach. "I'm real happy for Papa George," he said. "He's a helluva man."

"They beat us both ways," Lombardi continued. "Their offensive line beat us, and their defensive line beat us. They beat the hell out of us."

"It was the only game I can recall during Lombardi's nine years of coaching there where the team was flat," veteran CBS broadcaster Ray Scott observed. "After the game I went down to the Packers' dressing room. Just as I walked in, Phil Bengtson turned to Lombardi and said, 'Vince, we were flat out there.' I thought Lombardi would bite his head off. He looked at him and he said, 'How can you be flat for a game like this!'"

The race for the Western Division will go down in history as one of the greatest runs for a championship. After fourteen league games, Chicago finished one-half game ahead of the Packers. The Bears' record was 11 wins, 1 loss, and 2 ties, while the Packers record was 11 wins, 2 losses, and 1 tie. As Halas had so accurately predicted, the Bears had won the Western Division championship by defeating the rival Packers twice.

On the frozen turf of Wrigley Field on December 29, 1963, George Halas saw his dream come true as his Chicago Bears defeated the bridesmaid New York Giants, 14-10, with a stingy defense and two Bill Wade touchdown runs.

In a noisy, exuberant Bears' locker room, a smiling Halas joked, "I just hope the All-Stars go easy on us next summer," referring to the annual exhibition opener between the NFL champion and the College All-Star team. Defensive Coach George Allen received the game ball. Under his tutelage, the Bears' defense had led the league in ten of nineteen defensive categories and were second in eight others. They are remembered as one of the greatest defensive units in NFL history.

A huge party honoring Halas and the Bears was arranged by Chicago Mayor Richard J. Daley for the next day at the courthouse. The entire city was encouraged to attend to celebrate and honor their NFL Champion Chicago Bears.

Packers' fans still speculate that the loss of Paul Hornung was just enough to help the Bears win the division and, ultimately, the title in 1963. Some of their players concur.

"We didn't have our best running back," said Packers' guard Fuzzy Thurston. "With Paul ... in my mind we would have won it. Tom Moore [Hornung's replacement] did a great job but he was no Hornung."

"Paul was such the heart and soul of our team," fellow guard Jerry Kramer said. "He was our leader as much as anyone else, other than Lombardi. He was such a smart football player. He didn't have a hell of a lot of speed or strength, but he was just so smart. I think it [his absence] hurt us.

"It was just the Bears' year," Kramer added. "Fumbles would bounce right into their hands. I was talking to Doug Atkins at the Pro Bowl that year and I said you lucky sons-a-bitches couldn't do anything wrong the last half of the season. He said, 'I know it, Jerry, I know it. I told the team to plan on the championship, we're going all the way.'

"It just seemed to be their year and the ball bounced the Bears' way."

One of the best football players to come out of the prestigious and renowned Ivy League was Yale center Mike Pyle. As a matter of fact, he was the first player to make an NFL team after the formal Ivy League began in 1956.

"As I often say, I'm the only guy who graduated from Yale who had to play football," Pyle jokingly said.

Mike Pyle grew up in the Chicago area and was already familiar to George Halas after he made All-State in three sports in high school. George Allen, who was personnel director, drafted Mike in 1961.

"I remember thinking that if I make it," Mike said of his first training camp, "I'd love to play a couple of years to see what it's like playing in the National Football League, then get out and get a job. When I made that 1961 team, I knew I was there until they dragged me off the field. I really felt good about playing with the Chicago Bears and I loved those guys."

Pyle anchored the center position for the Bears from 1961 until he retired after the 1969 season. During that time he went up against those great Lombardi teams. And who was the toughest of them all?

"It was Ray Nitschke," he said without hesitation. "I played across from Ray three games a year for nine years. I can assure you that was an experience. I can say playing against Nitschke shortened my career dramatically.

"I had a great respect for Nitschke. I thought he was one of the greatest linebackers to play the game. Raymond hit awfully hard, but he wasn't a dirty player. He played his position very well. The Packers had a defense where the linemen, all of whom were good, kept blockers off the middle linebacker, and the middle linebacker would fill the hole. On a straight 4-3 defense, you protected the middle linebacker so a center or a guard couldn't get out to block him. So, he filled the holes and made the tackles all the time. It was Ray's job to make the tackles on running plays and he did it very well. With Ray I'd win some and lose a lot, and anytime I went to hit him I knew there was going to be contact. He'd whack you real good."

Mike vividly recalled going up against some of the other Packer defenders in his day.

"The two tackles, the two ends: Willie Davis, Bill Quinlan for several years, Henry Jordan, Hawg Hanner, and then Ron Kostelnik. My rookie year up in Green Bay, I knew about Henry Jordan and Hawg Hanner and here I was playing against them. Hawg Hanner was one of the all-time greats. Jordan had been around awhile. Two of the best.

"We came down on the 5-yard line and I come out over the ball. There wasn't a lot of talking on the line in the Sixties. I get over the ball and I hear this voice saying, 'Hey, rook, I'm gonna knock your jock off.' I'm thinking that's coming from Hawg Hanner. What has he got against me? It really impacted me. I made my block, got up to go back to the huddle, and it's number 77, Ron Kostelnik, another rookie! It wasn't Hanner, it was another rookie!"

Mike remembers an incident in the early Sixties when Ray Nitschke and Mike Ditka met face to face.

"I don't remember what year, but we were up in Green Bay. I

remember I had just made a block on a pass play and all of a sudden I heard this CRUNCH!... CRACK! I looked downfield and here's Ditka flat on his back with Nitschke standing next to him. Nitschke had clotheslined him and just decked him. I saw Ditka jump up and you thought, uh huh ...we're gonna have a fight. But he didn't. He looked at him, probably said something, Nitschke gave it the glower, and he came back to the huddle. I was surprised Ditka didn't do anything.

"A year later in a game, I heard a similar CRACK! on a running play. This time I looked over and there's Ditka standing over Nitschke. Ditka said, 'This is for last year, Ray.' He never forgot. He remembered and did it the right way, with a legal block."

Mike even found humor in the worst loss in Bears' history, the 49-0 washout to Green Bay in 1962.

"Bill George, the all-time great middle linebacker, the guy who really created the position, played thirteen years with the Bears. Bill had had a minor car accident during the off-season and injured his back. He had practiced a few weeks in training camp and they put him in the hospital. Some of the guys went to the hospital to visit Bill before getting on the plane. They told Bill George that they were going to play this game for him. This one's for you. We're going up and beat those Packers.

"Well, we lost, 49-0. I often wondered what those friends of Bill's said to him after the game!"

Chicago entered their 1964 training camp still walking the walk of a champion. They had proven that the mighty Packers were not invincible after dominating them in both games in 1963. Green Bay, fattened by the utopia of being back-to-back champs, were out-played in '63. George Halas had firmly stated before the season began that his Bears would have to beat the Packers twice to have any chance of being champions. They did just that.

Although Chicago was one of the oldest teams in the league, opponents conceded that the defense would return as strong as ever and the offense, with running backs Ron Bull and Willie Galimore staying healthy, would be just as effective or better in the 1964 campaign to come.

Sadly, the Bears' fortunes for 1964 were determined not by a pass, a run, a missed field goal, or a coaching decision. Instead, the stage for the 1964 season was set on a dark, desolate country road near Rensselaer, Indiana.

On Sunday night, July 26, at 10:25 pm, a Volkswagen with a sun roof approached a tricky S curve while traveling down Bunkum Road, a couple of miles from the Bears' training camp facilities at St. Joseph's College. As the Volkswagen maneuvered the dangerous curves, the rear of the car slipped off the blacktop flanked by loose gravel, blowing out a rear tire and hurling the vehicle into a skid. The car turned over at least once, throwing its passenger and driver through the sun roof, killing them both instantly.

The passenger in the Volkswagen was Bears' receiver Bo Farrington. He died with multiple skull fractures. Found some sixty feet away from him was the Wisp, Willie Galimore. Galimore died of multiple skull fractures, internal injuries, and a crushed chest.

Officers said the pair would have survived the accident if they had been using seatbelts. Also, a highway marker on the S curve had been broken for nearly two weeks. When a reporter visited the crash site the next afternoon, the sign had been erected back into its proper place.

The Bears' squad, getting ready to play the annual College All-Star Game, went into shock. Two of the team's brightest stars had been lost in an instant. Word of the accident swept through St. Joseph's College around midnight leaving players and coaches stunned and disbelieving. Both Farrington and Galimore had been popular with their teammates, and the news of their death left the rest of the team numb.

"This is the saddest day in Bears' history," Halas told his players gathered around him the following afternoon. "Something like this reaches the heart and makes everything else seem petty. It's going to take a great deal of will power to carry on. A great honor can be bestowed on Willie and Bo if you will dedicate the season to them."

Quarterback Bill Wade stood up and suggested they have a minute of silent prayer and pointed out the impact that family life had on the lives of the two deceased players. Galimore left three children, all under ten years old. Farrington left a widow expecting the couple's first child in the fall. They had only been married five months.

Willie Galimore gained 2,985 yards and scored twenty-six touchdowns in his six seasons with the Bears. He had also tied a club record of four touchdowns in one game.

Farrington joined the Bears in 1961 and played in every league game through the 1962 and '63 seasons. He was known for his fleetness and pass catching, along with his downfield blocking.

With Galimore gone, the Bears now had no experienced break-awayback. It was certain that the loss of both players would weaken the champions. Bears' runners Billy Martin and Charlie Bivins would have to pick up the pace, while Rick Casares healed slowly from leg surgery.

A week-long rain in Green Bay made the turf soggy and loose before the season opening game with the Bears. While inspecting the field on Friday, Lombardi yelled at the groundskeeper, claiming that the field was the worst in the league and angrily suggested that he roll it with a steamroller. "That would put waves in the field," the pudgy groundskeeper meekly answered.

"It's wavy as a ribbon now," Lombardi shot back. "I want it hard!" The groundskeeper assured him the field would be hard by Sunday.

There was good reason for Lombardi to be worried and edgy about the slippery sod on which his warriors, one warrior in particular, were about to do battle. Sunday's game would mark the glorious return of Paul Hornung from NFL banishment. After nearly a year in exile, Commissioner Pete Rozelle had announced on March 16 that Hornung and Alex Karras would be reinstated. Rozelle said there was no evidence that Hornung or Karras ever bet against his own team.

Hornung had not been destitute or bored by any means in his year off. He had a lucrative endorsement contract with Jantzen Sportswear. He also did radio and TV work for stations in Louisville, Kentucky. In addition, he was in great demand for speaking engagements. Of course, the womanizing didn't stop, either.

Lombardi and his team were overjoyed at Hornung's return. In his absence the Packers had not only lost a big play man but they had also missed his leadership. Hornung had such an air about him that when he walked into the locker room, he immediately uplifted the team. That feeling had been sorely missed during the '63 season.

Sunday came bright and cool, and the groundskeeper had been proven right. The field had hardened and was in excellent shape.

As in 1963, Chicago opened the 1964 season against their rivals in Green Bay, and were humiliated, 23-12. It was the first time anybody had knocked the Bears out of first place in the Western Division since the '62 season.

Paul Hornung, the Golden Boy, garnered a thunderous ovation when introduced and would not disappoint the Packers' faithful. Hornung scored eleven points, booted three field goals—one a 52-yarder—rushed for 77 yards, threw two passes completing one for 9 yards, and kicked off five times—twice into the end zone and once over the end line. The Golden Boy was back, giving the Packers the leadership and poise it had lacked the year he was absent.

Hornung's 52-yard field goal was the fourth longest in league history at that time and was a rulebook rarity. The rule said that after a fair catch on a kickoff, the offensive team has an option of putting the ball in play with a free kick or by a scrimmage play. Hornung booted the ball and split the uprights, with some help from a brisk wind.

"We never practiced the play," Hornung said afterwards while puffing on a cigarette. "I didn't even know what the heck we were doing."

Lombardi stated that he doubted anyone would see the rare play again in their lifetimes. He also lauded the electrifying return of Hornung. "I've seen Paul play other good games," the coach said, "but none any better than his performance today."

The absence of Willie Galimore showed prominently in the Bears' final team statistics. They could only muster forty-six yards on the ground, with Ron Bull leading the inept running game with only twenty-five yards.

George Halas spoke honestly after the game about his team and his rivals. "The Packers did to us today what we did to them last year," the old man said. "It's going to be that kind of season—full of peaks and valleys. Today we were in a valley."

And there the Bears would stay. After a close victory the following week, they were trounced unmercifully by Baltimore, 52-0. It was all down hill as Halas saw his squad go 1-5 over the next six games.

The night before the game with the Bears in Chicago, Lombardi walked into the Red Carpet restaurant and found Paul Hornung drinking at the bar with his beautiful date. Lombardi strictly forbid his players to be seen standing at a bar, and to make matters worse, it was the night before a game. In front of a roomful of diners Lombardi shouted he was going to fine Hornung $500 for breaking rules. The fine was later reduced to $300 because Lombardi tasted the beverage after Hornung had left and found it to be only ginger ale.

Coming off a revitalizing three-game winning streak, the Bears met the Packers for the 90th time on December 5 at snowy Wrigley Field. Chicago, hoping to salvage something of their lost season, was silenced by Willie Wood, former school teacher and part-time Justice Department employee.

Wood, the Packers' All-Pro defensive safety, returned one punt sixty-four yards, another for forty-two yards, and intercepted a pass to set up the two touchdowns and field goal that beat the Bears, 17-3. He was practically a one-man offense.

Bruising back Jim Taylor passed the 1,000-yard mark for the fifth consecutive year, becoming the first man to accomplish the feat. Jarrin' Jim scored a touchdown and finished with eighty-nine yards in twenty-one carries.

Chicago Tribune writer George Strickler wrote that some of the Bears' players who made up the championship team of the year before played an exceptional game. Others, he said, "would have done better to moonlight at a neighborhood filling station."

Early in the fourth quarter, Bears' fans took out their frustrations on a drunken and obese Packers' devotee. Stupidly, this Green and Gold supporter paraded unwaveringly up and down the aisles waving a "Green Bay" pennant while being pelted with a barrage of snowballs and obscenities. Experts estimated he was hit with a ton and a half of snowballs until a Chicagoan broke his pennant "stick" and threw it on the ground. Undaunted, the Packers' fan picked up the slush-soiled pennant and danced merrily on his way.

The former champion Bears finished a disillusioned season with a 5-9 record. Green Bay also found disappointment as they went 8-5-1 for the season, finishing second to the Baltimore Colts, to whom they had lost to twice.

It was truly a season of ups and downs. "I don't know what happened," offensive lineman Ted Karras reflected. "When Willie and Bo died, it just took a lot out of everybody. It even seemed like the coaches weren't that anxious to win. It didn't seem right. It was just a weird year. And, everybody was laying for us because we were the world champions."

Bears' center Mike Pyle noted that, "When we lost Galimore and Farrington in the pre-season, it really cast a pall on the way we felt and there just wasn't the same enthusiasm for playing. There was almost no change in our team [from the year before], but we just didn't play the same way as we did in '63. I do feel the Farrington-Galimore incident effected our team more than anything."

Quarterback Bill Wade agrees with the notion that the team was just as good in 1964 as it was the previous year before the tragic accident occurred.

"To me, we had as good a team in 1964," said Wade. "Losing Galimore hurt us tremendously. As far as speed coming out of the backfield and other aspects of our team's effort, we were definitely handicapped. For instance, if you line up strong to the right and have a left halfback like Willie, who had speed and could put fear into a defensive team by getting downfield so fast, a linebacker could not cover him. That was a key to destroying the Packers. When Galimore zipped past a Packers' linebacker, then Green Bay's free safety wasn't free any more, thus with a man like Willie Galimore coming out of the backfield on the weak side, [the side opposite the tight end] you put the strong side [the side where the tight end is lined up] man-for-man. That enables you to have a Johnny Morris and a Mike Ditka man-for-man on the strong side. Both Johnny and Mike should be able to get clear ninety-five percent of the time. So, the loss from the technical point was a very harmful loss, as well as their deaths, which was a deep hurt."

With all that happened during the year, some started to believe the whole season had been jinxed. Wade disagrees. "It wasn't jinxed, in my personal opinion," he says. "There were a whole lot of factors. I could go over game by game and tell you exactly what did happen. I personally don't believe in jinxes. You cannot dwell on life's negatives and hurts—even death. All of us have had heartaches."

Over the years a few ex-Bears have depicted George Halas as being shrewd, businesslike, and at times very callous. Once a former player said he threw around nickels like they were manhole covers. His demeanor and no-nonsense attitude many times made him look very calculating and unforgiving. But Halas wasn't the kind who would do a good deed and then broadcast it to the world. He silently went about his business committing acts of generosity and unselfishness.

George Halas paid all funeral expenses for Willie Galimore and Bo Farrington. He gave each widow more than each player's salary and added a bonus to each check.

It was yet another unannounced humanitarian act by George Stanley Halas.

Penn State has produced many solid football players but few like linebacker Dave Robinson. He was the Green Bay Packer's first round draft pick in 1963 and would be a marauder on the Packers' defense until 1972.

"I'm from New Jersey originally so all my life I had followed the New York Giants," he said. "I wanted to play for the Giants but I was drafted by the Packers. I was happy to play in the NFL and extremely happy about going to the world's championship team. I was ecstatic about playing for Vince Lombardi.

"My first game against the Bears was in the Shriners' exhibition game in Milwaukee, a game we won, 26-7. I remember Bears' quarterback Rudy Bukich threw a pass that I intercepted and ran in for a touchdown. I thought I was hot stuff. Later, I looked at the game film and I saw [Chicago halfback] Angelo Coia was behind me. He could have hit me but it was an exhibition game. On the film you could see he covered twenty yards to my ten. I thought I was some hot shot and I was running all alone, but he was right on my back. He could have reached up and grabbed me but he didn't.

"The first regular season game at Green Bay was against the Bears. Wholly mackerel! I couldn't believe these guys were so fired up. I knew the Packers and the Bears had a rivalry, but this was something. I didn't think any rivalry could match the Penn State-Syracuse rivalry. The hitting and intensity in pro football was that way. And the Bears took it a notch above.

"The Bears beat us twice in '63. The first game we played I didn't play very much. In the second game, when they were beating us in Chicago, I guess Vince said we might as well get this guy so test under fire. He threw me into the game and I played most of the third and fourth quarters.

"I had played against Mike Ditka in college but I didn't realize what Mike was until I went into that second game in '63 at Wrigley Field. In the exhibition in Milwaukee and the opener game in '63 he had played, but the intensity wasn't there. That game in Wrigley Field was a different story. I thought, now this is the Mike Ditka everyone has talked about."

In Robinson's rookie season, he was a little awe struck when Bears' runner Willie Galimore came galloping his way. He would have the same respect for Gale Sayers two years later as he did with Galimore.

"Gale was quicker but I think Galimore was faster," Dave recalled. "I didn't think Gale was flat-out fast but he had all the moves. Sayers went from zero to sixty so quick. For the first ten yards no one could touch him. But Galimore ... if he ever got loose on you and broke it for five yards, he was going to get twenty-five.

"I really enjoyed playing against Bears' offensive guard George Seals. In fact, some made people thought George and I had a feud going. There was never a feud between us but it made good copy and it helped sell tickets and got me a couple of speaking engagements in Chicago. I remember one time we were playing in Wrigley and I was covering Gale Sayers. Gale was going down the sidelines as the Bears' quarterback threw the ball. I intercepted it. As I was bringing it back down the field I made a great move then turned back to the inside and George Seals hit me with a forearm. It was one of the hardest hits that I can remember. He knocked me to the ground. When I looked up and saw George, I started laughing and he started laughing. I told him I was going to get my revenge. I didn't get a good shot at him until the next game in Green Bay.

"There were always rumors that George Halas had spies. In those days we always practiced Saturday mornings at the stadium. Rumor was that Halas owned an apartment in a building that overlooked Wrigley Field and there were spies and cameras there. To counter that, Lombardi used to put in fake plays we weren't going to use. He also made us wear different numbers. I would wear "83" in practice and Willie Davis would wear a fake number, etc. It was really spy vs. spy... a weird situation.

"I remember during Bears' week we always had a ton of people at our open practice in Green Bay. One time Lombardi said, 'I don't know if you guys know this or not, but one of those cars down there with all of the "Go Pack" and "We Love You Packers" stickers on it had Illinois license plates. That's probably one of Halas' spies.' Sure enough, there was a green and gold car with stickers and banners and all of this and it had Illinois tags. Lombardi assumed it was one of Halas' spies, but it could have been a Packers' fan who lived in Illinois.

"Vince said one time that the word going around was that George Halas had offered $10,000 reward to anyone who turned over a Vince Lombardi playbook. Before it hit the papers Vince told us that he would give Halas a playbook and let him try to figure out when we were going to run the plays.

"I look back on it and realize how silly and stupid it was, but it all added to the fury and getting us ready for the game. And it worked. Vince was a master with physiology, so a lot of things he said about George Halas he did to fire us up. He was using our minds getting us ready for the game.

"But Vince said the only man he called "Coach" was George Halas."

1965-'67

The bidding war for players between the NFL and the upstart AFL was as heated as ever before November, 1964. The AFL, proving many an NFL expert wrong, had survived and was doing quite well ... so well, in fact, that there had been talk of a merger of the two leagues.

The annual draft of college flesh was now a wide open affair. Salaries had skyrocketed, mainly because of the number of dollars the rich AFL owners were throwing around. Many of the best college players were now playing in the new league. Alabama star quarterback Joe Namath, who had been courted by the St. Louis Cardinals, signed with the New York Jets for a then enormous sum of $400,000. Many wondered where it would all end.

In 1965, the Chicago Bears spawned one of the greatest drafts of talent ever. The job of drafting players wasn't one for which George Halas could take full credit. Many accolades for the Bears' class of 1965 goes to defensive coach George Allen, who would leave the Bears to coach the Los Angeles Rams the following year.

One day Allen and Halas watched a Kansas University game film where they saw a running back make a move they couldn't believe. They reversed the film projector over and over watching in amazement. "[He] started one way," Halas described the move, "left his feet and seemed to change direction in the air. When he landed, he was running the opposite direction. When I saw that move, I knew we had to get that young man."

Trouble was, Lamar Hunt, the head Geronimo of the Kansas City Chiefs, also wanted the talented runner. Halas decided to draft the talented running back and pay the money to get him to showcase his talents in NFL stadiums and not in the upstart AFL venues. In hindsight, Halas had nothing to worry about. The college standout, who had grown up watching Cleveland Browns' great Jim Brown run roughshod over a football gridiron, had no desire to play in the new league.

The young star who had so impressed George Halas was Gale Sayers, the "Kansas Comet." While being an All-American at Kansas, there were some naysayers who thought Gale was too meek to play pro football. "He's not tough enough," said some amateur experts. Otto Graham, who coached Sayers in an All-Star game, doubted claims by Sayers that he had a hurt leg. Nevertheless, Graham decided not to play him in the game and later said, "This boy has great natural talent, but unless he changes his attitude, he'll never make the Bears because George Halas won't have him." Otto Graham was terribly wrong.

With the offense taken care of, Halas and Allen turned their attention to the defensive side of the ball. Chicago, by a previous trade, had two picks in the third round of the '65 draft. Halas chose University of Illinois All-American linebacker Dick Butkus. Soon after the draft, Halas would prematurely but correctly call Butkus the greatest lineman the Bears have had since Bulldog Turner. "Butkus should hold down the middle [linebacker position] for Chicago for at least the next decade," Halas declared.

Once again, Halas was competing against the rival league for the services of the towering linebacker. The Denver Broncos also drafted him, but Butkus never really considered going there. "I just like the Bears," he said. "It's the hometown and everything."

If there ever was someone who was born to play football, it was Dick Butkus. "I never thought of anything else but playing pro football since I was about ten years old," he once recalled. He came from a large family of eight, of which he was the second smallest of five husky, strapping boys. One can only imagine what it was like growing up at the dinner table of the Butkus family! That must have been where he developed his fast moves and cat-like agility.

A magazine writer at Illinois gave Butkus an "animal image" that to this day follows him. The article portrayed him as being a cross between a knuckle-dragging ape man to a bloodthirsty headhunter. Baltimore Colts' wide receiver Alex Hawkins once called Dick Butkus an animal, adding that, "He doesn't shower after a game. He licks himself clean." Headlines like, "Butkus: Man or Monster?" certainly didn't help to dispel the image. There was also the reported airplane incident. After a game in Green Bay in the late Sixties, Butkus got angry at Bears' business manager Rudy Custer for scheduling the short return flight on an old-fashioned, stuffy DC-3. He took care of the problem by punching out a rear window to get some air!

Butkus played with a hard-driving tenacity that many in Chicago hadn't seen since Ed Sprinkle. When Butkus tackled, the one getting tackled always remembered it. He was so aggressive that on every play he would try to take someone's head off. Cooper Rollow, the great Chicago writer who followed Windy City sports, once asked Butkus if he was as mean as all the press clippings had made him out to be.

"I'm not so mean," Butkus said. "I wouldn't ever go out to hurt anybody deliberately. Unless it was...you know...important...like a league game or something."

The Chicago Bears had unknowingly drafted two future Hall of Famers. It was an astounding maneuver that would pay dividends for the next decade, just as Halas had predicted. Oddly, when Butkus was interviewed in early December by *Washington Evening Star* writer Steve Guback, he humbly stated that, "I think I could play offensive center but the Bears have Mike Pyle. I wouldn't mind getting a shot at defensive end. Everybody talks to me about playing linebacker, but I don't know. The Bears have Bill George ... maybe I'll wind up riding the bench."

In July 1965, Dick Butkus walked onto the practice field in Rensselaer, Indiana for the first time. Veteran Bill George, standing there sweating in the mid-summer heat, turned around to get a good look at the new rookie in camp. "The first time I saw Butkus," George recalled, "I started packing my gear. I knew my Bear days were numbered. There was no way that guy wasn't going to be great."

For the next nine seasons, Butkus became one of the most feared middle linebackers in the game. After the '65 season, Bill George was traded to the Los Angeles Rams where he played one year and retired.

In the summer of 1965, former Packer coach and leader Curly Lambeau was living at his summer home in Door County near Sturgeon Bay, on the Wisconsin peninsula.

On a sunny June 1st day, a cheerful Lambeau visited his neighbors, the Van Duyses, and kidded them about him needing a little exercise. He got their lawn mower and began cutting their grass. Afterwards, he was talking to them when he commented that he felt "kind of sick." Suddenly, Lambeau fell over on the grass.

Earl Louis "Curly" Lambeau was dead of a heart attack at the age of sixty-seven. A week before Lambeau had passed his annual physical with flying colors.

George Halas, his old league rival, wrote a special piece on Lambeau that was published in the *Green Bay Press-Gazette* shortly after his death. "There's a limit to everything," he wrote. "Life ends. Curly Lambeau is gone. It's a world of turns."

Others spoke in tribute to the man who had helped make football the popular sport it had become. Commissioner Rozelle called him "one of the true pioneers of the game and certainly a great part of what the National Football League is today is directly traceable to him."

Tony Canadeo, Lambeau's star running back of the Forties, said, "What he's done for Green Bay borders on the miraculous. He brought a small town into the big leagues."

At Schauer and Schumacher Funeral Home, Lambeau's honorary pallbearers included George Halas and two former Packer coaches, Gene Ronzani and Lisle Blackbourn. A light rain was falling as his casket was carried from the funeral home by former Packers Don Hutson, Johnny Blood, Arnie Herber, Buckets Goldenberg, Charley Brock, and Dick Weisgerber.

On June 8th, the Greater Green Bay Labor Council unanimously adopted a resolution to change the name of City Stadium to "Lambeau Field," in recognition of his contribution to the town and to his impact felt nationally and internationally.

"Be it resolved," the resolution read, "that the name of Green Bay City Stadium be changed to 'Lambeau Stadium' or 'Lambeau Field' in honor of Curly Lambeau." It was signed, "Clayton Smits, President, Greater Green Bay Labor Council."

Gale Sayers walked onto the sun-drenched grass of the newly christened Lambeau Field on the third day of October with great anticipation. The Kansas Comet had seen little action in the Bears' first two games, both losses on the West Coast. Today he would get his first start in the backfield. He would not disappoint.

A record crowd of 50,852 witnessed the emergence of an NFL star, but not before an older one took center stage. Late in the first quarter Paul Hornung plunged 1 yard for a touchdown, and with Don Chandler's extra point, the Bay's led, 7-0. On the last play of the first quarter, Bears' QB Bill Wade retreated seven yards to attempt a pass. Packers' defensive stalwarts Lionel Aldridge and Ron Kostelnik converged on Wade, sandwiching him as he released the ball. The wobbly pigskin fluttered into the hands of linebacker Lee Roy Caffey, who promptly trotted into the end zone for another Packers' touchdown. Late in the second half, Bart Starr lofted a beautiful spiral to receiver Bob Long. The "Wichita Wheat Shocker" corralled the ball for a 48-yard TD.

In the second half of the game, Sayers showed his wares. In the last minute of the third quarter he whizzed his way by a couple of would-be tacklers for a 6-yard TD. Then, late in the game, Sayers produced a run for the highlight reels. Rudy Bukich, in replacement of Wade, tossed a little flair pass to Sayers. Like a twisting tornado, Sayers spun his way into the Packers' secondary and raced sixty-five yards for a touchdown. It was a beautiful thing to watch, but it meant very little on the scoreboard; the Packers came away with a 23-14 victory.

Sayers garnered eighty rushing yards on seventeen attempts for the day while earning an NFL baptismal at the hands of Packer defenders Ray Nitschke and Willie Davis. On one sweep around left end, Sayers met up with Nitschke and Davis and decided to lower his head and ram into both of them. The next thing Sayers knew he was four feet off the ground with Davis holding his left leg and Nitschke pulling on the other. Make a wish.

With the Bears at 0-3, it was surprising to hear an upbeat Halas after the game. "This could be the real beginning of a good ball club," he said full of gusto. "We're not at all ashamed of this ball game," added Halas. "Lombardi, has a great ball club, they should go on to win it."

On the last day of October, the undefeated 6-0 Packers marched into Wrigley Field prepared to make it seven wins in a row. Instead, they walked right into a Bear trap. Although the Packers scored first on a patented Jim Taylor 1-yard run, it was an all Chicago afternoon as they shocked Green Bay, 31-10. Rushing yardage for the Bears was spread around evenly, with Jon Arnett accounting for seventy-three yards, Sayers sixty-six, Livingston forty, and Ron Bull with forty-seven. An Arnett 2-yard plunge was set up by an electrifying 62-yard punt return by Sayers in the third period.

Jim Taylor had his usual good day against the Bears. Rushing for fifty yards and the Green Bay's only touchdown, Taylor had some All-Pro encounters with Dick Butkus. On two vicious collisions, Taylor had the ball jarred loose by Butkus, only to be saved by a quick official's whistle. On other head-on collisions the two exchanged words. "He's just a hard-nosed football player," Butkus said after the game. "When you tackle him, you've got to hold on or he'll slip away. He plays hard. But then, so do I."

Lombardi's declaration after the game that this Bears' team was just as good as the '63 team was quite astute. Chicago lost only two of their remaining seven games to finish at 9-5 on the year, good for a third place finish in the Western Division.

The Packers and the Colts both ended the year at 10-3-1, forcing a playoff game to decide who would eventually face the Cleveland Browns in the championship game. With the score tied, 10-10, at game's end, it was only the second playoff game ever to go into overtime. Kicker Don Chandler finished the matter by booting a 25-yard field goal that to this day old Colts' fans swear went wide of the goal post.

On January 2, 1966, in the ankle-deep mud of Lambeau Field, the Packers and the Browns squared off to decide who was best. With the horrible field conditions, straight ahead running was the best choice. Hornung and Taylor, behind the crushing blocks of their offensive line, combined for 201 yards on the ground, while the Packers' defense held the great Jim Brown to fifty yards rushing. Green Bay controlled the game and won the championship, 23-12.

Green Bay, Wisconsin was Titletown USA again!

Jim Tunney, an NFL official for over thirty years, told this story in his book, *Impartial Judgment*. It, better than any other story, tells of a rivalry with no bounds:

"I remember one Sunday morning going to mass at St. Willebrord's in Green Bay before the game. Halas was on one side of the aisle with most of his team, and Vince Lombardi was on the other, with most of his players. The priest addressed us. I don't remember all that he said, but he preached on the Gospel of the Good Samaritan and brotherly love and how important it is that we all share the feeling of brotherhood.

"I got to thinking about competition, these two teams about to go out and try to kill each other in a few hours. The priest finished his sermon, banged his fist on the lectern, and said, 'And now, let's go out and beat those Bears!' That's how well accepted that rivalry was."

There was now talk that the Packers were getting to be an old team. It took just one sports writer to bring to everyone's attention that Bart Starr was now thirty-three, Hornung and Taylor were thirty and thirty-one, Ray Nitschke and Willie Wood were thirty, while Jerry Kramer and Fuzzy Thurston were now thirty-one and thirty-three. The Packers needed a blend of youth and experience to compete for another title.

That blend of youth was about to cost the Green Bay Packers about $1,000,000. Heralded rookie running backs Donny Anderson from Texas Tech and Jim Grabowski from the University of Illinois were signed to replace the running tandem of Hornung and Taylor. In looks and style, the twosome set of runners paralleled each other. Anderson, with a head of blond hair, had the same handsome looks as Hornung. He was going to be the second coming of the "Golden Boy." He was wooed by the Houston Oilers but left Texas for the frozen tundra of Green Bay. By signing a contract for a quoted $650,000, Anderson had enough money to keep himself warm.

Where Anderson displayed more finesse, Grabowski was a "Taylorish"-type runner, one who preferred to run over you than around you. At 6'2" and 225 pounds, the big Illinois fullback saw limited playing time in 1966, but in 1967, after Taylor and Hornung were gone, Grabowski led the Packers in rushing.

Both players saw very limited duty in the Packers' sixth game of the season against the Bears in Chicago. The Green Bay defense would win this one. Holding the Kansas Comet to a paltry twenty-nine yards on fifteen carries, the Packers shutout their foes, 17-0, the first Green Bay blanking of the Midway Monsters in Wrigley since 1932.

Rudy Bukich had a miserable day against Packer defenders, allowing three of his tosses to be picked off and returned for big yardage setting up ten points. Herb Adderley ran an interception back forty-four yards, Nitschke ran one for twenty-three yards that set up a Don Chandler field goal, and Willie Wood stepped in front of a Bears' receiver and raced twenty yards into the end zone. The Packers gang-tackled, corralled, and dominated the Bears.

Asked if he had planned to use rookies Anderson and Grabowski, Lombardi said, "I had every intention of playing them, but like many good intentions, they just remained intentions."

Five weeks later the Bears, with an odd record of 3 wins, 4 losses, and 2 ties, traveled to Lambeau Field to, as writer Cooper Rollow put it, "continue their inexorable plunge to oblivion."

The 94th installment of the rivalry would be a brutal fracas that saw the officials arm-tired from throwing penalty flags all day. "It looks like, instead of playing football, we're playing drop the handkerchief," Halas grimly said after the game.

It would be a day of quarterback shuffling. On the second play of the game, Starr lobbed a 40-yard pass to end Carroll Dale, but in the process pulled a hamstring muscle. Zeke to the rescue! Zeke Bratkowski trotted onto Lambeau Field's sacred turf and completed fourteen of twenty-five passes for 187 yards and two touchdowns, leading the Packers to a hard-fought, 13-6, win.

The Bears began the game being led by Rudy Bukich, but after a miserable performance he was replaced by Bill Wade. Wade, making his first appearance in a league game since the third game of 1965, produced little. It got so bad that in the fourth quarter Wade himself was replaced by Bukich.

Sometimes sarcasm helps get through the tough times. Interviewed after the game, burly Bear Doug Atkins cynically informed anyone in earshot that the Bears were, "... going to play Northwestern [University] for the city championship next week since the Cardinals moved out."

The NFL vs. AFL war had taken its toll on all involved. The fight for the best college players had sent salaries spiraling through the roof. The business of robbing established players from each league was brisk. NFL veterans like San Francisco quarterback John Brodie, Mike Ditka, and the Rams' Roman Gabriel all contemplated jumping to the AFL, while in 1966, the New York Giants stole soccer-style place kicker Pete Gololak from the AFL's Buffalo Bills.

Secret talks, under the watchful eye of Pete Rozelle, were under way between Dallas Cowboys' owner Tex Schramm and the Kansas City Chiefs' Lamar Hunt to merge the two leagues into one. Shortly before the 1966 season began, a merger was announced that installed Rozelle as league commissioner. The two leagues decided to have a common draft of college players and to play separate schedules. They also agreed to play a "Super Bowl" between the AFL champion and the NFL champion to decide which was the best pro football team in the world.

It was Pete Rozelle who took the ball and scored the merger when he convinced Congress to pass a bill that would intercept any problems of legality surrounding the merger. Wise legislators attached the bill as a rider on President Johnson's anti-inflation bill, which was a sure bet to pass.

The war that had started with the birth of the AFL in 1960, a war that had been fought in courtrooms, in back rooms, in subpoenas, and most of all in owners' wallets, was now over. Out of the chaos another war, an organized one, was sanctioned: the Super Bowl. Vince Lombardi and the Green Bay Packers had the distinction of being poised to play the AFL champion in the first Super Bowl.

To decide the NFL's entry into the championship, the Packers had to play a game against the Dallas Cowboys. Played in surprisingly bad weather conditions, the twenty-degree temperatures after a rain made the sward of the Cotton Bowl an ice skating rink. In a spirited, tense game, Green Bay defensive back Tom Brown intercepted a fourth down Don Meredith pass in the end zone to secure a Packers' win, 34-27.

On a sunny January 15, 1967, in Los Angeles, the Green Bay Packers met the Kansas City Chiefs in the league's first Super Bowl. With the Packers being heavy game favorites, many were surprised that the Packers were only ahead 14-10 at half-time. The opening moments of the third quarter, however, made believers out of the surprised. Chiefs' quarterback Len Dawson rifled a pass that was picked off by Willie Wood and returned it to the Chiefs' 5-yard line. Packers' running back Elijah Pitts scored from there and the game was more or less won. Packers 35, Chiefs 10!

In the crunch of press after the game Lombardi breathed a huge sigh of relief. He and his Packers had reinforced the pride and tradition of the league over the new up-start AFL by whipping the Chiefs. The old guard NFL still had bragging rights.

If any picture identifies the Green Bay Packers and their coach Vince Lombardi, it is the famed Packers Sweep. It's really a very simple play. The ball would be pitched to Paul Hornung or another running back and the two offensive guards would pull in the direction of the ball carrier was running to block for him downfield and create a seal that the ball carrier could run through. It was a play all Packers opponents knew was coming but most of the time were powerless to stop it. Green Bay's basic philosophy was: Here we come, now try to stop us.

In any old highlight film you can see a number "64" and a "63" out front leading the way on the Packers Sweep. They were Lombardi's "guardian angels," Jerry Kramer and Fred "Fuzzy" Thurston. Their line play personified the excellence that Vince Lombardi demanded.

Jerry Kramer's selection by the Packers was a surprise even to him. "There was an executive with Georgia Pacific that I think had an interest in a mill in Idaho, maybe in Lewiston," Kramer recalled. "A guy by the name of Mike Couman had scouted me. At that time, of course, scouting procedures were less sophisticated than they are today.

"I got a questionnaire from the Packers asking how big are you, how tall are you, how fast are you, what do you weigh, and if I wanted to play professional football. I got the same thing from San Francisco, Pittsburgh, and a few other teams.

"That was all I ever heard from Green Bay. Later, I got a telegram from San Francisco that said they were interested in me. That was a very serious sign.

"I had no idea as to why or how Green Bay scouted me. I found out later that this friend of a friend suggested they draft me. I don't think he was a paid scout. I think it was just a hobby for him. So I was drafted by Green Bay and immediately went to a map and tried to figure out where the hell Green Bay was."

Kramer, like many others on the Packers' team, saw their new coach Vince Lombardi as a gruff, strict totalitarian and they didn't like him. It's interesting that a whole team that started out loathing Lombardi, would end up loving him and sacrifice everything to win for him.

"I disliked Coach Lombardi a great deal ... initially," Kramer said. "Our relationship was certainly antagonistic. After three or four years he was still on my ass. I remember we were having a Thanksgiving party and he wanted everyone to bring their family, kids, and parents. Bring everybody. One big happy family kind of deal. Well, he just chewed my ass unmercifully on Tuesday morning when we were watching game films.

"Afterwards, he was going around the room getting a head count of how many people were going to be there Thanksgiving Day. So he calls Hornung's name. Paul answers one.

"'Starr!' he yells. Bart replies four.

"'Kramer!' he yells.

"'I don't know,' I snap back.

"'What do ya' mean you don't know?' he says.

"'I don't know if I'm coming,' I said.

"'You're coming!' he said.

"'Five,' I said.

"So, it was that kind of relationship for a long time. Within a year or two after that time we were having a scrimmage at training camp. We'd had a long, difficult day and he was on my ass again, giving me his concentration lecture about six inches from my nose. I jumped offsides and he gets on my ass again. Just chewing my ass.

"I went up to the locker room after practice and I'm sitting on the stool there looking at the floor and I'm thinking maybe this isn't my sport. Maybe it's not my game and maybe it's time I move on. Maybe I'll never be the football player he wants and maybe I'll never be able to play for him. I'd been there about twenty minutes or so very deep in thought about the situation. He came strolling into the locker room, saw me, came over and slapped me on the back of my neck, messed up my hair, and said, 'Son, one of these days you're going to be the best guard in football,' and walked off. Well, hell, he just filled me up with an incredible burst of energy, but I think more importantly he gave me a vision. A mission, a thought, or a focus. That was a very, very big day in my life. From that point on, I think I started pushing myself as much as he wanted me to, and he quit pushing me because he finally got my motor started and he didn't have to get on my ass anymore. After that, we became pretty good friends."

Kramer and Thurston seemed to get a great deal of Lombardi's attention. They also received a great deal of Lombardi's wrath.

"We were great pals and still are great pals today," Jerry said of his teammate Fuzzy Thurston. "We used to run a little bit off the field. We figured it out one day that since Lombardi was an offensive coach instead of a defensive coach, we got a hell of a lot more attention than defensive players. Since he himself was an offensive lineman and not a running back, we got a lot more attention as offensive linemen than running backs. And, since he was a guard instead of a tackle or tight end, the guards got a lot more attention than anyone else. And since he was a right guard, I felt he really focused on that position because that was the position he played. I think he felt he was absolutely qualified to discuss that position.

"I felt that we were a little more important part of the offense, with the guards and the Green Bay Sweep. Of course, everyone on the offense was important. But I think everyone felt that way. I think he made everyone feel like they were the most important part of the offense. I'm sure Forrest Gregg and Bob Skoronski felt that if they didn't do their job the offense would fail. He made us feel like if we didn't succeed, the team would not succeed."

Lombardi posted a 13-5 record against his rival George Halas, a man who he loved to beat but respected like no other. "He loved the Bears and competing against them," Kramer recalled. "He really admired Coach Halas tremendously. He held him in very high regard. It's like anybody you think a lot of, you want them to think a lot of you.

"He always got ready for the Bears. It was a challenge and his step seemed a little lighter. He'd smile a little wider and he seemed more alive during Bear Week.

"He brought us all together one time and he was talking about whipping the Bears and he said, 'You guys go out and whip the Bears and I'll whip old man Halas' ass!' Then he let out a hearty laugh.

"He was such a genius at measuring our readiness as a team. One time we were in Chicago getting ready to play the Bears for the divisional title. Well, we were nervous, tight as fiddles. He pulled us all together before the game for his usual inspirational thoughts and comments to pump us up. All of a sudden he asked, 'Do you all know why Belgians are so strong?' Everybody looked at him like ... What? Somebody said 'No, why?' He said, 'Because all they raise are dumbbells.' We all looked at one another and said that's the dumbest joke we've ever heard. But what it did was to pull us down a notch and took some of the edge off. He thought we were a little too tight. It was a silly joke, and he certainly wasn't the kind to tell an ethnic joke, being an Italian himself. He was just desperate for something to bring us down some.

"One of the first times I began to appreciate Bart Starr or really understand what he was made of was in a Bears' game in Chicago," Kramer went on to say. "Bart was a very quiet, almost invisible ball player in my first couple of years. We had Lamar McHan, Joe Francis, Babe Parilli at quarterback, and Bart was in there somewhere. We didn't know how much steel Bart had in him. He didn't talk that much, he wasn't loud, and he wasn't much of a leader at that time. There were some questions about Bart's competitive fire.

"We were playing Chicago, either in 1959 or '60. Bill George was playing at middle linebacker when Bart threw a long pass. I remember blocking, then watching the ball. The play was over as far as the linemen were concerned. Well, Bill George comes in late and hits Bart, who's unprotected and looking downfield. George hit him in the mouth with a forearm and cuts Starr's lip from the bottom of it to his nose. Starr's bleeding like a stuck hog. Blood is flowing down the front of his jersey. George just really decked him. He knocks Bart down on his ass and says, 'That ought to take care of you, Starr, you pussy.' Bart gets up and points a finger at him and says, 'Fuck you, Bill George, we're coming after you!' That was the only time I've ever heard Bart even mention a word like that in the forty years I've known him.

"Since Bart's bleeding, someone says he has to go to the sidelines. Starr hollered, 'Huddle up! We're taking it after them.' He stayed in there, took the club in for a score, bleeding all the way. After that, in my mind at least, that was when I found out what Bart Starr was made of. I thought, that boy is all right."

Jerry recalled a funny moment from a game with Chicago in the mid-Sixties.

"One year we were playing up in Green Bay and Ken Bowman was playing center and Butkus was at linebacker. The snap was on one and Bowman thought it was on two or three. I don't know what the hell he was thinking. Well, Bart barks out 'Hut!' and pulls out going backwards without the ball. Fuzzy and I both come up in pass blocking position. The defensive tackles come across the line and we're all engaged in combat. And Bowman has still got the ball under center. He didn't know what the hell to do with it. He looks from side to side and he sees where everybody has gone then looks up at Butkus at about the same time Butkus looks at him. They both realize the situation. Butkus takes about a three-yard run and hits Bowman in the face with a forearm and knocks his ass right back where Bart is. Bowman said he looked up, saw Butkus coming, and said, 'Oh shit!'"

Lombardi's other "guardian angel" was Fred "Fuzzy" Thurston. Fuzzy? "When I was a baby," Thurston said, "I had real curly, fuzzy hair. My sister used to say, 'Look at that little fuzzy wuzzy.' It stuck with me. I went to college and thought I'd get rid of it. I knew this girl from Altoona, Wisconsin who came to Valparaiso University where I was in school. One day I was walking with some football players when she walked by and yelled out, 'Hey, Fuzzy, how are ya!' So I got the nickname back."

Fuzzy Thurston was drafted out of Valparaiso by the Philadelphia Eagles in 1956. Thurston was drafted into military service and shared the soldier life in Texas with Harlon Hill, the

Bears' great pass receiver. He played with Hill on the Army football team in 1957 where he made the All-Army team. Hill mentioned to him that he ought to become a Chicago Bear when his service duty was done. In 1957, the Bears were playing an exhibition game in Texas and Thurston had an opportunity to talk to George Halas. Halas wanted to offer Fuzzy a contract. Thurston played four exhibition games with Chicago where, oddly, he lined up at defensive end, the same position Doug Atkins was playing. It was one of Halas' rare mistakes. He traded Thurston back to Philadelphia.

Things didn't work out in the City of Brotherly Love; Thurston was cut from the team. In search of a place to play, he traveled to Canada. Before the 1958 season, the Baltimore Colts came calling. He was lucky enough to start on special teams and win a championship, the infamous 1958 overtime win over the Giants. Before the 1959 season, Thurston was traded to the worst team in the league located in the worst weather, the Green Bay Packers.

"They all said, 'poor ol' Fuzzy, got traded up to Green Bay, nobody wanted him,' Thurston recalled. "Well, Vince Lombardi wanted me and he made me into a hell of a football player. I was very happy to be in Green Bay." From the second exhibition game in Lombardi's first year, 1959, Thurston started at guard and stayed there until he retired in 1967.

Fuzzy banged heads with some of the greatest Bears of all time in his twenty-seven games he played against them. "Fred Williams was the main guy I played against," Thurston recalled. "I had to block Doug Atkins and Ed O'Bradovich on trap plays and I had to pull up the middle and block Hall of Fame linebacker Bill George. I knew all of these guys because I had played there for six weeks and they all knew me. I had the chance to drink a lot of beer with them and got to know them well. To this day, I'm still friends with them.

"The Bears' defensive line was tough. They were hard to hold. There was a special element there because of George Halas, who had the knack of getting his Bears prepared to play the Green Bay Packers. That rivalry was there waiting for us and it's still here, and is without a doubt the greatest rivalry in football as far as I'm concerned."

Like the other Packers who played for Lombardi, Thurston talks in a reverent tone when asked how Lombardi changed his life, both in football and every day living. "With out question, he brought out the best in me," Thurston stated. "I don't know what would have happened to me. I probably would have played in the league after Baltimore but I don't know if I ever would have had the great accomplishments playing for another coach. He put together a great team unity that we didn't have. He made the players very close and he was by far the smartest and most intelligent offensive-minded coach. By putting this all together, he made a great football team."

After the 1967 Super Bowl, Fuzzy retired. "Lombardi was going to retire and I thought what a better time to do it," he said. "The big guy was going and I would go along with him. Plus, I had a lot of injuries and I had lost my starting job to Gale Gillingham, who was a marvelous football player. It was time."

Fellow guardian angel Jerry Kramer tells a great story that typifies the fanatical nature of the Bears-Packers rivalry. Not even young children are excluded.

"Chicago was playing the Packers on a Monday night in 1986 (Bears 25, Packers 12) at Lambeau Field. My wife is from Chicago and she bought my boys some Bears' shirts after they had won the Super Bowl in January.

"We were staying out at the Radisson where the Bears were staying and my boys wanted to wear their Bears' shirts. I told them it wasn't a real good idea. They said, 'C'mon, Dad, chill out, relax.' I reminded them that it really wasn't a good idea.

"We went down to a restaurant that Fuzzy had at the time across town. We walked in and there must have been at least 300 people in there and they all turned, saw me and the kids, and they go, 'Boooooooooo!' The whole restaurant resounded in a chorus of boo's. It just continued and continued until the boys started to tear up. They didn't understand what the hell was going on.

"Then this lady walks by with a boy about ten years old, about the age of mine then. 'Are those your boys?' she asked.

"Well, I'm proud of my boys so I throw my shoulders back and say, 'Yep, those are my boys.'

"She said, 'You're a horse's ass! How could you put Bear shirts on your boys?' She gave me a hell of a cussing.

"Finally, Fuzzy came over and brought two Green Bay T-shirts and put them over the top of the Bears' shirts and the crowd starting cheering!"

Big changes were in store for Chicago in 1967. The Midway Monsters would see the retirement of quarterback Bill Wade, and the trading of All-Pros Doug Atkins and Mike Ditka.

"I retired after my knees started going bad and I had to have some operations," Wade recalled. "I was not activated and I ended up as the Bears' quarterback coach in 1967."

Doug Atkins, unhappy in Chicago, was traded to the expansion New Orleans Saints. "I was a little dissatisfied," Doug said. "You could play good ball for him [Halas] and he wouldn't give you enough of a raise. I always talked about getting traded but he'd say, 'Kid, I'd like to trade you but nobody wants you.' I think the only reason he traded me after twelve years was that he thought I was about through."

Doug Atkins' departure wasn't the only change in the Bruins' defensive makeup. Ed O'Bradovich was now the only remaining starting lineman or linebacker from that great '63 championship team, although being in the company of linebackers Dick Butkus and Doug Buffone wasn't a difference to complain about.

George Halas also traded tight end Mike Ditka to Philadelphia for Eagles' backup quarterback Jack Concannon. Concannon started most of Chicago's games in 1967, taking over for the often erratic Rudy Bukich, and finished third in rushing yardage for the Bears with 279 yards. There were no other changes in the backfield as Ron Bull, Andy Livingston, Brian Piccolo, and Gale Sayers handled the running duties. Sayers was coming off an All-Pro season, having set an NFL record for combined total yardage with 2,440 yards. Sayers had run for 1,231 yards, caught thirty-four passes, averaged thirty-one yards per kickoff return and fielded six punts. Another All-Pro year awaited Sayers in 1967.

With a new expansion team beginning play, the NFL Conferences realigned and divided into two four divisions. Both Chicago and Green Bay were placed in the Central Division along with Detroit and Minnesota, and competed for the Conference title with Los Angeles, Baltimore, San Francisco, and Atlanta.

Anyone who had the misfortune to come in crushing contact with Dick Butkus has a story to tell about the encounter. Packers' wide receiver Bob Long is no different.

Long wore the Packers' Green and Gold from 1964 to 1967, after being drafted out of Wichita. His Butkus memory is reminiscent of many that are told.

"It was my first game back after a knee operation," Bob recalled. "I was a secondary receiver on this play. My job was to occupy the cornerback because Bart Starr was trying to hit tight end Ron Kramer on a zig-in or a zig-out. I came off on a short route, kind of lazily underneath the line of scrimmage. There was a fierce rush on Bart. While being in a hurry he apparently saw me coming underneath and flipped me the ball. I caught it and as I turned upfield, all I could see was number "51." Butkus just knocked me upside-down, flipping me over on my back.

"As I came off the field there was Lombardi—in typical Lombardi style—saying, 'Well, I guess your knee is all right now, isn't it?' It had nothing to do with my knee, catching the ball and getting killed. I heard from players later that this play made the Dick Butkus highlight film."

Rumors had swirled during the 1966 season that Lombardi was set to retire from coaching. Feelings of Lombardi's possible departure permeated throughout the players, the fans, and the state of Wisconsin itself.

Vince's mind was occupied with what he considered more important matters than retirement talk in the summer of '67. Jim Taylor had wanted a three-year contract where he could end his career in Green Bay. If he didn't get it, he wanted to play near his home in Louisiana. Taylor had also taken offense to the huge signing money paid out to the "Gold Dust Twins," Anderson and Grabowski.

As Taylor mentioned earlier, his relationship with Lombardi had more or less hit a now low at the same time. Lombardi, maybe thinking Taylor was in the twilight of his career, wanted one more year out of the bayou basher. The "I need Taylor for one more year" thinking was probably because Vince himself saw 1967 as his last year. What a better way than to retire from coaching along with the other players he had molded into one of the greatest teams football had ever seen.

The reality of that neatly packaged scenario was not to be. After tiring from the Taylor impasse, Lombardi traded him to the New Orleans Saints. Vince was stung by what he thought was Taylor's insubordination.

Another off the field distraction probably hurt Vince more than anything ever in his coaching career. Lombardi loved Paul Hornung and had taken him under his wing when he had arrived in 1959. He had saved Hornung's career, a football career that had been marked by two years of ineptness.

Paul Hornung was selected in the 1967 expansion draft by the New Orleans Saints. Lombardi had to put his star player on a list of players available for the draft to help stock players for the new franchise. The Saints, wanting a name player, nabbed Hornung from the list.

Hornung had been bothered by nagging injuries for the past two seasons. In 1965 and '66, his rushing totals and point production had dropped dramatically. The most serious of Hornung's ailments was a pinched nerve in his neck that was a continuing problem. It was reported that his left arm had shrunk because of the reoccurring injury to the nerves that controlled it.

Hornung retired without ever donning a Saints' uniform. Just as well. Paul Hornung is first, foremost, and forever, a Green Bay Packer.

After a surprising tie with the Lions on opening day, the Packers took to the sacrosanct sod of Lambeau Field to battle the Bears, a game that would be decided by the foot of Green Bay kicker Don Chandler.

The Packers tried their best to give the game away, turning the ball over five times on interceptions and three times on fumbles. Bears' defensive back and pass robbery suspect Ritchie Pettibon fleeced Bart Starr out of three of the five interceptions on the day. It was truly an unwonted performance for "Mr. Quarterback." The week before Starr had been intercepted three times by Detroit. What made his poor play even more eyebrow-raising was that he had only been intercepted three times in all of 1966.

This would be a day for the young "Grabo." Jim Grabowski, transformed into a work horse, rumbled for 111 yards, his first 100-yard rushing day in the pros, and set a Packers' record for attempts, with thirty-two. In the second quarter it was Grabowski who swept around the right end from two yards out to open the scoring.

With the score tied, 10-10, late in the fourth quarter, Starr began a methodical drive downfield. Near the 40-yard line, Starr went back to pass and got tremendous pressure from mouth-frothing Bears' Ed O'Bradovich and Dick Evey. Somehow avoiding a huge loss behind the line that would have taken them out of field goal range, Starr broke away and gained 4 yards on the play.

With only 1:03 remaining, Chandler trotted on and lined up to try a 46-yard field goal. As the ball hung in the air, hearts stopped and silence reigned as all eyes watched the ball float over the cross-bar like a dying duck, and the Packers won, 13-10. "I knew it was straight ... I didn't know if it was long enough," Chandler said of the kick afterwards. "I didn't know it was good until I heard the crowd roar."

The Bears had recovered from an early season slump by the time the rivals met again in Chicago on November 26. They had put together three straight wins and brought a 5-5 tally into the contest while the Packers were at 7-2-1.

In the first quarter, Chicago behind, 7-0, but on their rival's 44-yard line, Bears' quarterback Jack Concannon called on Gale Sayers to hit the Packers on the left side of the line. Sayers burst through a hole, pulled out of Lionel Aldridge's grab, and zipped past a line-backer into the secondary. Only Packers' defensive back Tom Brown stood between Sayers and the goal line. It was no contest. Sayers gave a hip switch and Brown was left twisted on the Wrigley Field turf. Sayers pranced into the end zone tying the score.

The deciding touchdown came after an interception by Packers' linebacker Dave Robinson. "Jack Concannon," *Chicago Tribune* writer George Strickler wrote, "still thinks he can throw a football accurately without getting set." Concannon's overthrown aerial landed right in the hands of Robinson at the Chicago 31-yard line, and he returned it to the nineteen. A Donny Anderson 1-yard plunge and a field goal by Chandler iced the game, 17-13, clinching the Central Division title for the Packers.

The Packers were jocund and happy in the locker room confines of Wrigley, but not overly jubilant. This was almost old hat to them now. Their calm celebration was the revelry of a champion. No champagne, no wild merry-making bash. Just a feeling of a job well done and the knowing that the big push back to the Super Bowl would begin after the season.

Some 2,500 Packers fans braved 15 mph winds in fifteen degree temperatures to welcome their Central Division champs home to Austin Straubel Air Field. As Green Bay's heroes deplaned, fans cheered, fire sirens wailed, and "Love Those Packers" banners popped and crackled in the bitter wind.

When asked how they felt about clinching the division title, offensive tackle Forrest Gregg and defensive standout Henry Jordan spoke the truth. "All I know is we get the day off Monday," Gregg said.

"Yeah," Jordan chimed in, "and when we walk in there Tuesday, Lombardi will glare at us like we're losers."

Jordan was correct. At practice on Tuesday Lombardi gave his team unmerciful hell, telling them they were crazy if they thought they were going to lay down. He cussed, he ranted, and he screamed. Things were certainly back to normal in Green Bay.

The Packers defeated the Rams in the first round of the playoffs and readied themselves for a rematch in the NFL championship game with Dallas. The Cowboys had blasted Cleveland, 52-14, to earn the right to challenge the Packers, this time in Green Bay.

Much has been said and written of the game now known as "The Ice Bowl." Its images are frozen in our minds, frozen like the field and the breath of the 50,861 diehards who sat in minus thirteen degree temperatures on New Year's Eve 1967 and saw a piece of football folklore.

The Cowboys won the toss of the coin, leading one writer to predict that instead of receiving the opening kickoff, the Cowboys should elect to go home. In the fourth quarter, the Packers got the ball on their own 31-yard line with 4:50 on the clock. Starr mastermined a drive that took them down to the 1-yard line with twenty seconds remaining. On fourth down, Starr's surprise quarterback sneak iced the Ice Bowl and another trip to the Super Bowl, this time to face the Oakland Raiders.

That final drive may very well have been the greatest test of will ever seen on a football field.

Like the previous year, most considered the Dallas-Green Bay game as the real championship. The Raiders were no slouches, having posted a 13-1 regular season record.

Super Bowl II was never really a game. The Packers led, 16-7, after the first half and settled the matter when Herb Adderley returned an interception for sixty yards in the fourth quarter to win, 33-14.

Jerry Kramer and Forrest Gregg carried Vince Lombardi off the field on their shoulders, and into the land of football legends.

1968-'69

On Thursday, February 1, 1968, the Oneida Golf and Riding Club just outside Green Bay was the site of a torch being passed. Vince Lombardi stepped into the bright lights of the television cameras and announced he was retiring from the head coaching duties with the Packers, but he would stay on as general manager. His successor would be 54-year old Phil Bengtson, the only remaining assistant coach who had come to Green Bay with Lombardi in 1959.

Although some speculated that health was a reason Lombardi had retired, he assured everyone that he was in excellent health. He added that the requirements of being a head coach was a determining factor.

"It was an easy decision to make," Phil Bengtson, the new Packers' skipper responded, upon being asked about inheriting the best team in football. "I'm elated, excited," he said. Bengtson had some huge shoes to fill and he knew it. Upon hearing someone say that taking over after Lombardi was not going to be easy, Bengtson laughed, "There's only one way to go," but added, "it really doesn't bother me. Four in a row, that's my ambition. I see no reason why we can't continue winning."

Nearly five months later, George Halas arrived at the Bears' headquarters at West Madison Street in Chicago and shocked everyone by announcing he was stepping down as head coach of his Chicago Bears. Unlike Lombardi, Halas cited medical reasons for retiring.

"The arthritic condition in my hip has progressed to the point where I simply cannot move quickly enough on the sidelines," Halas noted. "Looking at practical realities, I am stepping aside now because I can no longer keep up with the physical demands of coaching the team on Sunday afternoons. I suppose I began to realize this in one of our final games last season when I started rushing after the referee who was pacing off a penalty and it suddenly dawned on me that I wasn't gaining on him. I began to wonder whether the officials were speeding up or I was slowing down.

"I have made this decision with considerable reluctance but no regrets," he continued. "There was a strong temptation to continue for another season. Next year is the Bears' golden jubilee and I would liked to have been on the field in 1969, rounding out fifty years as a player and a coach."

When asked if his successor would be from inside the Bears' family, Halas smiled and said, "Yes."

Fact is, former Bears' quarterback Bill Wade wanted the job. He recalled a surreptitious meeting several months before Halas' public announcement. "At the end of the season, all the coaches got together and sat in coach Halas' board room," Wade recalled. "He said, 'I'm going to get a new overcoat, who do you think should get my overcoat?' Abe Gibron [Bears' assistant coach], who was sitting at the table, said, 'I think Bill Wade ought to have his overcoat.' Halas gave me his overcoat. I was thrilled to have anything he owned.

"Coach Halas told me in our personal conversations that if I called him May 1st and I come back, 'something very nice will happen.' I said I'd call him May 1st. I called him and told him I couldn't come back. He said: 'If you come back, something very nice will happen to you.' I said, 'Coach, I just can't do it.'

"Two years later I was talking to someone about Bohemians—Coach Halas was a Bohemian—and in Bohemia, when a man gives you his overcoat, it means you're going to take his place in his business. If he had told me that he wanted me to be the head coach of the Bears, then I would have done that. I would have loved to have coached the Chicago Bears, although my father had asked me never to become a coach."

Soon after his announced retirement, George Halas named 38-year old Bears' assistant Jim Dooley as head coach of the Chicago Bears. Dooley, an end for the Bears for nine years beginning in 1952, had been the team's offensive coach from 1963 to '65, and then had coached the defense for two years.

Dooley's first tenure as the Bears' head honcho was marred by key injuries. Rookie BYU quarterback Virgil Carter was to prematurely shoulder the responsibilities as field general after ailments sidelined quarterbacks Rudy Bukich and Jack Concannon.

In Green Bay, even though some of the old guard were now retired, others returned for yet another year, determined to capture an unprecedented fourth championship. Bengtson had regulars Jerry Kramer, Forrest Gregg, and Bob Skoronski on the offensive line; Bart Starr, Travis Williams, Elijah Pitts, Donny Anderson and Jim Grabowski in the offensive backfield; and Ray Nitschke, Henry Jordan, Herb Adderley, and Willie Davis anchoring an imposing defense.

The Packers would be most vulnerable at the place-kicking position. The usually sure-footed Don Chandler was now in business in Kansas City, but had offered to play on Sundays if he could only come in to practice on Fridays, becoming a long weekend football player. General Manager Lombardi, probably forgetting that he had done the same for Hornung when he had military duties during the season, refused Chandler's request. It was a costly decision.

The kicking situation deteriorated from a concern early in training camp to complete desperation, with some comical events thrown in. Bengtson went through a host of flaky kickers. At one point he even agreed to try out a radio disc jockey in nearby Appleton who was known to have kicked a little in high school!

Nineteen sixty-eight became a season of tough breaks for the Packers. After an opening day win over the Eagles, they sputtered all the way to the November 3 meeting with Chicago, walking on to Lambeau Field with a disappointing 3-3-1 record. The Bears, having rebounded from a poor start, brought a 3-4 tally into battle with the Packers. To the capacity crowd watching, which included Paul Hornung in the press box, this game would bring reminders of the opening day game in 1964.

Chicago, with no problems with their kicker, took a 3-0 lead at the half when Mac Percival toed a chip-shot field goal. The Packers' kicking woes continued as recent recruit Errol Mann missed two field goals from twenty seven and forty-four yards out. With the score tied 10-10 midway in the fourth quarter, Gale Sayers fumbled in Packers' territory and Herb Adderley scooped the ball up and returned it to the Chicago fourteen. After the Packers' offense failed, Chuck Mercein, full-time running back and part-time place kicker, ran onto the field—and promptly shanked a 22-yard field goal. Bengtson could do nothing but kick the Lambeau Field sod and watch his hair grow gray. In the waning moments, Green Bay's Donny Anderson punted from deep in his own territory to where Bears' receiver Cecil Turner immediately made a fair catch. Hornung, sitting above the rim of Lambeau Field, knew what was coming.

It reminded Hornung of his 1964 game against the Bears when he had kicked a 51-yard field goal at the end of the first half. That field goal was set up by the little known rule of a free kick after any fair catch. This day, it would be Mac Percival's attempt that could win the game.

Ritchie Petitbon, dazed and wobbly after being smacked hard in the third quarter, held the ball on the 43-yard line as Percival stood three yards behind him ready to kick. The Packers could do nothing. Standing ten yards downfield, they, like the rest of the crowd, were nothing but bystanders.

Percival hit the heart of the uprights and won the game for

Chicago, 13-10. It was a poignant, torturous loss for the Packers, one that destroyed any chance of defending their Central Division championship.

The Packers had no one to blame but themselves. While the free kick by Percival was something they were powerless to prevent, their attempt to contain Gale Sayers failed miserably. The Kansas Comet, enjoying his greatest day as a pro, galloped for a smashing 205 yards on the ground. Sayers completely shredded the Packers' defense, leaving empty-armed tacklers watching his heels, as his cleats ripped up the turf, sending it high into the air in clumps.

The next day the *Green Bay Press-Gazette* noted that it was the first time since 1945, when George Halas was serving as a Naval officer, that he had not made the trip to Green Bay for the Packers-Bears game. Instead, Papa Bear had watched the game on TV from his apartment in Chicago; a satisfied smile crossed his face as Percival knocked the free kick over the goal post for the win.

Sadly, Halas' smile would be wiped away in the following week's game with San Francisco. It is one of the darkest moments in the Bears' history. Gale Sayers took a pitch-out from Virgil Carter and swung to his left. San Francisco defensive back Kermit Alexander hit Sayers on the side of his right knee just as the Kansas Comet planted his right foot in the ground. It was a loathsome sight as Sayers lay prone on the ground. From that moment on, the Comet would be forever robbed of his streaking breakaway speed.

On the last day of the season, the Packers came to Wrigley Field to play the part of spoilers. A Bears' win on this day would not only tie them for the Central Division title with Minnesota, but would send them to the playoffs; Halas' Bears had defeated the Vikings twice during the season.

After Mac Percival's first quarter field goal put the Bears in the lead, Packers' fill-in quarterback Don Horn lofted two long bombs for touchdowns, one of 67 yards to Jim Grabowski and the other to Boyd Dowler for seventy-two yards. Chuck Mercein added a 1-yard blast that put the Pack out in front, 21-10, at half-time. Another TD pass from Horn to Dowler seemingly put the game away, ending the Bears' chances.

Suddenly, the Bears came alive after an incident involving Packers' linebacker Ray Nitschke. "Early in the second half [offen-

sive left guard] George Seals had his knee completely blown out,"
Bears' center Mike Pyle remembered. "He was lying on the ground
as I came up to him, and Ray Nitschke was standing over him laughing, making some comment about not being so sorry he was hurt.
That enraged our offense."

The Bears, led by Jack Concannon, went on a 17-point tear to
make it 28-27 late in the fourth quarter. On the Packers 47-yard
line with 1:13 left to play, Concannon faced a fourth and fourteen
situation. There was confusion and second-guessing on the Bears'
sideline, leading them to call a time-out to decide whether to try a
long field goal or go for the first down. Percival trotted on the field,
then was called off. The Bears were going to go for it. Concannon
faded back and threw the ball downfield. The nimble-fingered Ray
Nitschke picked off the pass and ruined any chance of Chicago
going to the playoffs.

"It was the most inspired football game I've ever played in my
entire life," Mike Pyle said. "When people ask me what was the
greatest game, I've gotta say the championship game (1963), but
other than that, the final game in 1968 was."

Bengtson, seeing the huge win as a precursor of things to come
in 1969, termed the victory, "a real boost in that respect." The season had been a true heartbreak for both him and the Packers. They
lost five games by a total of only twenty-two points, and they tied
another. Their horrible kicking game was greatly responsible for
Green Bay's less than sterling 6-7-1 record. With better kicking,
and a few breaks here and there, they easily could have been 12-2.

The 1968 season had been a great disappointment for Green
Bay veteran Jerry Kramer, who took off his Packers' uniform for the
last time under the grimy girders of Wrigley Field. Tragically, to
top off what had been quite a rueful season, the next day Kramer
saw his house in Green Bay burn to the ground.

The name Fido Murphy won't ring a bell for many, but his
name certainly comes up in any conversations with former BYU and
ex-Bears' quarterback Virgil Carter. Fido was one of the Bears'
scouts who worked the Utah area for Halas. Murphy began show-

ing up at BYU's training facility, watching Carter perform. The more Murphy showed up at practice, the more Carter began to realize he would probably be drafted by Chicago.

In 1967 Carter went to active duty for the National Guard but he still got to practice with the Bears' taxi squad. The taxi squad was a small band of players who were allowed to practice with the team but were not allowed to suit up for any games. Carter first became aware of the Packers-Bears rivalry at a Tuesday practice session at Wrigley Field before the September 24 game.

"I still remember the coaches and some of the players were a little uptight about the Green Bay rivalry and they talked about it, which they had not done in the preceding game," Carter recalled. "So, we're standing there in Wrigley Field. If you're familiar with the scenario, once the baseball Cubs left Wrigley, they built temporary bleachers on the east side. While this construction was going on, we were down there practicing on the field. We were running through some drills when all of a sudden I noticed [coaches] Phil Handler, Luke Johnsos, and George Halas started going around whispering to players. It caught my attention and I wasn't sure why. Then suddenly they gave a shout, 'Go get him!' With that, the defensive team stormed the temporary bleachers. What had happened was that there was a fellow working on the bleachers sitting in the tunnel having his lunch. All they could see was his head kind of looking down on the field. Of course, they thought he was a spy! And we weren't doing anything special. From that time on they couldn't work on the bleachers' construction during our practice time.

"Paranoia prevailed on the team that week. There are some brown stone, two-story buildings with roofs that look down on to Wrigley field. They assigned a coach to use binoculars on those windows and roofs looking for someone who may be paying attention, filming, or making notes of the practice."

One of Carter's biggest pro career thrills was quarterbacking against and defeating his hero Bart Starr at Lambeau Field on November 3, 1968, in the 13-10 Bears' victory.

"The night before the game in Green Bay at the Northland Hotel—where they gave you skeleton keys to open the door to your room—the fire alarms went off a couple of times, initiated by Green

Bay fans, I'm sure," Carter remembered. "That got us up a couple of times in the night, but it obviously didn't affect the outcome of the game."

"We were unconsciously playing to avoid losing last year," Phil Bengtson was quoted in the 1969 Packers' yearbook. "I thought that we had a tendency to be too conservative. Hopefully, the attitude would be a little more reckless, not worrying so much about making a mistake, about making a certain move."

Writer Lee Remmel queried Bengtson about what other self-proclaimed football sages were saying about the Packers: that it was an over-the-hill team. "There's no question about that," Bengtson replied, "we are. But we feel we're taking care of that. We've gone through that transition in the backfield with Taylor and Hornung, by bringing in Anderson and Grabowski. Now it's in the offensive line."

There had been changes in the offensive line since the Packers' Super Bowl II victory. Gone were the "guardian angels," Kramer and Thurston, while tackles Bob Skoronski and Forrest Gregg were very near the end of their head-butting days.

Center Ken Bowman, Gale Gillingham and Bill Lueck at guard, and Dick Himes, Francis Peay, and rookie Bill Hayhoe at tackle rounded out a rugged front line that opened holes for rushing backs Travis Williams, Dave Hampton, and the Gold Dust Twins, Donny Anderson and Jim Grabowski.

The continuing thorn in the side of Bengtson was the kicking game. He had acquired Mike Mercer from the AFL's Buffalo Bills in 1968, but Mercer booted only seven of twelve field goal attempts. In 1969, Mercer would share the kicking duties with Booth Lusteg, a journeyman player acquired from Pittsburgh, where in 1968 he had only made eight of twenty field goal tries. *Green Bay Press-Gazette* writer Don Langenkamp recalled in a piece he wrote in August 1993, of a strange incident involving Lusteg. "Booth Lusteg," Langenkamp wrote, "would wake up his wife at 2:00 a.m. and make her hold footballs so he could practice in the back yard."

Like Green Bay, the Chicago Bears held high hopes for the

upcoming season. The 1968 season had been marred by a rash of injuries. If most of the Bears team had not had to train by running up and down hospital corridors, they would have finished better than their 7-7 mark in '68.

After lengthy and concentrated knee rehabilitation, Gale Sayers returned to lead the league in rushing with 1,032 yards, but he was not the same Kansas Comet. His longest run from scrimmage was only 28 yards and his 4.4 average rushing yards was the lowest of his career.

The defense, now anchored by the All-Pro linebacker Dick Butkus, absolutely terrorized opposing teams. If for some reason Butkus found himself occupied on a play, Coach Jim Dooley could count on linebacker Doug Buffone, or linemen Dick Evey, Ed O'Bradovich, Willie Holman, or Frank Cornish to corral an opponent's ball carrier or passer.

Although he only played in sixty-eight league games, Chicago Bears' running back Gale Sayers is considered one of the greatest runners of all-time. He was named to Pro Football's All 75-Year Team and was the youngest inductee into the Hall of Fame, bronzed in Canton, Ohio in 1977 when he was only 34-years old.

What was so exciting about Gale was that at any moment of a game, in a split second, he could burst through a defense and score. Many a fan who had the privilege of seeing Sayers play live were left crossing their legs by the fourth quarter, not wanting to visit the bathroom in fear of missing the "Kansas Comet" break one in the open.

His 4,956 yards rushing may not measure up to some gifted runners who have come after him, but Gale Sayers had a tremendous impact on the game. He is still the NFL's leading kickoff returner with a 30-yard average. He averaged five yards per attempt and lead the league in rushing in 1966 and 1969.

"The first time I saw Gale Sayers ... I could not believe what I had seen," said Papa Bear George Halas. "If you want to see perfection as a running back, you had best get a hold of a film of Gale Sayers. He was poetry in motion. His like will never be seen again."

Gale was born in Wichita, but when he was seven, his family moved to a little town in northwestern Kansas called Speed. How appropriate. After a stellar career at Kansas, where he was All-American his junior and senior year, he was drafted by Chicago in 1965. A student information director at Kansas tagged him with the nickname "The Kansas Comet." It stuck with him the rest of this career.

Oddly, some believe Gale wasn't tough enough to play pro football, especially for George Halas. "It didn't bother me, I had confidence in my ability to play," he said. "It's bad to go into training camp with a tag on you like that. When I got to the Bears' training camp I saw they had good football players—Ronnie Bull, John Arnet, Andy Livingston, Joe Marconi—but the first day there I saw I could do things quicker, I was faster, and I could see the holes better. I knew right then—just give me a chance and I'll prove I can play the game. Even though those players had three and four years experience on me, I knew they couldn't do what I did on the football field. I was ready."

George Halas wasn't the only one interested in Gale. Lamar Hunt, owner of the AFL's Kansas City Chiefs, also drafted him in 1965. Gale had no intentions of playing in the AFL. "I knew Lamar Hunt and the Chiefs were scouting me but unbeknownst to them I always felt that to better myself as a football player, I had to play against the best," Sayers admitted. "I felt at that time the best football was being played in the NFL. I signed a four year contract with the Bears for $25,000 a year. The Chiefs offered me $27,500 a year. Twenty-five hundred dollars didn't make a difference to me. They could have offered me $40,000 and I still would have signed with the Bears."

Sayers' first pro start came against Green Bay on October 3, 1965. He once confessed that before every game in his rookie year he would vomit because of nerves. "George Halas would call out the starting lineup in the locker room before the game," Gale recalled. "He never let anybody know before. On that day he called Gale Sayers. I didn't know I was going to start. I was nervous but ready.

"I didn't know of the Packers-Bears rivalry, I just knew that eleven people were going to be after me. They [the Packers] knew about Gale Sayers. I was no surprise to them. I had a good game the first ball game. They knew I was a pretty good football player and they tried to take it out on me."

Gale names defensive back Willie Wood as the toughest Packer he ever played against.

"Although he played free safety, he could recognize plays," Sayers said. "If you were running an end sweep you knew the linebackers or defensive end wouldn't be there. But all of a sudden, there was Willie Wood because he could recognize plays very early. That gave me something else to look for. They [Packers' defense] were all tough—Ray Nitschke, Willie Davis, Herb Adderley—but for me you had to watch where Willie Wood was on the field."

On November 3, 1968, Sayers stunned a capacity crowd at Lambeau Field by rushing for 205 yards. "It was a great ball game," Gale recalled. "It was one of those games where I ran up a lot of yards but couldn't score. I had a couple of long runs to help us maintain momentum and field position."

Many believe that Gale Sayers was the most beautiful runner to ever carry a football. Gale has heard this from the first day he walked onto the practice field in Rensselaer, Indiana.

"No question about it, it does make me feel good because my career was so short," Gale said. "When they start naming top five running backs of all time, Gale Sayers is in there. It also makes you realize that you did have something special when you played the game.

"People would say that 'I have never seen a back do the things you did on the field,'" Gale said. "Well, my friends back in high school did. I did that on the sandlots before high school. I did it in college. I had God-given instincts. I didn't work on any moves. I didn't work on faking left or right or twisting and turning. I got myself in shape and went out there and played. That's all I did."

Ironically, it would be the same God-given talent that enabled Sayers to twist, turn, fake, and run that would eventually be his downfall. Although Sayers would lead the league in rushing in 1969, his 1968 knee injury robbed him of some of his great cutting ability. An injury to his other leg in 1970 severely shortened his career.

"The way I ran, all the cuts I made in grade school, high school, college, and pro ball, my knees were so loose, I was a knee injury waiting to happen," Gale confessed. "All the cuts I had made over the years had made my knees loose. One day I was very unlucky.

"The only regret I have about my football career is that I wish weight training had been around at that time," Gale said. "Back then they didn't believe that running backs and wide receivers should be lifting weights because they thought weights would tie you up, bulk you up, and make you slower. Today, it's been proven that weights can build quickness, speed, and strength."

And what would have happened if injuries had not ended his career prematurely?

"I could have played another four or five years, gained more yards, scored more touchdowns," Gale says. "But the honors I have today I probably would have still gotten if I had played another four or five years. I had nothing else to prove."

A tavern in Kenosha, Wisconsin had been threatened in August 1969, by customers who were calling on a "friendly boycott" of the bar. The proposed sit-out strike wasn't because Don Lambrecht's Tavern served warm beer or his pickled eggs weren't pickled enough. His patrons wanted Don to purchase a color television set to watch the Packers-Bears game on, instead of the fuzzy black and white set that flickered above the bar. Thursday before opening day, Don yielded to the call of the wild and bought a brand new color set, tossing the old black and white out in the alley.

Patrons of Lambrecht's tavern congregated on Sunday, September 21, to watch the Packers and Bears scrap for the 99th time. The capacity crowd at Lambeau Field, which included eighty "delighted" Packers' alumni and Commissioner Pete Rozelle on hand to celebrate the Packers' 50th year anniversary, saw a new Green Bay team that at times resembled those of the past. In flawless fashion, the Packers dismantled Chicago, 17-0, never allowing the now de-clawed Bears to penetrate past their 30-yard line.

It was a masterful performance of ball control and defense by the Packers. In the third quarter, the Bart Starr-led offense hogged the pigskin for all but six of the quarter's twenty-seven plays. In the process, Starr hit nine passes for ninety yards, one of them a 31-yard scoring toss to Travis Williams.

The defense literally showed some "Hart" as veteran Doug Hart intercepted two passes, one in the fourth quarter that he returned forty-four yards to set up a 1-yard Grabowski blast for a game-icing touchdown.

In regard to Green Bay's supremacy on the day, Lee Remmel wrote that, "In the process, they dispelled whatever doubts may have remained that the Pack, as the faithful have been contending, would be back. The chastened Bruins, in fact, are wondering if their ancient adversaries ever had been away."

When they met again in mid-December, the Chicago Bears were in the thralls of their worst season ever. As they trotted on to the brownish turf of Wrigley Field to face the Packers, they brought along with them an atrocious 1-11 record. It was hard to believe that just six years before they had been the champions of the world. Now they, along with the hapless Steelers, were the champion door-mats of the league.

The Packers had started off well in 1969, then hit a three-game losing streak in middle of the season, and were now trying to rebound and finish the season on a high note.

An uneventful and inept first half produced a scoreless tie at half-time. For the intermission's entertainment, the Wheeling, Illinois High School band marched on the turf and played the opti-mistic "Everything Is Coming Up Roses." Writer Lee Remmel wrote that the band would, "deliver a musical prediction" that was, "prophetic."

Led by quarterback Don Horn, filling in for the injured Bart Starr, the Packers ambushed the Bears in the third quarter. First, Travis Williams broke open for a 39-yard TD run making it 7-0. Then Horn got hot, throwing touchdown passes of ten and sixty yards to tight end Marv Fleming and running back Travis Williams. The Bears could only manage a fourth quarter Mac Percival field goal. The Packers' final 21-3 margin would have been larger if kicker Booth Lusteg hadn't missed on his three first half field goal attempts.

"Bears Lose To Packers In Dullsville," was the headline in the

Chicago Tribune the following day. It had been a completely futile effort on the Bears' part and was no joy to witness for the Chicago faithful as the malady of boredom and freezing temperatures drove them to the exits before the game was over.

The scene in the Bears' locker room was not a pretty one. An angry Virgil Carter highlighted, or rather "lowlighted," a distraught Bears' team after the game. Carter claimed he had been assured by head coach Jim Dooley that he would play the entire game. When the Bears got the ball to begin the second half, Dooley sent in rookie Bobby Douglass to jump start the offense.

"It's the third time they've screwed me and that will be the last; I won't give them another chance," an angry Carter said. The boiling Carter in a roundabout way, called Dooley a "liar" and said he possessed no guts. "It said in the papers this week I would be the quarterback for the whole game and that Douglass was not going to play," he continued. "I would consider that being a liar. The first thing on my list of things to do is ask to be traded."

George Halas stepped in, suspended Carter for the last game of the season, then traded him to the Cincinnati Bengals.

Veteran center Mike Pyle was nearly at the end of his rope. The experience of his final season with the Bears was not an enjoyable one. "Statistically in 1969, we were almost the same as in '68," Pyle recalled. "We made mistakes and lost them, but we weren't that bad a team to go 1-13."

The Bears couldn't do anything right in 1969. Even their one win against Pittsburgh turned on them. The woebegone Steelers, like the Bears, had also finished the season at 1-13. Because the Bears had beaten the Steelers, Chicago got to chose first in the 1970 NFL draft.

History records that Pittsburgh drafted a balding quarterback from the swamps of Louisiana named Terry Bradshaw, who would be the field general for the great Steelers teams of the Seventies. History also records that the Bears didn't even get a first round choice in 1970. Winning the only game against Pittsburgh in '69 cost the Bears the chance to draft the quality quarterback they desperately needed.

1969 was a complete nightmare for the Chicago Bears. George Halas had to do something.

The 1970s

Sweetness, Abe, State Street Jack, and a Polish Prince

The NFL's merger with the AFL was consummated in February 1970, as the two leagues officially became the National Football League, consisting of the National Conference and the American Conference. Each conference was sectioned into three divisions: the Eastern, the Central, and the Western Division. The Baltimore Colts, the Pittsburgh Steelers, and the Cleveland Browns moved over to the AFC. The NFC's Central Division remained unchanged with the Minnesota Vikings, the Detroit Lions, the Green Bay Packers and the Chicago Bears.

Another big change was the emergence of televised Monday night games on the ABC Network. CBS, which had the rights to NFL football since 1956, turned down the idea of bidding for the Monday night telecast. With college football on Saturdays and pro football on Sundays, the brain trust at CBS feared overexposure of the sport. Maverick ABC won the rights to televise Monday Night Football, and the rest is history.

George Halas' Bears had just finished the worst season in their history. It had been embarrassing. The once proud franchise was now in total disarray, badly in need of repair.

Halas began to try to rebuild the team by trades. Ex-Packers Elijah Pitts, Lee Roy Caffey, and Bob Hyland found themselves in the Bears' 1970 pre-season camp. Chicago acquired halfbacks Craig Baynham from Dallas and Don Shy from New Orleans. They snatched Pittsburgh quarterback Kent Nix to fill the position left by the departure of Virgil Carter. The Bears' draft of 1970 yielded a fine receiver from UCLA, George Farmer. Halas believed the new blood would help rejuvenate the team.

Three more of Lombardi's old guard Green Bay Packers retired before the '70 season began. Zeke Bratkowski, Boyd Dowler, and the aforementioned Jerry Kramer hung up their cleats for good. Aging Packer stars Forrest Gregg, Bart Starr, Ray Nitschke, and

Willie Wood decided to hang on, trying to bring another title back to Green Bay.

The 1970 draft would be a remedy for the transitional Packers' squad. Four of the first five picks were for defensive men. Notre Dame defensive tackle Mike McCoy, the first player chosen, became a pillar of the defensive line for the next seven seasons. Texas A&I cornerback Al Matthews, Minnesota linebacker Jim Carter, and Ken Ellis from Southern University were talented picks that would pay dividends. Sandwiched in between was Elon University tight end Rich McGeorge. McGeorge would spend nine seasons catching balls in Green Bay.

Now entering his third and final contract season as head coach, Bengtson had reason for optimism. The Packers had finished the 1969 season with two wins, bringing their season record to a respectful 8-6. Also, Bengtson finally found a halfway reliable place kicker in Dale Livingston.

In the spring, Bengtson went into the hospital for a bleeding ulcer. It was obvious that the pressures of being head coach and general manager were beginning to wear on the reserved Norwegian. Rumors had him resigning because of his health before the season even began. Proving the rumors wrong, the fedora-wearing Bengtson guided the Packers into the 1970 season.

Washington, DC was abuzz about their football Redskins in the summer of 1970. Under the direction of Vince Lombardi, the once hapless franchise that hadn't had a winning season since 1955 recorded a very respectful 7-5-2. They finished second place in the NFC Eastern Division in the 1969 campaign, and looked to only improve.

Saint Vincent had started doing in Washington exactly what he had done in 1959 when he took on the Packers' head position. He immediately started weeding out the players from the non-players, the men from the boys, the strong from the weak. He had put the Redskins through as grueling a training camp in 1969 as he had with the Packers years before. It was an average but hungry team that needed a driving leader to believe in and follow. They had found just the man in Lombardi.

But, in the summer of 1970, Vince Lombardi met an opponent he couldn't beat. During training camp Vince complained of abdominal pains and went into Georgetown University Hospital on June 24 for a battery of test. The following day Dr. Robert Coffey performed a sigmoidoscopy. The exploratory surgery found he had contracted terminal intestinal cancer. He had symptoms for just a week. His health immediately went downhill. On July 10, Vince was released and went home to recuperate, and even made a public appearance in New York at a NFL owners' meeting. On July 27, Dr. Coffey readmitted him. Dr. Coffey was shocked by how fast and ruthlessly the cancer had spread. Vince had undergone two operations within a month to battle the disease. He was pale, gaunt, and frail.

It was very difficult for anyone who had known Vince and had been a part of his life to suddenly see the man they thought of as being indestructible now lying in a hospital bed weak and languished. Lombardi determinedly continued to fight.

In early September, two weeks before the start of the 1970 football season he had so anticipated, Lombardi fell into a deep coma. On September 3, a spokesman at Georgetown University Hospital announced that he had succumbed at 7:20 am with his wife Marie at his side. Marie said afterwards that the cancer had been "extraordinarily virulent."

Reactions from those who knew him were immediate and conciliatory. "The death of Vince Lombardi is a deep, personal loss to all in professional football, but those who will miss him the most are those who still had yet to play for him, who might have been taught by him, led by him, and counseled by him," said Commissioner Pete Rozelle.

To Bart Starr, Lombardi's passing was particularly poignant. "I told my wife before I left the house this morning that it was like losing a father. I felt that strongly about him," Bart said. "Fellows who had the pleasure of playing under him are better people for it."

George Halas was distraught over the loss of his old coaching rival. "It is a great loss not only to football, but to the entire country," Papa Bear said. "I regret that I really became closer to Vince only within the last five years. That was all too short a time to enjoy and admire his great qualities. All too few men are around to match his forceful leadership and competitive qualities. I loved him as a friend and as a man."

Vince Lombardi's funeral Mass at St. Patrick's Cathedral was attended by three thousand mourners. The entire Executive Committee of the Packers were in attendance. Archbishop Terence Cooke led the Mass saying, "Vince had fought the good fight. He has finished the course; he has kept the faith."

A string of forty limousines drove down Fifth Avenue to make the forty-five mile journey to Mt. Olivet Cemetery in New Jersey. Vince was buried on a small slope near a crabapple tree.

There's a tragic postscript to the death of Vince Lombardi. A doctor had been treating Vince for rectal problems before he left Green Bay. On one occasion the doctor had recommended a proctoscopic exam. Vince steadfastly answered, "You are not going to shove that thing up my rectum."

If he would have allowed them to perform the procedure, there's a good chance they would have been able to find the cancer in its early stages and restored his health.

Vincent Thomas Lombardi was fifty-seven years old.

When Lombardi tabbed Bart Starr at the beginning of the 1960 season to be Green Bay's leader and field general, the shy but wily veteran had performed feats of valor and heroism. For ten seasons, Starr had proven to be a great leader, the pied-piper of the great championship teams of the Sixties.

As the Seventies began, age was creeping up on Starr. At 37, he felt hurt on every hit, every tackle, and with every pass he threw. Since the 1968 season, Bart had been slowed by nagging injuries. During the 1968 campaign, a sore arm hampered his play. In 1969, a shoulder injury sidelined him. In the middle of the 1970 season, with his arm throbbing in pain, he once again showed why he was still Green Bay's *generalissimo*.

On November 15, the sacred sward of Lambeau Field saw the 101st meeting of football's best rivalry, played before 56,263 screaming fans. To the delight of Phil Bengtson, the Packers' kicking game would pull this one out.

Dale Livingston's 17-yard field goal and a Donny Anderson 14-yard gallop put the Pack up front, 10-0, at half-time. The Bears retaliated in the third period with a Mac Percival field goal and a beautiful 69-yard touchdown pass from Jack Concannon to flanker Dick Gordon. Livingston added another field goal but was bested by Percival, who kicked three between the uprights, giving the Bears a 19-13 lead.

With the ball resting on the Green Bay's 23-yard line with 1:33 to play, commander Starr took to the field and started the drive. Starr whipped a pass to Carroll Dale for 18 yards and out of bounds. A tricky pass over the middle to tight end John Hilton netted 29-yards, moving the ball to Chicago's 33-yard line. Pow, an eleven yard out-pass to back Larry Krause for a first down at the twenty-two. A 6-yard pass to Travis Williams was followed by an 11-yard scamper by Krause down to the Bears' 5-yard line with twenty-nine seconds left. After a half the distance penalty against Chicago, Bart came to the line with only three seconds remaining.

Standing on the other side of the line with his hands on his hips was former Packer linebacker Lee Roy Caffey. Caffey had played for the championship teams of the mid-Sixties. Now his job was to keep his former teammates from scoring a touchdown. "When I was standing there waiting for the next play," he later recalled, "I couldn't help thinking: this is like the 1967 playoff game against Dallas all over again, except here I am on the other side of the line from Bart."

Starr took the snap and rolled out to his right. His intended receiver, John Hilton, was suddenly knocked to the ground by Bears' linebacker Doug Buffone, who himself went down in the collision.

"All I could see was green grass ahead of me," Starr recalled. When Bart saw Hilton on the ground, he, as writer Cooper Rollow wrote, "leaped like a startled fawn from the underbrush," and ran untouched into the end zone for the touchdown.

Bengtson held his breath. The erratic kicking game had put more than a few gray hairs on his fedora-adorned head. Livingston ran onto the field to try the extra point with the game knotted, 19-19. "We've got to have this," he said to Starr in the huddle.

"No penetration," the quarterback barked in the huddle to his linemen. "We need this!"

Livingston's toe met the ball, sailing it through the uprights for a heart-stopping Hollywood ending, 20-19.

Calling the game three seconds too long, Bears' coach Jim Dooley said, "Starr's been the best."

Doug Buffone, powerless to prevent the score, said, "Only one in three million quarterbacks could do what Starr did. He's a classic."

In the rematch in mid-December, the Bears' defense began to make Starr consider retirement. Late in the first quarter, Starr drifted back to pass and had his cleats unearthed forcefully by a double-sandwiched hammer hit by Willie Holman and Dick Butkus. The force of the blow knocked Starr's helmet off, with his head almost still in it. Mr. Quarterback groggily got to his feet and began to limp off the field—in the direction of the Bears' sideline. After teammates helped him make a 180 degree turn, Starr left the field.

After the Bears' next punt, Starr hit Carroll Dale for a 33-yard gain. After throwing the pass, Starr sat down on the turf, deciding to take a short siesta. At this point, Bart couldn't remember his plays, his wife's name, or if Phil Bengtson or Twiggy was the Packers' coach. He was helped off the field with a concussion, not to return.

This was to be the day for Bears' quarterback Jack Concannon, or "State Street Jack," as Chicagoans had begun to call him. Concannon had surprised many by running onto the field wearing white cleats, `a la Joe Namath. The cocky QB wisecracked after the game saying he wore the whites because, "I wanted to jazz up the game. You never know when it's going to be your last."

Concannon connected on twenty-one of thirty-four passes for 338 yards and four TD's, ran for a touchdown, and added 31 yards rushing in a 35-17 thumping of the hapless Pack. Bears' receivers Dick Gordon and George Farmer ran freely in the Packers' secondary, catching every ball thrown at them. Green Bay's defense was filled with more holes than a colander.

Some credited the Bears' impressive performance on a special, much-publicized pep talk before the game by philanthropist and writer W. Clement Stone. Stone had been invited to address the team on the benefits of Positive Mental Attitude.

"A little P.M.A., Jack's white bucks, team defense, and excellent pass receiving were what did it," a happy Head Coach Dooley said after the game. Although the pep talk may have helped some, most of the Bears' players sat there looking at each other thinking, "Who's this guy?"

The December 13 game would be the last pro football game played in antiquated Wrigley Field. How time flies. Fifty years had passed since George Halas had signed to lease Wrigley for his then young Chicago Staleys. Halas had decided that it was time to move to Soldier Field on the banks of Lake Michigan. Soldier Field, built in 1919 as a tribute to soldiers of WWI, had the seating capacity of 100,000. College teams like Notre Dame and Army often drew over capacity. It had also been the site of the first big boxing event, the 1927 Dempsey/Tunney fight. After the 1970 season, the Bears left Wrigley Field to its original home team, the baseball Cubs.

Former CBS broadcaster Ray Scott recalls this wonderful story about Chicago Bears' running back Brian Piccolo.

"Ed McCaskey, who is now chairman of the Bears, and I are good friends," Ray said. "We were together in Canton, Ohio a couple of years ago and we sat down and started reminiscing.

"He was very close to Brian Piccolo. Brian had had the surgery and he knew he was dying. Brian's wife called Ed and said Brian wanted to see him. Ed went to the hospital. He told me, 'Ray, he cheered me up.' Piccolo had said, 'Ed, don't worry about me. I'm gonna be all right. Look at it this way. I never have to face that damn Nitschke again!'"

Brian Piccolo's inspiring and tragic life was depicted in the movie "Brian's Song." The story was based on the book *I Am Third*, written by his loyal teammate and very close friend, Gale Sayers.

Phil Bengtson's record in his three years at the helm of the Packers had been an unspectacular 20-21-1. In Bengtson's first training camp in 1968, many players noticed the torturous drills and schedule they had endured under Lombardi had greatly lessened.

When it became obvious that the Executive Committee was not going to renew his contract, Bengtson resigned the head coaching job at Green Bay shortly after the 1970 season. In many ways Bengtson's tenure as head coach was much like that of Gene Ronzani's. Both had the misfortune to follow in the footsteps of coaching legends. It was an impossible task for both. Like Ronzani, Bengtson was a good coach and a nice guy in the wrong place at the wrong time.

Three coaches were being mentioned as the top candidates to succeed Bengtson. From the pro ranks, LA Rams' coach George Allen was thought to be the front-runner for the job. From the college ranks, Dan Devine from Missouri and Joe Paterno of Penn State had the inside track.

Paterno, being of Italian extraction and from the East, reminded some of the committee members of Lombardi. Paterno had turned down pro offers before but had hinted that if the job in Green Bay ever came open he might be interested.

On January 14, 1971, to the surprise of many, Minnesota native Dan Devine was introduced as the new head coach of the Green Bay Packers. Devine's experience as coach and athletic director at Missouri was a large determining factor.

The relationship between Devine and the Packers' Executive Committee got off to a rocky start when Packers' President Dominic Olejniczak invited Devine and his family along with other committee members and their wives over to his home for a social evening. Devine spent more time in Olejniczak's pool room playing billiards with his family than socializing with committee members. That didn't go over well with the members.

When Devine drove to the Packers' headquarters and practice field across from Lambeau Field, he couldn't help but notice that he had to travel down Lombardi Avenue to get there.

Ray Nitschke became one of the game's greatest middle linebackers while anchoring the Packers' defense from his rookie season in 1958 through the 1972 season. Ray became one of the most feared hitters and tacklers, pulverizing ball carriers and anyone else who got in his way.

"Ray was a great football player," Bears' great Mike Ditka said. "I put some hits on him and he put a lot of hits on me that left marks. Nitschke hit me so hard in the first quarter of a game once that I don't remember the football game. When I looked at the game films I couldn't remember three quarters of it. I wasn't completely out but I certainly wasn't right. I never competed against anybody day-in and day-out that played any harder than Nitschke."

Ray was somewhat surprised when Jack Vainisi and the Packers drafted him out of Illinois in 1958. No one with the Packers had even spoken to him about the team's interest in drafting him. He wasn't happy about going to Green Bay. Since Ray had starred at Illinois, he was hoping George Halas would come calling.

"Initially, I wasn't too pleased because I really wanted to play in Chicago," Ray said. "I wanted to play for the Bears but Halas never approached me. You would think he would have said hello or something."

Nitschke got a special hello from the Papa Bear early in his career. "The first time I played the Bears was in a scrimmage," Nitschke recalled. "I was playing with the college All-Stars and we scrimmaged the Bears in Rensselaer, Indiana. Before that I was awed by playing against the big teams. I looked at Doug Atkins and thought oh my God—this was my first taste of professional football. I was kind of nervous but after a few plays I relaxed. I remember knocking [Rick] Casares out of bounds near the Bears' bench. I couldn't believe what Halas called me. He called me some bad names. I never forgot that."

Ray is quick to add that the games with Chicago each year were the most physical of the season.

"No question, no question. I know when I was playing, our biggest game was the Bears' game. It was the toughest game we played. No matter how good or bad the Bears were, we always knew that we were going to get hit. So it was a real physical football game."

Chicago tight end Mike Ditka was instrumental in making the rivalry violent for Nitschke. Ray recalled an incident where he and

Ditka exchanged pleasantries.

"Ditka had the temperament of a linebacker," Nitschke remembers. "Ditka hit me on a screen play; it was kind of a cheap shot. He hit me in the back when I wasn't looking. He put me out of a game in Green Bay. I couldn't wait for the next time to play the Bears. I got him back!"

When Mike Ditka wasn't slamming him, Nitschke had the formidable task of trying to contain the great Gale Sayers.

"He was the best I've ever seen. He was the greatest instinctive runner, a natural runner. You couldn't read Gale Sayers. He never did the same thing twice. You would study him in the movies and film and then you would play against him and he wouldn't do the same thing twice. He was really spontaneous. He had tremendous ability and great vision. He was stronger than he looked but he was nimble on his feet."

Nitschke, a man of few words, says what he wants and leaves it at that. This was evident when he was asked his opinion of Dan Devine as head coach of the Packers.

"He belonged in college," Ray snapped.

Devine and the Packers had one of their better drafts in 1971 when they chose Ohio State running back John Brockington and Alabama quarterback Scott Hunter. Under the tutelage of old veterans Bart Starr and Zeke Bratkowski, Hunter became the Packers' starting quarterback during the 1971 and '72 seasons, and, in 1973, shared that duty with Jerry Tagge.

Brockington, however, would be the real find. The "Buckeye Battering Ram" became the first running back in NFL history to rush for 1,000 yards or more in his first three seasons. In 1971, he rushed for 1,105 yards and led the league. Backed by Donny Anderson's 757 yards, the Packers finished third in the league in team rushing.

It was these two rookies, Brockington and Hunter, who led the Packers against their old nemesis on November 7.

The surprising 5-2 Chicago Bears hosted Green Bay, taking on a Packers' team who, in its last four games, had lost three and tied one. After a scoreless first quarter, the Packers lit up the scoreboard in the second when Scott Hunter drilled a 32-yard TD pass to Carroll Dale. John Brockington capped off a 60-yard drive by running a play called "42-outside," resulting in a 7-yard scoring dash, making it 14-0. It would stay that way until late in the fourth quarter.

"For more than 54 minutes yesterday," wrote Cooper Rollow, "it wasn't the Bears and Packers. The maniacal blocking, the murderous tackles, the blood and gore and adrenaline that had characterized the 102 previous games in pro football's most historic rivalry were missing. There wasn't even a single fist fight."

Then the game turned completely around. Bears' quarterback Bobby Douglass rifled a 30-yard pass to George Farmer for a score. On the Packers' next possession, running back Dave Hampton was handed the ball and was promptly leveled by Dick Butkus, who recovered Hampton's fumble at the Green Bay 11-yard line. Douglass leaned in from the 1-yard line to tie the game, 14-14.

Hampton made quick restitution on the ensuing kickoff, returning it to the Bears' thirty-nine. With fifty-nine seconds left, Green Bay kicker Lou Michaels toed a 22-yard field that narrowly grazed the out-stretched hand of Garry Lyle who leaped above the cross bar trying to block it. The Packers had turned away another miraculous Bears' comeback attempt, 17-14.

The week before the rematch with the Packers, Chicago's offense put on a pitiful exhibition in a 6-3 loss to the Denver Broncos, their fourth loss in five games. Jim Dooley, with rumors swirling that he was going to be fired, stood shoulders squared the Tuesday morning afterwards and said, "I believe I am as good a coach as there is in the league. My staff and my players are preparing for this Green Bay game Sunday as if it were the most important of our lives."

It was "Ray Nitschke Day" in Green Bay for the December 12 rematch. The Packers' old work horse linebacker had been benched most of the 1971 season in favor of second-year man Jim Carter. Carter brashly stated earlier in the year that, "I'm going to be the next middle linebacker for the Green Bay Packers. Ray Nitschke has been a great All-Pro, but it's no secret he's nearing the end." That head-strong attitude cost Carter. In his first years in the league Carter heard boos when he played and cheers when he was injured for his disobedient comments towards the popular Nitschke.

Ray Nitschke stood on the Lambeau Field turf along with his family and Ray Eliot, his University of Illinois football coach, and spoke to the fans who had seen him anchor the defense of Lombardi's great teams. Obviously moved, tough guy Nitschke wiped away tears in front of the 56,263 there.

Carter moved from middle to outside linebacker so Nitschke could start on defense on his day. Carter, Nitschke, and the rest of the Packer's defense held the Bears to only 61 yards rushing in a 31-10 shellacking of the Chicagoans. A 77-yard pass to Carroll Dale, and short runs by Brockington and the two quarterbacks Starr and Hunter, lifted the Packers to only their fourth win of the season.

The Bears had completely come apart. The loss was their fourth in a row and they would lose to Minnesota the next week to finish a disappointing 6-8.

Saying that "the record speaks for itself," Papa Bear Halas fired Coach Jim Dooley on December 29. The record Halas spoke of was Dooley's .357 winning percentage since he had taken over in 1968.

"It was a terrible decision for me to have to make," Halas said. Dooley was the first coach he had to fire in the club's fifty-year history. Someone at the hastily called press conference asked Halas if he had thought about returning to coaching.

"Only for a flicker of a second," Halas said.

Willie Wood wasn't drafted by the Green Bay Packers or anyone else for that matter. Willie, a smallish, 160-pound quarterback and defensive back at USC, was basically a free agent when he entered the league in 1960. Another reason he may have been passed up in the draft was because of racism.

"At the time I was one of the first black guys to come out of college who played quarterback," Willie said. "I think that had something to do with it."

His scouting reports didn't help either. A few unknowing scouts said he didn't have good speed and plainly stated that he was no pro prospect.

Enter Bill Butler. Butler was with the Police Boy's Club in Washington, DC. In early December 1959, Butler wrote a long letter to Vince Lombardi telling him about Wood and his desire to play football. Butler called Willie, "a thinking man's ballplayer," and challenged Lombardi to, "try him one time, you'll be glad you did." Lombardi did, and it paid off greatly for the Packers.

From 1960 through 1971, Wood played against some mighty tough Bears. The toughest, Willie confessed, was tight end Mike Ditka.

"Mike was the NFL's tough man when I was playing. He was a very physical player as well as a very talented player. At every level of the game, Mike was very dangerous and could hurt you. He wasn't a blazing speed guy but he could go deep on you. You had to focus in on him.

"You had to get yourself mentally prepared to play against the Bears. We always felt we could out-man them in terms of talent. But when it got to be 'Bears Week,' the best team didn't necessarily have to win."

Gale Sayers admitted that Wood was the toughest Packer he ever had to face because he always seemed to be at the line of scrimmage when he was running the ball. Coming from Sayers, Willie took that as a great compliment.

"There were certain positions on the field that you could not allow him to get to," Wood reminisced of Sayers. "You had to beat him to the point where he would cut upfield. Once he got squared up on you, he was tough to handle. We would try to keep his shoulders pointed to the sidelines."

Willie remembered Lombardi's concern about Halas' infamous spying escapades. "We would change jerseys during the Bears Week," he said. "Often we would change our practice times and a couple of times we changed our practice facilities. We knew that Halas had some of his people up there spying on us."

Summing up the Bears-Packers rivalry, Willie said of the encounters, "It was kill or be killed."

"I'm a Halas man and a Bears man, but not a yes man: I am the boss. This is going to be the Abe Gibron show." With that, Abe Gibron, the 46-year old, 300 pound, Bears' assistant became the new head coach of the Chicago Bears in late January 1972. Gibron had been Halas' first choice out of some thirty applicants. "We have to restore the Bears' reputation as a physically-tough team," Gibron said. "I will make all the football decisions. I am a football man and this is the way I want it to be."

The portly, potbellied Gibron had been an outstanding lineman for the Cleveland Browns for six seasons in the early Fifties and had finished his playing days with Philadelphia and the Bears. He had been an assistant with the Washington Redskins until 1965, when he joined the Bears' staff with Halas.

"Twenty-three years and over a thousand head-on blocks, and I'm finally a head coach, so I don't propose to blow this shot," Gibron wryly remarked.

"Abe is a naturally funny man," wrote *Chicago Today* writer Ed Stone, "partly because he looks as though he should be funny, but mostly because he doesn't try to be."

"I'm a stickler on conditioning, even though I don't look it," the 300-pound coach once said.

Gibron became known as "the first fat genius since Winston Churchill." Being almost as wide as he was tall, he became the butt of many jokes. "Until the autumnal equinox," said Chicago writer Bill Gleason, "the rays never strike below Abe's belt line. His belly eclipses the entire solar system."

Dan Devine had an immediate crisis upon entering the Packers' 1972 training camp. Veteran defensive backs Doug Hart and Willie Wood both retired, leaving a huge void in the defense. A shrewd trade and an excellent draft choice, however, would remedy the situation.

Traded to San Diego was Lombardi hold-over Lionel Aldridge for defensive safety Jim Hill. Only twenty-six years old, Hill became the elder statesman of the group that consisted of third year pros Ken Ellis and Al Matthews. The biggest surprise was rookie Willie Buchanon from San Diego State, who, with his 9.4 speed in the 100-yard dash and four interceptions, garnered Rookie of the Year honors. This young, brash defensive back field blended together and allowed only seven touchdown passes against the Packers in 1972, leading the league.

Big changes had taken place on the offensive side of the ball as well. Bart Starr officially retired and became the quarterback coach with Devine. Second-year man Scott Hunter, who had been tossed into the lineup as a sacrificial lamb in 1971, handled most of the quarterbacking duties, being subbed for on occasion by Nebraska rookie Jerry Tagge. To find a new running mate for John Brockington, Donny Anderson, the remaining "Gold Dust Twin," was traded to St. Louis for running back MacArthur Lane.

The Packers' third round draft choice was Chester Marcol, a Polish-born kicker from tiny Hillsdale College in Michigan. Marcol wore thick, black glasses under his helmet, giving him a somewhat comical look. Opponents quit laughing when, by season's end, he led the league in both field goal attempts with forty-eight, thirty-three of those splitting the uprights. Also, Marcol never missed an extra point attempt all season. For five of the next six seasons, Marcol led the team in scoring. His highest point total, 128, would come in 1972.

Devine's young team won two of its first three games and hosted the Bears on October 8. This was truly a case of two teams going in opposite directions. Abe Gibron's Bears had started off slowly, losing two and tying one.

In the tenth minute of the opening period, Packer Dave Robinson smacked into Bears' runner Jim Harrison, jarring the ball loose. Clarence Williams reached his big claw of a hand down, swept it up, and raced 21 yards for the touchdown.

After a Mac Percival boot made it 7-3, the Packers had the ball on the Chicago 48-yard line with two minutes remaining. Hunter faded back to pass and lofted a bomb to end Dave Davis. Davis and Bears' cornerback Joe Taylor leaped for the ball, batting it into the arms of Green Bay receiver Jon Staggers. The Packers' receiver made a rolling catch, regained his footing at the Chicago 3-yard line, and walked into the end zone.

After intermission, the Bears' offense returned to score on a 2-yard smash run by Cyril Pinder. With the score 17-10 and 9:47 on the clock, quarterback Bobby Douglass drove the Bears to the Packers' 2-yard line. Instead of going for the sure field goal, Gibron elected to chance it for the touchdown. Douglass rolled out, dodged linebacker Fred Carr, and pranced into the end zone, tying the game.

With time running out, Hunter marched the Pack downfield until the ball rested on the Bear's 37-yard line with thirty seconds remaining. In a swirling, gusty, 20 mph wind, Chester Marcol trotted onto the field.

"When I went out on the field to try that last field goal, I said to myself, 'you could be a hero or a bum on this day.'" Showing remarkable aplomb, the Polish cannon blasted the ball between the post for a 20-17 Packers lead.

Marcol wasn't done. On the ensuing kickoff, with two Bears waiting to run the ball back, Chester boomed the kick off the upright of the goal post, making it a dead ball, forcing the Bears to start at their own 20-yard line. In a last desperation kick, Percival missed short and to the left from 51 yards out, and the Packers preserved the win.

Before joust number two in November, Marcol received a letter that bore a Chicago postmark. Obviously from a devoted Bears' fan irritated by Chester's game-winning kick five weeks prior, the letter made one simple plea:

"Dear Chester, go back to Poland."

On Sunday, Marcol would send a special delivery reply.

After John Brockington and Scott Hunter ran for touchdowns, Bears' runner Cyril Pinder ran up the gut of the Packers' line from 4 yards out making it 14-7, Packers. Late in the first quarter, Jim Carter intercepted a pass that set up a 51-yard field goal try by Marcol. The bespectacled kicker booted the ball free and clear for the three points.

Later in the second period, Green Bay QB Scott Hunter was knocked silly by Dick Butkus and was replaced by Jerry Tagge. Tagge, who in his younger days was a peanut salesman at Packers' home games, lead the team on a long drive in the third period that culminated in another Marcol three-pointer. The Polish Prince added a 21-yarder late in the game to ice the victory for the Packers, 23-17. The final field goal was Marcol's twentieth, a new club record, eclipsing Don Chandler's record of nineteen three-pointers.

Clearly caught for a loss of words after the game, portly Abe Gibron shook his head and calmly stated, "What the hell."

What in the hell had happened to the Bears? They now were mired in a losing streak that would see them drop six of their last seven games of the season. One sports writer called the Bears' offense, "absolutely schizophrenic."

Although leading Chicago in rushing with an amazing 976 yards, Bears' quarterback Bobby Douglass only completed seventy-five passes on the year for 1,246 yards, dead last in the league. Near mid-season, opponent's defenses began playing the Bears up near the line, knowing that Douglass rarely passed the ball. The Bears began dropping games and dropped out of sight, finishing Gibron's maiden season at 4-9-1.

Dan Devine's Packers were another story. A win over the New Orleans Saints in the season finale sealed the NFC Central Division crown for the Packers, their first since the championship team of 1967.

At 10-4, and possessing one of the best ground games in the league, the Packers traveled to Washington to battle the Redskins in the playoffs. Sadly for Devine, his team met the same fate as Gibron's Bears had during the season. George Allen put five of his defenders on the line specifically to stop the Packers' rushing attack. It worked. John Brockington was held to only 9 yards in thirteen attempts as the Redskins thumped the Packers back to Wisconsin, 17-3.

At half-time, assistant coach Bart Starr's recommendation of changing the offensive scheme to get the team moving was rebuffed by Devine. Starr, feeling helpless and irritated, watched silently from the sidelines as the Packers went down in defeat.

"In retrospect, that game was probably my fault due to my inexperience," Packers' quarterback Scott Hunter recalled. "When Washington went to that five-man line I should have just kept throwing. Bart and Devine got into a disagreement about what we should be doing."

The rift between Starr and Devine was never mended. Starr left

Devine's staff after the game to devote time to his many business interests. But football and Green Bay had not heard the last from Mr. Quarterback.

The 1972 season would be the pinnacle for Dan Devine. Even from the standpoint of the Green Bay franchise it would be a peak, for it would not be until the final play of the 1995 season that the Green Bay Packers could call themselves Central Division champions again.

While growing up in the South during the 1950s, Scott Hunter would go over to a neighbor's house to watch pro football on television every Sunday in the fall. At the time, seven-year old Scott never dreamed he would once play against the Chicago Bears and beat them. "The Bears were always broadcast into the deep South," Hunter recalls. "I saw Harlon Hill, Ed Brown, and all those guys."

The Green Bay Packers drafted Hunter in the sixth round of the 1971 draft from Bear Bryant's Alabama team. It would make for good print to say that the Packers drafted Hunter from Alabama to be the successor to ailing Hall of Famer Bart Starr, also an Alabama product. One Alabama quarterback for another. Fact is, Dan Devine probably chose Hunter because he remembered him from the Gator Bowl when Devine's Missouri squad had played against Hunter and the Crimson Tide.

Hunter was thrown into battle in his rookie season, starting seven games for the injured Bart Starr. He got his first win as a starting quarterback against the Bears in 1971, the 17-14 win on November 7.

"It was a very special win for me," Hunter said of the victory over the team he'd watched as a youngster. "I was excited about playing the game but I didn't tell anyone about watching the Bears while growing up. I was excited because I knew I was going to start.

"On Saturday night before the game me, John Brockington, and [defensive back] Charlie Hall went to a steak house restaurant in Chicago. We sat down and we had our green jackets on and all. Well, on the menu they had a 32 oz. steak. John proceeds to order it. I said, 'John, you can't do that—we got a game tomorrow! You can't eat a 32 oz. steak, don't do this.' Well, he ordered it and ate it. I was thinking, he may make it to the second quarter. He went out and gained 142 yards and scored two touchdowns. Every time we went down there I'd ask him, 'Ya wanna go and get one of those steaks?'"

Hunter and Bears' linebacker Dick Butkus had met at a Packers-Bears charity golf tournament in Lake Geneva, Wisconsin where they struck up a conversation. That was on the golf course. Butkus let his hitting do the talking on the football field. Hunter remembers vividly the second Packers-Bears game in 1972 when he was knocked out by Butkus, and was later given sage advice from the old pro linebacker.

"It was third down and three and I was scrambling to my left. I looked up and one of our receivers was chicken fighting with one of the Bears' cornerbacks. I had my eye on him but I thought I could make the first down. I couldn't make it going out of bounds so I had to turn it upfield. When I did, I looked to my right and here came that black-jerseyed torpedo. I put my head down and the next thing I knew I was sitting on the sideline with smelling salts under my nose. I thought I had made the first down but I'd missed the next series of downs. After the game I was walking out on the field and Butkus came over and looked at me and said: 'Ya need to go out of bounds.'"

The once proud Chicago Bears' organization was in hibernation. They hadn't posted a winning record since 1967 and wouldn't again until 1977. This constant losing was all new to the 78-year old George Halas. Only once in their history had the Bears gone more than a year without winning over fifty percent of their games.

Halas and Gibron decided to rebuild through both the draft and trades. Chicago's first round choice was a talented defensive tackle from Eastern Kentucky University named Wally Chambers, who became a fixture in the Bruin's line for the next five years. Chosen in the second round was Florida State quarterback Gary Huff. He would help the Bears' inept offense and share the quarterbacking duties with Douglass. Also helping the offense was the acquisition of running back Carl Garrett from the New England Patriots. In 1973, Garrett led the Bears in rushing with 655 yards.

The Packers came into the '73 campaign with high hopes after their defense had lead them to the Central Division crown and the playoffs the previous year. But during the summer of 1973 Dan Devine became, according to Executive Committee member John Torinus, "a completely different man." That summer his wife was diagnosed with multiple sclerosis. A devoted family man, Devine was devastated by the news.

Devine also became combative with the press when asked certain questions. An interview he gave to *Time Magazine* was criticized because he made some derogatory comments about the Green Bay townsfolk. He alienated himself even more when he claimed that an irate fan had shot his dog. It was later learned that a neighboring farmer had shot the dog because it was raiding his chicken coop. A strange aura existed in Titletown USA.

Another typical "Bears-Packers incident" happened in the annual Shrine exhibition game with the Bears in Milwaukee before the 1973 season. During a Green Bay kickoff, Bears' coach Abe Gibron sent halfback and kickoff team participant Gary Kosins to block Chester Marcol and rough him up on kickoffs. The chances of Marcol making a tackle or even wanting to get near Cecil Turner, the Bears' speedy return man, were slim and none. The Packers protested vehemently, leading Gibron to reply, "What does he [Marcol] think he is, a Polish Prince or something?"

Green Bay wobbled through the first half of the season and into their showdown with the Bears at 2-3-2. Chicago came to Green Bay having only two wins to show in its seven games.

The crowd that turned out for the contest witnessed the worst second half offensive performance in Green Bay history, fitting for a team ranked last in offense. Pun intended, the Packer offense would be "rank" on this day. Somehow leading at the half, 17-10, the Packers forgot to bring out anything that resembled an offense for the second stanza. They managed only one first down in the second half, that coming late in the fourth quarter. The offense gained less than 100 yards for the third consecutive week and the passing yardage total for the game was a pathetic minus 12 yards.

On the other side of the ball, Bears' signal caller Bobby

Douglass was having his best day as a pro. The elusive Douglass scored four touchdowns on short runs, ran for 100 yards, and completed ten of fifteen passes for another 118 yards in Chicago's 31-17 thumping of the Bays.

It was redemption for Douglass, who had on many occasions suffered boos and catcalls from the Chicago faithful since entering the league in 1969. "I've heard the fans for years," he commented after the game. "Listen, I know how good a football player I am. I didn't play that much of a better game today. I've played as well this year."

The jeers from the Green Bay fans were not reserved for Douglass. The Packers' faithful vented their frustration on the home team with a lusty chorus of raspberries and howls in that wretched second half, unequaled at Lambeau Field.

"The Packers are in shreds," wrote *Press-Gazette* scribe Len Wagner. "They've got more cracks than a jigsaw puzzle."

Devine looked deflated after the game, leaving writer Lee Remmel to write that, "pain and anguish were mirrored in Dan Devine's coffee-colored eyes, reddened by an endless afternoon in the raw, November cold."

Defensive back Jim Hill stated wryly his intentions after the game. "I think I'll go home and kick my cat."

Long after the crowd had gone home, a white banner was found lying on the Lambeau Field turf. It read, "In Poland, they tell Bear jokes."

Hill and the Packers would kick the Bears in the final game in what had now become a nightmare season for both franchises. *Chicago Tribune* writer Don Pierson summed it up best with his opening comments. "The Bears threw their own funeral again yesterday in 'Soldier Tomb' and this time nobody came. The end was recorded mercifully at 4:02 pm. Cause of death was terminal incompetence after a long illness prolonged unnecessarily by the Green Bay Packers, 21-0. There were only 29,157 mourners on hand and the few that stuck around threw snowballs at the corpse. In lieu of flowers the owners ask that applications for next year's season tickets be sent immediately."

Some 26,544 folks decided not to even show up, opting to watch the game or the Sunday matinee on TV. Those who did watch saw a swarming Packers' defensive line tee off on quarterback Gary Huff, sacking him six times and harassing him the entire afternoon. Green Bay got two TD passes from the tandem of quarterback Jerry Tagge and receiver Jon Staggers, while John Brockington added 142 pounding yards on the ground.

It seemed that on the field inept antics of his Chicago Bears were just too much for the patriarch Halas to take. In the third quarter he watched as Packers' back MacArthur Lane snaked his way through the Bears' defense for an 18-yard gain. Halas stood up and yelled from the press box, "Tell the (bleeping) players to play!" It was too late. The Bears were well on their way to losing their last six games of the season.

It was a welcomed swan song for both teams. These were the two worst squads these old rivals had fielded since those mediocre Packers-Bears teams of the early Fifties.

"It's been a disappointing season," Dan Devine said, to no one's surprise. "The most disappointing one I've ever gone through." Devine didn't stop there. For some reason he felt it necessary to mention an incident the previous spring while in St. Paul, Minnesota accepting a Coach of the Year award. "There were 1,200 people in the audience and when the Vikings' coaches were introduced, they got a standing ovation," Devine said. "That's the big difference."

A remorseful Abe Gibron tried to shine a ray of light on a very gloomy situation. "The guys that played, played like hell for us." Finally giving into resignation, he quietly echoed Dan Devine's words. "It's been a tough year. To say I'm not disappointed would be goddamn lying."

You won't find Dayton, Ohio's own Gary Kosins in the football Hall of Fame. In his three-year career with Chicago as a running back, Gary didn't see a lot of playing time on offense. He did spend time on special teams for the Bears during the Abe Gibron era, which is where his name pops up in the story of the rivalry.

Remember, it was the rotund Gibron who ordered Kosins to go after the "Polish Prince," Packers' kicker Chester Marcol, in that

1973 exhibition game. "I always went after Chester Marcol; that was my job," Gary said. "He was the guy I was in charge of blocking. Chester was a fine place kicker at that time and if we could rattle him a little bit that was to our benefit. Gibron always had a way of trying to make his words act as a catalyst as far as my play. Gibron used to say about Marcol, 'That sucker isn't a Polish Prince, go after him and knock his ass off.'

"He [Marcol] knew that as soon as he got done kicking that he was going to be blocked on the play. So, you're hoping he was thinking that as he was approaching the ball, making for a less than perfect kick. It's more intimidation than blocking out a good player that could tackle the guy with the ball.

"Chester ran pretty good," Gary laughingly recalled. "He had no problem running to the sidelines completely off the field. So I think from that standpoint, he was intimidated and he knew I was coming every play after him."

And what about Gibron's "Polish Prince" comment?

"I think that's more of a compliment," Gary stated ironically, "My family name is Kosinski but we dropped the 'ki' making it Kosins!"

Packers' president Dominic Olejniczak was watching television one night in October 1974, when he heard that Dan Devine had just made a huge trade in an effort to put the Green Bay Packers back on top. Devine believed what the team needed was a veteran quarterback and proven leader. During the 1973 season, Devine played a game of revolving quarterbacks, which resulted in a lack of continuity. Scott Hunter, Jerry Tagge, and Jim Del Gaizo had all seen about the same amount of duty under center.

Devine, in a desperate move, traded the Packers' five top draft choices over the next two years to acquire former San Diego and Los Angeles quarterback John Hadl. Hadl had been a bomb thrower in the wide-open early days of the AFL, leading the Chargers for ten years before being traded to Los Angeles. Very likely, Hadl's best playing days were behind him. Devine might as well have traded for Sid Luckman, it would have been the about the same.

It would be one of the worst trades in NFL history. Devine had literally mortgaged the team's future on an aging quarterback. Plus, he had once again angered the Executive Committee. In the past, the head coach usually had informed the Committee about any trades being carried out that might involve the trading of a future asset of the corporation.

Another problem developed over running back John Brockington. Devine went to the carpet and told the Committee that they had to re-sign the big running back for any price. They ended up paying Brockington a very handsome salary while giving him a guaranteed three-year contract. Brockington would go from the penthouse to the outhouse, becoming a huge disappointment before being traded to Kansas City after the three years ran out.

After a 3-2 start, Devine and his Packers traveled south to play the struggling 2-3 Bears for the 109th time in front of ABC announcer Howard Cosell and a nationally televised Monday night audience. They would be witness to the typical Bears-Packers contest, one that the Midway Monsters would win, 10-9.

Chicago's defense won this game. Led by Wally Chambers, Jim Osborne, and Don Hultz on the line, and linebackers Doug Buffone and Waymond Bryant, and defensive backs Joe Taylor, Craig Clemons, and Gary Lyle, the Bears' defense stopped the Packers five times inside their own 20-yard line. Twice the Pack was inside their rival's 5-yard line and came away with no points.

The biggest play of the game came with only six minutes remaining when Packers' QB Jerry Tagge lofted a spiral intended for open receiver Barry Smith. As Smith crossed the goal line ready to catch the certain touchdown, Chicago's Craig Clemons came from out of nowhere to bat the pigskin away. The Packers had to settle for a Marcol field goal instead of a touchdown that would have won the game.

The rematch three weeks later marked the first, and the last time, that the Packers hosted the Bears in Milwaukee, where they now played three of their seven "home" games. The appearances in Milwaukee began in 1933 when the Packers hosted the Giants. Gradually, the number of games increased to two, then three games, in the town that suds made famous. It had been a tradition that the Bears always played in Green Bay. This game is the lone exception.

A driving rain and the sad fact of watching two poor teams. made many stay home for this one. The 48,000 who did show saw, what the *Chicago Tribune* said was, "a woeful contest between two struggling, panicky, uptight teams scrambling and sliding around muddy County Stadium like one of those electric football games gone haywire."

"A game-long rain turned the field into a slippery swamp, better suited to alligators and ducks rather than Packers and Bears," wrote *Green Bay Press-Gazette* writer Dick Karbon.

In an ugly 20-3 Packers win, speedster Steve Odom made a spectacular 95-yard kickoff return at the end of the first half. Dropping the ball on the five, Odom scooped it up, along with a handful of Milwaukee mud, and splashed his way to the end zone for a 10-3 Packers lead at the half. The run set a club record for a kick-off return, breaking the mark set by Veryl Switzer, whose 93-yard return on November 7, 1954 had also been against the Bears.

By this time, both Dan Devine and Abe Gibron knew their employment as head coaches was on very shaky ground. Devine's plight and odd behavior has already been mentioned. For Gibron, his downfall may have begun in the summer of 1974 when Halas hired former Vikings' vice-president and general manager Jim Finks to be the Bears' new general manager, VP, and chief operating officer. It would be his job to rebuild the team back to respectability. He would also become Abe Gibron's executioner.

The Bears lost seven of their last eight games in 1974, the final one being a 42-0 trouncing at the hands of the Washington Redskins. Under Gibron's rule, the Bears had compiled a 11-30-1 record. Two days later, Finks fired Gibron, stating that he "would not remain in the Bears organization in any capacity." Finks said he had told owner George Halas about his decision to fire Gibron and that the Papa Bear "offered no opinion of any consequence."

"Well, it's not the end of the world," Gibron said. "I definitely think I'll be back as a head coach." Abe even disclosed plans to apply for the two coaching jobs that had recently become vacated. "If they don't contact me," he said, referring to the two teams, "I'll contact them.

"We gave it a hell of a shot. Let's go get a steak," Gibron added.

Gibron never got the call, and the two teams with coaching

vacancies were Cleveland and Green Bay.

Yes, Green Bay. The Sunday night after the Packers' game with Atlanta, a 10-3 Green Bay loss, Dan Devine called Packers' president Olejniczak and asked him about his status for the 1975 season. Olejniczak talked to an impatient Devine the next day and invited committee members to his home to discuss the future. They decided to put off a vote until later in the month but Devine kept insisting, wanting a decision. The committee, obviously having had enough of Devine, chose to buy out the last year of his contract.

Later that week Devine and his attorney met with Olejniczak to endorse the agreement for the one year buy out. After signing, hands were shaken and Devine and his counsel exited. A minute later Devine opened the door, popped his head in, and said, "Oh, by the way, I'm going to Notre Dame."

It's theorized that Devine knew all along he was going to coach the Fighting Irish. In fact, a news conference in South Bend had already been scheduled for that very afternoon.

Devine had seemingly negotiated one year's salary from the Packers, then just walked away. He would go on to win a National Championship at Notre Dame in 1979 while the Packers floundered in the late Seventies, in part to the trade that sent five draft picks elsewhere for the aging John Hadl.

"I'm leaving a much better team than I inherited," Devine told reporters. "I'm leaving a potential championship ball club."

Nothing could have been further from the truth.

Offensive guard Bill Lueck was as surprised as anyone when the Packers drafted him in the first round out of Arizona in 1968. "I never knew they were interested," Lueck admits. "The only team that really scouted me was the San Francisco 49ers. I was quite surprised when the Packers drafted me because I had never had any contact with them."

Lueck saw quite a bit of playing time his rookie year because All-Pro guard Jerry Kramer was having knee problems. From 1969 through 1974, Lueck would be the starting left guard on the offensive line and would not miss a single regular season game.

Lueck found the wars he fought against the rival Bears were always physical. "More than a little bit," Bill recalled. "There was no love lost. But we had a healthy respect for each other, also."

Bill rapidly learned of the quickness and strength of Dick Butkus. "Dick dished out so much punishment but not to the linemen. He used to tear a ball carrier apart. But with the offensive linemen he used more of his matador-style move. What made him so great was that he could avoid or shed the block. Just with his quickness he could make plays."

Lueck recalled an incident in a 1969 game with the Bears. At that time the Bears were 1-11 on the year and a team of frustration. "In 1969 we were playing in Wrigley Field," Lueck recalled. "I was playing left guard and Bears' right tackle Dick Evey was over me. Of course, there was Butkus and Doug Buffone ... and defensive end Loyd Phillips. Well, we had a long run between the tackles on Evey and Phillips' side. They started jawing at each other about whose responsibility it was and who should have made the play. By the time we broke the huddle and came up to the line of scrimmage, they were there yelling and screaming at each other. And Abe Gibron [Bears' assistant coach] was over on the sidelines yelling at them, some real choice words that shouldn't be published. They were ready to fight each other."

Whenever Lueck looks into a mirror these days, he can't help but think of Bears' defensive tackle George Seals. "I still have a notch out of my nose because he used to like to head slap," Lueck said. "He head slapped me in a game in Green Bay and his little finger landed in my nose. When it came out, it took a chunk out of my nose! I bled like someone had committed hara-kiri on me. I still have the scar."

1975-'79

Immediately after the Dan Devine fiasco, the Packers' Executive Committee felt pressure from fans to hire Bart Starr as the head coach. Rumors began to circulate that Starr was about to be named coach.

"Yes, I'm interested in the job," Starr replied at the time. He said his interest was, "...an emotional thing, although I feel it's wrong to make a major decision based strictly on emotion." A small contingent pushed for the former Green Bay great to be chosen and the committee felt good about the straight-arrow Starr.

Although Starr hadn't coached since resigning after the '72 season with Devine, because of his work that year with the quarterbacks and his total service to the Packers, Green Bay fans were rewarded with an early Christmas present. On December 24, 1974 Bart Starr was named to the head post of the team he had led to five championships in the Sixties.

"To every man there comes in his lifetime, that special moment when he is figuratively tapped on the shoulder and offered the chance to do a very special thing, unique to him and fitted to his talents: what a tragedy if that moment finds him unprepared or unqualified for the work which would be his finest hour." Borrowing a quote from Winston Churchill, Bart Starr met the press for the first time as the franchise's eighth head coach.

"I'm absolutely ecstatic about this opportunity," he added. "I'm extremely thrilled and very honored ... but I'm not awed by it."

When asked about his lack of coaching experience, Starr replied, "I'm not as qualified as I'd like to be, but I'm willing." He had only one year of coaching experience, coaching quarterbacks for Devine's '72 squad. Time would show that Bart was not qualified to be a head coach so soon, but would gain experience and become a respected coach in his last years at Green Bay.

A week before Bart was named coach, his wife Cherry denied that he was about to take the job. "He absolutely has not talked to them about it and that is the truth," she said. "In fact, we just heard that Jack Pardee was the new coach."

As she predicted, Jack Pardee was appointed head coach, but not for the Packers. On the last day of 1974, Jack Pardee was named the head coach of the Chicago Bears, becoming the youngest head coach in the league at 38-years old. Like Starr with the Packers, Pardee also became the eighth head coach of the storied club. Pardee had been a player for fifteen years in the league, had coached with the Redskins in 1972, and was head coach of the World

Football League's Florida Blazers in 1974.

Pardee inherited a changing football team. Even the surroundings were different in 1975. After thirty-one years of holding preseason training camp in Rensselaer, Indiana, the Bears moved to Lake Forest College, a suburb of North Chicago. It was a welcomed change from Rensselaer's cornfields, stifling heat, and boring locale.

The Chicago Bears' squad had a new look us well. With ex-World Football League players, trades, and the college draft, players like quarterback Bob Avellini, running back Roland Harper, cornerback Virgil Livers, and defensive end Mike Hartenstine joined the Bears' roster.

Chicago's first round choice became a cornerstone player and future Hall of Famer, Jackson State running back Walter Payton. Payton earned the nickname "Sweetness" in college because of his sweet running moves. He was also a punishing runner, bowling over anyone or anything that got in his way. Also, his durability became a great asset to the team. In his first nine years in the league, he missed only one of the 131 games the Bears played. When he retired after the 1987 season, Walter Payton owned NFL records in attempted rushes (3,838); rushing yards (16,726); and rushing TD's (110). He would remind everyone of Gale Sayers, another great back who, because of injuries, never had the chance to run up impressive statistics like Payton.

Bart Starr defined the 1975 season as "a learning experience." First, he had the task of trying to add new talent after Dan Devine had given most of it away for the next two years in the Hadl trade. The Packers found some help in USC guard Bill Bain and running back Willard Harrell, who finished second behind John Brockington for team rushing honors.

Starr was bequeathed a bad team. There were holes everywhere and not enough people to fill them. The defense would give up more rushing yardage than any other team in 1975, and be ranked twentieth in league defense. There were problems on offense too. A porous offensive line allowed forty-two quarterback sacks, forcing signal callers John Hadl and Don Milan to run for their lives.

The Packers also suffered from an atrocious kicking game. Star kicker Chester Marcol missed the entire season due to a leg injury. He was replaced by Joe Danelo, who kicked only eleven of sixteen field goal attempts.

Both teams carried horrible 1-6 records into their first meeting in 1975. "In a contest to determine which team was the worst," wrote *Press-Gazette* sports writer Cliff Christl, "the Packers won in a landslide."

Bart Starr gave the starting quarterback nod to rookie Don Milan, replacing injured veteran John Hadl. Milan suffered a tough baptismal. With the Bears comfortably ahead, 20-7, in the fourth quarter, Milan lofted a pass towards tight end Rich McGeorge. Bears' defensive back Craig Clemons stepped in front of McGeorge and raced down the sideline for 76 yards, icing the game. Milan's job was made harder because of the paltry 41 yards rushing the Packers amassed in the game. Pressured into passing, Milan spent most of the day running from hard-charging Bears' defenders.

Three weeks later the Bears recaptured the worst team award by a landslide. In a swirling, 30 mph Wisconsin wind and a chill factor of minus two, Hadl took the Packers down the field for 84 yards on the game's opening drive, culminating with a short plunge for a touchdown by John Brockington. The Ohio State battering ram scored again on the second play of the second quarter after Green Bay defensive tackle Mike McCoy jarred the ball loose from Walter Payton. Dave Pureifory recovered the ball at the Bears' 10-yard line and four plays later Brockington scored.

Leading 28-0 at half-time, the Packers' defense pinned their ears back and put heavy pressure on Bears' rookie quarterback Bob Avellini, intercepting him three times. In the miserable cold and wind of Lambeau Field, Avellini only completed nine passes. His first completed pass came after the Packers already had a 21-0 lead.

Payton added a meaningless 1-yard touchdown run in a 28-7 loss to the Pack. At half-time, with the Packers safely ahead, many of the 47,104 fans who had braved the cold left early, leaving the stadium at the end of the game barren and silent. "The ones who stayed," wrote *Tribune* writer Don Pierson, "gave an indication of the mental state of Green Bay zealots by stripping to the waist and providing one of the few highlights of the second half."

It was a season of few highlights for both franchises. Both teams finished the year 4-10, the worst records the two teams ever recorded collectively in one year.

Before the 1976 season, Bart Starr knew he had to get a reliable quarterback in order to bring glory back to Titletown USA. In the off season, Starr picked up quarterback Lynn Dickey from the Houston Oilers in a trade for John Hadl and cornerback Ken Ellis. Dickey was a talented, accurate thrower who had played second fiddle to Dan Pastorini in Houston since 1971. Suffering from a severe hip injury, he didn't play at all in '72 and had missed most of the '75 season with a broken leg. Starr was taking a risk with Dickey but he had little choice.

Dickey's receivers were a talented but unspectacular bunch. Ken Payne led all receivers with thirty-three catches, while tight end Rich McGeorge snagged twenty-four. Also in the backfield, Willard Harrell and John Brockington would handle the running load along with replacements Barty Smith and Eric Torkelson adding extra yardage.

The offensive line was vastly improved. Third-year man Larry McCarren anchored the center position while veterans Gale Gillingham and Steve Knutson held down the guard positions. At tackle were Dick Himes and rookie Mark Koncar.

Two 4-5 squads met in Soldier Field for the 113th time on November 14, a game Bart Starr said, "upheld the tradition of a Packers-Bears game.

"There were mistakes by both teams," Starr added, "but if you put that aside and look at the effort, this game was in keeping with games of the past."

Green Bay fell behind early, coughing up the ball on their first two drives and allowing Chicago to turn both miscues into touchdowns. The Packers bravely fought back. Dickey found the middle of the field open on the Bears' defense and exploited it by tossing pass after pass to Steve Odom and Ken Payne. Bruising back John Brockington, showing some of that old form, stung his way to 71 yards on the day.

But this was to be a day for Walter Payton and the Chicago Bears. On a 42-yard burst late in the game, Payton became the first NFL player that year, and the first Bear since Gale Sayers in 1969, to reach 1,000 yards. Ending the day with 109 yards, Payton led the Bruins to a 24-13 victory.

Unfortunately for Starr's Packers, it would be a costly lost. With eight minutes remaining, Lynn Dickey separated his shoulder when he was hammered into the Astroturf by Bears' defensive tackle Jim Osborne. Second-string quarterback Carlos Brown came into the game but couldn't pull out a win.

A few Packers protested that the hit on Dickey had been late and intentional. "I don't think it was a late hit, but I'll have to wait until I see the films," Dickey said after the game." When asked if he thought Dickey had been hit late, Bart Starr tersely replied, "I don't have any comment on that."

Packers' defensive tackle Mike McCoy saw the crowd at Soldier Field as a determining factor in the Bears' win. "This is the first time I've come here when the fans have been behind them," McCoy said after the game. "They're not the Bears I used to know. They used to be clipping and holding and biting and punching. I always felt we could beat those teams, and we usually did. But now the Bears are playing basic football, and they're better for it."

In the rematch game two weeks later, it would be too damned cold for anyone to clip, hold, bite, or punch.

"Those who attended this game," wrote *Green Bay Press-Gazette* writer Don Langenkamp, "deserve a game ball." Dressed in woolen shirts, blankets, snowmobile suits, and deer hunting parkas, 50,000 came out to see the second coldest game in Green Bay history, losing out to the infamous Ice Bowl Game. How cold was it? It was so cold the stadium turnstiles froze up. The underground electric system that kept the field thawed had been on since Friday. The Green Bay West High School band, the game's half-time entertainment, found their instruments frozen and unusable.

At kickoff, the temperature was six degrees and the wind chill factor minus fourteen. "The cold might have persuaded more clear-thinking people to stay at home and watch on TV," wrote *Tribune* writer Don Pierson, "but this is Green Bay, and if you're crazy enough to live here, you might as well torture yourself."

Actually, a statement by Green Bay defensive tackle Dave Roller may have given the Bears the extra advantage to win. Roller proclaimed earlier that week that he would "get" Chicago quarterback Bob Avellini. As the frozen, and by now quite lubricated, Packers' faithful began to shout, "We want Roller! We want Roller!" the defensive giant sat quietly on the bench.

"We wanted him, too," Bears' guard Noah Jackson said. "When the fans started yelling, I think that really picked our club up." Jackson had stood in the middle of Lambeau Field motioning for Roller to come out and play.

The combination of the harsh cold, bad play by the Packers, and three field goals by Chicago kicker Bob Thomas resulted in a 16-10 Bears' win. "At times our tackling was atrocious," Starr admitted. On the offensive side, the Pack couldn't get their running game going nor could quarterback Carlos Brown complete many passes.

The Bears' game was the Packers' third of four straight losses that helped plummet them into a 5-9 regular season mark. The Bears finished the season at 7-7, their best record since 1968.

In 1974, Chicago drafted Tennessee State linebacker Waymond Bryant to replace an aging and injury-slowed Dick Butkus. After playing one year at middle linebacker, Bryant was moved to outside linebacker, where he played for three more years. A shoulder injury in 1978 ended his playing career.

Bryant played only eight league games against the Packers but he quickly came to understand the intense rivalry. "It doesn't matter who's on top or on bottom," Waymond said. "To me, it was like a mini-Super Bowl against each other. I enjoyed the rivalry. What I liked the most about it were the fans. They were behind their teams 100 percent. I think the fans were more into the game than some of the players. There's nothing like Chicago and Green Bay fans.

"One of my funniest experiences was a Packers' game when I first played in snow. I'd played in cold, but never played in that much snow. It was just unreal. It was in Green Bay during either the 1976 or '77 season. When the game started the temperature may have been around thirty degrees. When we went in at half-time, there were some flakes. When we came out, there was three inches of snow on the ground. It looked like a blizzard had just hit. I wish they had been able to clear the field. It was like, find a line. I was too cold to remember if we won the game or not."

Examining the 1977 seasons of the Green Bay Packers and the Chicago Bears is a study of two teams going in different directions. The Packers' ground game in 1977 would be second worst in the league, last being the lowly Tampa Bay Buccaneers. Also, finishing second to Tampa Bay, Green Bay had only 469 rushing attempts, a clear sign that quarterbacks Lynn Dickey and later on rookie David Whitehurst were behind early and forced to throw often.

Chicago had Walter Payton. Since his rookie year in 1975, Payton's rushing totals had been climbing. There were 679 yards in 1975 and 1,390 yards in 1976. 1977 would see Payton chasing after O. J. Simpson's season rushing record of 2,003 yards. Only three times would he finish a day's work by not rushing for more than one hundred yards. No one in the league could stop him.

Green Bay's defense, like the rest of the league, would not be spared.

Both 2-4 teams met in Green Bay on October 30 for the 115th time, a game that saw animosity return between the two old rivals comparable to the days of Ed Sprinkle and Lee Artoe. It had started to heat up the previous season with, what the Packers claim was a late hit on Lynn Dickey and Dave Roller's comment that he was going to "get" Bears' quarterback Bob Avellini and "throw out the rule book when we play."

"I don't like Avellini and you can say that," Roller stated. "It's a personal thing. It's something he said about me at a banquet in the off-season. It was an off-color remark in front of 800 people."

Bears' middle linebacker Don Rives countered with a guarantee that they would beat the Packers. "We don't even have to play that good a game because we're so much better than Green Bay," he boldly stated. "It's just a matter of going up there and not giving the game away."

Maybe Roller should have been more worried about stopping Walter Payton than trying to get to Avellini. At the end of the first quarter, Payton had already amassed 117 yards on ten carries. *Green Bay Press-Gazette* writer Cliff Christl wrote that as gifted as Payton was, "he could not have achieved what he did without the assistance of the Packers' Swiss cheese defense."

As the Packers left the field at half-time behind 16-0, a steady chorus of boos rang throughout Lambeau Field as never heard before. "The boos?" Bart Starr asked. "You're damn right I heard the boos. I hope they were directed at us (coaches) instead of at the team." As the Packers walked back out for the second half, the last notes of "Send in the Clowns" were being played by the half-time entertainment band.

Things didn't get any better as the Bears added ten points in the fourth and shutout the punchless Pack, 26-0. Walter Payton tied Gale Sayers' record for yardage in one game, 205 yards, set on the same field on November 3, 1968 against the Packers. "He (Payton) could have gained 300 yards," said Bears' safety Gary Fencik.

Payton could have. Pardee took him out of the game with eleven minutes still remaining. In the process, he also surpassed Bronko Nagurski and Ronnie Bull on the all-time Bears' rushing list.

In a mid-December clash, 33,557 fans sat in minus seven degree temperatures chanting "Let's go, Bears! Let's go, Bears!" The team answered when quarterback Bob Avellini tossed an 11-yard touchdown pass to James Scott in the corner of the Packers' end zone.

It was again Payton who inflicted the most damage. For an eighteen minute stretch the Packers stopped Payton for 21 yards on seven carries. For the remaining forty-two minutes, Payton ran for scores of 1 and 7 yards, garnering 142 yards.

The 21-10 victory over the Packers was the Bears' fifth straight win and catapulted them into the first round of the playoffs against Dallas. There, they would be hammered by the Super Bowl-bound Cowboys, 37-7.

For Bart Starr and the lowly Packers it was another 4-10 season finish.

Bob Avellini was a 6'2", 208-pound quarterback out of Maryland, chosen by the Chicago Bears in the sixth round in 1975, Jim Finks' first year working on the draft with Chicago. Looking to rebuild the Bears back to Midway Monster form, Finks went for youth. Bob Avellini, along with first round draft choice Walter Payton, would be a part of that youth movement in '75.

"Lots of guys made the team that year," Avellini recalls. "Basically, we were a very young team ... a team in transition. As far as the rivalry, it's tough if you're a young team and you're not sure if you should be hating another team like the Green Bay Packers. We didn't have older players to tell us how much we were supposed to dislike the Packers. We didn't know we were supposed to go to war when we played them."

The only incident for Avellini that came close to a rivalry was with the aforementioned Dave Roller. "You're always going to run into someone who wants more publicity than they're getting," Avellini said. "Dave Roller was an average defensive tackle who would come out and say, 'I'm gonna knock Avellini out of the game.' I never took him seriously because he wasn't that good. There's always going to be some big mouth, there's one on every team. Some guys can back it up. Dave Roller wasn't one. If he ever did get a quarterback sack, he'd do his little Bear dance. He looked like a dancing Bear. He was a none-issue in a game."

What did Avellini say at that banquet that had so riled Dave Roller? "I have no idea," he said, exasperatingly. "I didn't realize that anything was said at a banquet. I don't know."

Avellini speaks highly of Packers' fans who fill the seats at Lambeau Field even in the worst weather. "I had the utmost respect for the people in Green Bay," he said. "They supported their teams. I remember one game (the November 30 contest in 1975) when it was about twenty-five below, and we were up like 28-0 in the fourth quarter. Not one person had left the stadium. So, I've learned to respect the people of Green Bay."

Avellini had his best year as a pro in 1977. He completed fifty-three percent of his passes for 2,004 yards and eleven touchdowns, and rushed for 109 yards. He led the Bears into the playoffs for the first time since the 1963 championship game against the Giants.

Unfortunately, Avellini tossed four interceptions and his team was blasted by Dallas. He cites the impending departure of Coach Jack Pardee as a reason for the Bears' poor showing.

"We had kind of a lame duck coach," Bob said. "I know Pardee had already signed with Washington [Redskins] and he sold us down the tubes in the playoffs. We never really had a chance to practice. We got killed."

Jack Pardee wasn't denying or confirming that he was about to become the coach of the Washington Redskins. "I think I'm the prime candidate," Pardee said.

In a written commentary, *Chicago Tribune* writer David Condon stated that the Bears "deserved" the disloyalty of Pardee. "I submit," he wrote, "that loyalty hasn't been as cardinal a mark in the new Bears' regime as it was in the old."

In mid-January 1978, Pardee signed on to be the new head coach of Washington. Twenty-eight days later Jim Finks named Neill Armstrong to be the Bears' ninth head coach in fifty-nine years. Armstrong had been the defensive coach for the Minnesota Vikings since 1969. Before that, he had coached the Edmonton Eskimos of the Canadian Football League.

Armstrong reminds one of ex-Packers Coach Phil Bengtson. He was a nice guy who failed to instill discipline on the team. He would lead Chicago to the playoffs in 1979, but that would be the only high point in his four-year stay in Chicago.

Chicago Bears' linebacker Doug Buffone grew up in Western Pennsylvania, the same fertile football country that also produced Mike Ditka, and quarterbacks Joe Namath, Jim Kelly, Johnny Unitas, Dan Marino, and Joe Montana.

Buffone fits the blue collar stereotype of the tough area from where he came. During his career, which began in 1966 and lasted all the way through the 1979 season, Buffone played in 186 games, more than any other Chicago Bear other than Steve McMichael and

Walter Payton. "I really worked hard at the game and stayed in shape," Buffone says of his lengthy career in pro football. "As far as my longevity, I think I was fundamentally strong."

Buffone's first year in the league was a bittersweet one. The talented rookie linebacker immediately began working himself into the lineup, spot playing for Joe Fortunato. Later, in a game against the Packers on October 16, 1966, Buffone hit Paul Hornung on a goal line play and unwittingly assisted in ending Hornung's football career.

"We were in a goal line defense and you knew what was going to happen," Buffone recalled. "They were going to give Paul Hornung the ball. So the first play they gave Hornung the ball and I stacked him up. They gave him the ball again and this time I really drilled him. He scored but that was his last game. I hurt him and he never played again. I felt good and bad at the same time. His pinched nerve was bad and when I hit him he never played after that. Although I wanted to make that great hit, it was like seeing a legend go out."

From 1966 through 1979, Doug played in thirty-eight Packers-Bears games, including pre-season contests. It was the kind of football Doug loved to play: rough, tough, and all out.

"We used to call it 'Packers' Panic Week.' The guys were just totally different in attitude going into that game. That's when I learned it just wasn't another game. It was take-no-prisoners; whoever is left standing, wins. Even in exhibition games. There was one exhibition game we played against them that was in pouring rain. It was just a dog fight. They had three plays, we had three plays. That was it. That's what I loved about the games. There was nothing fancy about it. It was two old warriors going at it. After it's said and done with, you respect each other."

During the mid-Seventies, the rivalry appeared to simmer somewhat, but not to Doug and some of his older teammates. "During that whole era there were always coaches around who had been involved with the Packers or ball players who played for the Packers. The rivalry was continuing as far as the players were concerned.

"Two years ago when Bears' quarterback (Eric) Kramer came out and made the statement the Packers game was just another game, for us ex-players, it made your hair stand up because, in our minds, it never was just a game."

Doug laughingly recalled the days when the team would go up to Green Bay and stay in the Northland Hotel before the game. The hometown Packers' fans would do their best to see to it that the visiting Bears got as little sleep as possible. "It was nothing to be staying at the old Northland Hotel and at 3 o'clock in the morning hear someone playing 'Bear Down Chicago Bears' with a trombone. Or someone pulls the fire alarm at 4 o'clock and players in their shorts started running out the door, then stood there in front of a bunch of Packers' fans wearing antlers on their heads. I used to get a chuckle out of that."

The Packers' draft of 1978 yielded some needed talent for Bart Starr. Defense got most of the attention as Starr and his staff drafted linebackers John Anderson of Michigan and Mike Douglass of San Diego State, and Illinois State defensive back Estus Hood. But it was the Packers' first round choice that gave them a new lethal weapon on offense. In Stanford wide receiver James Lofton, the Packers found the deep scoring threat they desperately needed.

Green Bay's passing game took a serious blow when Lynn Dickey suffered a serious broken leg on the last play in the ninth game of the 1977 season against the Los Angeles Rams. It caused him to sit out the entire 1978 season. Thrust in his place was second-year man David Whitehurst, who did a commendable job at quarterback. To add some experience at the position, the Packers hired ex-Bears' quarterback Bobby Douglass, who brought nine years of pro ball knowledge to help Whitehurst.

The 1978 Green Bay Packers were a talented and underrated team. The offense was one to be reckoned with. Second-year running back Terdell Middleton became only the fourth running back in Packers' history to rush for over 1,000 yards in a season, gathering 1,116 yards in '78. It wouldn't be until the 1995 season that the Packers would have another 1,000 yard rusher. Their receiving corps consisted of Lofton, Aundra Thompson, and tight end Rich McGeorge. Running backs Middleton and Barty Smith would combine to catch seventy-one passes themselves.

Green Bay's defensive line was solid with Mike Butler, Ezra Johnson, and Carl Barzilauskas punishing quarterbacks and ball carriers. Jim Carter and John Anderson led the linebacking crew while Willie Buchanon, Johnny Grey, and Steve Luke anchored positions in the defensive backfield. It would be Luke who would lead the Packers to a win in their first game with Chicago.

The streaking 4-1 Packers hosted the 3-2 Bears on October 8 at Lambeau Field. Before the game someone posted a quote on a bulletin board in the Packers' locker room. The quote was from Bears' star running back Walter Payton. "After they (the Packers) lose on Sunday," Payton was quoted as saying, "they'll have to regroup and put things back together, and I don't think they'll be able to do this." Payton had just committed the reprehensible sin of football. Never say anything that will anger an entire team and give them more impetus to beat the hell out of you.

"That quote in the paper fired us up," Steve Luke said. "Anytime you tamper with a man's pride, he's gonna fight you."

Early in the game, Payton was running a sweep around end when he was met by Luke and the ball came loose. "I didn't fumble," fumed Payton after the game. "I was getting up and I let the ball go." Luke recovered the ball, setting up a Chester Marcol 41-yard field goal.

With the Packers ahead 10-0 in the third quarter, Bears' quarterback Bob Avellini drifted back to throw. As his arm came forward, Packers' linebacker John Anderson belted him, causing the ball to flutter. Racing down the sideline to defend, Steve Luke jumped in front of the ball and glided 63 yards into the end zone.

Sandwiched between two Avellini-to-James Scott touchdown passes, was a Whitehurst-to-James Lofton lob over the middle for a score. Lofton was all alone in the Bears' secondary as he hauled in the ball and galloped untouched into the end zone for the score.

The 24-14 victory had the 55,352 Green Bay faithful chanting, "We Beat The Bears!" as the final minutes ticked away. They had reason to celebrate. Their Packers had not been 5-1 since Lombardi's 1966 squad.

"We're working our way back," a beaming Bart Starr said afterwards, "and our record indicates we have made some progress."

Two weeks after that, in what would later be a critical game, the

Packers lost to Minnesota, 21-7. The roof began to cave in. Two wins over hapless Tampa Bay, three losses and a tie with the Vikings had the Packers 8-5-1 going into Chicago for a December 10 game. The Bears, at 5-9, were cast into the role of spoilers, determined to slap the Pack and keep them out of the playoffs.

Soldier Field's artificial turf was slick and icy in the fifteen degree temperatures, turning the game into one of field position and conservative play calling. Midway through the first quarter, Packers' running back Terdell Middleton broke loose and was romping for a touchdown when he tried to stiff-arm Bears' defensive back Doug Plank. Plank stripped the ball away and the Bears recovered the fumble. With fifteen seconds left in the half, Payton crawled over from one yard out and Chicago had a 7-0 lead.

Early in the third, the Packers' Johnnie Gray attempted to field a Bears' punt. Choosing not to call a fair catch, Gray was annihilated with a vicious hit by Steve Schubert, causing Gray to fumble. Chicago's Len Waltersheid recovered, and, on the next play, James Scott caught a 35-yard touchdown pass for a 14-0 Bears' lead.

In the fourth quarter, Packers' quarterback David Whitehurst was injured by defensive end Mike Hartenstine. Hartenstine got a game ball after the *Chicago Tribune* said he "personified the intensity," by jumping on Whitehurst while he was flat on his back, injuring his shoulder.

Whitehurst's backup was quite familiar with the surroundings of Soldier Field. Ex-Bears' quarterback Bobby Douglass entered the game to a chorus of boos-birds, of which he had become accustomed to while playing for the Bears. The Chicago fans showed no mercy. Douglass promptly changed boos to cheers when he attempted a patented Douglass quarterback bootleg, stiff-arming Bears' linebacker Gary Campbell. Later in the drive after completing a pass to Lofton, Douglass ran down the field and met Bears' safety Doug Plank. The two collided and Plank was the one who limped away. "He caught me right on top of the head," Plank said. "It was embarrassing. I didn't even know the score."

Plank and the Bears hung on for a 14-0 shutout, damaging the Packers' playoff hopes. In the final game of the season, the Packers needed only a win against the Rams to win the Central Division over Minnesota. The Los Angeles Coliseum became a mausoleum for the Packers, as they were thumped by the Rams, 31-14. Even though the Vikings lost on the same day, the two teams finished in a tie for the Central Division lead. That mid-season 21-7 loss to the Vikings had been enough to send the Packers back home with their hats in their hands and no playoff game.

All coaches know that the fine line between a championship contender and an also-ran are injuries. When key players are out and the bench player isn't as strong as a starter, that position becomes the weak link in the chain. Overall conditioning gives the player a better chance that injury will not occur but many times it's just a freakish play. Cleats get caught in the turf twisting knees, players roll on the leg of another player after the whistle, and fingers get caught between two helmets crashing together. The game is played by men who know that the probability of injury is very high.

In 1979, both Chicago and Green Bay would be injury plagued. In the Bears' last game of the pre-season, fullback Roland Harper suffered a knee injury that sidelined him for the entire year. Harper had gained nearly a thousand yards the previous season and was the primary blocker for Walter Payton. Fullback Dave Williams became Harper's replacement.

The injury jinx continued on opening day at newly renovated Soldier Field as the Packers came to town to do battle. The day turned out to be a scorcher with humid temperatures in the mid-eighties. Heat prostration, instead of frostbite, became the concern for this Bears-Packers match.

Midway through the second period Green Bay's number one draft choice, Georgia Tech running back Eddie Lee Ivery, swung around left end and crumbled to the artificial turf, fumbling the ball into the hands of Chicago's Alan Page at Green Bay's 29-yard line. After the game Ivery blamed the new artificial turf of Soldier Field.

"I tried to make a cut back and I planted my left foot," he remembered. "On natural turf my foot would have slid. On this stuff, it stuck. I wrenched my knee and I dropped the ball. Nobody popped it loose, I just dropped it when I felt the pain. I never felt anything like that in my life." Later in the quarter, Bears' running backs John Skibinski and Robin Earl also had to leave the game hurting.

One could look on the Bears' 6-3 win as a great defensive game between two old Central Division foes or a listless game showcasing two inept offenses. Two Bob Thomas field goals would be all the Bears needed to win. Green Bay had a chance in the third period to tie the game but Chester Marcol's field goal attempt was blocked by Virgil Livers.

Three months later it was a drastic change in weather and venue as the Bears traveled to Lambeau Field in the thick of playoff contention. The Bears had started well, then slid in mid-season, only to regroup and win five of their last six games.

It was a different story in Green Bay. The Packers had fallen apart due to injuries. Nearly everyone on the team had been hurt or nicked-up at some time during the year. Although they now had Lynn Dickey back at quarterback, the team was in a mess and once-loyal Bart Starr backers were starting to call for his head.

The Packers showed what an undisciplined and maladroit team they were when they were penalized nine times in the first half, with four of the flags giving the Bears a first down. Only penalized once in the second half, they made up for it by turning the ball over four times.

Somehow, Green Bay was leading 7-6 with 11:10 to go in the game. In Bears' territory and threatening, Lynn Dickey threw a screen pass in the direction of reserve back Ricky Patton. It never got there. Chicago linebacker Tom Hicks intercepted and raced 66 yards for a back-breaking touchdown. The Packers blocked the extra point, making it 12-7, Chicago.

On the ensuing kickoff, Packers' defensive back Mike McCoy fumbled and Wentford Gaines recovered for the Bears at the Packers' 31-yard line. Three plays later Bob Thomas kicked a 44-yard field goal and it was 15-7.

The Packers weren't done. Lynn Dickey tossed a 22-yard scoring pass to tight end Paul Coffman with 1:33 left to play. Reserve defensive back Wylie Turner recovered the subsequent onside kick setting up a 52-yard field goal try by Packers' kicker Tim Birney with thirty-seven seconds left. The kick was short and wide left. Final: Chicago 15, Green Bay 14.

Green Bay had just set a club record for most defeats in a season with eleven. Three times—1958, '75 and '77—the franchise had lost ten games. The Packers lost seven of their final nine games, a complete collapse.

Injuries certainly played a part in the season's bad performance. After running for over 1,000 yards in 1978, Terdell Middleton was nagged with injuries in '79 and only gathered 495 yards. Veteran running back Barty Smith went out with a knee injury in October along with defensive tackle Carl Barzilauskas. Barzilauskas' knee injury ended his career.

By the end of the decade, the once-proud Green Bay Packers were one of the worst teams in the league. Bart Starr, the supposed savior of the franchise, had just wallowed in his fourth losing season in five years and the wolves were howling at his door.

The Bears knocked off the St. Louis Cardinals in the last game of the season and won a playoff berth against Philadelphia. After playing quarterback shuffle between Mike Phipps, Vince Evans, and Bob Avellini for most of the year, the Bears settled on Mike Phipps to lead them into the playoffs and to the Super Bowl. Leading 17-10 at half-time, the Bears squandered the lead and lost to the Eagles, 27-17.

It had been a positive season for the Midway Monsters. At 10-6, Chicago tied for the Central Division lead with Tampa Bay and began learning how to be winners again, and Walter Payton had had his fourth consecutive 1,000-yard season. Things were looking up in Chicago

In Green Bay, they were looking up from the bottom of the league's standings.

The 1980s

The Fridge, Iron Mike, Terrible Towels, and Lucky Lindy

The 1980s became a decade of change for pro football. From its early beginnings in the 1920s, pro football had slowly but steadily climbed to the top of American sport. The advent of television in the Fifties led to the heightened popularity of the game in the Sixties. In the Seventies the game became sophisticated with more complex offensive and defensive formations. Also, the Super Bowl had now become the premiere and most watched sporting event in America. Pro football had certainly come a long way, baby, since Harold "Red" Grange had run on a football gridiron.

In the Seventies, the heat on the rivalry between Green Bay and Chicago had been turned down to a simmer. Green Bay coaches Phil Bengtson, Dan Devine and Bart Starr toned down the feud to a point where it almost was non-existent. After Abe Gibron was ousted, Chicago coaches Jack Pardee and Neill Armstrong, having no past history of the rivalry, did nothing to rattle the cages of anyone connected with Green Bay. The rivalry became downright tame.

It would soon change. Beginning with the 1980 season, the heat would slowly start to be turned up to a point where, by mid-decade, it would get ugly and dangerous.

Bart Starr and the Packers were plagued by injuries and bad luck. Their first round draft choice, Penn State defensive tackle Bruce Clark, decided to play football in Canada. Linebacker George Cumby, their second pick, went out with a knee injury in November, while other key injuries to offensive tackle Mark Koncar and linebacker Rich Wingo damaged any hopes of Green Bay competing for a championship.

The only bright spot was the emergence of receiver James Lofton. With Lynn Dickey healthy and throwing better than ever,

Lofton caught seventy-one passes for a league-leading 1,226 yards. Dickey finished third in passing yardage with 3,529 yards on 278 completions. The passing game that Curly Lambeau had long ago pioneered had certainly progressed.

The Chicago Bears had high hopes for the upcoming season. Two of the last three seasons the Bears had made the playoffs only to lose in the first round. Chicago had the best running back in the game with Walter Payton. His 1,460 yards in 1980 crowned the fifth year in a row that he led the league in rushing. The Bears were going as far as Walter Payton's legs would take them.

The week before the opening day game with Chicago, the Packers were in turmoil after suffering through a 0-4-1 pre-season and being outscored, 86-17. The annual Hall of Fame game in Canton, Ohio turned into an omen of things to come when a dangerous electrical thunderstorm chased fans out of the stadium and players into their locker rooms. Soon after, the scoreless game was canceled.

Many Green Bay fans had now lost hope that Bart Starr would coach their team back to the Super Bowl. All week long rumors and speculation ran rampant about Starr and the team's future. There was also trouble inside the team as well. Players had factioned off into small groups, leaving the team fragmented and cliquish. Thursday before the Bears' game, Green Bay's squad met after practice in an attempt to mend the team.

"We had a few beers and loosened up," said center and offensive captain Larry McCarren. "The offense, the defense ... everybody was well represented. I left there with a good feeling."

On opening day, 54,381 fans witnessed one of the strangest sights ever seen at Lambeau Field. The first sixty minutes of regulation were an example of how not to play professional football. Due to both team's inept offenses, the game was knotted 6-6 at the end of regulation.

In overtime, after a three and out Bears' series, the Packers got the ball and moved downfield where the drive stalled in Chicago territory. Out trotted the "Polish Prince," Chester Marcol, to attempt a 35-yard game-winning field goal.

In the Bears' huddle, former Vikings' great and now Chicago defensive tackle Alan Page bellowed, "I'm going to block it."

Chicago put an all-out rush from the right side, leaving the left side open. With the snap good and the ball on the ground, Marcol connected, sending the ball flying—right into the helmet of the hard-charging Page. Just as quickly as it had left his foot, the ball, without hitting the ground, flew right back into the hands of Marcol who was completing his follow through. "The ball came into my hands and I ran to daylight," Marcol said after the game.

While no one could mistake Chester Marcol for Walter Payton, Marcol did see an opening and dashed for it. Spotting daylight on the left side of the Bears' line, the bespectacled bantam kicker took off, scampering for the end zone, his eyes behind his glasses bigger than a car's headlights. "I had no choice but to go left," Marcol remembered. "I played a lot in high school and college and it gave me some football sense. There wasn't much time left on the clock so I was thinking first down. But six points were better than a first down."

It certainly was. The Polish Prince pranced into the end zone untouched with a huge smile on his face while Green Bay players and fans went delirious. Green Bay had won the game in one of football's most unusual turn of events.

"Life evens things up for you and it evened it up for us today," Bart Starr said. "You may live your lives out and never see another play like that. What we had to overcome today and the way we won makes this game even better. No rivalry in pro football matches the Packers and the Bears and our defense responded magnificently. With the injuries the Packers had sustained and all the flak we've been getting from the fans and the media, starting the season against the Bears just added to the challenge."

The euphoria didn't last long. The Packers settled into their usual losing ways, dropping seven of their next eleven games before facing the Bears again in Chicago on December 7. The Bears came into the game playing for a playoff spot with a record of 5-8, with two games behind the division-leading Vikings. It was a long shot, but they still had a chance. That fact would set the stage for a contest that would turn the burners up on the rivalry, and fast.

57,176 football fans sat in a steady drizzling rain in Soldier Field and saw a complete massacre. It became Green Bay's worst loss since the 56-0 drubbing by Baltimore in 1958, and their worst loss to the Bears in the 122 game series.

After a quiet and scoreless first quarter, the roof fell in on the Packers. Two Vince Evans touchdown passes and two rushing scores put the Bears in front, 28-7, at half-time. Chicago clearly had the out-manned Packers on the ropes and beaten, but they kept pouring it on. Two more touchdown passes, a couple of rushing scores, an interception return, and 594 total offensive yards put the Bears embarrassingly ahead, 61-7!

When the game ended, Starr met Bears' coach Neill Armstrong at mid-field for the post-game handshake. Starr was upset at the way the Bears had piled up the score. With the score 55-7 and the game firmly in his hands, Armstrong inserted Walter Payton back into the game. To that point, Payton had run for 118 yards and three touchdowns. The Packers considered Payton's return as rubbing the team's nose right in the ground, or Soldier Field's artificial turf, in this case. Asked about the incident after the game, Starr calmly said, "I don't comment on things like that publicly."

"When you see guys like him (Payton) come back in with the score lopsided, it kind of sticks in your mind," Packers' cornerback Estus Hood said. "Yeah, we'll remember it next time we play the Bears."

Starr was also upset that the Bears, even in the fourth quarter, were still blitzing their linebackers. It's an unwritten rule in any sport: When you have a team down and beaten, don't humiliate them. Defensive coach Buddy Ryan was sending his defense full force into the Packers' offense even when the score was 55-7.

"We were trying to get into the playoffs that year and it did come down to a point thing," Bears' defensive tackle Mike Hartenstine stated. "We had to win by thirty points or so and we needed the Washington Redskins to win. We had to score a certain amount of points because of the tie breaker. Things were just rolling for us that day and we needed to win by so much. That part of destiny was in our hands. We had control of that."

Armstrong had some explaining to do when questioned after the game. As for putting Payton back in late in the game, Armstrong said it was done with the league rushing title in mind. "He wanted a few more yards," Armstrong said. "I told him I didn't want him to go back in, but he wanted to."

When asked why he had backup quarterback Mike Phipps throw two passes on Chicago's final possession, Armstrong said, "We were just trying to get the first down so we could continue to run out the clock."

Run out the clock? His team was leading 61-7! The Bears could have just played defense in the fourth quarter and the Packers would not have beaten them.

"I should be exuberant, but I'm not," Armstrong added. "I don't enjoy running the score up on anybody. It just happened that way."

Green Bay Press-Gazette writer Cliff Christl summed it up in the headline of his column the following morning.

"Green Bay Packers — R.I.P."

Todd Bell was an All-Pro safety who played for the Chicago Bears for six years beginning in 1981. Bell knows about football rivalries all too well. He played safety for the Ohio State Buckeyes, whose nemesis were the Wolverines of Michigan.

"If I could equate any of the Green Bay-Chicago games to a college atmosphere, it would be an Ohio State-Michigan type rivalry," Bell said. "These teams have been playing each other for years. As a result, there are traditions, rivals, certain memories and stories that are told about the rivalry between the Packers and the Bears. No one pulls any punches. If you had the opportunity to hit someone, you did."

Bell recalls a funny story about teammate Al Harris, a defensive end who played nine years with Chicago.

"Al Harris was always imitating Bruce Lee, all the Kung Fu stuff," Bell said. "You know... Iiiiiiii Eeeeeeeee! This became a regular routine. We'd be coming in the locker room and he'd act like Bruce Lee. So, we were playing the Packers up at Lambeau Field, and we were punting the ball. On this play, Al Harris was going down the field when, out of nowhere, defensive back Maurice Harvey spear-headed big Al. He knocked him out. Al didn't remember what happened or who hit him. Imagine. Big Al, 6' 5" and 250 pounds, running down the field and being hit by this small, skimpy defensive back.

"We were watching the special teams film and they slow-motioned the play. In the dark, someone hollered out, 'Whooopieeeeeee Pow!' Everybody in the room started laughing. It just took us all back to when Al would go through the locker room doing his Bruce Lee imitation. We all started teasing big Al. He never lived it down!"

In late December, 1980, the Executive Committee gathered to discuss the future of Bart Starr and the Packers. Some members clearly wanted Starr's scalp while others were not so fast to condemn him. Finally, in a move that placated the entire board, it was decided that Starr would finish out the last year of his contract as head coach, but be relieved of his general manager duties. It was purely a move to give Starr time to devote all of his attention to football operations and give him the best possible chance to have a winning season in the final year of his contract.

Although not as drastic, change was in the air in Chicago. George Halas, the 86-year old owner, was going to take a more active role in the running of the club. For the entire season, Halas oversaw the progress and operations of the entire franchise. After the Bears won only six of sixteen games in 1981, the decision for a coaching change became an easy one.

On September 6 the two rivals opened the season against each other for the third straight year. It was a comedy of errors as Chicago fumbled six times, losing it on four occasions. The costliest fumble came with thirty-two seconds left in the game. With the ball on the Packers' 3-yard line, Bears' quarterback Vince Evans handed off to fullback Matt Suhey. Packers' defensive lineman Mike McCoy planted Suhey at the half-yard line, jarring the ball loose and Packers' safety Johnnie Gray recovered. There was confusion between two officials about whether Suhey had been down when the ball popped loose or had he not hit the turf yet. Both officials conversed and finally decided that Suhey had fumbled. Green Bay won, 16-7.

Suhey's comment after the game concurred with the official's decision. "I think I hit the ball with my knee," he said.

Overall, both teams' performance were quite unremarkable. *Chicago Tribune* writer Steve Daley called it a "yawner," and went on to say that, "if there were any football justice, this game would have been hauled into court for forgery. When the Great Book of NFL History is written, this affair will not get a mention."

Neither would the mid-November's rematch in Green Bay. Although Walter Payton gained 105 yards rushing, the rest of the Bears' offense was listless, leading *Tribune* writer Bob Verdi to offer the best line of the day when he called the Bears "Motleys of the Midway."

The Packers' attack, if you can call it that, was led by quarterback David Whitehurst. His two TD throws to running back Harlan Huckleby and one to Terdell Middleton put the Packers on top, 21-17, late in the fourth quarter. During the last nine minutes of the game, quarterback Vince Evans and the Bears' offense had the ball on the 49-, the 36-, and the 20-yard lines, only to gain a total of 11 yards.

On a play befitting the game and the season for Chicago, Vince Evans threw a strike late in the game to Bears' receiver Ken Margerum at the Packers' 23-yard line. The catch would have put the Bruins in good shape for a possible game-winning score. Instead of catching the ball with his hands, Margerum let it come into his chest, popping off him and into the hands of Green Bay cornerback Mark Lee.

The Packers were now on a roll. After starting out a dismal 2-6, Starr's troops rebounded to win six of their last eight games and finished a respectable 8-8. Two losses to the Central Division champion Tampa Bay Buccaneers cost the Packers a shot at the title. The big finish helped extend Bart Starr's job for another two years.

In Chicago, the season had been a running soap opera. All year long, while the team on the field played terribly, George Halas was busy poking his nose into all team operations. He had a decision to make. Either keep both General Manager Jim Finks and Coach Neill Armstrong, fire both of them, or keep one and not the other.

Even though the Bears went on to win the last three games of the season, they finished with a lackluster 6-10 record. Winds of change were blowing in the Windy City.

On Monday, January 4, 1982, Head Coach Neill Armstrong was fired by George Halas. Papa Bear's decision was done without the consultation of Jim Finks. Armstrong's record with the Bears had been 30-34, and Halas saw the team going backwards instead of forwards.

Soon after the firing, names of potential new coaches began to be thrown around. USC's John Robinson and Hugh Campbell, head coach of Edmonton in the Canadian League were being mentioned, but the leading candidate was ex-Bears' tight end and Dallas Cowboys' offensive coach Mike Ditka. Ditka had been an assistant coach with Tom Landry's Cowboys since retiring as a player in Dallas in 1973. After being in charge of special teams, Ditka was hired as offensive coach, a position he would hold for nine years.

On January 20, the *Chicago Tribune* reported that Ditka would be named the Bears' tenth head coach in a press conference that day.

"I will be in control," Ditka announced in front of the Chicago media. "I know where the buck stops."

It was an odd re-pairing of Ditka and the Papa Bear. They had parted ways in 1967 with a "clash of personalities," as Ditka put it. "I didn't fit in with the empire he built," Ditka said of Halas. "They made it plain that there is no place for me in their organization." After a lengthy contract dispute, Halas traded Ditka to Philadelphia where he played for two years. The Eagles then traded Ditka to Dallas.

Halas may have had his fill of Ditka then but he was sure "Iron Mike" was the right man to coach his Bears. Halas, as usual, was ready to put any petty differences aside if it would make the Bears winners again.

Ditka was a tough disciplinarian who had come by it honestly. His upbringing in the blue collar area of Carnegie, Pennsylvania had toughened him into a no-nonsense player and coach. After the lenient coaching regimes of Neill Armstrong and Jack Pardee, Mike Ditka's demeanor was a drastic change, and, for the Bears' team, a much needed one.

"I like his ability to handle himself and handle other people," Halas was quoted as saying. "I know he'll do a good job getting people to play according to his desires."

It would become Halas' last great decision for the franchise. It was a choice that would eventually have people calling them the "Monsters of the Midway," again. Sadly, the Papa Bear would not live to see it.

Reaction around the league was mostly in favor of the naming of Ditka as head coach. Luke Johnsos, longtime Halas assistant, said, "He won't take any guff from anybody. He has the winning spirit."

Two ex-Packers who had battled on the football field with Ditka spoke their minds when they heard of the selection.

"If anybody can work for George Halas, Mike Ditka can," said Fuzzy Thurston. "It's a difficult job, but Mike is tough enough to handle it."

Ray Nitschke, in his own way, put the hiring into an oddly honest perspective. "As long as Halas didn't hire Howard Cosell, it's a step forward."

In 1977, the NFL and the players' union, the NFLPA, endorsed a five-year bargaining agreement. Five years later owners and players were back at the table as the 1982 expiration date loomed. Jack Donlan, the NFL owners' negotiator, and Ed Garvey, representing the players' union, pleaded their case. The worker-management snag was the players' insistence of a less restrictive free-agency agreement, and the players' radical salary demands based on incentive clauses and years played in the league.

Two weeks into the '82 season, players walked out and pro football was on strike. For fifty-seven days the walkout dragged on. By November 8, the chances of the season being salvaged were becoming less and less. George Halas was hopeful that the season could be saved. "I don't see why not, unless Garvey screws it up," Halas said.

Finally, an agreement was hammered out between the two warring factions. Although none of the radical proposals were adopted, there would be more money for the players.

It was not the way Mike Ditka wanted to start his first season as a head coach. After the strike was settled, his team would go 3-4, and finish 3-6 on the year.

It was a rebirth of sorts for Bart Starr and the Packers. Playing only .500 football after the strike, the Pack ended up with the third best record in the NFC, going 5-3-1. In the revamped playoff system imposed because of the strike, the Packers made the playoffs and beat the St. Louis Cardinals, 41-16. A week later, Dallas put an end to Green Bay's Super Bowl dreams by beating them, 37-26.

For the first time since 1922, the rivalry between the Packers and the Bears had been interrupted. They didn't play against each other at all in 1982. The players' strike wiped out both games between the rivals.

If there is a name that is synonymous with the Green Bay Packers it is undoubtedly Bart Starr. Bart's history with the franchise dates from when he was drafted in 1956, until he was released from the head coaching position after the 1983 season. Bart was not only a hero to many a young kid growing up, like this author, but was also a man of great personal and religious conviction. If one had to have a hero as a kid, there was no one better to idolize than Bart Starr.

Bart has nothing but praise for the Bears and the rivalry itself.

"We were always extremely proud and privileged to be a part of a rivalry like that," Bart said. "You didn't have to work too hard to get up for the Bears because you knew they would be ready to play. It was a great David and Goliath-type of happening; a small town team playing another from one of the country's largest cites.

"Equally important is the history associated with the rivalry," Bart said. "From the beginning, a fierce rivalry developed. It has grown over the years and today is exceptional. There was a true uniqueness about it, and I always felt that way because coaches and veterans conveyed the challenge to us when we came in as rookies.

"It was great playing them twice a year. When you're in the same division you're going to face each other at each other's home. That really adds depth to a continuing rivalry. It's incredible to see how long these two teams have competed against each other. It's a marvelous story."

After he became Green Bay's coach, Bart instilled the history of the rivalry to his players.

"Yes, but again, veteran players also conveyed that well [the rivalry]to the younger ones," Starr added. "You're proud of those kinds of match-ups and pieces of history. When you have tradition at work in a league and in a sport as popular as professional football, a rivalry such as the Bears and Packers is truly special.

"I always enjoyed playing in Wrigley Field," Bart added. "A loud, hostile crowd in a small baseball stadium. It was tough and challenging. Not many are aware that one of the end zones was inadequately sized because one of the baseball dugouts was in the south end zone of the field. Little things like that will always be remembered. With the rivalry having the impact that it did, it was thrilling to compete on their turf.

"One of the things I'd like to have noted is that when they are not playing the Packers, I'm a big Bears' fan. I like them. Being a history buff, I enjoyed reading about the Bears, Coach Halas and others. The Bears, like the Packers, are an interesting story in professional sports.

"Additionally, over the years, Mike Ditka and I became good friends. I admired Mike as a player. His competitiveness has been well documented. I also admired him as a coach for the same reasons. Mike is one of those great straight-shooters who you enjoy being around."

George Halas hired Mike Ditka to turn things around in the Windy City. Ditka, along with General Manager Jim Finks, began immediately to draft and trade for players to make the Bears contenders again.

The Bears began to acquire the nucleus of a great team during the 1982 draft of college players. Chosen in the first round was quarterback Jim McMahon out of BYU. The free-wheeling McMahon was tabbed to be the team's quarterback of the future. Also chosen in the '82 draft was talented running back Dennis Gentry and offensive guard Kurt Becker.

The draft of 1983 proved to be one of Chicago's best. Many of the rookies drafted that year would start for the Bears' Super Bowl team three years later. Offensive tackle Jimbo Covert, wide receiver Willie Gault, defensive backs Mike Richardson and Dave Duerson, defensive tackle Richard Dent, and guard Mark Bortz were the fresh harvest of talent the Bears reaped in 1983.

Coming off a playoff year, the Packers had a surge of new life. Maybe Bart Starr could save the day in Titletown, after all. Starr had put together one of the most feared passing games in football, with quarterback Lynn Dickey lobbing bombs to the "Glitter Twins," receivers John Jefferson and James Lofton, and to tight end Paul Coffman. In 1983, Dickey threw for an amazing 4,458 yards and thirty-two touchdowns, both league leaders. A total of eleven players caught ten or more of Lynn Dickey's throws.

Basically, the running game was used to set up the passing game. Gerry Ellis led the team with 696 yards, while Eddie Lee Ivery, Jesse Clark, and Mike Meade contributed.

Even with the great passing game, the Packers' performance was erratic. Never playing two good games together, the Packers would win a game then lose a game as the season progressed. Chicago had the same problem. Like the Packers, they were a good team but inconsistent. Both squads brought mediocre records into the first match on December 4 in Green Bay.

The anti-Bart Starr group was out in full force at Lambeau Field as some fans held up cardboard signs that read, "Fresh Start Without Bart," and "Retire No. 15 Forever." The latter was prompted by the pre-game ceremony that officially retired Ray Nitschke's old number "66." Bart Starr was one of the three other Packers who had had his number retired. It was such a volatile gathering that even Packers' president Judge Robert Parins was booed as he introduced Nitschke to the crowd.

On Green Bay's first play, Gerry Ellis rumbled off on a 71-yard run setting up the first of two touchdown runs by halfback Harlan Huckleby. With the Packers securely ahead, 28-14, and in control of the ball with 5:30 left in the game, offensive coordinator Bob Schnelker called a play that bordered on bizarre. Running back Gerry Ellis took a pitch-out, then threw the ball across the field in the direction of Paul Coffman. It never arrived. Chicago defensive back Leslie Frazier made his second interception of the day and returned it to the Green Bay 24-yard line. A few plays later, Chicago fullback Matt Suhey plunged over from the 1-yard line for the score.

With 1:50 left, Chicago's Dennis McKinnon darted his way through the Packers' punt team on his way to a 59-yard punt return tying the game, 28-28. On the next series, Dickey faded back to pass and threw a 67-yard bullet to receiver James Lofton, putting the Pack on the Bears' 10-yard line. On the last play of the game, Green Bay kicker Jan Stenerud booted a 19-yard field goal and Green Bay had the heart-stopping victory.

The loss ended what little post-season hopes the Bears had. "It's not over until the fat lady sings," said Walter Payton after the game, "but I guess she's backstage warming up."

The fat lady was also warming up for Coach Bart Starr. As the final game of the season against the Bears approached, all knew that a loss would leave the Packers with an 8-8 record, out of the play-offs, and Bart Starr out of a job. A win would put them at 9-7, in the playoffs for the second straight year, and secure Starr another contract.

But Bart Starr was about to be reminded of an old sport adage: There's a fine line that separates winners from also-rans.

With Green Bay leading 21-20 with just under four minutes left, Bears' quarterback Jim McMahon began marching his troops down-field. He had help in the fact that Green Bay's defense had more holes than a block of Swiss cheese. Rated eleventh worst of the fourteen NFL team defenses, Green Bay was totally out-manned. With Walter Payton running the ball and McMahon completing short passes to Matt Suhey, and tight ends Jay Saldi and Emery Moorehead, the Bears moved into field goal range. With ten seconds left, Chicago kicker Bob Thomas soccer-styled a 22-yard field goal between the uprights, and Chicago won, 23-21.

It was an agonizing loss for Starr and the Packers. They had been a mere ten seconds away from the playoffs. Instead, like Chicago, they would watch the playoffs at home. Bart Starr had just suffered what he called, "my most disappointing, bitter defeat."

On Monday, December 19, Packers' president Robert Parins fired Bart Starr. Several members of the board of directors praised Parins' decision, calling it, "the right decision" and "it's time for a change." One of the members had recently been sent a five-page pocket guide from a group wanting Bart Starr fired. The guide listed the records of coaches in the NFL for eight or more years—and Bart Starr was on the bottom.

Bears' coach Mike Ditka commented about Starr's firing, saying, "I don't feel they'll get a man who will fill his shoes that will bring to the organization the same class and character."

Bart Starr had alluded to his inexperience when he had taken the head coaching job in 1974. That, plus some questionable trades by his predecessor Dan Devine, put Starr at a great disadvantage from the beginning. By the time Starr was fired, he had become a good head coach.

Starr's overall coaching record over nine seasons was 52-76-3. Although it appears a cold-hearted Robert Parins fired Starr for losing the Chicago game and not getting in the playoffs, the truth is that a change was needed in Titletown USA. And no one can say that Parins or the governing body of the Green Bay Packers didn't give Starr the time and opportunity to produce a winner.

On October 23, 1983, the Chicago Bears were holding on to a slim 7-6 lead over the Philadelphia Eagles at Veterans Stadium in Philadelphia. Papa Bear George Halas was watching the game from his North Sheridan Road apartment screaming at the television set, rooting on his beloved Bears like he always had when he sat in the press box. Although losing a battle with cancer, Halas wasn't about to miss his Bears win another game.

By next Sunday's game against Detroit, Halas could only concentrate on the game for a few minutes. On Monday, October 31 at 8:25 pm, George Halas died at the age of 88.

"He was an immortal man who made the National Football League," Sid Luckman said. "I just didn't have the heart to be there when he died. He loved the Bears with all his heart. He lived for them. He died for them."

"He was a leader among men and had all of our respect," said Bears' Hall of Famer George Connor. "But he was also our friend and advisor. He never forgot any one of his players over the years."

Legendary running back Bronko Nagurski paid homage to Halas saying, "I'm sure gonna miss the old guy. He was the best coach I ever had, and I had some good ones. He knew football."

Mike Ditka said, "I had my differences but I never lost my respect for him. There's a big difference there. You don't have to agree with somebody as long as you respect him. He is the reason the league is what it is today."

Dominic Olejniczak, Chairman of the Board of the Green Bay Packers, said, "The Packers could not have had a better friend than George Halas. When the Packers needed help at the time of building a stadium in the 1950s, Halas came and talked to the citizens of Green Bay and spoke in favor of a bond issue. He gave an impassioned plea for pro football in our little city. The result was Lambeau Field, built in 1957."

According to plan, the Chicago Bears remained in the Halas family, with 89% of the stock being controlled by Halas' only daughter, Virginia McCaskey.

It may be impossible to write of everything George Halas did for pro football. It's best to simply say that he was and is pro football. He was instrumental in beginning the league, saw it through its leaner days, was involved in many rule changes, and presided over the league for sixty-three years.

Ed McCaskey, Chairman of the Board of the Chicago Bears, recently told a story about Halas that shows the pride and the fight he had in him all his life.

"We were still going up to Green Bay by train," McCaskey recalled. "Green Bay killed the Bears that day and Coach Halas and I were at the Green Bay train station, walking down the platform to our car. As we approached the Bears' car, some guy wearing a heavy red and black woolen shirt comes down the steps and says, 'Hey, Halas, why don't you quit?' Coach Halas dropped his bag and said, 'I'll show you why' and hit the guy right in the chin, then got on the train."

Papa Bear—rest in peace.

"Ever since I left Green Bay, I always hoped that some day I would get the opportunity to coach this football team," said a beaming Forrest Gregg, just named the ninth head coach of the Green Bay Packers. Gregg, a disciple of Vince Lombardi, was given a five-year contract and full control of the franchise's operations.

The differences between the choice of Bart Starr as Packers' head coach in 1974 and Forrest Gregg in 1984 was night and day. Starr began with little coaching experience while Forrest Gregg did his apprenticeship on the sidelines. The former Packers' offensive lineman began coaching as an assistant with the San Diego Chargers in 1972. After the 1973 season, he moved to Cleveland where he was an offensive line coach. One year later he was named head coach of the Browns. He turned the Browns around and won "Coach of the Year" honors. He coached the Cincinnati Bengals in 1981 and '82, leading them to Super Bowl XVI.

"I'm not a prophet, so I can't tell you what is going to happen in the next year," he said. "I can tell you that I didn't take this job to field a losing football team."

Gregg inherited a talented but inconsistent Packers' squad, vastly different from the grind-it-out, run-to-daylight Lombardi teams he had helped build. This was a passing team. During the 1984 season, Lynn Dickey, passing to receivers James Lofton, John Jefferson, and tight end Paul Coffman, once again filled the air with footballs. Gerry Ellis managed to gain 581 yards on the ground, while Eddie Lee Ivery tallied 552 yards, but both were used sparingly in between Lynn Dickey spirals.

There was a new feeling in Green Bay. Bart Starr's regime had gotten a little old for some and a new coach was a big shot in the arm for the franchise. It was a fresh start.

It was also the beginning of a competitive feud between two players who had played against each other back in the Sixties and now were going to use their heads to try to out-smart each other in the Eighties. The one-on-one rivalry between Mike Ditka and Forrest Gregg was a natural one. They came from the old school. They played football in the days of Vince Lombardi, George Halas, Dick Butkus, Ray Nitschke, Jim Taylor, and Doug Atkins. As coaches in the 1980s, they would bring that same break-neck spirit back to the rivalry.

"I think the problem with Forrest was his dislike for Ditka," said

Packers' receiver Walter Stanley. "I think those were two coaches who really didn't care for each other. With Forrest, it was brought on to the players. One of the things he did emphasize with us was the Bears and his dislike for them. He didn't emphasize cheap shots, he just wanted us to play hard, aggressive football. He just thought, an eye for an eye."

Bears' quarterback Bob Avellini recalled an incident that clearly shows how Mike Ditka and Forrest Gregg stirred up the smoldering embers of the rivalry to a red-hot pitch. It happened in an exhibition game in Milwaukee on August 11, 1984, a game won by the Packers, 17-10.

"In Milwaukee you had both teams on the same side of the field on the sidelines. Just ten yards away there's Forrest Gregg and Ditka. It's late in the second quarter and the Packers hadn't gotten a first down yet. They hadn't even gotten past mid-field. The Packers had the ball and it was third and fifteen and Buddy Ryan (defensive coach) sends in a blitz. We blitzed them and they completed a pass for their first first down of the game. Mike Ditka goes up to Buddy Ryan and jumps in his face and starts cursing at him, saying, 'How could you do that, how could you blitz on third and fifteen?' Ditka snapped. Buddy just ignored him.

"Three downs later we sacked Lynn Dickey and they punted the ball. With that, Buddy takes off his headphones and goes up to Mike Ditka, gets in his face, and calls him every name in the book and says, 'Don't you ever bother me when I'm calling defensive plays!' He's saying this in front of the whole team. You could see the veins in Ditka's neck getting bigger and bigger and he wanted to kill this guy. We had to separate them on the sidelines.

"Then, Ditka gets in a shouting match with Forrest Gregg. This is an exhibition game! You can see that we go from playing Green Bay in an exhibition to playing them like they were our hated enemy. Exhibition games should be a time to make the team and work on your timing. It shouldn't be life or death. Mike Ditka made it like that."

By 1984, Mike Ditka had assembled a group that was ready to challenge for the NFL championship. Although injuries sidelined key players on offense, opponents feared the Bears' defense even more. Behind the driving force of defensive coordinator Buddy Ryan, Chicago now had one of the best defenses ever seen on a football field. It became known as the "46 Defense." It wouldn't win every game for Chicago, but an opponent's offense certainly knew they had been into a game after tangling with the Bears.

At defensive end were Richard Dent and Mike Hartenstine, and at tackles were the punishing Dan Hampton and Steve McMichael. Chicago possessed the best linebacking group in the game, with middle linebacker Mike Singletary being sandwiched on the outside by Otis Wilson and Wilber Marshall. The Bears carried ten players listed as defensive backs. Todd Bell, Dave Duerson, Gary Fencik, and Shawn Gayle headed up the squad that would steal twenty-one interceptions on the year. Chicago's second team defense was better than some first teamers on their opponent's squad. They were unforgiving.

Ditka's Bears won their first two games, one a shutout of Denver, and brought their spotless record to Lambeau Field for game 127 of the rivalry. The contest saw the return of the white and dark blue pant road uniforms the Bears hadn't worn since the 1940s.

Both teams' offenses had an off day because both were sporting two quarterbacks with bum backs. Jim McMahon could only last a half until he took himself out because of pain. "He took a real shot early, and he had a late hit on his back," Ditka said after the game. "He was losing color he was in so much pain." Bob Avellini relieved, but the inept Bears' offense could only muster three Bob Thomas field goals.

The Packers' Lynn Dickey did last the entire game, although he was mostly ineffective. Green Bay's only score on the day was a 1-yard dive from Jesse Clark just before the half. Their total yardage on the ground was a paltry 32 yards.

With the Bears leading 9-7 and only 4:37 left in the game, the 55,942 fans in Lambeau Field held their breath as Packers' kicker

Eddie Garcia lined up for a 47-yard field goal attempt. With the flags atop the stadium motionless, Garcia was kicking in the most desirable of circumstances. Garcia smacked the ball but hooked it to the left, wide of the goal post.

Garcia was in his second year with the Packers. In 1983, he watched from the sidelines as veteran All-Pro kicker Jan Stenerud hit every one of his fifty-two extra point tries and twenty-one of twenty-six field goal attempts. Forrest Gregg traded the veteran Stenerud to Minnesota before the season began. Garcia made only three of nine field goal attempts before being replaced by Al Del Greco. As Garcia's kick was sailing wide, Stenerud was at that same moment kicking field goals from 54- and 22-yards out, helping Minnesota defeat the Atlanta Falcons.

"Another sterling offensive performance out of our football team," a sarcastic Forrest Gregg stated after the game. "Just sterling. A memorable occasion."

It was the usual physical Packers-Bears game as a number of fights broke out during the contest. Bears' defensive stalwarts Mike Singletary and Gary Fencik were warned about shoving and pushing opposing Packers.

"Ditka set the tone during the week," said Fencik. "He's the one who said he hated the Green Bay Packers. We're not going to take any type of late hits. I kicked a guy [Green Bay offensive tackle Karl Swanke], I don't know why. I'm not proud of it. It was something someone did."

"They [Green Bay] are going to try to muscle you where they can, and we're just not a team that can be muscled very easily," Ditka said after the game. "We respond back to what they do, and they respond back to what we do. When we play the Packers, you notice their players don't pick anybody off the ground and ours don't pick any of theirs up."

Green Bay didn't pick themselves up until halfway through the season. Poised at a dismal 1-7 record, Green Bay suddenly got hot, won five of six games, and traveled to Chicago to meet the 9-5 Bears.

By this time in the season the Bears were banged up at the quarterback position. Starter Jim McMahon had suffered a lacerated kidney that had ended his season. Backup Steve Fuller separated his shoulder the previous week against San Diego. That put the ball in the hands of an unproven Rusty Lisch.

In the first half the Bears had a chance to score but botched it when Lisch attempted a hand-off to fullback Matt Suhey at the Packer 3-yard line. The ball hit Suhey's face guard and bounced into the hands of a Packers' defender. After Lisch fumbled three more times, Ditka got desperate and put Walter Payton in at quarterback in shotgun formation with 1:51 left in the half. As a quarterback, Payton rushed for 25 yards, threw an incomplete pass, and then threw an interception to Green Bay defensive back Tom Flynn. Payton finished the day with 175 yards rushing.

With the score 14-13, backup Packers' quarterback Rich Campbell faded back to pass with heavy pressure from a blitzing Bears' defense. Campbell evaded a head-twisting tackle attempt by Jeff Fisher and threw a rocket to wide receiver Phillip Epps. Epps, at only 5' 8" and 150 pounds, broke his pass pattern and caught the ball on the Bears' 9-yard line. He spun around, breaking tackle attempts by Gary Fencik and Terry Schmidt, and landed in the end zone, winning the game for the Packers, 20-14.

"The Bears are advancing towards the playoffs with all the momentum of Napoleon on Moscow," wrote *Chicago Tribune*'s Bernie Lincicome.

The loss assured that Chicago would not host a playoff game in Soldier Field. After a season-ending win, the Bears whipped the Redskins in the first round of the playoffs and then were demoralized by the 49ers, 23-0.

The Packers had finished in grand fashion, winning seven of their final eight games to finish again at 8-8.

1985

The 1985 Chicago Bears became one of the NFL's greatest teams. A Monday night loss to Miami on December 2 was the only blemish on an otherwise perfect season. This great Bears' team is mentioned in the same breath as the undefeated 1934 and '42 squads, and the champion '63 team. Some believe they were the best Bears' team ever.

The heart of this team was defense. Linebackers Mike Singletary and Otis Wilson, safety Dave Duerson, and defensive linemen Richard Dent and Dan Hampton would all go to the Pro Bowl, while other Chicago defenders could have been honored. They were defensive league leaders in points allowed (198), fewest first downs (236), fewest rushing touchdowns (6), fewest yards allowed (1,319), and most interceptions, stealing thirty-four opponents' passes. They simply ran roughshod over the entire league.

In striking comparison were the Green Bay Packers, who had become the NFL's unnotables. 1985 was yet another year of inconsistent play by mediocre talent. It would be the third year in a row that the team finished 8-8, their fourth in five seasons. The only break in that string was the strike-shortened campaign of 1982.

Two of the eight losses that year were two of the more memorable games the Packers have ever played against their rivals to the south. The games rekindled the rivalry's fiery emotions, cheap shots, fights, personal fouls, game ejections, and, in the meantime, made a folk hero out of a man nicknamed after a kitchen appliance.

On Monday night, October 21, a nationwide audience and 65,000 in Soldier Field witnessed the emergence of a new folk hero who brought new meaning to the word "fullback."

In the first quarter, the Bears had the ball on the Packers' 2-yard line. Waddling into the game from the sidelines came a 325-pound rookie defensive lineman from Clemson named William Perry, whose enormous weight and width of body had brought him the nickname "The Refrigerator." Perry lined up in the fullback position and with the snap, lunged forward, carrying his massive weight into Packers' linebacker George Cumby.

"I tried to hit him at an angle," Cumby said later. "I wanted to take the blow away from me. I hit him pretty good, but he outweighed me by 100 pounds. I tried to take him on one side, but I soon discovered that one side was as big as the other." Walter Payton calmly walked into the end zone behind the huge hole Perry had produced.

Less than four minutes later the Bears once again had the ball near the Packers' goal line. A chant of, "Perry! Perry!" echoed through the ancient pillars of Soldier Field as "The Refrigerator" again waddled back onto the turf for offensive duty. Tom Thayer, the Bears' offensive guard, heard a Green Bay linebacker daring Perry to run. "He said, 'Come at me, big boy,'" Thayer recalled.

McMahon handed off to the hulking Perry who blasted into the line and over for a touchdown, giving the Bears a 14-7 lead. After rising to his feet, Perry spiked the ball, nearly deflating it.

The idea of installing Perry as an offensive weapon had been fostered the year before in the NFC Championship game when the 49ers put in offensive guard Guy McIntyre as a blocking back in their 23-0 romp over the Bears. Although Ditka didn't like it, he also saw the advantages of such a ploy. The week before the Packers game, Perry carried the ball twice for 4 yards in a retaliatory 25-10 win over the 49ers.

"I'm just a straight-ahead runner at the goal line," a smiling Refrigerator said after the game. "I was just out there having fun. I hit the linebacker or whoever else was in my way." When asked if Cumby had spoken to him during the crushing blocks, Perry said, "He didn't say anything, I think I rung his bell."

Outside of the fun Perry was having, the game featured a number of fights that nearly saw the game turn into a boxing match instead of a football game. Chicago's Jay Hilgenberg, and Green Bay's Charles Martin, Keith Van Horne and Ezra Johnson, Dennis Gentry and Mark Murphy, and Wilber Marshall and Packers' quarterback Jim Zorn all became amateur pugilists by involving themselves in sparring matches. Green Bay wasn't upset that the Bears had used Perry in the backfield. They did take exception to Richard Dent and Dan Hampton physically abusing starting quarterback Lynn Dickey, bruising his shoulder and putting him out of the game. The Packers also took offense when Chicago called a time-out with twelve seconds left in the game, then attempted a pass, all this while leading, 23-7.

"They're a good team, they don't have to do that stuff," Packers' tight end Paul Coffman said afterwards. "That shows a lack of class when they do something like that. Fortunately, we get to play them again."

"What were they going to do?" Forrest Gregg pondered in the locker room. "Beat us by another touchdown? What does that do?"

Bears' defensive tackle Steve McMichael correctly identified the focal point of the hostilities. "Mike (Ditka) and Forrest (Gregg) don't have the greatest desire to like each other and it stems to the players."

Summing up his feelings on the rival Packers, defensive lineman Dan Hampton said, "I wouldn't give you two cents for the whole Green Bay team."

On this night, William Perry was officially dubbed "America's Mascot." *Chicago Sun Times* columnist Ray Sons won the award for the best post-game quote. On the newly knighted America star, he said Perry was, "the best thing to happen to fat since the invention of bacon."

During the two weeks before the November 3 rematch at Lambeau Field, taunts and braggadocio were traded between players on both teams, giving the game good advertisement. Bears' wide receiver Dennis McKinnon referred to their rivals as the Green Bay Quackers, "because they cry a lot." Quarterback Jim McMahon chimed in calling them crybabies. Said Packers' linebacker Randy Scott of the Bears' pre-game comments, "It's like somebody calling your mamma a name, like downgrading your family."

The scene outside the stadium was an odd one. Fans tailgating and meandering around before the game could lay down a dollar and whack a refrigerator with a mallet, with all proceeds going to cerebral palsy. The refrigerator was painted with a big "72" on it's side, William Perry's uniform number. One Bears' fan brought his own refrigerator, and wore it! The gutted appliance had a hole cut out for the fan's head. Imagine the fun as a few of the Packers' faithful attempted to tip over the "fridge-wearing" Bears' fan. Later, reports of a Kenmore running around the parking lot of Lambeau Field were substantiated.

The scene inside both teams' locker rooms was equally strange. All during Bear Week, a full-sized poster of Perry, dating back to his Clemson days, was tacked on a wall in one of the Packers' meeting rooms as a motivational tool.

As Chicago players silently dressed in the visitors locker room, a special delivery package arrived addressed to, "Mike and the Boys." Upon closer inspection, the bag contained horse manure with a note saying, "Here's what you're already full of."

"I didn't actually sniff it," Bears' defensive lineman Dan Hampton said, "but it was manure, all right."

Offensive tackle Keith Van Horne recalled, "It was funny, but I think it worked against them. I think it got some of us fired up."

It didn't take long for the donnybrook to begin. On the second play of the game, Walter Payton was stripped of the ball, and Packers' defensive lineman Ezra Johnson recovered. Rookie free safety Ken Stills took aim at quarterback Jim McMahon, walloping him hard. Five minutes later Walter Payton was slammed by Green Bay defender Mark Lee while running out of bounds with the ball. Referee Bob McElwee immediately ejected Lee from the game. "Walter was pulling on my jersey," Lee pleaded. "I hit him just as he was going out of bounds. He grabbed my shirt and started yanking me. So I pushed him more. He grabbed me and we went over the bench together."

A few minutes later Packers' offensive guard Ron Hallstrom was called for unnecessary roughness on Bears' linebacker Wilber Marshall. Hallstrom said the cheap shot was in retaliation to Marshall's spearing of a Packers' player.

On the Bears' third possession Chicago fullback Matt Suhey was watching Walter Payton get up off the ground after being held to a 2-yard gain. Out of nowhere again came Ken Stills, who unloaded on Suhey in full view of the world. "I didn't feel like stopping," Stills said later. "They've been doing it to our players, and they get away with leg-whipping us and that stuff."

Astonishingly, Forrest Gregg seemed to wink at the hit. "I don't mind that," he said. "He [Stills] took a crack at somebody. That's aggressive football."

Stills was flagged for a personal foul but not thrown out of the game. "It was simply a late hit off the ball," said field judge Ed Merrifield. "It was not deemed as unsportsmanlike to eject."

After the officials began to regain some order by calling six personal fouls, an actual game was played. After being thrown over the bench, Payton ran amuck through the Packers' defense for 192 yards, as a capacity Lambeau Field crowd watched in reverence. "I thought Payton's exhibition was maybe as good as I've ever seen a guy with a football under his arm," Ditka said.

The Packers were surprisingly ahead 3-0 near the end of the

half, when the Bears mounted a drive. With the ball resting in the shadow of the Packers' goal line, William Perry joined the offensive unit. Although the Packers had practiced in anticipation of Perry running the ball again after their Monday night embarrassment, they were not prepared for the Fridge to lineup as a slotback receiver.

"I had to keep a straight face when I got on the line," Perry recalled later.

As McMahon barked the signals, Perry lumbered in motion behind the line. At the snap, Perry turned upfield and ran into the end zone. McMahon spotted him and lobbed a pass towards the NFL's only appliance. With the soft touch of an All-Pro receiver, Perry caught the ball for an "in your face" touchdown. Once again, George Cumby was victimized. Perry had been Cumby's man to cover.

With 10:31 to play, Payton darted through a bevy of yellow-helmeted Green Bay defenders for a 27-yard touchdown, sealing a 16-10 victory, and keeping the Bears perfect with a 9-0 record.

"The Packers ought to reevaluate themselves," Bears' linebacker Otis Wilson said in the locker room. "If they're pros, they should conduct themselves in a professional manner. All they wanted to do is come out and fight."

"I thought everybody should have taken off their face masks and put on black high tops [cleats] today," said Chicago tackle Steve McMichael.

Keith Van Horne had his own view of the game. "This is a great rivalry, but, geez, you saw what happened. It was just a brawl."

"This was by far the toughest football game of the year for us," Coach Ditka theorized. "This was old-fashioned football and we won it."

Ditka would prove to be correct. Other than the Miami loss, the Bears tore through the regular season, shut out the Giants and the Rams in the NFC playoffs, and completely destroyed the New England Patriots, 46-10, in Super Bowl XX in New Orleans on January 26, 1986. To that point it was the widest winning margin in Super Bowl history. The Bears' defense was so dominating that they sacked Patriots' quarterback Steve Grogan seven times, stole two interceptions, and surrendered a grand total of 7 yards rushing on the day. Even Perry got into the act. The "Fridge" scored his final touchdown of the year on a 1-yard run plunge after the game was out of the Patroits' reach.

One has to believe that somewhere Papa Bear George Halas was indeed watching over the Bears, taking notes—with a huge grin on his face.

1986-'89

With Green Bay finishing 8-8 in four of the past five seasons, changes were needed to get the Packers over the hump and back into the playoffs. Forrest Gregg's answer was to cut some veterans and start new players. Quarterback Lynn Dickey and tight end Paul Coffman were now gone. In Dickey's place would be the untested Randy Wright, a 200-pound quarterback from Wisconsin. Backing Wright up was the strong-armed ex-Rams' QB Vince Ferragamo. In Coffman's place were third year men Ed West and Dan Ross. Ross was a journeyman player who had played for Gregg at Cincinnati.

Offensively, the Packers suffered because of the changes. They scored eighty-three less points in 1986 than the previous year, and James Lofton had under a thousand yards in receiving for the first time since 1982. Kicker Al Del Greco also had an off year, making only sixty-three percent of his field goals. The result would be a 4-12 season, finishing just above the 4-11-1 Tampa Bay Buccaneers for the worst team in the NFC.

The Super Bowl champion Chicago Bears would have to do without some key personnel. First and foremost was the parting of the two volatile coaches, Mike Ditka and defensive coach Buddy Ryan. Ryan accepted the Philadelphia Eagles' head coaching position. Although Ditka shed no tears for Ryan's leaving, Buddy had been credited with putting together one of the best defensive units in NFL history. Even without Ryan, the 1986 Bears' defense proved to be as stout as ever.

Another loss came early and was costly to the Bears' fortunes in

1986. In the Bears' opening game with Cleveland at Soldier Field, quarterback Jim McMahon suffered a shoulder injury that plagued him all season. Because of his injury, McMahon played only about half of the year, with the offense being led by a trio of quarterbacks, Mike Tomczak, Steve Fuller, and Doug Flutie. They were all instrumental in getting the Bears to playoffs, only to see them lose to Washington, 27-13.

The hostilities that punctuated both games in 1985 would not be carried over to the first meeting of the rivals in 1986. Compared to the last two games, this one would be downright tame. "Both Gregg and Ditka said we wanted to make this thing clean," Bears' safety Dave Duerson said. "A Bears-Packers game always is, and this was no exception. The play on the field was indicative of it. The hits were very crisp and clean."

"The Bears played more like diplomats than bullies, as if they had gathered to negotiate rather than eradicate," wrote *Tribune* writer Bernie Lincicome. "Maybe the Packers are no longer worth the effort it takes to hate them."

The Packers and the Bears returned to Monday Night Football for the game, this time in Lambeau Field. Green Bay was out to make amends for the embarrassing "Refrigerator Perry" episode of last year.

"There wasn't anyone who gave us an ice cube's chance in hell tonight," said Packers' quarterback Randy Wright. "Everyone thought we'd get beat by thirty-five points."

The Packers did play well. Although they could only muster four field goals by Al Del Greco, they led the champion Bears 12-10 early in the fourth quarter.

On the last play of the third quarter, Chicago's Steve Fuller threw a 6-yard pass that was caught by Willie Gault. Gault turned and headed upfield and lowered his helmet into Packers' defender Tim Lewis. The blow knocked Lewis backwards where he lay prone on the grass. In a very scary moment, Lewis lay still, having lost all feeling in his arms. Lewis was carried from the field on a stretcher to the hospital. Lewis would recover, but it was the last game he ever played.

In the fourth quarter, Del Greco lined up for another long field goal attempt. The conditions for kicking on this night were perfect.

Most of the evening a light breeze blew, barely moving the flag stationed on top of the stadium. As Del Greco met the ball, Bears' lineman Dan Hampton blocked it back in his face. From there, the Bears gained all momentum, scored fifteen unanswered points, and won, 25-12.

Game two of the series on November 23 at Soldier Field would be different. In game one, both sides had downplayed the antagonism and got back to playing football. Just as quickly as the cheap shots and hyperbole had stopped, they returned in a flash in the form of Packers' defensive end Charles Martin and two terrible towels.

The Packers entered the game with an atrocious 2-9 record. The youth movement that Forrest Gregg believed would return the Packers back into a contender was not happening. In fact, this was turning out to be one of the worst teams in franchise history. At the opposite end of the spectrum were the Bears at 9-2, and cruising to another Central Division title.

As the Packers came onto the field, some of the Bears noticed that Packers' safety Ken Stills and defensive end Charles Martin were wearing towels on their belts. Stills, a marked man now for his alleged late hit on Matt Suhey the year before, wore a knee-length towel he called his "terrible towel." After making a tackle, Stills would wave his towel in a circular, taunting motion at his victim.

Martin's towel was more ominous. Allegedly, it featured a hit list. On his belt he wore a towel listing the numbers 9, 34, 29, 83, 63, and a mysterious "M." They were jersey numbers for Jim McMahon, Walter Payton, Dennis Gentry, Willie Gault, and Jay Hilgenberg. No one knows what the "M" stood for.

At Friday's practice before the game, Martin said, "We always go for the gun-like Payton and McMahon. We put those guys out, it's to our advantage."

Early in the second quarter, Chicago offensive tackle Jim Covert was hit from behind by Stills. No flag was thrown. With 7:55 remaining in the second quarter, the Bears had the ball and were driving behind an ailing Jim McMahon. McMahon drifted to his right after being chased by Martin, and threw a pass that was intercepted by cornerback Mark Lee. With the play on the other side of the field, McMahon casually stood there watching. Suddenly,

Martin bear-hugged McMahon, picked him up, and threw him down onto the hard Soldier Field artificial turf. McMahon lay hurting as Martin towered over his kill. A shoving match ensued that took officials some time to bring under control.

Referee Jerry Markbreit threw a flag and disqualified Martin from the game. "The ball had been thrown, the quarterback was at rest," Markbreit explained. "He came in and took the quarterback, picked him up and stuffed him, which is our term for slamming him to the ground. I flagged it and felt that it was a disqualifying foul."

Markbreit went over and told Martin he was ejected from the game. Martin shot back, "No, I'm not going." For a moment the stunned Markbreit didn't know what to do. When Martin was finally convinced he was no longer going to be allowed to play, he walked off the field to a chorus of boos from a vigilant Chicago crowd. The Bears' faithful threw everything they could at Martin as he walked to the dressing room. Beer, programs, batteries, cups, coins, you name it. "I think I got about a case of beer dumped on me," Martin said later.

"At that time," said Mike Singletary, "I have to be honest, we were ready to go fist-fight because there is no room in football for that."

The game proceeded with the Packers giving the Bears all the work they needed. With six minutes left and the Packers leading 10-9, Packers' running back Gary Ellerson fumbled after being annihilated by linebacker Mike Singletary. With 2:37 left, Kevin Butler's 32-yard field goal settled the game and Chicago won, 12-10.

Most of the post-game comments concerned Martin's cheap shot on McMahon. Bears' defensive tackle Steve McMichael questioned the wisdom of Martin's actions. "I guess that guy [Martin] isn't in any position to win the Nobel Peace Prize for intelligence."

Otis Wilson said, "I can't understand Forrest Gregg. A lot of his players do this consistently. That doesn't show too much character."

"Worst late hit I've ever seen," said Walter Payton.

Jim McMahon commented after the game that, "You could tell it was a blatant thing to do. The guys on my side tell me he was giving high fives going off the field. They were excited about it."

Charles Martin, already dressed after his early shower, met

reporters afterwards. Decked out in a canary-yellow suit, he looked more like *Sesame Street*'s Big Bird than he did a football player who had just initiated one of the worst cheap shots the league had ever seen. "I didn't want to hurt him; I was just spaced out," he said.

Forrest Gregg agreed with Markbreit that ejection was warranted. "What he did was flagrant," Gregg said. "To grab him and throw him down, that's costly. It cost us his services for the whole day."

It was also unfortunate. After the cheap shots and dirty play in both games of 1985, the Monday night game in September had been a clean game. It was as though both sides had seen the folly in continuing the dangerous play and had decided to simmer things down. That was all forgotten the second McMahon hit the ground, shoulder first.

League Commissioner Pete Rozelle reviewed the tape of the cheap shot and decided to fine and suspend Martin. While Martin served out his suspension, there was an allegation of a sexual assault at a bar in Green Bay that never resulted in an arrest. During the '87 season, Martin was traded to the Houston Oilers and then, in 1988, went to Atlanta where his career silently ended.

A few Bears thought Forrest Gregg and his coaching staff were responsible for what many saw as dirty play. Ex-Packers' linebacker and Packer Report columnist Ray Nitschke disagreed. "He inherited a bad group of guys. There were a few bad apples. But Forrest didn't teach that kind of stuff."

A *Chicago Tribune* writer asked this question in his column two days after the game. "If Martin was dumb enough to broadcast his wanton designs, or too dumb to remember enemy jerseys without writing them down, where were Forrest Gregg and his fellow deep thinkers? No coach worth his headset should condone it or ignore it."

Ditka certainly didn't hold back his anger towards the Green Bay Packers. He called them a bunch of thugs. Forrest Gregg resented Ditka's statement and called it a reflection on him as a person and a football coach.

In summation, *Press-Gazette* writer Don Langenkamp may have had the best idea of all. "If you worship the American way of making a quick buck, think about this; Charles Martin versus William

Perry in a wrestling ring. It definitely would play in Green Bay and Chicago. All-Star Wrestling would eat it up; it makes about as much sense as some of the things in Sunday's game did."

Green Bay defensive back Ken Stills had a heart-pounding introduction to professional football. His first game in a Packers' uniform was on October 21, 1985, in front of a nationally televised audience on Monday Night Football. It was the infamous "Refrigerator" game where William Perry became an American hero in the Bears' backfield.

Stills was drafted by Green Bay in the eighth round out of Wisconsin, where he had led the Big-Ten Conference in interceptions his senior year. He was released from the team on the last cut before the regular season after the Packers signed another rookie defensive back, Mossy Cade.

Forrest Gregg told him that if he needed a player he would come calling again. A couple of key injuries to the Packers' defense had Coach Gregg on the phone to Stills in mid-October looking for help.

Stills was involved in an incident in the second Packers-Bears game in 1985, won by the Bears, 16-10. It came after Packers' defensive cornerback Mark Lee was pulled out of bounds and over the Bears' bench by Walter Payton. An official thought that Lee had hit Payton late out of bounds and ejected him from the game.

"I remember the next series everybody was cussing in the huddle," Stills said. "They were just going off. I said, 'Let's make a big play, let's get 'em.' The next play started and it was a sweep to my right. Payton got the toss and he had a lead blocker. I started coming up from about fifteen yards deep. Well, Charles Martin had knifed through, hit Payton in the backfield, and Payton had fallen. I was already running full speed and Matt Suhey had gotten into the lane where the sweep was going. I just caught him under the chin and took him for a ride for about 5 yards. You could hear whistles and flags flying everywhere. I heard [Packer assistant coach] Dick Modzelewski cussing, 'You dumb SOB; what the hell are you doing!' Forrest Gregg grabbed him and said, 'Leave him alone; he's the only one being aggressive.' From that point on Forrest recognized that I was an aggressive player and he needed more players like me.

"We played aggressive and Forrest liked that. He believed in eleven guys at the ball; every guy should touch the ball; there should not be one guy back waiting. He believed there were no friends on the football field. You covered your eyes and said 'Hey, the other guy is not my friend now.' When it was time to take the field, it was time to go to war. That's the way Forrest saw it and how he taught us to play the game."

Stills was on the field when Charles Martin threw Bears' quarterback Jim McMahon to the turf in that November game in 1986. He offered some kind of explanation for Martin's behavior.

"I really think that goes back to the coaches," he said. "Every day in practice Dick Modzelewski would say the quarterback is always the last one to make the tackle. Charlie's job, since he was the nose tackle, was to block the quarterback. So Modzelewski would always say, 'Charlie, the quarterback's the last one to make the tackle, block him!' If you watch the film of the game, you can see that Charlie kind of snapped. He tackled McMahon and drilled him to the turf. You can see him jump a little bit as he grabbed him. He was thinking, 'Oh, Coach said the quarterback is the last guy, I better block him.'

And what of Charles Martin's hit list towel labeled with numbers of Bears' players?

"Charlie was the kind of guy that got everybody fired up," Stills said. "He said here's the guys we have to stop and I'm gonna write them down for you. So he wrote them down on a towel and the next thing we know it's hanging on the side of his pants out on the field. It wasn't a hit list. It was a list of players that we needed to keep our eyes on to win the game."

Stills is conciliatory when asked about Mike Ditka calling the Packers' defense a bunch of thugs.

"He might have a point," Stills confessed. "We wore the towels and we did some things. Mike had the right to call us thuggish. I wish that he could see the difference in us and see how we are. That was part of our young, wild mentality."

Labor trouble reared its ugly head again in 1987 when new contract negotiations broke down between team owners and the NFL Players Association. The players union held strong five years before when their walkout had lasted fifty-seven days. This time the owners were ready.

After the second game of the season, players walked out wanting a new contract. The owner's reply was to form teams made up of "replacement players" who would play games that were to count in the standings. Union officials and players dubbed the replacements "scabs" and denounced them and the farcical contests they were playing. After a week where one season game was canceled, play continued.

It was a terrible situation for all involved. The players wanted a contract; the owners wanted their players back; and fans were being cheated out of the best professional football had to offer. During the three-week strike, attendance fell and tempers flared. It was fast becoming the season of unreason.

As the owners held tightly together, soon a few union players began to cross the picket line. Then a few more crossed. Finally, the union gave in and allowed players to return, vowing to take their case to court. While it's agreed that nobody won this standoff, it was a damaging defeat for the union.

Luckily, the three replacement games did not affect the Packers-Bears series. The strike and the replacement games were over when the two rivals met for the 133rd time on November 8 in Green Bay. The game would be Walter Payton's final appearance at Lambeau Field.

The 3-3-1 Packers gave the 6-1 Bears a great game. In the first half, Randy Wright threw touchdown passes of 27 and 26 yards to tight end Ed West and receiver Phil Epps. Number one draft choice Brent Fullwood added a rushing touchdown. The Bears scored on a 59-yard pass from McMahon to running back Neal Anderson, and the sure-footed Kevin Butler added two field goals, making the score 21-13 at the half.

With less than a minute to play, and the Packers ahead 24-23, McMahon had his Bears' offense huddled up at their own 24-yard line and in possession of their three time-outs. In workmanship fashion, McMahon led Chicago downfield with passes to Ron

Morris and Dennis McKinnon.

With only four seconds left, Kevin Butler came in to attempt a 52-yard field goal. In his first three seasons he had made only one of twelve field goal attempts for 50 yards and beyond. To try to ice the kicker, the Packers called a time out. The steely-eyed Butler used the extra time to his advantage. "The ground where I was going to kick from was torn up, holes and everything," he said post game. "So, actually that time-out helped me. I built a little mound and smoothed it out and had a clean spot to kick from."

With a 12 mph wind at his back, Butler smacked the ball perfectly, sending it between the south uprights of Lambeau Field and winning the contest for the Bears, 26-24.

It was a crushing defeat for the Northmen. Once again they had played the mighty Bears close but at the final gun were short on the scoreboard. "We're jinxed," said receiver Walter Stanley.

Three weeks later in rainy, cold, and dreary Chicago, the 12-point underdog Packers would have another respectful showing against the Bears in a losing cause. Once again it was the Packers' kicking game that would derail them. Place kicker Al Del Greco had been replaced by Max Zendejas, who, in his first five games at starting kicker, had made ten of ten field goal attempts. That streak was about to end. On the other side, Chicago kicker Kevin Butler hit field goals from 21, 27, and 52 yards out.

Early in the game quarterback Randy Wright uncorked a 66-yard bomb to Walter Stanley giving the Packers a 7-0 lead. Jim McMahon answered that with a 20-yard lob to running back Neal Anderson, tying the score.

Max Zendejas' nightmare began in the second quarter with the score knotted, 10-10. The soccer-style kicker swung his leg from 50 yards out and had the ball blocked by Chicago's Todd Bell. The Ohio State safety began running with the ball, eventually fumbling it back to Green Bay's Brian Noble.

Later, Zendejas missed a 42-yarder when he tried to aim the ball in the swirling wind of Soldier Field. In the fourth quarter, he toed an attempt from the 37-yard line that was so low that it hit Chicago defensive lineman Al Harris in the thigh. After that, Zendejas made a 32-yard field goal but by now Forrest Gregg could no longer count on him. In the middle of the fourth quarter and trailing 20-

10, Gregg decided to go on a fourth and six from the Bears' 21-yard line. His decision not to attempt a field goal clearly showed his lack of confidence in the kicking game. Green Bay failed to make the first down and the game was decided: Bears 23, Packers 10.

This was Walter Payton's last game against the rival Packers. His 22-yards rushing ended up being his lowest total ever against Green Bay, despite the fact that Sir Walter had made a career running through the Packers' defense in his thirteen years in the league. His twenty-four game rushing total against Green Bay had been 2,484 yards. That figure alone would have been enough to rank him ninth on the Bears' all-time rushing list.

It was also be the last Bears' game Forrest Gregg would coach. The Packers lost three of their last four games and finished third in the NFC Central Division in 1987 at 5-9-1. In January of 1988, Forrest Gregg resigned the head coaching position at Green Bay and returned to his alma mater, Southern Methodist University, as football coach.

For Mike Ditka and the Bears, it would be another playoff appearance. After finishing the season at 11-4, Chicago took on the Washington Redskins at Soldier Field. The hometown faithful saw the Bears jump out to a 14-0 lead in the second period, only to lose, 21-17, at the gun.

Although a successful one, it had been a rough season for Ditka and his Bears. The strike, internal fighting, and a sieve-like defense had caused dissension and hard feelings on the team. But even in the grip of adversity, the Midway Monsters were still one of the best teams in the league.

In the seventy-five years that the Bears and the Packers have butted heads on the gridiron, at no time was the rivalry any more vindictive, revengeful, malicious, and downright dangerous than in the mid-1980s.

Behind both teams were two coaches from the old school. They brought a fiery, competitive spirit back to the rivalry that hadn't been seen for some years.

Mike Ditka became coach of the Bears in 1982. In Ditka's first two years of coaching he matched minds with Green Bay coach Bart Starr. Both coaches had enormous respect for each other and were friends. Chicago-Green Bay games were the competitive contest they had always been but there were no allegations of cheap shots.

In 1984, when Forrest Gregg replaced the fired Starr, the rivalry entered an ominous stage. There were hostile accusations and charges of cheap shots and a rough style of play exhibited by both teams. Mike Ditka even called the Packers' team a bunch of thugs.

"We had some incidents I didn't like," Forrest Gregg recalls. "I certainly didn't consider our guys thugs. There were some things that happened on both sides that weren't pretty."

"When we went up there to play them, we never played outside of the rules," the Bears' Mike Ditka remembers. "I don't care what people say or what they thought about me. We never taught anything outside of the rules. They played outside of the rules.

"I just think you can't let guys put those towels on and have them hanging down to their ankles," Ditka continued. "They had numbers written on there and that was a bounty list. That doesn't belong in the National Football League. It doesn't even belong out on the street. It's childish."

"These guys wear towels all the time," Gregg says. "You don't pay attention to it. We used to have one kid who wore nearly a whole towel down to his feet almost. Just because you have a towel don't mean you're a dirty football player."

It was only natural to think that because of the hostilities, both coaches had a feud going. Both downplay it.

"It was blown out of proportion," Gregg said. "I don't know how Mike felt about me, but I certainly had no real dislike for him. I played with him one year in Dallas and have known him since he was a player. There was a rivalry and competitiveness. I don't consider it a feud."

"I really had a lot of respect for Forrest," Ditka admitted. "There were some things I didn't understand and that was earlier in my coaching career. One incident happened in a game in Milwaukee. They called a time-out with fourteen seconds left to go in the half. In a pre-season game, I'm not sure I understand that. My whole concern was to get off the field and don't have an injury. It bugged me. I probably said something I shouldn't have said, and he said something he shouldn't have said."

The most notorious cheap shots were the Charles Martin incident, where Martin turned Bears' quarterback Jim McMahon into an accordion, Ken Stills alleged late hit on Bears' fullback Matt Suhey, and Packers' cornerback Mark Lee getting ejected for his encounter with Walter Payton on the sideline.

"I don't think [Lee] meant to hit Payton on the sidelines when he knocked him over the bench," Ditka says. "I don't think he was trying to do that and I told the official that. I said I don't think he could stop.

"But the other two were bad shots; the one on Suhey and the one on McMahon. I guess that's why I feel better about life now because I don't have to worry about winning. If that's what winning is all about then I don't need to win anymore."

"Ken Stills had been with us in training camp," Gregg recalls. "He'd been released and we called him back. He had one week's practice and ended up starting against the Bears. Ken wanted to make an impression. His timing was a little off and he hit Suhey. There was a lot of hitting out of bounds and stuff like that by the Bears' players. That's what kind of started all of that," Gregg theorizes.

Some members of the Bears questioned Gregg's coaching style, thinking he condoned unsportsmanlike play. "I'm not on trial here," Gregg snaps. "I don't give a damn what the Bears' players say. I never told anybody to hit late. I never told anybody to take cheap shots."

Ditka used to refer to the northern rivals as the "Red Bay Packers." Actually, it was not meant in a derogatory way.

"In the old days when he played the Packers, our coaching staff used to get so uptight. So, we [the players] walked around calling them the Red Bay Packers instead of the Green Bay Packers so the coaches wouldn't be so uptight. We just did it as a joke. I didn't call them that as a slight. I mean Packers' week wasn't like any other week. Everything was secretive. We had closed practices and all. It was crazy."

Ditka even had kind words for the Green Bay fans.

"The Green Bay fans are great," he said. "Whether they like me or they hate me, they're great fans. I think that's what has kept this [the rivalry] going, the fans. Mostly the Green Bay fans."

Both coaches are in agreement about one thing. The Packers-Bears rivalry isn't what it used to be.

"I don't think it's the same," Gregg says. "It doesn't seem to be. Of course, I'm not there."

"It's not the same anymore," Ditka admits. "There really are no old Bears and old Packers anymore. The tradition is gone. They're good people: Dave [Wannstedt, Bears' coach] and Mike [Holmgren, Packers' coach], but I don't think they really understand what the Packers-Bears rivalry is."

Mike Ditka relayed to his Bears' players the importance of the rivalry and not socializing with any Packers before a game.

"I think the players respected us for what we got across to them, a sense that the Packers were not your friends," Ditka said. "My players always knew where I stood with all of our opponents. Life is about brotherly love, but football isn't. On the field let's play the game the way it's meant to be played. That's not meant to be disrespectful. It's a great rivalry that went back for years in the National Football League and it has transcended all of these years. So why should we let it become just another game now? That's what Halas always talked about, that's what Lombardi always talked about, and that's what I've always talked about. So, let's keep it going."

Even though offensive tackle Karl Swanke was recruited at Boston College by a number of pro teams, he wanted nothing more than to be chosen in the 1980 NFL draft by the Green Bay Packers. The mountainous offensive star had good reason.

"I wanted to play for the Packers since my dad had grown up in Wisconsin," he said. "He loved the Packers and I did, too. It was a dream come true. Getting drafted by them was a great thrill."

Swanke anchored Green Bay's offensive line for six seasons, punishing defenders. On twelve different occasions the defenders were the tough Bears' defense.

"That year they went to the Super Bowl and won, I think that was the best defense I had ever played against in the NFL," Swanke said. "If you didn't get the points in the first half, they would completely shut you down in the second. They were always good at blocking field goals. They always had a way of disrupting our special teams.

"Buddy Ryan [Bears' assistant coach] was a genius as far as defenses were concerned. As an offensive lineman, I would watch his defensive play calling. He was innovative. A lot of guys [coaches] have the same old defense but he was willing to try all kinds of crazy defenses."

And who was the orneriest Bear he ever faced?

"I think Richard Dent was the best pass rusher I ever went up against. But for just shear toughness I think Dan Hampton was as tough as any guy I played against."

Swanke easily recalled the Bears-Packers game in 1986 when Charles Martin dumped McMahon, stoking the rivalry to a fever pitch.

"That was the only time I was ever afraid to be on a football field. I didn't see it until after it happened. After watching it I can see why the fans got upset. I guess fans had televisions in the stands. They got upset at the whole thing. The whole stadium in unison was chanting, 'Green Bay Sucks.' The security guy with the Packers told us to put our helmets on when you leave the field."

Swanke recalled a game in 1984 where he unknowingly put a Bears' defender out of the game.

"The only time I ever broke anyone's leg was in Chicago. I didn't even realize it until the next day. I went out on a wide screen—where the offensive linemen run out to block a safety—I came out and blocked [Shaun Gayle]. It seemed like he wanted to take a dive underneath me and then at the last second he tried to jump around me. I hit him right as he was thinking. I didn't think anything of it as I went back to the huddle. The next morning we were watching the game films and Greg Koch said, 'Here's where the guy broke his leg.' I looked closer and said, 'Is that me blocking him?' I didn't even remember them pulling him off to the sideline."

On February 3, 1988, Gelindo "Lindy" Infante became the tenth head coach of the Green Bay Packers' franchise. He was the third Packers' head coach of Italian extraction, preceded by Gene Ronzani and Vince Lombardi. In many ways his coaching history was very much like Forrest Gregg's. He was plucked from the Cleveland Browns where he was offensive coach. The Browns' high scoring offense put them in the AFC championship game the two previous years. Before Cleveland, he was a head coach for two years with the Jacksonville Bulls of the rival United States Football League. From 1980 to 1982, Infante had coached side-by-side with Forrest Gregg in Cincinnati.

The selection of an offensive-minded coach was no coincidence. Green Bay's sputtering offense had finished at the bottom of the league for the past two seasons. Although they would finish there again in 1988, in 1989 they would be near the top in offensive production.

Needed most was a replacement for James Lofton. After nine seasons, 530 catches, 9,656 yards, and fifty touchdowns, Lofton was cut from the team and sent packing. In his place, the Packers drafted a fast possession receiver from South Carolina named Sterling Sharpe. Sharpe would immediately step up and fill the shoes of the departed Lofton, snagging fifty-five passes for 791 yards.

A brash kid drafted out of Virginia in 1987 slowly took over Randy Wright's reigns as signal caller. Don "Majik Man" Majkowski threw for over 2,000 yards in 1988, gearing up for a splendid season in 1989. Majkowski's star would shine for the briefest of times until quickly burning out in 1992.

The Bears came into the 1988 season loaded as usual. Running back Neal Anderson had solidified himself as the heir-apparent to Walter Payton. The often-injured Jim McMahon split quarterbacking duties with backup Mike Tomczak, both throwing to talented receivers such as Ron Morris, Dennis McKinnon, and Dennis Gentry.

The season saw the return of the rugged defense that had dominated opponents a few years earlier. Although they lost linebacker's Wilbur Marshall to free-agency and Otis Wilson to injury, the Bears once again led the league in less points allowed with 215.

Another Bear that would miss a game due to illness was Head Coach Mike Ditka. In mid-season Ditka had a heart attack, but he returned to the sidelines after missing only one game. He promised a calmer, more docile Ditka.

The Bears visited the land of dairy farms in late September for a therapeutic trouncing of the hapless Packers, their seventh straight victory over their rivals. Chicago even committed three turnovers in the first seventeen minutes of play giving the Northmen great field position, but the Packers could not capitalize.

With Chicago ahead 7-6, Neal Anderson got great blocking up front and sprinted 45 yards for a touchdown, the longest run of his career. Kevin Butler added a field goal just before the half ended, giving the Bears a 17-6 lead. The only scoring in the second half was a 5-yard scamper by running back Thomas Sanders, set up by Green Bay's lone fumble on the day.

Chicago's defense completely shut down the Packers, allowing only 99 yards passing and thirty-four on the ground. On the flip side, the Bears garnered 116 yards through the air and a ground-churning 242 yards rushing. The Packers' offense couldn't move against the relentless Bears' defense, and they couldn't stop their offense.

After the game Ditka ran off the field, ignoring Lindy Infante's attempt at the customary post-game handshake.

The day's only real excitement was a verbal battle between Mike Ditka and Packers' linebacker Tim Harris. Harris got into a shouting match with the Bears' coach near the sideline late in the game.

"The animated Harris kept retreating to the middle of the field in full battle regalia while the unarmed Ditka unleashed his verbal barrage," wrote writer and witness Fred Mitchell.

The problem was that Harris was spouting off while his team was getting hammered. "Harris is a good player but he vocalizes a lot," said one Bear. "And, when you're down 24-6, you probably should not do a lot of talking."

To give their husbands needed inspiration before the game, some of the Packer players' wives hung a sign in the team's locker room that read, "Kick the Bears' Butts!" After the resounding defeat, Packer players were ushered home by the same wives while passing another sign hanging on a fence at Lambeau Field that read, "Green Bay: Home of more dog teams than the Yukon."

It was the 10-2 Bears meeting the 2-10 Dogs at Soldier Field on November 27 for another go-around. On the sideline was a calmer

Mike Ditka, this game being his third following his heart attack.

The inept Packers' offense managed one first down in the first quarter and only four by half-time. In that time, the Packers' ground game managed to gain a measly 16 yards. At the end of the game they only had 22 rushing yards. Not since 1956 had the Packers rushed for so little yardage in one game.

In contrast, the longest run in Soldier Field history happened when Neal Anderson galloped 80 yards through the Packers' defense for a score. Anderson added another one yard score. The Bears' defense swarmed quarterback Don Majkowski all day, eventually chasing him out of the end zone for a safety. Majkowski might as well have just kept on running out of the stadium and down Lake Shore Drive. Bears in a rout, 16-0.

The Packers' defense tried to make up for the ineffective offense by playing aggressive football. Late in the second quarter, Bears' quarterback Mike Tomczak separated his shoulder after being slammed to the ground on a sack by Tim Harris. That was a clean hit. Ken Stills' hit on Chicago center Jay Hilgenberg, some Bears thought, was questionable. "The play was over and he ran in from the side and hit me in the ribs," Hilgenberg complained after the game. "Some guys, when you block them legally, the only way they can come back is to cheap-shot you. It's ridiculous."

Stills, who at the time had taken a vow of silence towards the press, said nothing.

The Bears marched on into the playoffs after posting a 12-4 regular season record. They whipped the Eagles, 20-12, in the first round, but were routed by the 49ers, 28-3, the next week.

The Packers, of course, watched all of this at home. The 4-12 Green Bay team of 1988 was one of the worst in team history. There was nowhere to go but up for Infante's group, and that's just where they were headed.

In 1986, the NFL adopted instant replay for use in all league games. With the use of television cameras, officials in the booth upstairs could overrule their counterparts on the field if the camera showed a difference in the official's call and what was seen on camera. Since the advent of the experiment, only a handful of calls had been reversed, some replays were inconclusive, and the rest showed officials making the correct call. Fans approved of instant replay while owners grudgingly went along with it. The down side was that many times it would delay a game and stop whatever momentum one team may have had.

On November 5, 1989, the officials in the press box at Lambeau Field would decide this 137th replay of the rivalry. The 5-4 Packers had begun to earn some respect coming into the game. They had finally found an offense, led by Don Majkowski and rookie offense tackle Tony Mandarich. Wide receiver Sterling Sharpe was turning into the star the Packers had hoped he would become. The sure-handed South Carolinian led the league in receiving with ninety catches and crossed the goal line for twelve touchdowns.

Fullback Brent Fullwood rushed for 821 yards, the most for any Green Bay running back since 1981. The Packers were no longer the doormats of the league. They were an exciting band of players who began to taste the sweetness of success.

The Bears were on an erratic course that would eventually see them descend into the also-rans of the league. Before the beginning of the season, Jim McMahon was traded to San Diego. Many thought the Bears' offense would suffer. Surprisingly, Chicago started off like giant killers, notching blowout victories over their first four opponents. Then the bottom fell out. Key injuries on defense exposed their secondary and opponents keyed on Bears' defenders Richard Dent and Mike Singletary. The once dependable defense finished twenty-fifth in the league, losing three games in the final two minutes. The Bears lost their final six games, and ten of their final twelve.

Green Bay scored first as Don Majkowski rifled a 24-yard TD pass to tight end Clint Didier. Chicago's Kevin Butler added a 25-yard field goal making it a 7-3 game at half-time. In the third period, Brad Muster plunged over from the two and Butler booted another three pointer putting the Bears ahead 13-7, entering the fourth quarter.

Most of the Packers' offense came from the arm of Majkowski. While the rushing game was having its usual troubles, the Majik Man was picking apart Chicago's defense for 299 yards, throwing to ten different receivers in the process.

With only minutes remaining, Majkowski huddled his troops around his own 20-yard line and began a systematic march down the field. With 1:26 left, the Packers had a first and goal at the seven. Three plays later it would be fourth and goal at the 14-yard line with forty-one seconds showing on the game clock.

On fourth down, Majkowski tried to quiet the crowd as he stood behind center trying to read the defense. On the snap Majkowski drifted back to pass. The play was supposed to be a slant-in pattern to Jeff Query, one of the four receivers lined up on the play. Finding him covered, Majkowski scrambled. Bears' defensive line-man Trace Armstrong charged in hot pursuit, narrowly missing the Packers' quarterback. As Majkowski ran to his right looking for an open man, he saw Perry Kemp in the corner of the end zone. He almost threw the ball, but in the last split second his eyes caught the speedy Sterling Sharpe cutting across the middle of the end zone. Majkowski planted his right foot into the Lambeau Field turf and zinged a pass to Sharpe, who was surrounded by three Bears' defenders. "All I had to do was look it in," Sharpe said afterwards. "He put it right in my stomach." Sharpe caught the ball for the game-tying touchdown.

All 56,556 in attendance roared as the Packers celebrated the score. The roar quickly turned to silence after an official's yellow flag lie crumpled on the ground. Line judge Jim Quirk had thrown a penalty flag against Majkowski for stepping across the line of scrimmage before he had thrown the pass. The touchdown was called back and the ball given to the Bears.

As the Bears came on the field to run out the clock, word filtered down to the officials that replay official Bill Parkinson was reviewing the penalty call against the Packers' quarterback. Play was halted and, as four agonizing minutes crept by, players and fans turned their attention to Parkinson in the press box.

Parkinson finally ruled that Majkowski had not stepped across the line of scrimmage, therefore, the touchdown pass would count. Kicker Chris Jacke trotted onto the field, booted the extra point, and the Packers beat the Bears for the first time in nine tries.

Views on the call reversal differed, of course. "I can't wait for them to get rid of instant replay," Bears' linebacker Ron Rivera said.

"I was taught that a judgment call could not be overruled. They're taking human error out of the game."

"If anybody doesn't like the instant replay right now, they're crazy," Lindy Infante said with a smile.

Ditka took a more middle-of-the-road approach saying that there was, "No use crying. We had chances out there to make something happen and we had some penalties that hurt us at crucial times. They did what they had to do to win the game."

Evidence of the Bears' displeasure over the "official" outcome of the game can still be found in the team's press guide. In the guide's all-time regular season results, the game is marked with an asterisk and labeled "Instant Replay Game."

The victory was a great boost of confidence for the young Packers' team. The traveling Lindy Infante show continued to gain respect as they rolled into Chicago on December 17 to face the hosting Bruins. The Chicago fans who braved the minus seven degree wind chill factor sat through five Bears' turnovers and watched a bulldozing Packers' team out rush, out hit, and out muscle the now "Midway Motleys."

The two Packers' stars were Majkowski and running back Keith Woodside. The Majik Man tossed for 244 yards and one touchdown, becoming only the second passer in Green Bay history to pass for over 4,000 yards in a season. Woodside, who had only rushed for a total of 149 yards all season, put on a dazzling show, shredding the once stout Bears' defense for 116 yards on ten carries. His lone score was a run of 68 yards.

With the score 30-28 in the fourth quarter, Chicago had the ball deep in Green Bay territory. Bears' quarterback Jim Harbaugh tossed a pass in the direction of tight end Cap Boso. The ball fluttered into the hands of Packers' linebacker Scott Stephan, thwarting the Bears' drive. After the huge interception, Majkowski led his troops downfield where he would eventually score from the 1-yard line. Jacke added an insurance field goal, and the Packers held on to whip the Bears, 40-28.

The last time the Packers had scored that many points against the Bears, Vince Lombardi and George Halas were the coaches and John F. Kennedy was president. "They said we couldn't win, they said we couldn't beat the Bears," bellowed Coach Infante. "We refused to believe it."

Free-tongued Packers' linebacker Tim Harris raged in the lock-er room, shouting at TV cameramen to remove their Chicago hats because the Packers had "just kicked the Bears' ass."

For the first time since the strike season of 1982, the Packers were in position for a wildcard spot in the playoffs. All they had to do was defeat the Cowboys in Dallas in the final week of the season and hope the Minnesota Vikings would lose to Cincinnati on Monday night. The Packers did their job, downing the Cowboys, 20-10. Cincinnati failed to do its job. The Vikings defeated the Bengals, 21-9, knocking the Packers out of the playoffs.

Although disappointed, Infante and the Packers had come a long way from that awful 4-12 squad the previous year. The Packers had found an offense and a rifle-armed star in quarterback Don Majkowski, who was being compared to San Francisco great Joe Montana. Infante was rewarded for his efforts by being named Coach of the Year. The future was definitely getting brighter in Green Bay.

In Chicago, the future was less clear. A few began to question Ditka and wondered if he could still lead the team. It was the first losing season the team had suffered through since the 3-6 strike sea-son in 1982 and the 7-9 team in 1980.

Mike Ditka was not a loser, and he was determined to prove it to the skeptics.

The 1990s

Bozo, Majik Man, Big Play Dante,
and the Minister of Defense

In the early days of pro football, instances of players refusing to play or holding out for a better contract were very rare. A few brazen souls did, risking their athletic futures with a tight-knit, cliquish group of team owners who could collectively blackball a player they deemed unloyal or uncooperative.

That was long ago. As pro football entered the 1990s, players' rights, wants, needs, and demands were negotiated and many times met by team owners. Players' salaries had risen steadily during the 1980s and ballooned astronomically with the advent of free-agency in 1993. Long gone were the days of players selling used cars or insurance in the off-season to make ends meet.

Any momentum Lindy Infante and his Packers had in 1989 quickly disappeared in the summer of 1990 when the team began to be eaten away from the inside out by player's demands. A total of sixteen veterans held out a total of 302 days in contract squabbles with management. Leading the group was the hero of the 1989 season, "Majik Man" Don Majkowski. The free-spirited quarterback held out at home for the first forty-five days of training camp. No quarterback, not even a Majik Man, could return after such a long layoff and be effective in the early games of a season.

Majkowski had a disappointing season. After an erratic early season performance, Majkowski suffered a tear in the rotator cuff of his shoulder in the eighth game. Anthony Dilwig, his backup, was pressed into action and finished out the season.

Majkowski and Dilwig got little help from the rushing offense. "Pathetic" would best describe the Packers' running game. Green Bay's leading rusher, Michael Haddix, ranked 58th overall with a paltry 311 yards. The team itself was dead last in rushing in the NFC. If they had been in the AFC, the Packers would have been last there, as well.

Mike Ditka had no such problem with the running game in Chicago. Neal Anderson, although slowed by nagging injuries in 1990, managed to gain 1,078 yards. His blocking back, Brad Muster, added another 664 yards. To reemphasize the ground game troubles in Green Bay, Bears' quarterback Jim Harbaugh gained more yardage scrambling east and west away from defenders than the Packers' Michael Haddix did actually running the ball north and south.

Both teams posted opening day wins and met in dairyland on September 16 for game 139 of the rivalry. It was a game that saw the return of the swarming Bears' defense of old and the return of hold-out Packers' quarterback Don Majkowski, as well.

On the first play of the game, Bears' field general Jim Harbaugh lofted a pass intended for tight end James Thornton. Green Bay cornerback Jerry Holmes intercepted and returned it to the Packers' 37-yard line. "Totally messed up, bad read, terrible throw," Harbaugh would say later. The interception set up Keith Woodside's 10-yard scamper and a 7-0 Packers' lead.

After a Kevin Butler field goal, Neal Anderson drove his way over a bunched-up Packers' defense for a 1-yard score and a 10-7 Bears lead. The touchdown was set up by a roughing-the-kicker penalty against the Packers that gave the ball back to the Bears.

On Green Bay's next series, Chicago again quickly regained possession. Starting Packers' quarterback Anthony Dilweg went back to pass from his own 15-yard line and was pounded by "Refrigerator" Perry, causing a fumble. Bears' defensive lineman Trace Armstrong recovered and, six plays later, Harbaugh bootlegged for a 2-yard scoring run.

Later in the third period Dilweg was again rushed hard and fumbled while being sacked by the Bears' Jim Morrissey. Another Packers' turnover turned into another Bears' touchdown, with Harbaugh hitting Ron Morris for a score on a 40-yard fly pattern. Completing the scoring, Harbaugh tossed a TD pass to Neal Anderson in the fourth and the Bears had a decisive 31-13 victory.

Chicago's defense was unmerciful, recording six sacks, three fumble recoveries, and two interceptions. A ravaged Dilweg was replaced late in the fourth quarter by Majkowski, who led a drive downfield only to see it end with an interception in the end zone.

Fans were glad to see the Majik Man back in action. After sitting out the first game of the year, Majkowski had reported to the Packers the Wednesday before the Bears' game. Although rusty, he did enter the game and complete eight of twelve passes for eighty-four yards in the fourth quarter.

Possibly assisting in the Bears' motivation to win was, of all things, a McDonald's commercial that played in Green Bay and Chicago the week prior to the game. The ad featured Packers' offensive lineman and hamburger huckster Tony Mandarich in a Bear-baiting commercial. In the commercial, Mandarich made fun of the Bears' quarterback situation, and in one of them referred to Illinois as "Illa-noise." Adding to the insult, Mandarich sneered through the ad spots.

After seeing the commercial, Mike Ditka started referring to Mandarich as "Bozo" in the press. "I'll say what I want to say, even if it sounds arrogant and controversial," Mandarich shot back. "If Mike Ditka wants to call me Bozo, then I'm a $35,000 (McDonald's commercial fee) Bozo. I'd do it again. I'm not going to stoop to his level by calling him a Bozo for doing his soup commercials (referring to Ditka's Campbell's Chunky Soup ads) or whatever it is he does. It's a business. He's out to make money and I'm out to make money."

Not only were Packers' fans riled at Ditka's "Bozo" remark, a few even complained that he spit too much on the sidelines! Some of the fans' comments phoned into the *Green Bay Press-Gazette* after the game grumbled that they "didn't understand why Mike Ditka is allowed to spit on the sidelines." Another said, "I am disgusted with Ditka's spitting all over our field. Fine on his turf, but this is ours and he should have permission."

It's doubtful that the city issues spitting permits.

Lindy Infante and his Packers paid a visit to Mike "the mad spitter" Ditka in Chicago on October 7. As Infante and his Packers went through their pre-game warmups, a plane circled Soldier Field pulling a sign that read: "Lindy's a girl's name," signed Jim Shorts.

A drizzling rain and 22 mph winds aided Chicago's superior running game, since field conditions warranted using the ground game rather than throwing the ball in the swirling Soldier Field wind. On the ground the Bears dominated with 202 yards rushing. In comparison, Green Bay's ineffective rushing attack tallied just thirty-two yards, forcing Majkowski to throw early and often.

Late in the first quarter, with Chicago at Green Bay's 2-yard line, William Perry lumbered onto the field to the deafening cheers of the Bears' faithful. Perry was going to try to score in the very same end zone and on the very same kind of play he had five years before. At the snap, Harbaugh handed off to the Fridge, who was immediately gang-tackled by Green Bay defenders, lead by linebacker Brian Noble. Perry's minus 1-yard carry would be his first and last on the day.

With Chicago in command and ahead 14-6, Majkowski stung the Bears with a 76-yard TD pass to Sterling Sharpe on the first play of the fourth quarter. Coming up to tackle Sharpe, Bears' safety man Mark Carrier slammed into the Packers' receiver, suffering a concussion. Sharpe, now with open field in front of him, turned on the speed and found the end zone. "I just remember driving into him and waking up on the sidelines," Carrier recalled.

On the Bears' next possession, Kevin Butler smacked a 51-yard field goal through the now dark, rainy skies over Soldier Field. It was his fifth field goal from over fifty yards out against the Packers in Butler's career.

Majkowski faced constant pressure the entire afternoon. At times in the game he yelled at his offensive linemen to, "Keep those [blank] guys out of my face." His yellow and white uniform now muddied and grass-stained, Majkowski attempted to rally his troops but couldn't. After the long scoring pass to Sharpe, Majkowski aired twelve straight incompletions. A late game-clinching TD pass from Mike Tomczak to tight end Cap Boso settled the score. Bears 27, Packers 13.

Afterwards, the Bears' locker room was the scene of an odd prank by two radio personalities from Milwaukee. The two buffoons burst in with microphones complete with their station's call letters—wearing nothing but bow ties and athletic supporters! Apparently there to support the locker room ban of female reporters, one said, "We're in solidarity with the players. If they have to be naked, we should have to be naked, too." Both were sporting press credentials, although they had no clothes to pin them to. Brian Harlan, the Bears' Public Relations Director, promptly threw them out anyway.

Unfortunately for the Packers, 1990 would not see a return to the playoffs. After winning four of six games after the Bears' contest they went into a tailspin, losing their last five to finish 6-10, a reversal of the previous year.

The Bears' big machine marched through the regular season winning eleven of sixteen league games, rebounding from their poor showing in 1989. In the first round of the playoffs, the Midway Monsters thumped New Orleans, 16-6, but were dismantled a week later by the New York Giants, 31-3.

Ditka and his Bears were again in the elite class of league teams. Their defense struck fear in opponents, led by Pro Bowl safety Mark Carrier's league-high ten interceptions. Running back Neal Anderson headed up an offense that led the league in rushing touchdowns and second in rushing yardage.

In Green Bay, the simple act of a quarterback handing a football to a running back and watching him run to daylight had become a distant memory. Again in 1991, the Packers had the worst ground game in the league.

The Don Majkowski "Majik Show" had now become a disappearing act, leaving Packers' fans hypnotized in a trance-like stupor from losing. The excitement of 1989 was now long forgotten, replaced by the fan's cry of "What have you done for me lately?"

Green Bay's defense was the only bright spot in 1991. Packers' defenders shackled opponent's offenses, allowing only ninety-six yards per game, the best since Curly Lambeau's 1940 squad.

On Thursday, October 17, game 144 of the rivalry placed the Green Bay Packers squarely on ground zero in both franchise stature and game score. In Lambeau Field, children laughed and grown men cried after sitting through the Packers' dismal performance. It prompted Head Coach Lindy Infante to apologize for his team's inept exhibition, declaring it "an all-time low."

A national audience saw the Bears' defense pull the plug early on Green Bay's offense, allowing only one first down in the first half.

To the observer it was difficult to tell if Chicago's defense was that good or the Packers' offense was that bad.

A 60-yard drive in the second quarter was capped off with a Jim Harbaugh 8-yard TD pass to tight end James Thorton. Early in the fourth, Bears' kicker Kevin Butler booted a 22-yard field goal to close out the scoring. Bears 10, Packers 0.

The Green Bay faithful became restless early, soundly booing Majkowski and later his replacement, former Bear Mike Tomczak. "Every pro quarterback gets booed sometime in his life," Majkowski said afterwards. "I can handle it. It's sure not going to be the last time. They're just frustrated." Majkowski and Tomczak looked like men running out of a burning building trying to get away from the relentless Bear defenders.

The Packers set a team record by posting the twelfth straight game in which they had not gained over 100 yards rushing. Bears' defensive linemen William Perry and Richard Dent stuffed the Packers' running game, and if they missed a tackle, linebackers John Roper, Mike Singletary, and Ron Rivera were there to plant the Packer.

A combination of alcohol and fan frustration made some Green Bay fans turn uncharacteristically ugly. Officers arrested seventeen people and bounced another 170 out of the gates for unruly behavior. Police Lieutenant Bob Boncher's personal assessment of the fans was, "They're fed up."

Late in the game, a few fans turned on some Packer players on the bench. Tony Mandarich got into a shouting match with some fans who were taunting him. Yelling obscenities, Mandarich threw a cup of water into the crowd.

In early December, a lame duck Lindy Infante brought his disjointed 3-10 squad to Chicago to face a 9-4 Bears' team. The Midway Monsters were coming off a two-game losing streak and needed a victory to keep pace with the Detroit Lions for the Central Division title.

Bears' fullback Brad Muster leaped over one tackler and rumbled eight yards for the game's first score after Green Bay safety Chuck Cecil had an interception nullified by a holding penalty. In the second quarter, Muster banged his way to a 6-yard TD, set up after a roughing-the-passer penalty was called against Packers' defensive end Robert Brown. The Packers continued to shoot themselves in the foot, amassing eleven penalties for eighty-seven yards, allowing the Bears to keep drives alive.

Green Bay's lone touchdown came on a 1-yard TD pass from Tomzcak to tight end Jackie Harris in the second period. Turning the tables, the Packers' touchdown was made possible by a Vinnie Clark interception that he returned twenty yards to the Bears' 30-yard line.

In the end, Green Bay could not overcome the rash of penalties and mistakes. Late in the third period, Bears' receiver Wendell Davis out-dueled Clark for a Harbaugh loft in the end zone that ended the day's scoring.

The 27-13 win was a milestone for Mike Ditka. The leather-jacketed Ditka walked off the Soldier Field turf, thumb in the air in approval, for his 100th victory as a head coach. "I'm happy," Ditka said, all smiles. "It would be foolish of me to stand up here and say you don't know it." Of his 100 victories, fourteen had come against the Packers.

Bears' linebacker Ron Rivera commented after the game that the dangerous cheap shots that were the norm in the rivalry during the 1980s had mostly disappeared. "It has changed from an almost cheap, dirty type of rivalry to more of a competitive, respective kind of thing," he said. "It's a lot better for the game. You don't see the chicken stuff or cheap shots anymore. I don't know if it's the personnel or the coaches' attitudes towards one another. There was no love lost between Coach [Forrest] Gregg and Coach Ditka."

Lindy Infante and some of his players knew they were facing possible unemployment in the winter. The Packers had lost twelve of their last fourteen games against Chicago and hadn't beaten a team with a winning record in twenty-two games. "I don't know about my job after Mr. [Ron] Wolf [Green Bay's new General Manage] sees that," Tony Mandarich said.

Infante was well on his way to tying a record for team futility. The twelve losses in 1991 would stand in the record books along with his twelve losses in 1988, and Forrest Gregg's 4-12 team of 1986, as the most losses in a season by a Packers' team.

Ditka and the Bears were about to see the end of their success. After splitting the final two games, they were beaten by a revamped

Dallas Cowboy team that now featured running back Emmitt Smith, wide receiver Michael Irvin, and quarterback Troy Aikman. It would be Mike Ditka's last playoff appearance.

It didn't take long for General Manager Ron Wolf to drop the ax on Lindy Infante. On December 23, two days after a season-ending win at Minnesota, Wolf released "Lucky Lindy" from his job as Packers' head coach. "Doing this is very distasteful," Wolf said.

Nineteen days later Wolf named San Francisco offensive coordinator Mike Holmgren as the Green Bay Packers' eleventh head coach in their 74-year history. At 6' 5," he was also the tallest head coach ever to coach the Packers.

The forty-four-year-old Holmgren had come to the 49ers from BYU, where he had been offensive coordinator. For three years Holmgren tutored Joe Montana and Steve Young, then was named offensive coordinator in 1989. After the '89 season, Holmgren turned down head coaching jobs in Phoenix and with the New York Jets.

Ron Wolf's other ingenious move was to obtain a husky, devil-may-care quarterback who, in his rookie season with the Atlanta Falcons, had thrown only five passes, all incomplete. Wolf's pairing of the offensive-minded Holmgren and quarterback Brett Farve would pay great dividends for Green Bay. The reckless Farve both dazzled and disappointed Holmgren in his first two years, but eventually settled down and became one of the premiere quarterbacks in the game.

Green Bay's 1992 season showcased their gun-slinging quarterback Farve and speedy wide receiver Sterling Sharpe. Farve threw for 3,227 yards and eighteen touchdowns, and tied with Dallas quarterback Troy Aikmen for completions at 302. On the receiving end of a record-breaking 108 catches was Sharpe, who also led the league with 1,451 receiving yards and thirteen touchdowns.

Although Green Bay's passing game was one of the league's best, their inept running game was still a problem. The Packers had not had a thousand yard runner since 1978. Vince Workman led the Packers with 631 yards while Darrell Thompson assisted with 255 yards.

Mike Ditka and his Bears were about to embark on a topsy-turvy season that saw the franchise sputter and then completely collapse in the second half of the season. The reasons were simple. The once unbendable defense was now aging, one reason why they would finish the season in the lower bracket of team defenses. Also, veteran quarterback Jim Harbaugh led an offense that had difficulties scoring. Star running back Neal Anderson had a mediocre year, finally losing his starting job to Daren Lewis.

On October 25, the 3-3 Bears and the 2-4 Packers met for the 143rd time, both needing a win to keep pace with the streaking Minnesota Vikings in the Central Division.

With the score 3-3 midway through the second quarter, the Packers had no idea they were about to have their pants pulled down in front of the hometown crowd. Bears' punter Chris Gardocki set up to punt near midfield after a Bears' drive stalled. As Gardocki waited for the ball, special team's player Mark Green ran onto the field like he had forgotten to come in. Ron Rivera, quarterback of the punt team, began yelling, "Get out of here, get out of here; we have enough." Green began running back to the sidelines. Suddenly, with the snap of the ball, Green headed upfield. Gardocki, seeing Green wide open, threw a pass that Green caught for a 43-yard gain and a first down.

The fake punt had been called by special team's coach Dan Abramowicz, who called it the "Rambo Play." He had used the same play when he coached at a high school in New Orleans the previous season. It worked then, also.

"That was a key play, no question about it," Ditka said after the game. "It's a great play if it works but if it doesn't work, it's back to high school."

Two plays later, Brad Muster slammed over from the 1-yard line and the Bears were out in front to stay.

Green Bay's last gasp came with Chicago leading, 20-10. On third down and goal to go at the Bears' 3-yard line, Farve drifted back to pass, trying to find Sterling Sharpe in the end zone. Bears' defensive standout Richard Dent muscled through the Packers' line and sacked Farve for a 7-yard loss. On fourth down, kicker Chris Jacke came in to kick a 28-yard field goal to draw the Pack a little closer. He missed it.

"At that point that series of events leading up to the missed field goal really took the wind out of our sails," Green Bay Coach Mike Holmgren confessed.

The 30-10 win put the Bears in good shape to play the division-leading Vikings the following week. Although not playing spectacularly, they were playing consistently.

Now at 2-5, the Packers and their fans began to question themselves and the season. Some fans were ready to concede the season then and there, falling back on the old excuse of "it's a rebuilding year."

When the two teams met a month later in Chicago, the pendulum had swung in the opposite direction. The Bears were mired in a three-game losing streak and on the brink of total disaster. In the meantime, Green Bay had won two of three and were on a hot streak.

In front of 56,170 rain-soaked fans and 10,780 empty Soldier Field seats, the Packers slapped the slumping Bears 17-3 behind the ball-rushing exploits of rookie Edgar Bennett. Bennett slithered through Chicago's defense for 107 yards, the first Packers' runner to tally a hundred yards in a game in more than three seasons. He was also the first rookie to run for a hundred yards in his debut as a starter since Jim Taylor had done it some thirty-four seasons before.

"I've been waiting years to do this, and I was ready," a grinning Bennett said after the game. "It was sweet, man. I used to watch the Bears on TV all the time when I was growing up. I thought they were awesome."

Brett Farve did a marvelous job at the controls, tossing twenty-four balls in the air and completing sixteen for 209 yards and a touchdown. His touchdown throw came late in the first quarter. Holmgren called for a play-action pass to fool the Bears. Farve faked a hand-off to Bennett and lofted the ball in the direction of Sterling Sharpe. Sharpe corralled the ball for a 49-yard touchdown, making it 10-3.

In the third period Green Bay became stingy, controlling the ball for thirteen of the quarter's fifteen minutes of action. The frustrated Bears' offense could do nothing but watch from the sidelines.

"There are a lot of players on this team who have never beaten the Bears," Packers' coach Mike Holmgren said. "In our division, the Bears have been the mark of excellence for a long time, so it was important for many reasons. This win gives us some respect in the division."

The Chicago Bears fell completely apart. After their first win over the Packers in mid-October, Ditka's Bruins lost eight of their final nine games to finish a dismal 5-11.

On the other hand, Holmgren and his Packers had turned it around after the first Bears' game. They won seven of their final nine games, narrowly missing the playoffs after a season-ending loss to the Vikings.

It appeared the Packers now had the coach and quarterback to lead them back to the top of the Central Division.

In Chicago, Mike Ditka was about to be fired.

Chicago Bears' President Michael McCaskey made the decision in mid-January to replace Mike Ditka with another Dallas Cowboy assistant coach, defensive coordinator Dave Wannstedt.

Tabbed the eleventh head coach in the team's history, Wannstedt came to Chicago with impressive credentials. His announced hiring came eleven days before his number-one ranked Dallas defense helped win the 1992 Super Bowl for the Cowboys.

Wannstedt, like his hero Mike Ditka, grew up in the Pittsburgh area. After playing offensive tackle at the University of Pittsburgh from 1970 to '73, he had seen coaching stints at Albany State, Bridgeport, Central Connecticut State, Washington State, Pittsburgh, Oklahoma State, Syracuse, Miami, and then with the Dallas Cowboys.

Wannstedt even had a connection to the Green Bay Packers. He was selected by the Packers in the fifteenth round of the 1974 draft but spent the season on injured reserve with a foot injury.

"I'm very excited about the opportunity and challenge that lies ahead," Wannstedt said. "The great tradition of football in Chicago and the pride involved in being a part of the Chicago Bears' organization made this a very attractive job. I will work extremely hard to make this a very competitive team and hopefully a Super

Bowl champion."

In 1993, free agency came into its own with 120 players changing teams. A player with five or more years of duty to the league would be able to negotiate with another team after his contract had expired.

One of the most sought-after free agents was Philadelphia Eagles' defensive end Reggie White. The bull-strong, 6' 5", 285-pound White had registered 124 quarterback sacks since arriving in the NFL in 1985. In the process of terrorizing opponents' offensive lines, White had been to seven straight Pro Bowl games.

White's whirlwind thirty-seven day tour of the NFL had head coaches and owners salivating for his services. For Reggie, a very religious man, it was a wrenching decision.

"There were times I almost cried, I was so desperate to make the right decision," White said of the time.

In May, Reggie White, dubbed the "Minister of Defense" and the most sought-after free agent in the league, was in a Green Bay Packers uniform. General Manager Ron Wolf had won the contest to land White, digging deep into the team's coffers. Wolf made White the highest-paid non-quarterback player in the league by signing him to a four year, $17 million dollar contract, with White getting a cool $9 million up front.

"I think we can compete for the NFL Central Division title, that's what we're in it for," Wolf commented at a press conference. "With Reggie in place, we're going to be considered a serious contender."

Reggie was instrumental in turning Green Bay's defense into the second best defense in the league in '93, recording thirteen quarterback sacks. With White on the line were stalwarts John Jurkovic, Matt Brock, and Gilbert Brown. Green Bay's linebackers were considered some of the best in the NFL. Tony Bennett, Johnny Holland, George Koonce, Brian Noble, and Bryce Paup made life miserable for league offenses all year long. Defensive backs LeRoy Butler, rookie starter George Teague, Doug Evans, Terrell Buckley, and Mike Prior stole eleven interceptions on the year. It would be

George Teague who would make the big play in the 145th revival of the series on Halloween, October 31.

The 58,945 in attendance at Lambeau Field were all given masks in the likeness of Coach Holmgren for Halloween. Through the eye holes of the masks they watched two mistake-prone teams. Green Bay capitalized on Chicago miscues while the Bruins had trouble converting.

On the second play of the game, Packers' quarterback Brett Farve called an audible at the line of scrimmage, changing to a play he thought would work against the Bears' defense. Farve misread the coverage and threw an interception to Chicago's Mark Carrier on the Packers' 17-yard line. When the drive stalled, kicker Mike Butler came on to attempt a 27-yard field goal. Butler's holder, Chris Gardocki, fumbled the snap, grabbed the ball, scrambled around until throwing an incomplete pass. "I lost control of it. It was my fault totally," Gardocki said.

After a Chris Jacke 40-yard field goal, the Packers took a 10-0 lead when Farve found receiver Sterling Sharpe for a 21-yard touchdown pass in the second quarter.

The Bears missed another opportunity when on the next series, halfback Neal Anderson threw a surprise pass to tight end Ryan Wetnight. Wetnight, wide open at the Packers' 10-yard line, had the ball hit his hands and bounce to the ground incomplete. The Bears ended up with three points, behind 10-3 at the half.

The game's deciding play came in the fourth quarter with the Bears' offense stationed at the Packers' 12-yard line. In Green Bay's huddle, linebacker Johnny Holland said in desperation, "Somebody's got to make a play, who'll it be?"

LeRoy Butler raised his hand and said, "I'll try."

At the snap, Bears' quarterback Jim Harbaugh drifted back to pass. He had no idea that the Packer defense was coming on a full blitz. Safety LeRoy Butler came unmolested through the Bears' line and nailed Harbaugh while his arm was in throwing motion. The ball popped loose, was nearly intercepted by Reggie White, then was inadvertently kicked back to the Bears' 37-yard line where Butler fell on it.

On the next series, the Packers put the game away by going ninety-one yards in twelve plays, culminating in Darrell

Thompson's 17-yard touchdown run. Final: Green Bay 17, Chicago 3.

Packers' nose tackle John Jurkovic's jersey was checked by referee Gary Lane during the game after complaints by Bears' left guard Mark Bortz and center Jerry Fontenot. The two Bruins theorized that Jurkovic's jersey had grease spread over it, making it hard for them to block him. "They were complaining I had some type of foreign substance on my jersey," Jurkovic said after the game. "That's simply ludicrous. There was nothing there except perspiration from hard work, hard sweat. Fontenot and Bortz are a couple of wily veterans. They weren't complaining until I made a tackle."

In early December, game 146 of the rivalry saw Brett Farve set a Packers' team record for completions, throw for 402 yards and two touchdowns—and lose, 30-17, to the Bears. The unpredictable Green Bay quarterback would, in the process of trying to win the game, lost the game on three critical turnovers.

Seven minutes into the game and with the Packers driving, Bears' cornerback Jeremy Lincoln intercepted a Farve pass on the 14-yard line. On the verge of being tackled near the twenty, Lincoln spotted linebacker Dante Jones approaching near the sideline. Lincoln flipped Jones the ball. Jones leaped over an attempted tackle by Farve and high-stepped upfield eighty yards for a score.

"Big Play Dante" was far from being done. With less than a minute left and the Packers again inside the Bears' 20-yard line, Jones picked off a pass intended for tight end Jackie Harris, preventing a Green Bay score.

The next Packers' mistake was, as *Chicago Tribune* writer Bernie Lincicome put it, "what could be the most atrocious pass ever attempted by a professional; so grotesque that it was called a fumble so as not to shame any authentic passes Farve may make in the future." Under heavy pressure, Farve had the idea of getting off a pass, but simply dropped the ball instead. The ever-present Dante Jones picked up the ball and rolled into the end zone for another score.

Even with all the miscues, Green Bay was still in the game. Down 23-17 and in a fourth-and-one situation with 5:19 left, Farve let loose a perfect pass to the usually sure-handed Sterling Sharpe at the Chicago 20-yard line. Sharpe dropped the ball, ending the rally.

The final nail in the coffin came after the Packers got the ball back with 1:53 left. On the series' first play, Farve misread the opportunistic Bears' defense. His throw was intercepted by Mark Carrier and returned thirty-four yards for a touchdown. Chicago 30, Green Bay 17.

"The way our offense played today, I thought we were part of a new government giveaway program," said Packers' left tackle Ken Ruettgers.

It was the first time the Bears had scored three defensive touchdowns in a game since the infamous 1940 championship game, when they goose-egged the Washington Redskins, 73-0. The feat hadn't been done in the league since 1981.

At 7-5, the Chicago Bears were in first place in the Central Division and poised to give Coach Dave Wannstedt a playoff appearance in his maiden season. In the last four games of the year, the Bears punchless offense scored a measly thirty-three points and lost all four games. It was a disappointing end to an exciting season in Chicago.

After a 1-4 start, Holmgren's young squad rebounded and won a wildcard spot in the playoffs against the Detroit Lions. The Packers were going only as far as their sometimes erratic, sometimes brilliant quarterback could take them. Farve showed the brilliant side against the Lions late in the game when he threw a bomb to Sterling Sharpe, who caught it for a score and the Packers first playoff win since the strike-shortened 1982 season.

Unfortunately for Packers' fans, just like in the 1982 playoffs, the Dallas Cowboys spoiled Green Bay's wish to play in another championship game by beating the Northmen, 27-17.

Both the Bears and the Packers had reasons to be satisfied with the 1993 campaign. Although the Midway Monsters had pulled the plug on their season early, it was obvious that their new head coach had them going in the right direction.

In Green Bay, credit had to be given to Coach Mike Holmgren for not giving up on his fluky quarterback. Brett Farve's nineteen TD passes were offset by his league leading twenty-four interceptions. But there was a bonding between the coach and the quarterback; and it was going to continue to pay off for the Green Bay Packers.

The often-used maxims of "The good ol' days" and "Things aren't what they used to be" fairly well describe pro football in the 1990s. Many stadiums and sports venues showcasing pro football have artificial turf instead of real sod and have domed roofs to protect the players and fans from the elements of mother nature.

In Green Bay and Chicago, pro football comes to a historic standstill. Attending a game in ancient Soldier Field or walking through the turnstiles of Lambeau Field is a return trip to the days of, what *Chicago Tribune* writer Bernie Lincicome called, "when men were men and misery was a magnet." To this day Green Bay and Chicago still play on real grass, open-aired without a dome, completely at the mercy of the unpredictable skies above. If it rains, it rains. If it snows, it snows. Either way the game goes on.

On Halloween night, October 31, 1994, the Packers, the Bears, some 47,381 brave—no, foolish—football fans and a nationally televised Monday Night Football audience witnessed a game played in some of the worst weather ever seen for a football game. Even before the game started Soldier Field was the scene of a monsoon. Then it got worse.

Officially, the wind at game time was 36 mph but Green Bay quarterback Brett Farve turned into an amateur weatherman with his own post-game weather report. "The guy was lying when he was saying it was gusts of 36 mph," Farve said. "I live on the Gulf of Mexico. I've seen gusts. Hell, that was 50, 60 mph. It was ridiculous." Farve was right on target. Professional weather predictors clocked wind gusts of up to 53 mph during the game. Chicago: the Windy City.

Not only were there gale-force winds, it was sleeting, as well. At times it appeared to be raining sideways. Temperatures in the thirty degree area only added to the miserable conditions. *Green Bay Press-Gazette* scribe Chris Havel coined it the "Mudder" of all football games.

Also adding to a night of oddities were the teams' uniforms. Both clubs wore their throwback uniforms for the game. During the 1994 season every NFL team wore uniforms from days past for some of their games. The Packers' outfits were white travel jerseys topped with yellow around the shoulder pads, khaki-colored pants, and dull yellow helmets, minus the "G" decal. Chicago wore replicas of their 1920s uniforms. The dark blue jerseys were enhanced by orange vertical stripes, leading Bernie Lincicome to say the Bears looked like "vertical bumblebees."

Both teams found it nearly impossible to move the ball early on. In the second quarter, Packers' fullback Edgar Bennett splashed for a 3-yard touchdown after Bears' signal caller Erik Kramer had fumbled the soggy pigskin. Kicker Chris Jacke added the extra point, 7-0.

Six minutes later Green Bay was poised at Chicago's 36-yard line. Farve took the snap and faded back to pass. "I thought he was going to dump it off to me," Edgar Bennett said. "I was looking for him to throw it and he yelled, 'Go, go, go...'"

And go, go, go he did. Farve tucked the ball under his arm and boot-legged around the right end headed for the goal line. After picking up good blocks from Bennett, tight end Ed West, and receiver Anthony Morgan, Farve hurdled the Bears' Jeremy Lincoln and landed head first into the end zone for the score.

"The last time I ran one that long was against North Bay in the fifth grade," Farve said.

In the third quarter, a rumbling Edgar Bennett scored on a short run and caught a wind-blown pass from Farve for another score. All Chicago could muster was a 5-yard touchdown pass to Jeff Graham from quarterback Steve Walsh, who had replaced Erik Kramer. Final: Green Bay 33, Chicago 6.

The monsoon-like weather dominated the post-game interviews. "It was like playing in a park," Packers' offensive lineman Guy McIntyre said. "It was all football, baby. Just breaking it down to the bare elements and the love of the game. That's what it was tonight. With the uniforms, the weather, the whole ambiance of the game was old-fashioned. It was great to be a part of it."

To Green Bay defensive lineman John Jurkovic, winning the game made the miserable conditions bearable. "It's fun when you're winning, but I tell you what, I'd hate to have been the Bears tonight," he said.

Obviously, the weather, plus their annihilation on the field, made for a remorseful Bears' locker room.

"It's tough to get your butt kicked on national TV," said Bears' linebacker Joe Cain. "It's embarrassing. It stinks."

Amazingly, the Packers' ground game slopped their way to 223 yards on forty-five carries through the soupy turf of Soldier Field, with Edgar Bennett garnering 105 of those. Packers' runners shredded the Bears' defense, leaving the Midway Monsters face down in the mud.

Adding to the throwback feeling of the evening was the retirement of Gale Sayers' and Dick Butkus' jersey numbers. Sayers' #40 and Butkus' #51 jerseys were retired at half-time as the rain and wind whipped around both Hall of Famers standing at midfield. The only thing the memorably nostalgic evening lacked was seeing Sayers and Butkus suit up and actually play.

The win brought the Packers up to a 4-4 record at mid-season, still very much in the playoff race in the Central Division. Tied with the Packers at 4-4 were the Chicago Bears. Both teams were two games behind the division-leading Minnesota Vikings when they met again in dairyland in mid-December.

This time there was no rain, little wind, and sunny skies for the contest. But when playing in Green Bay, Wisconsin, one expects to play outside in the cold. Temperatures hovered around fifteen degrees for the game.

Despite the freezing cold, thousands tailgated prior to the game outside Lambeau Field, turning the parking lot into a camp of mostly Bear-hating, merry revelers, many being entertained by a rock-polka band called the Happy Schnapps Combo. One bearded Packers' fan, dressed in a red hunting outfit and red toboggan, was surrounded by his brew-drinking friends watching him play "Bearball": a game played by taking a baseball bat and smacking a stuffed bear, dressed in a blue and orange sweater, into the air. Also, near the parking lot's entrance, a huge stuffed bear sat on the roof of a van—with an arrow protruding from its back.

The Bears led off the scoring with a Kevin Butler 25-yard field goal in the first quarter. Little did they know that would be all the scoring they would do that day.

Green Bay's rushing attack picked up where it left off in the Halloween hurricane. Edgar Bennett led the way with 106 yards while Reggie Cobb added seventy-eight and Leshon Johnson forty-two. Registering 259 yards rushing, the Packers' offense ran roughshod over Bear defenders.

The ground game served as a setup for Brett Farve's rifle arm. In the first quarter, Robert Brooks snagged a 12-yard pass for the go-ahead score. With less than a minute to play in the first half, fusilier Farve fired a 13-yard pass to Sterling Sharpe in the end zone, ending a nine play, 88-yard drive.

The passing tandem of Farve to Sharpe wasn't done yet. In the third period, Sharpe caught a 22-yard touchdown pass, making it the thirty-seventh time in their careers that the two connected to score.

Farve's three touchdown passes, a rushing touchdown by Bennett, and four Chris Jacke field goals were more than enough to throttle the outgunned Bears, 40-3.

Toward the end of the game a few thoughtless Packer fans, smelling blood and wanting the Packers to run up the score, began booing when they failed to go for a touchdown while deep in Bears' territory. After the boos died down many started chanting, "Bears Still Suck! Bears Still Suck!"

At least one Chicago Bear agreed with the chanting throng. "Hey, we did," Bears' linebacker Joe Cain said after the game. "I'm not going to lie to you."

The Bears would be home watching the playoffs. After the Packers beat Atlanta and Tampa Bay to end their season 9-7, Holmgren's gang won a wildcard playoff berth against Detroit. After disposing of Barry Sanders and the Lions, the Packers traveled to Dallas, only to get beaten again by the Cowboys.

Both the Bears and the Packers eagerly looked forward to the '95 campaign. Dave Wannstedt had shown he was the coach the Chicago Bears needed to get back to the top. Green Bay's Mike Holmgren had made the playoffs in 1993 and '94, and was now ready to make a run for the NFC championship and the Super Bowl.

The last time the Green Bay Packers could call themselves

Central Division champions, Richard Nixon was president. Since Dan Devine's 1972 divisional winner, Packer fans had endured some lean years. Except for the playoff appearance in the strike-shortened 1982 season, the Packers were always in the category of also-rans, and, often, the league's doormats.

Not any longer. Head Coach Mike Holmgren had molded a winning squad led by his "throwback" quarterback Brett Farve. After suffering through a couple of topsy-turvy years under center, Farve came into his own in 1995. By year's end he would be named the league's Most Valuable Player, lead his team into the championship game against Dallas, and narrowly miss a trip to the Super Bowl. The Pack was back.

Holmgren and the Packers traveled to the Windy City on September 11 to take on the rival Bears at Soldier Field.

Bears' coach Dave Wannstedt was fully aware of his team's 0-7 record in their past seven appearances on Monday Night Football. Thanks to the rifle-arm of Brett Farve, it was about to become 0-8.

Actually, Wannstedt's squad played two games, a terrible one in the first half and a comeback one in the second. Early in the first quarter, Farve lobbed a 4-yard scoring pass to Robert Brooks in the corner of the end zone. Later in the quarter, crowning a ten-play, 83-yard drive, Farve again connected through the air for a touchdown, this one a 15-yard pass to former Bear Anthony Morgan.

No one was prepared for Robert Brooks' second touchdown of the night. After an interception by LeRoy Butler at the 3-yard line, Packer running back Edgar Bennett lost yardage with two running plays up the middle in the shadow of his own goal post. On third down from his own 1-yard line, Packers' coach Mike Holmgren called an old sandlot play, the pump-and-go. Fading back into the end zone, Farve pumped his arm once, then fired a pass in the direction of Robert Brooks near the 20-yard line. Bears' defensive back Donnell Woolford took the bait of Brooks' fake to the inside.

"I was going for the interception," Woolford said after the game. "I wasn't expecting it and they got behind me. I gambled and I missed."

Brooks was five yards behind Woolford when the ball landed in his hands. Reminiscent of Sterling Sharpe, the speedy Brooks took off like a rocket, streaking down the sideline for an amazing 99-yard touchdown. The long completion was a Packers' team record, besting the a 96-yard TD toss from Tobin Rote to Willie Grimes in 1950. As kicker Chris Jacke booted the extra point, a chorus of boos directed at the Bears echoed through the ancient pillars of Soldier Field.

Embarrassingly behind at half-time, 24-7, the Bears regrouped in the locker room and came out a different team. Capitalizing on Green Bay's mistakes, the Bears fought their way back into the game.

Bears' quarterback Eric Kramer lobbed a 2-yard pass to Jim Flanigan, a defensive tackle sometimes inserted as blocker and tight end on offense. Flanigan, a Green Bay native in the off-season, hauled in the ball for the score. After Donnell Woolford redeemed himself by intercepting a Farve pass near the Packers' goal line, Bears' rookie running back Rashaan Salaam darted his way for an 8-yard touchdown, drawing the Bears to within six points, 27-21.

The ceiling continued to fall in on the Packers after Craig Hentrich's punt was blocked by the Bears' Anthony Marshall, giving Chicago a first-and-goal at the 2-yard line. Twice Salaam slammed into the line, only to be repelled by Reggie White and the hardened Packers' defense. On third down, Kramer lofted a pass to Jeff Graham who caught the ball, but out of bounds. The Bears settled for a Kevin Butler field goal, 27-24.

Green Bay was doing everything it could to give the game to Chicago. Late in the game Packers' kicker Chris Jacke readied for a field goal attempt, but holder Ty Detmer mishandled the snap, giving the Bears the ball and 2:40 to either tie or win the game.

On the third play of the drive, Erik Kramer drifted back to pass and suddenly felt the huge presence of Reggie White. As Kramer stepped into the pocket, White stuck out a big paw, stripping the ball from Kramer. Packers' linebacker Wayne Simmons landed on the bouncing pigskin, sealing a victory for Green Bay.

"It was a toe-to-toe, blow-by-blow type of game," Green Bay offensive tackle Ken Ruettgers said in the locker room.

"There were some strange things that happened on that field tonight, and it was a heckuva game from a spectator's standpoint," Packers' coach Mike Holmgren added. "But very difficult and very rewarding at the same time, because the Bears are a fine football team and it's a great rivalry. I'm glad we could hold on with our fingernails and get it done."

"I don't think anything can make me feel good," Bears' defensive tackle Jim Flanigan said. "Not after losing to Green Bay."

In the 150th renewal of the rivalry one month later, injured Green Bay standouts Reggie White and Brett Farve made 59,996 delirious fans at Lambeau Field stand in reverence. Farve had suffered a badly sprained ankle, had not practiced during the week, and remained doubtful for the Bears' game. The Minister of Defense was hobbling with a strained medial collateral ligament in his knee. Knowing it would limit his movement, White brushed off the idea of wearing a knee brace, but was convinced by the team doctor to at least wear a small one.

Farve stood with the rest of his squad in the tunnel ready to trot onto the field. "I've never had butterflies like this in my stomach for a long time," he told a teammate. Brett Farve turned his apprehension and nervousness into a performance worthy of a Hollywood script.

Press-Gazette sports columnist Chris Havel christened the gun-slinging Green Bay quarterback, "Moses with a limp."

After Chicago struck first with a TD pass from quarterback Erik Kramer to receiver Curtis Conway, Farve's rifle-arm began to fire. In the first quarter, he tossed a screen pass to Edgar Bennett who rumbled into the end zone from seventeen yards out. Six minutes later, Farve connected with speedy Robert Brooks for a 29-yard score.

Erik Kramer and the Bears owned the second quarter. After a Rashaan Salaam 2-yard scoring run, Kramer again hit Conway for a 46-yard touchdown, tying the game 21-21 just before the half. Repeating his first half tactics, Conway badly fooled Packers' rookie defensive back Craig Newsome and waltzed into the end zone.

With only 3:48 left in the regulation and the score knotted, 28-28, Farve lobbed another screen pass to Edgar Bennett who pranced in for the go-ahead score. It was Farve's fifth touchdown pass of the game, his twenty-fifth completion in thirty-three attempts, amassing 336 yards.

Nearly equaling Farve's numbers was Bears' sharp-shooter Erik Kramer. Completing twenty-three of thirty-eight passes for 318 yards, Kramer was a reminder that Brett Farve wasn't the only out-standing signal caller in the Central Division.

As the game clock ticked down, Kramer moved his Bears down-field. With eleven seconds left in the game, Packers' defender Doug Evans was flagged for holding Bears' receiver Jeff Graham near the goal line, giving Chicago a first down at the Green Bay 14-yard line.

It was not to be for the Bears. Kramer threw three incomple-tions and the Packers won a thriller, 35-28.

Pro football had gone through a metamorphosis in the rivalry's seventy-five years. Like most games of that era, the first game of the series at Cubs Park on November 27, 1921, was dominated by the running game with an occasional forward pass. In this, the 150th game, the two quarterbacks together attempted seventy-one passes, completed forty-eight, and amassed 617 passing yards. It was the first time in the series that the rivals had collectively thrown seven touchdown passes. Combined, both teams tallied 800 yards in total offense. Certainly, a lot had changed since the days of Curly Lambeau, Cub Buck, Red Grange, and George Trafton.

Fittingly, NFL Commissioner Paul Tagliabue was at Lambeau Field to watch the 150th meeting of the arch rivals, and the 1,000th professional regular season and post-season played by the Packers. Before the game, Tagliabue commented on the Green Bay-Chicago series.

"As far as tradition, history, and rivalry, this is THE football game."

Seasons come and seasons go. Franchises move; players migrate and depart. But one component of pro football is perpetual—the Green Bay Packers' and the Chicago Bears' rivalry.

So it has gone ... and so it continues.

Sources

1920–'22

"George Trafton," Pro Football Hall of Fame profile; Canton, Ohio.

Chicago Tribune, 28 November 1921.

George Calhoun, *Green Bay Press-Gazette*, 28 November 1921.

Bob Wolf, "Strong Man Buck High Scorer For Lineman," *Milwaukee Journal*, December 1964.

Chicago Tribune, 28 January 1922.

Torinus, John B. *The Packer Legend.* Neshkoro: Laranmark Press, 1982, pp. 3, 22-23.

Names, Larry. *The History of the Green Bay Packers, The Lambeau Years-Part One.* Wautoma: Angel Press of Wisconsin, 1989, pp. 36, 88, 99.

"Curly Lambeau," Pro Football Hall of Fame profile, 23 August 1980.

"Fiery Leader," *Green Bay Press-Gazette*, 21 October 1969.

George Calhoun, *Green Bay Press-Gazette*, 29 August 1921.

1923–'24

Terry Bledsoe, "Earp's Career Dates Back to Infancy of Pro Football," *Milwaukee Journal*, 1 November 1965, Sports section, p. 14.

Chicago Tribune, 22 September 1924.

Green Bay Press-Gazette, 15 October 1923.

Chicago Tribune, 15 October 1923.

Chicago Tribune, 24 November 1924.

Green Bay Press-Gazette, 24 November 1924.

1925

George Calhoun, *Green Bay Press-Gazette*, 23 November 1925.

George Calhoun, *Green Bay Press-Gazette*, 28 September 1925.

"Grange Warns of Danger Ahead," *Chicago Tribune*, 23 November 1925.

Irving Vaughan, *Chicago Tribune*, 23 November 1925.

George Calhoun, *Green Bay Press-Gazette*, 28 September 1925.

1926–'28

George Calhoun, *Green Bay Press-Gazette*, 27 September 1926.

George Calhoun, *Green Bay Press-Gazette*, 22 November 1926.

George Calhoun, *Green Bay Press-Gazette*, 13 October 1927.

George Calhoun, *Green Bay Press-Gazette*, 21 November 1927.

Chicago Tribune, 20 December 1926.

Chicago Tribune, 22 November 1926.

Don Maxwell, "Speaking of Sports," *Chicago Tribune*, 27 September 1926.

Bob Carroll. *The Coffin Corner* 2, no. 3. Pro Football Researcher's Association. Huntingdon, PA.

Arthur Bystrom, *Green Bay Press-Gazette*, 1 October 1928.

Arthur Bystrom, *Green Bay Press-Gazette*, 22 October 1928.

Arthur, Bystrom, *Green Bay Press-Gazette*, 10 November 1928.

Chicago Tribune, 1 October 1928.

Wilfrid Smith, *Chicago Tribune*, 22 October 1928.

Wilfrid Smith, *Chicago Tribune*, 10 December 1928.

1929

"Game Day: Chiefs vs. Steelers," Pro Football Hall of Fame profile, 5 December 1982.

Lee Remmel, *Green Bay Press-Gazette*, 7 April 1965, Personality Parade.

Arthur Bystrom, *Green Bay press-Gazette*, 30 September 1929.

Torinus, John B. *The Packer Legend*. Neshkoro: Laranmark Press, 1982, p. 33.

Wilfrid Smith, *Chicago Tribune*, 9 December 1929.

Wilfrid Smith, *Chicago Tribune*, 11 November 1929.

Gerald Holland. "Is That You Up There Johnny Blood?" Reprinted courtesy of Sports Illustrated, 12 September 1963, 23. ©1963 Time Inc. All rights reserved.

1930–'34

Greg Kukish, "Along Came Jones." *The Coffin Corner* 10, no. 1-2. January/February 1988.

Chicago Bears Press Guide, 1936. Pro Football Hall of Fame archives.

Harold Rosenthal, "The College Boy Who Knocked Out Nagurski," *College & Pro Football Newsletter* 14, no. 19 (1988): 12, 15-21.

Lee Remmel, *Green Bay Press-Gazette*, 17 April 1965, Personality Parade.

Gerald Holland. "Is That You Up There Johnny Blood?" Reprinted courtesy of *Sports Illustrated*, 12 September 1963, 18. ©1963 Time Inc. All rights reserved.

Green Bay Press-Gazette, 29 September 1930.

A. W. Bystrom, *Green Bay Press-Gazette*, 11 November 1930.

Wilfrid Smith, *Chicago Tribune*, 8 December 1930.

A. W. Bystrom, *Green Bay Press-Gazette*, 21 November 1931.

A. W. Bystrom, *Green Bay Press-Gazette*, 28 September 1931.

Wilfrid Smith, *Chicago Tribune*, 7 December 1931.

A. W. Bystrom, *Green Bay Press-Gazette*, 7 December 1931.

C. C. Staph, "When Stinky Stuffed The Pack." *The Coffin Corner* 9, no. 2.

Clarke Hinkle, "Playing for the Pack in the 30s," interview by C. Robert Barnett, *The Coffin Corner* 9, no. 5, May 1982. Reprinted by permission *Packer Report*, 13 August 1981.

Bob Barnett, "Clark Hinkle: Life After Pro Football," 2 February 1984. Reprinted by permission from *The Packer Report*.

Charlie Powell, "Football Great Clarke Hinkle Calls 'Em As He Sees 'Em," *Steubenville (Ohio) Herald Star*, 30 March 1975.

Cleon Walfoort, "Herber Couldn't Thread Needle With Ball ...," *Milwaukee Journal*, 4 November 1965, Sports section.

John F. Steadman, "Hall of Famer Herber Made $75 A Game," *News American*, 21 December 1966, Pro Football Hall of Fame archives.

Arthur Bystrom, *Green Bay Press-Gazette*, 26 September 1932.

Wilfrid Smith, *Chicago Tribune*, 26 September 1932.

Wilfrid Smith, *Chicago Tribune*, 17 October 1932.

Arthur Bystrom, *Green Bay Press-Gazette*, 17 October 1932.

Bob Braunwart and Bob Carroll, "Moose of the Bears." *The Coffin Corner* 3, no. 6.

Joe Meyer, "George Musso Named to Hall of Fame," *Edwardsville Intelligencer*, 29 January 1982. Pro Football Hall of Fame archives.

Arthur Bystrom, *Green Bay Press-Gazette*, 25 September 1933.

Wilfrid Smith, *Chicago Tribune*, 25 September 1933.

Arthur Bystrom, *Green Bay Press-Gazette*, 23 October 1933.

Wilfrid Smith, *Chicago Tribune*, 23 October 1933.

Wilfrid Smith, *Chicago Tribune*, 11 December 1933.

Arthur Bystrom, *Green Bay Press-Gazette*, 11 December 1933.

John M. Walter, *Green Bay Press-Gazette*, 29 October 1934.

Chicago Tribune, 24 September 1934.

George Strickler, *Chicago Tribune*, 29 October 1934.

Jim Klobucher, "Believe Everything You Hear," *Minneapolis Star*, 1974.

1935

Arthur Daley, "The Legend of Don Hutson," *Pro Football Almanac*, 1965, pp. 81-82.

George Strickler, "Don Hutson: See the Antelope Run," *Quarterback*, December 1969, pp. 61-62. Pro Football Hall of Fame archives.

George Strickler, *Green Bay Press-Gazette*, 23 September 1935.

John Walters, *Green Bay Press-Gazette*, 23 September 1935.

George Stricker, *Chicago Tribune*, 23 September 1935.

George Stricker, *Chicago Tribune*, 28 October 1935.

Joe Horrigan. Interview by author. 7 May 1995.

Names, Larry. *The History of the Green Bay Packers, The Lambeau Years-Part Two.* Wautoma: Angel Press of Wisconsin, 1989, p.79.

Hal Van Every. Interview by author. 8 July 1995.

1936–'37

David Adam, *Quincy (Iowa) Herald-Whig*, 18 September 1993.

Bill Bradshaw, *Quincy Herald-Whig.*

Herm Schneidman. Interview by author. 26 February 1995.

Frank Finch, "Jumbo Joe Stydahar Sits on Top of the World," *All-Sports News*, 16 January 1952. Pro Football Hall of Fame archives.

John Walter, *Green Bay Press-Gazette*, 2 November 1936.

George Strickler, *Chicago Tribune*, 2 November 1936.

"New Orleans vs Pittsburgh", Pro Football Hall of Fame profile, 5 November 1978.

Sam Francis. Interview by author. 24 January 1995.

George Strickler, *Chicago Tribune*, 20 September 1937.

George Strickler, *Chicago Tribune*, 8 November 1937.

John Walter, *Green Bay Press-Gazette*, 20 September 1937.

John Walter, *Green Bay Press-Gazette*, 8 November 1937.

Russell Thompson. Interview by author. 24 January 1995.

1938–'39

John Walter, *Green Bay Press-Gazette*, 19 September 1938.

John Walter, *Green Bay Press-Gazette*, 7 November 1938.

John Walter, *Green Bay Press-Gazette*, 25 September 1939.

John Walter, *Green Bay Press-Gazette*, 6 November 1939.

Dick Flatley, *Green Bay Press-Gazette*, 6 November 1939.

George Strickler, *Chicago Tribune*, 19 September 1938.

George Strickler, *Chicago Tribune*, 7 November 1938.

George Strickler, *Chicago Tribune*, 25 September 1939.

George Strickler, *Chicago Tribune*, 6 November 1939.

Gus Zarnas. Interview by author. 19 April 1995.

1940

Joe Maniaci. Interview by author. 12 July 1995.

Emil Klosinski, "A Hunk of History," *The Coffin Corner* 3, no. 2, February 1981.

"Sid Luckman," Pro Football Hall of Fame profile, 28 September 1980.

Sid Luckman. Interview by author. 31 August 1995.

Clyde "Bulldog" Turner. Interview by author. 21 December 1994.

Dick Flatley and John Walter, *Green Bay Press-Gazette*, 23 September 1940.

George Strickler, *Chicago Tribune*, 23 September 1940.

Winfrid Smith, *Chicago Tribune*, 8 December 1940.

1941

George McAfee. Interview by author. 10 August 1995.

Hugh Gallarneau. Interview by author. 2 August 1995.

Tony Canadeo. Interview by author. 12 June 1995.

Sid Luckman. Interview by author. 31 August 1995.

Harry Clark. Interview by author. 22 July 1995.

"George McAfee," Pro Football Hall of Fame profile.

Chicago Tribune, 29 September 1941.

John Walter, *Green Bay Press-Gazette*, 29 September 1941.

Ed Prell, *Chicago Tribune*, 3 November 1941.

Ray Pagel, *Green Bay Press-Gazette*, 3 November 1941.

Green Bay Press-Gazette, 8 August 1993, p. 23.

Edward Prell, *Chicago Tribune*, 15 December 1941.

Ray Pagel, *Green Bay Press-Gazette*, 15 December 1941.

Bob Barnett, "When the Packers Went to War," *The Coffin Corner* 10, no. 2,
    February. Reprinted by permission from *The Packer Report*.

Names, Larry. *The History of the Green Bay Packers, The Lambeau Years-Part Two.*
    Wautoma: Angel Press of Wisconsin, 1989, p. 181.

Green Bay Press-Gazette, 14 December 1942.

Don Hickok, R. Pagel, and A. Daley, *Green Bay Press-Gazette*, 28 September 1942.

Ray Pagel and Art Daley, *Green Bay Press-Gazette*, 16 November 1942.

Edward Prell, *Chicago Tribune*, 28 September 1942.

Edward Prell and Wilfrid Smith, *Chicago Tribune*, 16 November 1942.

Ray Pagel, *Green Bay Press-Gazette*, 15 November 1942.

Art Daley, *Green Bay Press-Gazette*, 10 December 1942.

Don Hickok and Dave Yuenger, *Green Bay Press-Gazette*, 27 September 1943.

Dave Yuenger, *Green Bay Press-Gazette*, 8 November 1943.

Edward Prell, *Chicago Tribune*, 27 September 1943.

Edward Prell, *Chicago Tribune*, 8 November 1943.

Names, Larry. *The History of the Green Bay Packers, The Lambeau Years-Part Two.*
    Wautoma: Angel Press of Wisconsin, 1989, p.196.

1944–'45

Names, Larry. *The History of the Green Bay Packers, The Lambeau Years-Part Two.*
    Wautoma: Angel Press of Wisconsin, 1989, p. 209.

"I Remember: 49ers vs Saints," *Pro Football Hall of Fame Game Program*, 17 October
    1976.

Jim Stewart, "The Era of Hutson," *The Coffin Corner* 10, no. 4.

Edward Prell, *Chicago Tribune*, 25 September 1944.

Don Hickok, *Green Bay Press-Gazette*, 25 September 1944.

Edward Prell, *Chicago Tribune*, 6 November 1944.

Dave Yuenger and Don Hickok, *Green Bay Press-Gazette*, 6 November 1944.

Chicago Tribune, 1 October 1945.

Wilfrid Smith, *Chicago Tribune*, 5 November 1945.

Lee Remmel, *Green Bay Press-Gazette*, 1 October 1945.

Dave Yuenger, *Green Bay Press-Gazette*, 5 November 1945.

Tony Canadeo. Interview by author. 11 June 1995.

1946–'49

Names, Larry. *The History of the Green Bay Packers, The Lambeau Years-Part Three.*
    Wautoma: Angel Press of Wisconsin, 1989, pp. 54, 130.

Lee Remmel, *Green Bay Press-Gazette*, 30 September 1946.

Don Hickok, *Green Bay Press-Gazette*, 30 September 1946.

Ed Prell, *Chicago Tribune*, 30 September 1946.

William Fay, *Chicago Tribune*, 4 November 1946.

Lee Remmel, *Green Bay Press-Gazette*, 4 November 1946.

Ed Sprinkle. Interview by author. 17 November 1994.

Green Bay Press-Gazette, 6 November 1944.

George Connor. Interview by author. 17 February 1995.

Bobby Dillon. Interview by author. 1 March 1995.

Art Daley. *Green Bay Press-Gazette*, 29 September 1947.

Lee Remmel, *Green Bay Press-Gazette*, 10 November 1947.

Edward Prell, *Chicago Tribune*, 29 September 1947.

Edward Prell, *Chicago Tribune*, 10 November 1947.

Tony Canadeo. Interview with author. 11 June 1995.

Edward Prell, *Chicago Tribune*, 27 September 1948.

Art Daley and Lee Remmel, *Green Bay Press-Gazette*, 27 September 1948.

Lee Remmel, *Green Bay Press-Gazette*, 15 November 1948.

Art Daley and Lee Remmel, *Green Bay Press-Gazette*, 26 September 1949.

Art Daley and Lee Remmel, *Green Bay Press-Gazette*, 7 November 1949.

Harry Warren, *Chicago Tribune*, 26 September 1949.

Harry Warren, *Chicago Tribune*, 7 November 1949.

1950–'55

Art Daley, *Green Bay Press-Gazette*, 1 February 1950.

Art Daley, *Green Bay Press-Gazette*, 20 January 1950.

Torinus, John B. *The Packer Legend*. Neshkoro: Laranmark Press, 1982, pp. 69, 73.

Green Bay Press-Gazette, 21 September 1969.

George McAfee. Interview by author. 10 July 1995.

Ken Kavanaugh. Interview by author. 10 May 1995.

Green Bay Packers Press Guide, 1950, p. 3.

Art Daley, *Green Bay Press-Gazette*, 2 October 1950.

Art Daley, *Green Bay Press-Gazette*, 16 October 1950.

Edward Prell, *Chicago Tribune*, 2 October 1950.

Harry Warren, *Chicago Tribune*, 16 October 1950.

Tony Canadeo. Interview by author. 12 June 1995.

Art Daley and Lee Remmel, *Green Bay Press-Gazette*, 1 October 1951.

Art Daley and Lee Remmel, *Green Bay Press-Gazette*, 19 November 1951.

Edward Prell, *Chicago Tribune*, 1 October 1951.

Edward Prell, *Chicago Tribune*, 19 November 1951.

Ed Prell, *Chicago Tribune*, 29 September 1952.

Ed Prell, *Chicago Tribune*, 10 November 1952.

Art Daley and Lee Remmel, *Green Bay Press-Gazette*, 29 September 1952.

Chicago Tribune, 10 November 1952.

Art Daley, D. Yuenger, and L. Remmel, *Green Bay Press-Gazette*, 10 November 1952.

Deral Teteak. Interview with author. 3 January 1995.

George Strickler, *Chicago Tribune*, 5 October 1953.

George Strickler, *Chicago Tribune*, 9 November 1953.

Art Daley and Lee Remmel, *Green Bay Press-Gazette*, 5 October 1953.

Art Daley and Lee Remmel, *Green Bay Press-Gazette*, 9 November 1953.

Harlon Hill. Interview by author. 21 November 1994.

Art Daley and Lee Remmel, *Green Bay Press-Gazette*, 8 November 1954.

Art Daley and Lee Remmel, *Green Bay Press-Gazette*, 4 October 1954.

George Strickler, *Chicago Tribune*, 4 October 1954.

Green Bay Packer Press Guide, 1955, p. 6-7.

Art Daley and Lee Remmel, *Green Bay Press-Gazette*, 3 October 1955.

George Strickler, *Chicago Tribune*, 3 October 1955.

George Strickler and Dave Condon, *Chicago Tribune*, 7 November 1955.

Art Daley and Lee Remmel, *Green Bay Press-Gazette*, 7 November 1955.

Gary Knafelc. Interview by author. July 1995.

Gene Schroeder. Interview by author. January 1995.

George Connor. Interview by author. January 1995.

Veryl Switzer. Interview by author. July 1995.

1956–'58

Don Langenkamp, "Lisle Blackbourn, The Hall of Fame Drafter," *Green Bay Packer Yearbook*, 1977.

Art Daley and Lee Remmel, *Green Bay Press-Gazette*, 8 October 1956.

Art Daley and Lee Remmel, *Green Bay Press-Gazette*, 12 November 1956.

Cooper Rollow, *Chicago Tribune*, 8 Ocotber 1956.

George Strickler, *Chicago Tribune*, 12 November 1956.

Gary Knafelc. Interview by author. July 1995.

Art Daley and Lee Remmel, *Green Bay Press-Gazette*, 30 September 1957.

Art Daley and Lee Remmel, *Green Bay Press-Gazette*, 11 November 1957.

George Strickler, *Chicago Tribune*, 30 September 1957.

George Strickler, *Chicago Tribune*, 11 November 1957.

Art Daley and Lee Remmel, *Green Bay Press-Gazette*, 29 September 1958.

Art Daley and Lee Remmel, *Green Bay Press-Gazette*, 10 November 1958.

Cooper Rollow, *Chicago Tribune*, 29 September 1958.

George Strickler and David Condon, *Chicago Tribune*, 10 November 1958.

Doug Atkins. Interview by author. 3 November 1994.

1959

Art Daley, *Green Bay Press-Gazette*, 3 February 1959.

Jerry Kramer. Interview by author. 14 February 1995.

Art Daley and Lee Remmel, *Green Bay Press-Gazette*, 28 Septebmer 1959.

Art Daley and Lee Remmel, *Green Bay Press-Gazette*, 5 December 1960.

Green Bay Press-Gazette, 21 September 1969.

Bill Wade. Interview by author. 26 December 1994.

Milton Gross, *New York Post*, 27 December 1963.

Lee Remmel and Art Daley, *Green Bay Press-Gazette*, 2 October 1961.

Lee Remmel and Art Daley, *Green Bay Press-Gazette*, 12 November 1961.

George Strickler, *Chicago Tribune*, 2 October 1961.

George Strickler, *Chicago Tribune*, 12 November 1961.

Don Smith, "Willie Davis, 1981 Enshrinee," Pro Football Hall of Fame news release.

Lee Remmel and Art Daley, *Green Bay Press-Gazette*, 1 October 1962.

Lee Remmel and Art Daley, *Green Bay Press-Gazette*, 5 November 1962.

George Strickler, *Chicago Tribune*, 1 October 1962.

George Stricker and Cooper Rollow, *Chicago Tribune*, 5 November 1962.

Edwin Pope, *Miami Herald*, 17 January 1967.

Jim Taylor. Interview by author. 3 March 1995.

1960–'64

Paul Hornung as told to Myron Cope, "My Longest Year," Pro Football Hall of Fame archives.

Bill Wade. Interview by author. 26 October 1994.

Mike Pyle. Interview by author. 30 October 1994.

Rollow, Cooper. *The Bear's Football Book*," Campaigne: Jameson Books, 1985, p. 37. Permission granted by Jameson Books.

Art Daley and Lee Remmel, *Green Bay Press-Gazette*, 16 September 1963.

Art Daley and Lee Remmel, *Green Bay Press-Gazette*, 18 November 1963.

George Strickler, *Chicago Tribune*, 16 September 1963.

Dick Hackenberg, J. Agrella, R. Smith, *Chicago Sun Times*, 18 November 1963.

Jerry Kramer. Interview by author. 14 February 1995.

Fred "Fuzzy" Thurston. Interview by author. 13 December 1994.

Ray Scott. Interview by author. 2 April 1996.

George Strickler, *Chicago Tribune*, 14 September 1964.

George Strickler, *Chicago Tribune*, 6 December 1964.

Art Daley and Lee Remmel, *Green Bay Press-Gazette*, 14 September 1964.

Art Daley and Lee Remmel, *Green Bay Press-Gazette*, 6 December 1964.

Tex Maule, "Shining Hour For Golden Boy," 21 September 1964. Reprinted courtesy of *Sports Illustrated* ©1964 Time Inc. All rights reserved.

Bill Wade. Interview by author. October 1994.

Ted Karras. Interview by author. December 1994.

Dave Robinson. Interview by author. April 1996.

Art Daley, *Green Bay Press-Gazette*, 16 March 1964.

1965–'67

Green Bay Press-Gazette, 10 June 1965.

Art Daley, *Green Bay Press-Gazette*, 6 June 1965.

Art Daley, *Green Bay Press-Gazette*, 1 June 1965.

Art Daley and Lee Remmel, *Green Bay Press-Gazette*, 9 November 1965.

Art Daley and Lee Remmel, *Green Bay Press-Gazette*, 4 October 1965.

George Strickler and Cooper Rollow, *Chicago Tribune*, 4 October 1965.

George Strickler and Cooper Rollow, *Chicago Tribune*, 9 November 1965.

George Strickler and Cooper Rollow, *Chicago Tribune*, 9 November 1966.

George Strickler and Cooper Rollow, *Chicago Tribune*, 21 November 1966.

Art Daley and Lee Remmel, *Green Bay Press-Gazette*, 17 October 1966.

Art Daley and Lee Remmel, *Green Bay Press-Gazette*, 21 November 1966.

George Strickler, *Chicago Tribune*, 25 September 1967.

George Strickler, *Chicago Tribune*, 27 November 1967.

Lee Remmel, *Green Bay Press-Gazette*, 25 September 1967.

Lee Remmel and Len Wagner, *Green Bay Press-Gazette*, 25 November 1967.

Cooper Rollow, "Class of '65—and All Time," *Chicago Tribune*, 31 October 1994.

Steve Guback, "Butkus Wonders if He Can Make It," *Washington Evening Star*, 2 December 1964.

"Dave Klein, "Bear's Best Draft Ever," *Sunday Star-Ledger*, 24 August 1969. Pro Football Hall of Fame archives.

Robert Morrison, "Butkus: Man or Monster," *St.Louis Post-Dispatch*, 19 November 1965.

James Spaulding, "Injury Leaves Hornung of Doubful Value to Saints," *Milwaukee Journal*, 12 February 1967.

Jerry Kramer. Interview by author. 14 February 1995.

Fred "Fuzzy" Thurston. Interview by author. 13 December 1995.

Bob Long. Interview by author. March 1995.

Tunney, Jim. *Impartial Judgment*, Glendale: Griffin Publishing, 1995. Permission granted *Impartial Judgment*, Griffin Publishing ©1995.

1968–'69

George Strickler, *Chicago Tribune*, 28 May 1968.

Len Wagner, *Green Bay Press-Gazette*, 2 February 1968.

Lee Remmel, "Phil Takes Over," *Green Bay Packer Yearbook*, 1969.

Len Wagner and Dave Devenport, *Green Bay Press-Gazette*, 4 November 1968.

Lee Remmel and Len Wagner, *Green Bay Press-Gazette*, 16 December 1968.

Cooper Rollow and George Strickler, *Chicago Tribune*, 4 November 1968.

Cooper Rollow, *Chicago Tribune*, 16 December 1968.

Mike Pyle. Interview by author. 30 October 1994.

Don Langenkamp, *Green Bay Press-Gazette*, 8 August 1993.

Lee Remmel, *Green Bay Press-Gazette*, 22 September 1969.

Lee Remmel, *Green Bay Press-Gazette*, 15 December 1969.

Cooper Rollow, *Chicago Tribune*, 22 September 1969.

Cooper Rollow and George Langford, *Chicago Tribune*, 15 December 1969.

1970–'74

Pete Waldmeir, "It Was An Impossible Task, and Packers' Coach Failed," *Detroit News*, 17 December 1970.

Torinus, John B. *The Packer Legend*, Neshkoro: Laranmark Press, 1982, p. 182.

Green Bay Press-Gazette, 3 September 1970.

Lee Remmel and Len Wagner, *Green Bay Press-Gazette*, 16 November 1970.

Lee Remmel, *Green Bay Press-Gazette*, 14 December 1970.

Cooper Rollow and George Langford, *Chicago Tribune*, 16 November 1970.

Cooper Rollow and George Langford, *Chicago Tribune*, 14 December 1970.

Cooper Rollow, "Jim Dooley Fired by Bears," *Chicago Tribune*, 30 December 1971.

Joe Zagorski, "Jim Carter, Former Packer Put Problems Behind Him," *The Coffin Corner* 10, no. 3 and 4.

Rollow, Cooper. *Cooper Rollow's Bears Football Book,"* Campaigne: Jameson Books, 1985, p. 63. Permission granted by Jameson Books.

George Langford, C. Rollow, and D. Pierson, *Chicago Tribune*, 8 November 1971.

Lee Remmel, *Green Bay Press-Gazette*, 7 November 1971.

Lee Remmel, *Green Bay Press-Gazette*, 13 December 1971.

George Langford and Don Pierson, *Chicago Tribune*, 13 December 1971.

Cooper Rollow, *Chicago Tribune*, 30 January 1972.

Bob Oates, *Los Angeles Times*, 2 December 1973.

Lee Remmel and Len Wagner, *Green Bay Press-Gazette*, 9 October 1972.

Lee Remmel and Len Wagner, *Green Bay Press-Gazette*, 13 November 1972.

Cooper Rollow and George Langford, *Chicago Tribune*, 9 October 1972.

Cooper Rollow, *Chicago Tribune*, 12 November 1972.

Lee Remmel and Len Wagner, *Green Bay Press-Gazette*, 5 November 1973.

Lee Remmel, *Green Bay Press-Gazette*, 17 December 1973.

Don Pierson, *Chicago Tribune*, 5 November 1973.

Don Pierson, *Chicago Tribune*, 17 December 1973.

Bud Lea, *Green Bay Packer Yearbook*, 1986.

Ed Stone, *Chicago Tribune*, 18 December 1974.

Green Bay Press-Gazette, 17 December 1974.

Gary Kosins. Interview by author. 5 January 1996.

Scott Hunter. Interview by author. 11 January 1996.

Ray Scott. Interview by author. 2 April 1996.

Willie Wood. Interview by author. 16 April 1996.

Bill Lueck. Interview by author. 22 March 1995.

Mike Ditka. Interview by author. 1 July 1996.

Ray Nitschke. Interview by author. 16 February 1996.

1975–'79

Cliff Christl, *Green Bay Press-Gazette*, 24 December 1974.

Don Pierson, *Chicago Tribune*, 10 November 1975.

Cliff Christl, *Green Bay Press-Gazette*, 10 November 1975.

Don Pierson, *Chicago Tribune*, 1 December 1975.

Green Bay Press-Gazette, 1 December 1975.

Cliff Christl, *Green Bay Press-Gazette*, 15 November 1976.

Cliff Christl and Don Langenkamp, *Green Bay Press-Gazette*, 29 November 1976.

Don Pierson and Ed Stone, *Chicago Tribune*, 15 November 1976.

Don Pierson, *Chicago Tribune*, 29 November 1976.

David Condon and Ed Stone, *Chicago Tribune*, 21 January 1978.

Don Pierson, *Chicago Tribune*, 31 October 1977.

Don Pierson, *Chicago Tribune*, 12 December 1977.

Cliff Christl and Don Langenkamp, *Green Bay Press-Gazette*, 31 October 1977.

Cliff Christl, *Green Bay Press-Gazette*, 12 December 1977.

Torinus, John B. *The Packer Legend*, Neshkoro: Laranmark Press, 1982, p. 216.

Bob Avellini. Interview by author. 4 January 1996.

Doug Buffone. Interview by author. 18 December 1995.

Waymond Bryant. Interview by author. 11 November 1994.

Joe Zagorski, "Jim Carter," *The Coffin Corner* 10, no. 3 and 4.

Don Langenkamp, *Green Bay Press-Gazette*, 9 October 1978.

Cliff Christl, *Green Bay Press-Gazette*, 11 December 1978.

Don Pierson, *Chicago Tribune*, 9 October 1978.

Don Pierson and Bill Jauss, *Chicago Tribune*, 11 December 1978.

Cliff Christl, *Green Bay Press-Gazette*, 3 September 1979.

Cliff Christl, *Green Bay Press-Gazette*, 10 December 1979.

Don Pierson and Dave Nightingale, *Chicago Tribune*, 3 September 1979.

Bob Verdi and Don Pierson, *Chicago Tribune*, 10 December 1979.

1980–'84

Todd Bell. Interview by author. 7 November 1994.

Mike Hartenstine. Interview by author. December 1994.

Bob Avellini. Interview by author. 4 January 1996.

Tony Walter and Cliff Christl, *Green Bay Press-Gazette*, 8 September 1980.

Cliff Christl and John Campbell, *Green Bay Press-Gazette*, 8 December 1980.

Don Pierson and Bob Logan, *Chicago Tribune*, 8 September 1980.

Bob Verdi, D. Pierson, and B. Logan, *Chicago Tribune*, 8 December 1980.

Cliff Christl, *Chicago Tribune*, 7 September 1981.

Green Bay Press-Gazette, 16 November 1981.

Steve Daley and Don Pierson, *Chicago Tribune*, 7 September 1981.

Bob Verdi and Don Pierson, *Chicago Tribune*, 16 November 1981.

John Husar and Don Pierson, *Chicago Tribune*, 5 January 1982.

David Condon, C. Rollow, and D. Pierson, *Chicago Tribune*, 20 January 1982.

Chicago Bears Media Guide, 1984.

Cooper Rollow, *Chicago Tribune*, 8 November 1982.

Don Pierson and Bob Verdi, *Chicago Tribune*, 5 December 1983.

Don Pierson and Bill Jauss, *Chicago Tribune*, 19 December 1983.

Cliff Christl and Bob McGinn, *Green Bay Press-Gazette*, 5 December 1983.

Cliff Christl and Bob McGinn, *Green Bay Press-Gazette*, 19 December 1983.

David Condon, D. Pierson, and B. Jauss, *Chicago Tribune*, 1 November 1983.

Tony Walter, "Packers vs. Bears" review, *Green Bay Press-Gazette*, 11 November 1995.

Packer Report, 3 October 1988, p. 13. Reprinted with permission.

Bob McGinn and Jim Egle, *Green Bay Press-Gazette*, 17 September 1984.

Bernie Lincicome, *Chicago Tribune*, 17 September 1984.

Bernie Lincicome and Bob Logan, *Chicago Tribune*, 10 December 1984.

1985

Bernie Lincicome, D. Pierson, and E. Sherman, *Chicago Tribune*, 22 October 1985.

D. Pierson, B. Verdi, and E. Sherman, *Chicago Tribune*, 4 November 1985.

Cliff Christl, B. McGinn, and J. Egle, *Green Bay Press-Gazette*, 22 October 1985.

Bob McGinn, B. White, and J. Egle, *Green Bay Press-Gazette*, 4 November 1985.

1986–'89

Jim Egle and Bob McGinn, *Green Bay Press-Gazette*, 23 September 1986.

Jim Egle, B. McGinn, and D. Langenkamp, *Green Bay Press-Gazette*, 24 November 1986.

Don Pierson, *Chicago Tribune*, 23 September 1986.

Bob Verdi, *Chicago Tribune*, 25 November 1986.

David Marran, "Big Plays Made by the Big Players Again," *Chicago Bear Report*, 1 December 1986, p. 18. Reprinted with permission.

Don Langenkamp, *Green Bay Press-Gazette*, 8 August 1993.

Bob McGinn, *Green Bay Press-Gazette*, 9 November 1987.

Bob McGinn, *Green Bay Press-Gazette*, 30 November 1987.

Bob Verdi, *Chicago Tribune*, 9 November 1987.

Robert Markus, L. Kay, and M. Conklin, *Chicago Tribune*, 30 November 1987.

Green Bay Packer Press Guide, 1988.

Fred Mitchell and Bob Sakamoto, *Chicago Tribune*, 26 September 1988.

Linda Kay et al., *Chicago Tribune*, 28 November 1988.

Bob McGinn, *Green Bay Press-Gazette*, 26 September 1988.

Bob McGinn, *Green Bay Press-Gazette*, 28 November 1988.

Tom Mulhern and Bob McGinn, *Green Bay Press-Gazette*, 6 November 1989.

Bob McGinn, *Green Bay Press-Gazette*, 18 December 1989.

Bernie Lincicome and Fred Mitchell, *Chicago Tribune*, 6 November 1989.

Bernie Lincicome, F. Mitchell, and B. Sakamoto, *Chicago Tribune*, 18 December 1989.

Karl Swanke. Interview by author. 13 April 1996.

Mike Ditka. Interview by author. 1 July 1996.

Forrest Gregg. Interview by author. 21 February 1996.

1990–'95

Bob McGinn, *Green Bay Press-Gazette*, 17 September 1990.

Bernie Lincicome, F. Mitchell, and B. Sakamoto, *Chicago Tribune*, 17 September 1990.

Brian Hanley, *Chicago Sun Times*, 8 October 1990.

Don Pierson and Paul Sullivan, *Chicago Tribune*, 18 October 1991.

Bob Verdi, F. Mitchell, and P., Sullivan, *Chicago Tribune*, 9 December 1991.

Chris Havel, *Green Bay Press-Gazette*, 18 October 1991.

Chris Havel, *Green Bay Press-Gazette*, 9 December 1991.

Chris Havel, *Green Bay Press-Gazette*, 23 December 1991.

Kevin Isaacson, *Green Bay Press-Gazette*, 11 January 1992.

Green Bay Packer Press Guide, 1992.

Chris Havel, *Green Bay Press-Gazette*, 26 October 1992.

Chris Havel and Kevin Isaacson, *Green Bay Press Gazette*, 23 November 1992.

Robert Markus and Fred Mitchell, *Chicago Tribune*, 26 October 1992.

Fred Mitchell and Bob Sakamoto, *Chicago Tribune*, 23 November 1992.

Tim Mulhern, "White Expects to Win in Green Bay," *Green Bay Packer Yearbook*, 1993.

Chris Havel, *Green Bay Press-Gazette*, 30 March 1993.

Bernie Lincicome, *Chicago Tribune*, 3 November 1993.

Paul Sullivan, D. Pierson, and F. Mitchell, *Chicago Tribune*, 16 December 1993.

Chris Havel and Kevin Isaacson, *Green Bay Press-Gazette*, 3 November 1993.

Chris Havel, *Green Bay Press-Gazette*, 16 December 1993

Chris Havel, *Green Bay Press-Gazette*, 1 November 1994.

Bernie Lincicome et al., *Chicago Tribune*, 1 November 1994.

Mike Vandermause and Brad Zimanek, "Packer Plus," *Milwaukee Sentinel*, 3-9 November 1994.

Paul Sullivan, *Chicago Tribune*, 12 December 1994.

Eric Goska and Chris Havel, *Green Bay Press-Gazette*, 12 December 1994.

Dan Bickley, *Chicago Sun Times*, 12 September 1995.

Chris Havel, *Green Bay Press-Gazette*, 12 September 1995.

Chris Havel et al., *Green Bay Press-Gazette*, 13 November 1995.

General References

Neft, D. S., Cohen, R. M. and Korch, R., *The Football Encyclopedia*, New York City: St. Martins Press, 1994.

O'Brien, Michael, *Vince*, New York City: William Morrow Co., 1987.

Whittingham, Richard, *Chicago Bears, An Illustrated History*, New York City: Simon and Schuster, 1986.

A Note from the Publisher

Publishing a book, like every other aspect of life, is the culmination of a series of decisions. It gives me pleasure to acknowledge those people whose participation had a significant impact on the publishing of this book:

Steve Bloch, Phil Swann, Susan Hathaway, Barbara Balch, Myra Westphall, Elaine Jesmer, David Land, Hal Larsen, Ed Bazel, Greg Athens, Robert and Jackie Epstein, Lurvie and Eileen Johnson, Frank and Lenore Finneran, Rick and Sally Orlando, Bob Holt, Ken Felderstein, Brendan Burns, Bill Chatz, Matt, Wendy, and Karen at the Conner Design Group, Oceanside Kinkos—especially Chris, Mary Settle at ATG, Laurie Antosy at KNI, Viki Mason at Victoria Graphics, Kevan Burks at NFL, Vernon Biever, Lee Lefebrve, Phyllis Gapen, Vivian Monroe, and Marc Jaffe.

Special appreciation to my family, Victor, David, Joseph and Lupe Villaseñor, and to my parents, Charles and Zita Bloch, who began Charles Publishing over twenty years ago, and continue to inspire its growth.

A very special thanks to Glenn Swain, for his contagious enthusiasm about these two teams, his diligence in research and writing, and his eagerness to contribute every way possible to produce this book. You made the project a joy.

Most especially, to all the Packers' fans and the Bears' fans, thank you for giving this book life!

To every one of you, my deepest gratitude. The end result would have been less without you; that's how important each of you are.

Barbara Bloch Villaseñor
Publisher